THE EVOLUTION OF PENOLOGY IN PENNSYLVANIA

PATTERSON SMITH

REPRINT SERIES IN

CRIMINOLOGY, LAW ENFORCEMENT, AND SOCIAL PROBLEMS

———

PUBLICATIONS

No. 1. Lewis, Orlando F. *The Development of American Prisons and Prison Customs, 1776-1845.*

No. 2. Carpenter, Mary. *Reformatory Prison Discipline.*

No. 3. Brace, Charles Loring. *The Dangerous Classes of New York.*

No. 4. Dix, Dorothea Lynde. *Remarks on Prisons and Prison Discipline in the United States.*

No. 5. Bruce, Andrew A., Albert J. Harno, Ernest W. Burgess, & John Landesco. *The Workings of the Indeterminate-Sentence Law and the Parole System in Illinois.*

No. 6. Wickersham Commission. *Complete Reports, Including the Mooney-Billings Report.* 14 Vols.

No. 7. Livingston, Edward. *Complete Works on Criminal Jurisprudence.* 2 Vols.

No. 8. Cleveland Foundation. *Criminal Justice in Cleveland.*

No. 9. Illinois Association for Criminal Justice. *The Illinois Crime Survey.*

No. 10. Missouri Association for Criminal Justice. *The Missouri Crime Survey.*

No. 11. Aschaffenburg, Gustav. *Crime and Its Repression.*

No. 12. Garofalo, Raffaele. *Criminology.*

No. 13. Gross, Hans. *Criminal Psychology.*

No. 14. Lombroso, Cesare. *Crime, Its Causes and Remedies.*

No. 15. Saleilles, Raymond. *The Individualization of Punishment.*

No. 16. Tarde, Gabriel. *Penal Philosophy.*

No. 17. McKelvey, Blake. *American Prisons.*

No. 18. Sanders, Wiley B. *Negro Child Welfare in North Carolina.*

No. 19. Pike, Luke Owen. *A History of Crime in England.* 2 Vols.

No. 20. Herring, Harriet L. *Welfare Work in Mill Villages.*

No. 21. Barnes, Harry Elmer. *The Evolution of Penology in Pennsylvania.*

No. 22. Puckett, Newbell N. *Folk Beliefs of the Southern Negro.*

No. 23. Fernald, Mabel Ruth, Mary Holmes Stevens Hayes, & Almena Dawley. *A Study of Women Delinquents in New York State.*

No. 24. Wines, Enoch Cobb. *The State of Prisons and of Child-Saving Institutions in the Civilized World.*

THE EASTERN STATE PENITENTIARY, 1829

PUBLICATION NO. 21: PATTERSON SMITH REPRINT SERIES IN
CRIMINOLOGY, LAW ENFORCEMENT, AND SOCIAL PROBLEMS

The Evolution of Penology in Pennsylvania

A STUDY IN AMERICAN SOCIAL HISTORY

By

HARRY ELMER BARNES, PH. D.

*Professor of Historical Sociology, Smith College, Northampton, Massachusetts;
Historian to the New Jersey Prison Inquiry Commission, 1917;
Historian to the Pennsylvania Committee to
Investigate Penal Systems, 1918*

AUTHOR OF

*"The History of the Penal, Reformatory and Correctional Institutions
of New Jersey," "The Repression of Crime," Etc.*

ILLUSTRATED

Montclair, New Jersey

PATTERSON SMITH

1968

Copyright 1927 by The Bobbs-Merrill Company
Reprinted 1968 by arrangement with
Harry Elmer Barnes
Patterson Smith Publishing Corporation
Montclair, New Jersey

Library of Congress Catalog Card Number: 68-55768

To

DWIGHT WHITNEY MORROW

Lawyer, scholar and enlightened student of criminal jurisprudence
and prison administration; to whom the author owes the origin
of his interest in the history of penology.

PREFACE

The present book is a revision and an elaboration of a historical study of the penal institutions and criminal law of Pennsylvania which was undertaken for the Pennsylvania Commission to Investigate Penal Systems in 1918. The delay in the completion of the book has enabled the author to take into account the progress in penological science and practice which has come about in Pennsylvania during the last decade as a result of the work of this Commission and other enlightened forces operating within the state. The work endeavors to present a comprehensive review of the development of penology in Pennsylvania, indicating the interaction between Pennsylvania and the rest of the western world in this field. The effort has been made to construct the book in such fashion that it is not merely a technical summary of penological development but a contribution to social history, of which the history of penology is conceived as a vital and integral element. The author has attempted to portray the social and intellectual developments that conditioned the ideas and practices which have emerged in the criminal codes and in the penal and correctional institutions that have existed in Pennsylvania since the first settlement by the whites. The first chapter of the book is devoted primarily to a statement of the importance of the history of penology in general and of the development of penology in Pennsylvania in particular. Therefore, no reason exists for further discussion of that subject in this place. It is hoped that the work will prove useful to students of American history, and to sociologists and criminologists who are concerned with the important and thus far baffling problem of the repression of anti-social action. It is also believed that the book may likewise interest those intelligent general readers whose acquaintance with the contemporary debates concerning crime, crime waves and criminals has aroused a curiosity to discover what has been attempted in this field in the past and what is the historical origin of the laws and institutions which are proving so futile and inadequate to-day in the matter of reducing crime and reforming criminals.

The author is under deep obligations to a number of persons who have rendered indispensable assistance to him in various stages of the prosecution of his studies. Most of all he is indebted to Mr.

PREFACE

Albert H. Votaw, the veteran Secretary of the Pennsylvania Prison Society and devoted laborer in the cause of scientific and humane prison administration. At no time during the last ten years has Mr. Votaw failed to give evidence of incredible patience in answering questions and putting valuable material at the disposal of the author. In gathering information concerning the developments of the last decade the author has received valuable aid from Dr. Ellen C. Potter, formerly Secretary of the Department of Public Welfare, Mr. B. L. Scott of the Bureau of Restoration, Dr. Louis N. Robinson and Mr. Leon Stern of the Pennsylvania Committee on Penal Affairs, Warden Stanley P. Ashe of the Western Penitentiary, Warden John C. Broome of the Eastern Penitentiary and Dean William E. Mikell of the University of Pennsylvania Law School. Acknowledgment of assistance and encouragement in various ways should be made to Rev. J. F. Ohl, Mr. Kenneth L. M. Pray, Dr. George W. Kirchwey, Librarian L. Beardsley of Swarthmore, former Warden John Francies, Judge William H. Staake, Superintendent W. F. Penn and Honorable William Draper Lewis.

I have greatly profited through the fact that Professor Rayner W. Kelsey has read the proofs of the second chapter, Mr. Albert H. Votaw the proofs of the third chapter, and Dr. Louis N. Robinson the proofs of the fourth chapter. I am, in particular, heavily indebted to my friend and former student, Mr. John Edward Ratigan, for reading with care the galley proofs of the entire volume, and to Mr. Robert W. Hankins for a patient examination of the page proofs.

HARRY ELMER BARNES.

Northampton, Mass.

CONTENTS

CONTENTS—*Continued*

CONTENTS—*Continued*

CONTENTS—*Continued*

CONTENTS—*Continued*

LIST OF ILLUSTRATIONS

THE EVOLUTION OF PENOLOGY IN PENNSYLVANIA

The Evolution of Penology in Pennsylvania

CHAPTER I

GENERAL INTRODUCTION

I. THE SIGNIFICANCE OF THE HISTORY OF PENOLOGY IN PENNSYLVANIA

A CONTRIBUTION to the history of penology no longer requires an apology for its aim and purpose. Though there has been no end of the making of books describing the institutions and processes involved in the making of laws, there has been an almost total neglect of the history of the breaking of laws and of the mode of imposing and executing the penalty for this violation. It is, then, a field which extends a twofold invitation to the student of history in that it is not only a fertile and significant subject, but also one that has been as yet little exploited and developed. On account of the intimate relation of crime and its treatment to the prevailing social and economic conditions and to the existing state of scientific knowledge, the historical study of penology affords not only a valuable excursion into one of the most undeveloped borderlands of jurisprudence, but also furnishes a most fruitful investigation in political, social, economic and intellectual history. No study in the evolution of penology can be regarded as fundamental or trustworthy if divorced from a careful consideration of the conditions and changes in the political, social, economic and intellectual environment.

If it is easy to justify a concern with the general field of historical penology, it is even less difficult to establish the value of a study of the history of the penal, reformatory and correctional institutions of the State of Pennsylvania. No community has been more significant in the history of penology than this commonwealth. Its Quaker colonists in the late seventeenth century introduced for the first time on an extended scale the practise of employing imprisonment at hard labor as the chief method of punishing anti-social action. The reversion in 1718 to the barbarous English criminal jurisprudence furnished for a half-century an example of the operation of this crude and brutal method of repressing crime. The

1

"common jail" and that rarer institution—the workhouse—well represented the typical penal institutions of the colonial period. In the generation following the American Revolution, Pennsylvania was the first state to abolish the cruelties of the English jurisprudence and to substitute imprisonment at hard labor for the various degrading types of corporal punishment. The Walnut Street Jail in 1790 was the earliest institution in America in which these principles were adopted. From 1790 to 1829 Pennsylvania was elaborating and perfecting one of the two great systems of prison administration which dominated the penology of the civilized world during the nineteenth century—the separate confinement of prisoners. Visited, admired and imitated by large numbers of eminent and enthusiastic European penologists, the Eastern Penitentiary at Cherry Hill was the pivotal point linking American and European penology for more than a generation after 1830.

Meanwhile, the Western Penitentiary, less affected by venerable administrative traditions, was losing faith in the system of separate confinement, as practised in Pennsylvania, and in the decade of the Civil War it adopted the congregate organization of the Auburn Prison system, combined with a partial acceptance of the classification procedure employed in Crofton's "Irish" system. From 1869 to 1913 Pennsylvania operated both of the two prevalent systems of prison administration in her state penitentiaries. At the present time a new state penitentiary has been erected and is designed to put into operation the best that has been evolved from the experience of a century in penal administration, not only in Pennsylvania, but also in Europe and America. In 1889, this time not as an originator, but as one of the first imitators of the neighboring commonwealth of New York, Pennsylvania adopted the justly famed "Elmira system" of penological principles in the reformatory at Huntingdon. This system combined in a single type of administration all the progressive features of a half-century of penological progress—the commutation system, the practise of the progressive classification of prisoners, the indeterminate sentence, parole, and productive and instructive labor. A half-century earlier Philadelphia had been one of the first three cities in America to provide institutions for separating juvenile from adult delinquents. In the progress of the evolution of its correctional institutions the experience of Pennsylvania has revealed the major advances of the last century, passing from the crude and repressive "house of refuge" to the flexible, reformative and educational farm colony and cottage system. Recently steps have been taken which look toward the final elimination of that last relic of penal barbarism—the county jail, which is doomed except as an institution for the detention of those accused of crime. The Allegheny County Workhouse is a model institution, pointing the way for the abolition of the menace of the county jail, and the recent District Farm Act makes this desirable step legally possible. Finally, the Pennsylvania Prison Society can point to the longest existence of any of the world's organizations for prison reform and its achievements have not been less notable than the duration of its labors. Even this scanty review of the outstanding phases of the penological development within the commonwealth of Pennsylvania will be sufficient to establish the contention that no modern community can more perfectly exhibit and recapitulate the essential features of the evolution of penology and of the general reform movements which have accompanied this development.

II. THE EVOLUTION OF PENAL INSTITUTIONS VIEWED AS A PROCESS OF SCIENTIFIC DIFFERENTIATION

While many scholars now hold that Herbert Spencer's formula of evolution as a passage from a crude and undifferentiated homogeneity to a differentiated and specialized heterogeneity possesses more virtue as a rhetorical flourish than as a scientific proposition, there can be no doubt that it admirably describes and summarizes the course of the development of the penal, reformatory and correctional institutions of Pennsylvania, as well as of those in the country as a whole.

For more than a century of its history the penal, reformatory and correctional institutions of Pennsylvania were limited to the county jails and the few and scattered workhouses, which were erected mainly in conjunction with the almshouses. In the jails there could be no approach to anything like a differentiated treatment of delinquents. In them were herded promiscuously those imprisoned for debt, those convicted of crime and those accused or held as witnesses; those of all ages and both sexes; those convicted of all categories and grades of crimes punishable by imprisonment; those of all mental states—normal, feeble-minded, neurotic, psychotic, epileptic. The few colonial workhouses were employed as little more than an agency for suppressing vagrancy.

The first step in a differentiated treatment of crime and criminals came with the erection of a semi-state prison in the Walnut Street Jail in 1789-90. This provided for a partial differentiation between those convicted of the more serious crimes and those convicted of petty offenses or awaiting trial, and separated debtors from criminals. It did not, however, attempt any scientific separation on the basis of age, sex or mental states. Children and adults, male and female, sane and insane, were confined in contiguity. The opening of the state penitentiaries at Allegheny and Philadelphia in 1826 and 1829, with their fundamental principle of solitary confinement, carried further the process of differentiation, but still continued to apply the same general type of treatment to all incarcerated inmates. It was a system of individual separation rather than of a differentiated treatment of special types of prisoners. The second important development in the direction of specialization in the provision of institutional treatment of delinquents appeared in the establishment of a House of Refuge for juvenile delinquents at Philadelphia in 1828. Though this was at first a private rather than a state institution and was of very limited capacity, it marked an epoch in the progress of Pennsylvania penology by making possible some elementary differentiation on the basis of age, degree of criminality and relative susceptibility to reformation.

The next attempt at further differentiation came with the erection of the state hospital for the insane at Harrisburg between 1841 and 1851, chiefly as a result of the agitation initiated by Dorothea L. Dix. This and the other state hospitals for the insane, subsequently erected, provided for a treatment of the more important types of mental disorder, though no adequate provision was made for removing the insane from the prison. Not until 1905 was an act passed ordering the erection of a state hospital for the criminal insane at Fairview, which was opened in 1912.

During the quarter of a century following 1850 there was an active agitation to provide a means of differentiating the treatment of criminals on the basis of age, sex and degree of criminality. The first important achievement in this direction was the further development of reform schools for juvenile delinquents through the removal and enlargement of the Philadelphia House of Refuge in 1850-54 and the erection of the Western House of Refuge at Allegheny during exactly the same period. Juvenile delinquents, if petty offenders, could thereafter be removed from their degrading confinement in the state prison or worse county jails and receive the properly specialized treatment which their circumstances demanded. No provision for the differentiated treatment of the less definite and confirmed types of adult delinquents was made until the opening of the reformatory for males at Huntingdon in 1889, and of that for females at Muncy in 1918. The provision of reformatories and juvenile correctional institutions marked a double process of differentiation, in that these institutions actually called for a diversity of treatment according to age, sex, and degree of criminality, and also from the fact that they were clearly differentiated from the state prisons and the county jails in making reformation rather than punishment or detention their chief aim.

Along with this development of a widely differentiated system of treating the delinquent population, has gone the growth of specialized institutions for dealing with the closely related class of defectives, which was once treated indiscriminately along with the delinquent classes when its members were guilty of criminal action. Though provision was made for some state aid to the Pennsylvania Training School for Idiotic and Feeble-minded Children at Elwyn, established in 1853, there was no formal state institution for the feeble-minded and idiotic provided in Pennsylvania until 1897. The state institution for the feeble-minded at Polk opened in 1897; the institution for epileptics and feeble-minded at Pennhurst, provided by an act of 1903; and the state village for feeble-minded women at Laurelton, opened during 1916, now furnish scientific treatment for large numbers of those who would to-day be confined in the state prison or county jails, if the ideas and institutions of 1840 prevailed. Even an institution for inebriates was contemplated in an act of 1913.

But this vital and all-important process of the differentiation, classification and specialized treatment of the delinquent and defective classes has now proceeded far beyond that most elementary stage of furnishing separate institutions for dealing with the most general classes of delinquents and defectives. It has been found that the general terms defective, delinquent, insane and criminal have only a precise legal significance and are practically useless when involving the problem of exact scientific analysis and treatment. Each general class of delinquent boys, of defective girls or of criminal adults, for instance, is made up of distinguishable and distinct types which demand specialized treatment in the same way that it is required for one general class as distinguished from another. Though it is as yet very imperfectly developed, the present tendency is for each institution to differentiate into a number of specialized departments, each designed to provide the proper treatment for one of these types.

Finally, within the last decade, beginnings have been made in what is likely to be an important future development, namely, the non-institutional care of the less pronounced and confirmed types of delinquents, particularly delinquent minors. The developments along this line have, up to the present, consisted chiefly in the adoption of parole systems by all the state penal, reformatory and correctional institutions and a more liberal use of the suspended sentence and probation. The recently established Municipal Probation

Court of Philadelphia is a pioneer in Pennsylvania in this promising new development in the preventive treatment of the less confirmed type of delinquents.

III. CHANGES IN THE ATTITUDE OF SOCIETY TOWARD THE NATURE OF THE CRIMINAL AND CRIMINAL BEHAVIOR

Accompanying, and to a large degree promoting, this differentiation and development of penal, reformatory and correctional institutions there has gone a series of transformations in the attitude of society toward delinquency and its treatment.

For the first century and a half of the history of Pennsylvania there prevailed generally the theological conception of the criminal as a "free moral agent" deliberately choosing his conduct, and, hence, deserving nothing better than the savage revenge of society. The whole system of criminal jurisprudence was founded upon this fundamental premise of punishment as social revenge, and the penal codes were crude and unscientific attempts to assess the mode and degree of social revenge which was appropriate to any particular crime. Little or no attempt was made to adjust the degree of punishment to the circumstances connected with the individual offender and his life-history, as it was confidently supposed that all criminals belonged to the one simple and undifferentiated class of perverse "free moral agents," who had deliberately and definitely chosen to violate the rules prescribed by the group for the control of individual action.

The first step in the development of an intelligent conception of delinquency and its treatment came not in an accurate conception of the nature of crime and its causes, but in a clearer and more correct notion of the function of punishment. By 1790 the element of deterrence in punishment was recognized and emphasized. The element of reformation was a cardinal point in the theory and practise of the Philadelphia Society for Alleviating the Miseries of Public Prisons, and this society did its best to infuse this doctrine into the Pennsylvania system of prison administration. Before 1830 it was very generally asserted that reformation, in addition to deterrence and social revenge, was to be regarded as a chief aim of punishment, though the offender was still regarded as an "unregenerate free moral agent." This theory of crime received a severe shock in the forties from the investigations of Dorothea L. Dix and others, who showed the great prevalence of insanity and idiocy among the delinquent classes. It could scarcely be denied by the theologians and the traditional jurists that the exercise of "free will" was likely to be seriously impeded by insanity or feeble-mindedness.

From 1850 to the beginning of the present century the most notable advances toward a more intelligent conception of crime and its treatment consisted in the gradual but definite triumph of the notion of detention and punishment as agencies for reformation rather than as instruments of social revenge, and in the accumulation of that technical information in biology, medicine, sociology, criminal anthropology and abnormal psychology which has made possible the modern rational doctrines regarding delinquency and its scientific treatment.

During the last two decades, the progress has consisted chiefly in securing a beginning of the public recognition and the practical application of these present-day ideas concerning delinquency and its treatment. It is now recognized that the term *criminal* as a juristic concept has only specific legal validity and possesses very limited significance for the sociologist, penologist, criminologist or psychologist. It is clearly perceived that within this general legal class of criminals there are numerous biological and psychological types, produced by hereditary or environmental influences or a combination of these, over which the particular individual has had little or no control. The responsibility for crime is thus conceived to be in its broadest sense social, and not individual, and from this transformation of the notion of criminal responsibility there has resulted the final destruction of the conception of punishment as social revenge. It has long been recognized that certain members of this legal class of criminals are amenable, though in different degrees, to reformatory influences, and that it is, therefore, the duty of society to supply these influences for its own welfare as well as for that of the individual offender. On the other hand, it is admitted with equal frankness that others of the class of so-called criminals are, by reason of unfavorable biological heredity or unfortunate individual experience, so hopelessly defective or abnormal as to defy any hope of ultimate reformation, and, as a consequence, demand permanent segregation and the prevention of propagation. It has thus become evident that carefully specialized institutions and management must be provided for the proper detection, differentiation, and treatment of these classes, now roughly grouped in a legal sense as criminal or delinquent. In short, the idea of individual perversity and responsibility has given way to that of hereditary and environmental influences, or social responsibility, and along with this change of view regarding the causation of delinquency has gone the substitution of the notion of social protection through reformation and segregation, for that of social revenge, as the goal of the treatment of delinquency. In its broadest sense, therefore, the development of the ideas and institutions relative to delinquency and its treatment, may, to employ a mathematical figure, be regarded as a function of the growth of technical knowledge and of social intelligence.

It is the purpose of the following historical sketch to indicate these successive stages or epochs in the development of penological concepts and practises in Pennsylvania and to show their relation to the general evolution of penology in Europe and America.

CHAPTER II

THE COLONIAL PERIOD

I. THE SETTLEMENT OF THE COLONY OF PENNSYLVANIA [1]

1. THE ORIGINS OF PENNSYLVANIA

ON THE fourth of March, 1681, "Charles the Second, by the Grace of God, King of England, Scotland, France and Ireland, Defender of the Faith," issued a letter patent at Westminster in which he declared:

"Whereas our trusty and well beloved subject, William Penn, Esquire, son and heir of Sir William Penn, deceased, out of a commendable desire to enlarge our English Empire, and promote such useful commodities as may be of benefit to us and our Dominions, as also to reduce the savage natives by gentle and just manners to the love of civil society and Christian religion has humbly besought leave of us to transport an ample colony unto a certain country hereinafter described in the parts of America not yet cultivated and planted. . . . Know ye, therefore, that we, favoring the petition and good purpose of the said William Penn, and having regard to the memory and merits of his late father, in diverse services, and particularly to his conduct, courage and discretion under our dearest brother, James, Duke of York, in that signal battle and victory, fought and obtained against the Dutch fleet, commanded by Herr Van Obdam, in the year one thousand six hundred and sixty-five, in consideration thereof, of our special grace, certain knowledge and mere motion, have given and granted, and by this our present Charter, for us, our heirs and successors, do give and grant unto the said William Penn, his heirs and assignees, all that tract or part of land in America, with all the islands therein contained, as the same is bounded. . . ." [2]

---

[1] The brief preliminary discussion of the historical background of the colonial jurisprudence and penology of Pennsylvania will be limited to that which is essential to an understanding of any phase of the institutional history of the province.

[2] *Charter to William Penn and Laws of the Province of Pennsylvania,* 1682-1700, edited by George, Nead and McCamant, Harrisburg, 1879, p. 81.

This grant is conventionally regarded as the origin of the colony of Pennsylvania and as the beginning of William Penn's direct interest in the colonization of America. It was neither. The first settlement along the Delaware River was made under the auspices of the Dutch West India Company in 1623 on the New Jersey side of the river opposite what is now Philadelphia. In 1635 a few English settlers came from Connecticut. Three years later a considerable number of Swedes founded a permanent settlement along the Delaware and disputed the possession of the region with the Dutch. By 1654 the Swedes had gained the military ascendency over the Dutch, only to lose it the next year when Stuyvesant reconquered the district. About this same time the Dutch also purchased from the Indians the site of Philadelphia. During the period before the English conquest the Swedes had the numerical preponderance, but it is estimated that the total European population about 1660 was only three hundred and sixty-eight. In 1664, James, Duke of York, conquered New Netherland from the Dutch and this conquest carried with it the claim to New Jersey, Delaware and the district which later came to be known as Pennsylvania. The control, thus established, persisted until the grant of the King to Penn in 1681, with the exception of a few months in 1673, when the region was reconquered by the Dutch. In the period of the Duke's control many more English settlers came, and it is estimated that at the time of Penn's arrival in America the population of the Delaware settlements was between two and three thousand. There was, thus, a very considerable European population already settled in the lands granted to Penn in 1681.[3]

Penn had also been interested in an American colony before he received the grant of Pennsylvania from Charles II.[4] In 1673 he had been one of the group of Quakers who had purchased West Jersey from Berkeley, and about the time that he obtained Pennsylvania from the Crown he also was a joint purchaser, with others of his sect, of East Jersey, from the heirs of Carteret.[5]

Though it is not historically accurate to regard the origin of Pennsylvania as dating from the Charter of 1681, the social history of the colony and state really begins with the arrival of Penn

---

[3] *Historical Notes on the Early Government and Legislative Councils and Assemblies of Pennsylvania,* by Benjamin Nead, Appendix B to *The Charter and Laws of the Province of Pennsylvania,* pp. 413ff.

[4] Sydney George Fisher, *The Making of Pennsylvania,* Chap. I. A. S. Bolles, *Pennsylvania, Province and State,* pp. 31-75.

[5] E. P. Tanner, *The Province of New Jersey,* 1664-1738, pp. 6, 10, 11. H. L. Osgood, *The American Colonies in the Seventeeth Century,* Vol II, p. 191.

and his fellow Quakers at New Castle on October 27, 1682. Mr. Fisher makes this point clear in the following paragraph:

"The Swedes, the Dutch, and the English under the Duke made no important settlement, so far as Pennsylvania was concerned, and did nothing which materially affected after events. Their peculiar laws and customs became completely obsolete; they and their descendants were absorbed in the rest of the population; and there is no institution in Pennsylvania that can be traced to their influence. They were not in the line of real beginning and progress of our Commonwealth. The Commonwealth was created by the Quakers." [6]

The basis for Penn's desire to obtain the grant of land known as Pennsylvania is to be explained by his inheritance and the experiences of his life. He inherited a debt due his father from the Crown to the amount of sixteen thousand pounds, and during his student days at Oxford he had joined the Quakers. A grant of land in America would allow him to establish a Quaker commonwealth, and this concession might be obtained in lieu of the sum which was owed to him by the ever-bankrupt Charles II. Accordingly, on June 1, 1680, he petitioned the King to cede to him the region he desired, and, as was pointed out in the opening paragraph, he obtained his request on the fourth day of the following March. The grant included not only what is now known as Pennsylvania, but also the present state of Delaware.[7] Penn had proposed to call the district Sylvania, but the King, in memory of Penn's father, insisted on calling it Pennsylvania, and the name so appears in the royal proclamation of April 2, 1681, commanding the inhabitants of the Province to render obedience to Penn.[8] Penn's chief purpose in founding the colony was to be able to offer a refuge for the persecuted members of his sect, in particular, and for all who were suffering from the bigotry and intolerance of the times. This is stated in one of his most famous letters, in which he says:

"I went thither to lay the foundation of a free colony for all mankind, more especially those of my own profession, not that I would lessen the civil liberties of others, because of their persuasion, but screen and defend our own from any infringement on that account." [9]

---

[6] Fisher, op, cit., p. 32.
[7] W. R. Shepherd, *A History of Proprietary Government in Pennsylvania*, pp. 9-10. Bolles, op. cit., pp. 109-10.
[8] Bolles, op. cit., p. 110. *Charter and Laws of the Province of Pennsylvania, 1682-1700*, p. 466.
[9] Quoted by Bolles, op. cit., p. 118.

2. The Elements that Settled in the Province of Pennsylvania

The unusual degree of tolerance which was accorded by Penn to all dissenters, as well as the liberal form of government which he established, attracted a large and varied group of immigrants. In no other American colony was the population as heterogeneous as in Pennsylvania. Mr. Fisher has well stated this significant fact:

"Most of the English Colonies in America were founded by people of pure Anglo-Saxon stock, and each colony had usually a religion of its own, with comparatively little intermixture of other faiths. . . . But Pennsylvania was altogether different, and no other colony had such a mixture of languages, nationalities, and religions. Dutch, Swedes, English, Germans, Scotch-Irish, Welsh; Quakers, Presbyterians, Episcopalians, Lutherans, Reformed, Mennonites, Tunkers, and Moravians all had a share in creating it." [10]

The first settlers, were, as has already been pointed out, the Dutch and Swedes who were distributed along the lower Delaware in the first half of the seventeenth century. They constituted an insignificant proportion of the later population of the colony. The two great colonizing groups were the English and the German elements which are estimated to have constituted about two-thirds of the total population during the eighteenth century. The English settled mainly in the eastern part of the province around Philadelphia. The two chief groups of the English settlers were the Quakers and the Episcopalians with a few Presbyterians. Until 1750 the Quakers were as numerous as all the other English elements combined. The German element, which was about equal in size to the English group, began to come in about the time of Penn's acquisition of the colony. The firstcomers were various minor dissident Germanic sects, but the later immigrants were chiefly the orthodox Protestants, Dutch Reformed and Lutheran. They settled in the valleys of the Lehigh and Schuylkill Rivers and have from that time to the present constituted one of the most persistently non-assimilable elements in the American population. The remaining third of the population of provincial Pennsylvania was constituted of various minor groups of the most diverse character. Racially akin to the Germans were the Moravians, a Bohemian sect which was a branch of the old Hussite heretics of the early fifteenth century. They began to come about 1739 and settled at Nazareth near the Lehigh River. Later they moved to Bethlehem, which has since remained the center of the activities of their fol-

---

[10] Fisher, op. cit., preface, p. iii.

lowers. Scotch-Irish Presbyterians began to come in considerable numbers about 1700. They furnished the majority of the settlers in the Cumberland Valley in the district around Gettysburg. One of the earliest of the various minor groups of immigrants was the Welsh. They began to come in as early at 1682 and until 1700 they constituted the most numerous of all the immigrants. After that time their immigration tended to die out. Penn had promised them in advance the grant of a tract of forty thousand acres. This was given to them near Philadelphia in what was later organized as Chester County. It was called the Welsh Barony and was established much as a feudal grant of the Middle Ages. The Welsh are said to have supplied all the physicians of the colony up to 1700, and one of their number was David Lloyd, Chief Justice of the province and one of the main figures in the early development of Pennsylvania jurisprudence. Among other things, he drafted some of the important judiciary acts of the early eighteenth century and the notorious penal code of 1718. For the nature of the latter, however, he was personally scarcely responsible. Finally, among the inhabitants of colonial Pennsylvania should be noted the Connecticut "invaders" who settled the beautiful Wyoming Valley. With respect to the total population of the province during the colonial period we have only estimates. These put the population in 1660 at about four hundred; in 1682, at about two thousand to three thousand; in 1730, at about fifty thousand; in 1750, at two hundred thousand to two hundred seventy-five thousand. In 1790 the population was four hundred and thirty-four thousand.[11]

There was very little assimilation of these groups into a common provincial population. They offer a striking example of the operation of the principle that Professor Giddings has called the "consciousness of kind." Each group tended to isolate itself in some well-defined geographic area and to resist any unifying impulses. Mr. Fisher thus summarizes this interesting situation:

"Many of these divisions led a more or less distinct life of their own in colonial times, some of them wishing to found a colony for themselves within the province. . . .

"The Scotch-Irish got as far away from the others as possible. The Connecticut people, in the fastness of their valley, held aloof from all association and intercourse with the rest of the province. The Germans congregated by themselves in the fertile valleys of

[11] Fisher, op. cit., passim. This extremely interesting book contains what is by far the best summary of the part played by the various European elements in the settlement of the colony of Pennsylvania.

the Schuylkill and the Lehigh, and the Welsh were at first isolated on their barony. Only two elements were brought in close contact— the Quakers and Episcopalians who occupied Philadelphia." [12]

In spite of the diversity of the early immigrants the Quakers constituted the dominating element until the middle of the eighteenth century. Professor Osgood says on this point:

"Pennsylvania was in the full sense of the word a Quaker province. Not only was the proprietor a Quaker, but the sect controlled the assembly until the middle of the eighteenth century." [13]

The result of this situation in the settlement of Pennsylvania was that two widely conflicting tendencies were brought into existence, which created a serious problem in maintaining an effective degree of social control. The mildness and tolerance of the Quaker régime attracted dissident and divergent groups and created a most heterogeneous population which required a vigorous public policy and administration to control it in an effective manner. The plastic and informal Quaker republic was peculiarly unadapted to such a task,[14] and its weakness in this respect was undoubtedly one of the causes of the downfall of its domination. The decline of the power of the Quakers is attributable to at least three influences. One of them was the submergence of the Quaker group by the immigration of other elements on a large scale. Another was the political weakness of the Quaker administrative system in the face of the difficult problem of bringing under firm political control the most diverse population of colonial America. A third was the fact that the proprietors themselves, with their dominating political powers, tended to desert the Quakers and go over to the Church of England. They then naturally threw the weight of their power into the Episcopalian group, which gradually ousted the Quakers from the control of provincial politics.[15] Mr. Applegarth has thus stated the problem that the Quakers faced in attempting to maintain their hold upon the political direction of the colony:

"Civil government, owing to their religious principles, was always very embarrassing to the Friends. It became more and more so, as the population became more heterogeneous. Great difficulty was experienced in providing for the public defense of the Colony,

---

[12] Fisher, op. cit., preface, p. iii, and p. 355.
[13] Osgood, op. cit., Vol. II, pp. 254-55. Cf. also Isaac Sharpless, A Quaker Experiment in Government, pp. 72ff.
[14] Cf. Isaac Sharpless, Quakerism and Politics, pp. 17-49, 79-110.
[15] Fisher, op. cit., p. 356. Shepherd, op. cit., pp. 496-97, 501. A. C. Applegarth, The Quakers in Pennsylvania, J. H. U. Studies, Vol. X, Numbers VIII-IX, pp. 47-8.

and it became every day more apparent that the time was rapidly approaching when they would be compelled to lay down the government, consigning it to hands whose owners did not share such scruples. . . . No longer was there any opportunity of halting between two conflicting opinions. One of two things must be done. They must either renounce their political capacity or they must consent to merge the Quaker into the politician. 'With a rare virtue,' avers Mr. Grahame, 'they adhered to their religious principles and resigned the political authority which they had enjoyed since the foundation of the colony.' " [16]

There is no general agreement among authorities as to just when the dominating power in the province slipped from the hands of the Quakers, but all agree that it took place at some time between the middle of the eighteenth century and the outbreak of the Revolution.[17]

II. THE POLITICAL ORGANIZATION OF COLONIAL PENNSYLVANIA

1. THE TYPES OF ENGLISH COLONIES IN AMERICA

There were two chief types of colonies founded by the English in America—the chartered colony and the royal colony. Of the chartered colonies there were two kinds. One was the civil corporation, which was practically an independent commonwealth, such as the several New England colonies. The other was the proprietary colony, which was really the medieval feudal grant of immunity transferred to America. In some cases the proprietors shared the granted power liberally with the people, as in Pennsylvania, but in others they withheld it. In the royal province the colony was brought under the direct control of the English crown, which governed through an appointive governor. The royal colony constituted an important step in the direction of imperial unity. A colony often changed from one type to another, as was the case with New Jersey, which originated as a proprietary colony and became a royal province in 1702. On the whole, the tendency in the eighteenth century was to transform the chartered colonies into royal provinces.[18]

---

[16] Applegarth, Ibid.
[17] Ibid. Fisher, op. cit., p. 356. Isaac Sharpless, *A Quaker Experiment in Government*, pp. 226ff.
[18] Osgood, op. cit., Vol. I, Introduction, pp. xxvff. Shepherd, op. cit., pp. 5ff.

2. Pennsylvania as a Proprietary Province

Pennsylvania was a proprietary colony and remained such until it became a state.[19] It was from the first that form of a proprietary colony which granted a large share of governing power to the people. It was not, however, entirely independent of royal power, as a clause in the royal charter declared that a duplicate of the laws passed by the provincial legislature was to be submitted to the privy council within five years after their passage. If they were not repealed by the council within six months from the time they were submitted they were to remain in force.[20] This provision probably introduced more confusion into the early government of Pennsylvania than any other single element. Among other things it prevented the establishment of a permanent court system until 1731.[21]

3. The Organization of the Provincial Government

A.   The Provincial Executive

It is difficult to describe briefly the organization of any branch of the provincial government of Pennsylvania because of the fact that it was frequently altered as a result of the necessity of experiment and compromise on the part of the proprietor and because of interference by the Crown. The provincial government was organized upon the basis of the "Frames of Government" of 1682 and 1683, drawn up and promulgated by Penn, and upon his Charter of Privileges issued in 1701. The latter remained as the "constitution" of the province until the formation of the state in the Revolutionary period.[22]

Under all of these different regulating instruments the proprietor was, of course, the head of the executive power, but he usually delegated his power to an acting executive who exercised the real functions of this branch of the government.

According to the provisions of the first Frame of Government, the executive power was to be vested in a governor or lieutenant-governor appointed by the proprietor. He was to have three votes in the provincial council, of which he was president, but he did not possess the veto power. The executive "departments" were filled by the governor's appointees, and from a list submitted to

---

[19] Shepherd, op. cit.

[20] *Charter and Laws of the Province of Pennsylvania, 1682-1700*, p. 85.

[21] W. T. Root, *The Relations of Pennsylvania with the British Government, 1696-1765*, pp. 158ff. Shepherd, op. cit., pp. 307ff.

[22] Osgood, op. cit., Vol. II, p. 256f. Shepherd, op. cit., pp. 225ff., 474ff.

him by the council he appointed the chief local officers, such as justices, treasurers and masters of the rolls.[23] By the terms of the second Frame of Government the governor was deprived of his triple vote in the council.[24] In 1687, on account of friction in the provincial government, Penn appointed five "commissioners of state" to supersede the governor and act as deputy governors.[25] This experiment did not prove satisfactory and at the close of the next year the single governor was restored. In 1692, owing to the growing confusion in administration, Penn was suspended from his control of the province and Benjamin Fletcher, Royal Governor of New York and New Jersey, was appointed in his stead. Penn was restored in 1694, and in 1701 he promulgated his Charter of Privileges which provided the organization of the government down to the Revolution. The executive power was continued essentially as it had existed before 1692, though the power of the governor was somewhat curtailed, especially in the matter of initiating legislation. After Penn's death in 1718 the proprietor either governed directly or through his appointed deputy. Associated with the governor was an advisory council appointed by the proprietor.[26]

B. The Provincial Legislature

In all the "constitutions" of provincial Pennsylvania very liberal concessions were made in the amount of power exercised by the elective branch of the legislature. As provided by the first Frame of Government, the all-important branch of the legislature was an elective council of seventy-two members constituted of those chosen annually because of "best repute for wisdom, virtue and ability." It was given wide executive power as well, being organized into committees on plantations, trade and finance, education and arts, and justice. In addition, it was given the authority to summon and dissolve the assembly. Finally, in it was vested the authority to nominate the double list of individuals from which the governor should select the leading local officers.[27] An elective assembly of two hundred members, chosen annually, constituted the other branch of the legislature, but it occupied a position decidedly inferior to that assigned to the council. Its functions were merely "to impeach

---

[23] Osgood, op. cit., Vol. II, pp. 257ff. Shepherd, op. cit., pp. 239ff.
[24] Shepherd, p. 251f.
[25] Osgood, pp. 262-63. Shepherd, pp. 261ff.
[26] Osgood, pp. 275-76. Shepherd, pp. 292ff., 317ff.
[27] Osgood, op. cit., Vol. II, pp. 257-59. Shepherd, op. cit., pp. 240-42.

offenders before the council, to prepare amendments to bills submitted to it and to accept or reject such bills." [28]

Under the second Frame of Government this arrangement was altered to some extent. The council was to be made up of eighteen members, three elected from each of the six existing counties. The assembly was to be constituted of thirty-six members, six elected from each county. The governor, council and assembly were to be known as the "General Assembly of the Province." The committees of the council were abolished.[29]

The period from 1683 to 1701 was one of continual friction and disputes between council and assembly which resulted in the confusion of the government of the province.[30]

By the Charter of Privileges of 1701 the council was made an appointive body and was deprived of all legislative and most judicial powers. Henceforth it was to be an executive council, advising the governor and discussing legislation, but never originating it. The seat of the actual legislative power in the eighteenth century was in the assembly, which was chosen annually and was made up of four persons from each county. Its sessions were held in Philadelphia. From 1701 to 1776 Pennsylvania was unique among the American colonies in having a legislature of but one house.[31]

C. The Provincial Judiciary

Almost from the beginning of the proprietary government, Pennsylvania was provided with a provincial court. As was the case with the whole judicial system, however, it was periodically interrupted or suspended, owing to the perversity of the Crown in repealing the successive judiciary acts. Not until 1722 did the Crown allow a provincial judiciary act to stand without repeal.[32] The first provincial court was established in 1684. It was made up of five judges appointed by the proprietor, and any three of them might constitute the provincial court. The court was to sit twice annually in Philadelphia and was to go out on the county circuits twice each year. It was to hear appeals from the county courts and to try the more important cases that could not be decided by the county tribunals. In the following year its appointment was

---

[28] Osgood, op. cit., Vol. II, pp. 257-59. Shepherd, op. cit., pp. 240-42.
[29] Osgood, op. cit., Vol. II, pp. 260-61. Shepherd, pp. 246ff.
[30] Shepherd, pp. 248ff.
[31] Osgood, p. 276. Shepherd, pp. 292ff.
[32] Shepherd, p. 396.

given to the governor and council and its jurisdiction was made chiefly appellate.[33] This organization of the provincial court was in general confirmed by the Charter of 1701 and, in spite of successive repeals by the Crown, it persisted until the judicial system was given some degree of permanency by the law of 1722. On May 22, 1722, a bill was signed which established the judicial system of the province and, unlike the earlier bills of 1701, 1706, 1710 and 1715, it was not repealed by the Crown. It provided for a supreme or provincial court of three members which should sit twice each year at Philadelphia and have general appellate jurisdiction.[34] The act of 1722 was repealed by the provincial authorities in 1727, but was re-enacted in 1731 and remained the basis for the organization of the judicial system until the creation of the state government.[35] In addition to the provincial court certain rather vague but important judicial powers were exercised by the provincial council from 1683 to 1701. Counterfeiting, sorcery and admiralty cases came under its jurisdiction. After 1701 the judicial as well as the legislative power of the council tended to disappear.[36]

4. LOCAL GOVERNMENT IN PROVINCIAL PENNSYLVANIA

A. Origins of Local Government, 1676-82

The significant origins of local government in Pennsylvania go back to the ordinance of September 25, 1676, by which Governor Andros put into application the laws which had been drawn up by the order of the Duke of York for the government of his domains in America. Two general local administrative units were provided for—the "riding" and the town or parish. The riding was a vague entity, apparently having little function except to serve as a district of jurisdiction for its chief officer, the sheriff, who was appointed annually by the governor from three nominees presented to him by the justices in the last previous session. The real unit of local government in this period was the town. County government could scarcely be held to exist. The chief officers of the town were the constable and the board of overseers, both elected directly by the people, the constable for one year and the overseers for two. The constables and overseers drew up the "constitution" and by-laws for each town which were binding as soon as they were sanctioned by the court of general sessions. They had almost complete charge

---

[33] Shepherd, op. cit., pp. 371ff. Osgood, op. cit., Vol. II, p. 281.
[34] Shepherd, pp. 373-97. Root, op. cit., pp. 159ff.
[35] Root, pp. 168ff.
[36] Bolles, op. cit., pp. 176-79.

of all local duties and interests of a political nature and, in addition, being ex-officio church wardens, they exercised supervision over the public morals of the community. They also formed the chief local judiciary, trying all petty offenses and minor disputes. They were to meet as a town court every two, three or four weeks as conditions necessitated.[37]

The institution which furnished a connecting link between the periods before and after 1682 in the history of local government in Pennsylvania was the court of sessions. Three of them were in existence in 1676, having come down from the Dutch period. They met at New Castle, Upland and Whorekill, respectively. They were not organized on the basis of the "ridings," but were really county courts and were so referred to in the court records. These courts of general sessions, then, mark the first beginnings of county institutions in Pennsylvania. In addition to general judicial powers these courts possessed extensive legislative authority which constituted the beginning of county legislation. Inasmuch as the town was the center of local government before Penn's occupation of the province in 1682, while the county became the all-important unit afterward, the court of general sessions may be regarded as the transitional institution between the two systems.[38]

B. The Institutions of Local Government in the Proprietary Province

With the establishment of Penn's authority in the province there came a revolution in the local government of the colony. The town lost most of its significance as a local institution and the county emerged as the center of local political life.[39] This transformation has been well summarized by Mr. Gould:

"We have seen that the tendency of the Duke of York's laws was to center local government in the towns. Under the Proprietary administration a totally different order of things was instituted. The county now became the element of primal importance. In fact

---

[37] E. R. L. Gould, *Local Government in Pennsylvania, Johns Hopkins University Studies in Historical and Political Science,* Vol. I, No. III, pp. 20ff. E. P. Allinson and Boies Penrose, *Philadelphia, 1681-1887, J. H. U. Studies,* Extra Volume II, Introduction, pp. xxxvff. *Charter and Laws of Pennsylvania, 1682-1700,* pp. 21-2, 44, 50, 60, 69.

[38] Gould, loc. cit., pp. 24ff. G. E. Howard, *An Introduction to the Local Constitutional History of the United States, J. H. U. Studies in Historical and Political Science,* Extra Volume IV, pp. 369ff. Allinson and Penrose, loc. cit., pp. xxxix-xl.

[39] Howard, loc. cit., p. 373.

it may be safely asserted, that, during nearly the entire portion of the first half-century of the government of Penn and his descendants, the town had little or no significance." [40]

This county organization, which was established after 1682, was the best example among the American colonies of the independent county system and it later became the model for this system when it was so extensively adopted in the western states. Professor Howard says with regard to this point:

"In almost every important respect the county organization of Pennsylvania is without a parallel during the colonial era. Nowhere else is there so clear a model for the independent county system since developed in the western states." [41]

The functions and organization of the county judiciary will be described in treating the origin and development of the judicial system of the province and may be passed over at this point.

The fiscal system of the Pennsylvania County was created by the laws of 1693 and 1696. It was provided that the amount to be raised by taxation each year was to be determined by the justices in the court of quarter sessions, aided by a grand jury and three assessors. Six assessors were then to be elected annually by the freemen from "substantial freeholders." These assessors were to appoint collectors and a county treasurer. The constables of the towns were to bring in a list of taxable persons and estates from which the assessors determined the rate and authorized the collectors to collect the taxes and turn the money over to the county treasurer.[42] An important alteration in this system took place in 1724. In that year a law was passed which removed the fiscal power from the court of quarter sessions and the grand jury and gave it to a board of three commissioners who were to be elected annually in the same election that chose the coroners, sheriffs, and assemblymen. The creation of these commissioners marks an epoch in the history of county government in Pennsylvania. They have remained from that time to this the body in charge of the general fiscal administration of the county, corresponding to the supervisors in New York and the board of chosen freeholders in New Jersey.[43] These commissioners were to meet annually in a joint session with the six assessors and determine the amount which it was necessary

[40] Gould, loc. cit., p. 27.
[41] Howard, loc. cit., p. 383.
[42] Charter and Laws of Pennsylvania, 1682-1700, pp. 221ff., 256ff. Howard, loc. cit., pp. 379-82.
[43] J. A. Fairlie, Local Government in Counties, Towns and Villages, p. 29.

to raise by taxation. The other phases of the fiscal mechanism established in 1693-96 were not seriously altered until 1779, when two assistant assessors were appointed in each town to take over the work of the constables in returning the lists of taxable persons and estates.[44]

In the general civil administration of the county, the county courts kept much of the broad supervisory and appointive power that had been exercised by the court of general sessions before 1682.[45] The chief administrative officer of the county was the sheriff, who had been provided for in the laws of the Duke of York. In the Frames of Government it was stipulated that the sheriff should be commissioned for one year by the governor from a list of nominees furnished originally by the assembly and later by the body of freemen. By the law of January 12, 1706, however, the office was given the elective character which it has since retained.[46] The system of local government created in Pennsylvania before the close of the first quarter of the eighteenth century has remained unchanged in fundamental outlines down to the present time. As Mr. Gould has pointed out, "the Revolution did not change the form of local government which had prevailed before the year 1776. There was no distinct difference between the administration of the province and of the commonwealth." [47]

The right to create counties was vested by the royal charter of March 4, 1681, in the proprietor.[48] At the time of the establishment of the proprietary rule in 1682 three counties were established in what is now the State of Pennsylvania, and the three counties which constituted what is now the State of Delaware were annexed. The three new counties which were created in Pennsylvania were Chester, Bucks and Philadelphia. The "lower counties" which were annexed were New Castle, Jones and Whorekill.[49] The lower counties refused to accept Penn's Charter of Privileges in 1701-02 and drifted away from the rest of the province, remaining united to it only through the common executive.[50] What the province lost in territory, at least, by the defection of the lower counties was more than compensated for by the creation of new counties. Lan-

---

[44] Howard, loc. cit., pp. 382-83. Gould, loc. cit., pp. 28-9.
[45] Howard, loc. cit., pp. 377-79.
[46] *Charter and Laws of Pennsylvania, 1682-1700*, pp. 97, 159. Fairlie, op. cit., p. 29. Shepherd, op. cit., p. 398 note. *Statutes at Large*, Vol. II, pp. 272ff. A. E. McKinley, *The Suffrage Franchise in the Thirteen English Colonies of America*, p. 283.
[47] Gould, loc. cit., p. 28.
[48] *Charter and Laws*, p. 86.
[49] Ibid., p. 104.
[50] Shepherd, op. cit., pp. 338ff.

caster County was created on May 10, 1729, being formed out of
a part of Chester County. York County was formed on August 19,
1749, out of Lancaster. Cumberland County was formed on January 27, 1750, also out of Lancaster. Berks County was created on
March 11, 1752, out of Philadelphia, Chester and Lancaster. Northampton County was also formed on March 11, 1752, being created
out of a part of Bucks County. Bedford County was formed on
March 9, 1771, out of Cumberland. Northumberland was created
out of Lancaster, Cumberland, Berks, Bedford and Northampton
on March 21, 1772. Finally, Westmoreland County was created out
of Bedford County on February 26, 1773. There were, thus, eleven
counties in the province at the close of the colonial period, exclusive of the lower counties.[51]

III. THE JUDICIAL ORGANIZATION, THE CRIMINAL
CODES AND THE PENAL INSTITUTIONS OF
PROVINCIAL PENNSYLVANIA

1. THE JUDICIAL ORGANIZATION

It is impossible to give a comprehensive account of the early
judicial history of the province of Pennsylvania in a brief compass.
It was changed too frequently to allow of a complete sketch except
at the expense of great length and tortuous details. It will here
suffice to describe the origin of the system and to indicate its
organization when it was given permanence in 1731.

In the royal charter the right of establishing courts and a judicial
system was vested solely in the proprietor, but he pursued his usual
liberal policy by leaving the organization of the judicial system to
the legislature.[52] The proprietor, however, exercised his right of
appointing all justices and judges, though up to 1701 he allowed
the assembly to nominate them.[53]

The basis for the provincial courts was laid in the law of March,
1683, though the supreme or provincial court was not created until
the following year.[54] The lowest judicial body created was the
"peacemakers," who were probably a perpetuation of the arbiters

---

[51] A complete account of the creation of all the counties in Pennsylvania
may be found in any recent issue of Smull's *Legislative Handbook of
Pennsylvania*.
[52] Shepherd, op. cit., p. 370. Root, op. cit., pp. 158-59.
[53] Shepherd, pp. 370, 373. Howard, loc. cit., p. 374.
[54] *Charter and Laws of Pennsylvania, 1682-1700*, pp. 128, 178. Sehpherd,
p. 371.

of the town courts of the earlier period under the provisions of the laws of the Duke of York.[55] Three of these peacemakers were to be appointed in each precinct in the county by the justices of the county court. They were given power to settle minor civil disputes, though their judgment was subject to review by the county court. This court of peacemakers became obsolete by 1692. The Quakers had special sectarian organs for settling their disputes.[56] The next stage in the judicial hierarchy was constituted by the justices, appointed by the governor. Up to 1701 they were appointed during good behavior from a popularly selected list of nominations. After that date they were appointed by the governor and commissioned by him to hold office during his pleasure, as was the practise in England.[57] Two justices were allowed to hold a court which could decide civil cases involving less than forty shillings, though the decision was subject to review by the county court. Later this power was conferred upon a single justice, but after 1701 justices sitting except in county court had only powers of taking acknowledgments and binding over to keep the peace.[58] As might be expected from the importance of the county in provincial Pennsylvania, the real center of judicial life and activity was the county court. The provincial county court was the direct perpetuation of the courts of the Duke of York, which had been holding sessions in New Castle, Uplands and Whorekill. They were accepted and continued by Penn and the provincial legislature in the law of March, 1683.[59] They were made up of all the justices of the county and held their sessions quarterly.[60] They had the power to try "all titles of land, all actions of debt, account or slander, actions personal, and all actions criminal or civil whatsoever, excepting treason, murder, manslaughter, and other heinous and enormous crimes." [61] In the earliest county courts, then, civil and criminal cases were tried by the same tribunal sitting in the same capacity. The organization of the supreme or provincial court, which was created in 1684, has been described above. In addition to its appellate jurisdiction it had original jurisdiction over the serious crimes which were excluded from the jurisdiction of the county courts.[62]

---

[55] See above, pp. 19-20. Howard, p. 374.
[56] *Charter and Laws*, p. 128. Bolles, op. cit., p. 180. Howard, pp. 373-74.
[57] Howard, p. 374. C. A. Beard, *The Office of the Justice of the Peace in England.*
[58] *Charter and Laws*, pp. 131, 186, 219. Howard, p. 374.
[59] *Charter and Laws*, p. 129. Howard, pp. 370-73.
[60] *Charter and Laws*, pp. 177-78.
[61] Ibid., p. 178.
[62] See above, pp. 18ff. *Charter and Laws*, pp. 178, 311.

These various organizing acts were brought together in the act of October 28, 1701, which for the first time established in a systematic manner the judicial system of the province.[63] This law might well have served as the basis for a permanent provincial judiciary, if it had not been repealed by the Crown in council on February 7, 1705. From that date until November, 1731, the judicial system of the province was in a chaotic condition. Judiciary bills were passed only to be repealed by the Crown, and were replaced by a new system established by the governor's ordinance power, which lasted until a new bill could be passed and put into operation, and in due time be repealed again by the Crown. After the repeal of the bill of 1701 in 1705, the system was continued by the ordinance power until the next judiciary bill was passed on February 28, 1710. This was repealed in 1713. The next act was passed on May 28, 1715. This was repealed in 1719. The judicial system was again established by the act of May 22, 1722, which was not repealed, but was superseded by the act of August 26, 1727. This law was repealed by the Crown in 1731. On November 27, 1731, an act was passed reviving the act of 1722, and this remained in force until the Revolution, except for amendments on September 29, 1759, and May 20, 1767.[64]

The only important development in the judicial system in the period of confusion between 1701 and 1722 was contained in the Ordinance of Governor John Evans of February, 1706, which provided a judicial system to take the place of that repealed in the previous year. This carried on the differentiating process in the evolution of the judiciary of the province. It created two county courts, one with civil and the other with criminal jurisdiction. The jurisdiction over civil cases was given to a county "court of common pleas" and the criminal jurisdiction was delegated to a county "court of general quarter sessions of peace and gaol delivery." While there were to be two distinct courts, they were to be composed of the same justices meeting at the same sessions.[65] This differentiating process was carried still further by the laws of 1722 and 1759, which not only provided for separate courts, but also for a different set of justices for each.[66] A minor development in this period was the provision in the law of March 27, 1713,

---

[63] *Charter and Laws of Pennsylvania, 1682-1700*, pp. 311-19. Root, op. cit., p. 159. Shepherd, op. cit., p. 373.

[64] *Compilation of the Laws and Ordinances Establishing the Several Courts of Judicature of the Province of Pennsylvania, in the Charter and Laws of Pennsylvania, 1682-1700*, pp. 296-410. See especially the Historical Introduction by Staughton George. Root, Chap. VI. Shepherd, Part II, Chap. VIII.

[65] *Charter and Laws of Pennsylvania, 1682-1700*, pp. 319-23.

[66] Ibid., pp. 387-94, 405-07.

which gave the court of general quarter sessions the power to sit as an orphans' court. It held this power until 1759 when the authority was transferred to the court of common pleas.[67]

The judicial organization, which was in force from 1722 to 1727 and from 1731 to 1776, may be ascertained by an analysis of the system created by the act of May 22, 1722. According to this law, criminal jurisdiction in each county, except in capital cases, was vested in a court of general quarter sessions of peace and gaol delivery which was to hold its sessions four times each year in the county for which it was created. The justices were commissioned by the governor or lieutenant-governor and, like all other provincial justices at the time, were to hold office at the pleasure of the governor. All the justices of the county, or any three, were to constitute a court.[68]

The jurisdiction over all civil cases was given to the county court of common pleas, which was to hold its sessions quarterly. Three justices constituted a court. Special justices were contemplated for this court, but in practice the justices of the quarter sessions were usually commissioned to act in this capacity, though both courts and sessions were now distinct and separate.[69]

The supreme or provincial court was composed of three justices commissioned by the governor, none of whom could be members of the inferior courts. Any two were to constitute the court. They were to meet twice annually in Philadelphia. The court was given appellate jurisdiction over all cases and original jurisdiction over all criminal cases involving capital offenses. The court was to meet as often as necessary to handle these criminal cases. All criminal trials under the jurisdiction of the supreme court were to be held in Philadelphia, regardless of the place of the commission of the crime. An appeal might be taken from a decision of the supreme court to the Crown.[70]

The act of 1722, as revived in 1731, was twice amended before the creation of the state. On September 29, 1759, an act was passed which provided that the court of common pleas should be composed of five justices, none of whom could be members of the court of general quarter sessions.[71] The act of May 20, 1767, stated that henceforth the supreme court was to be made up of four justices instead of three, that instead of holding all their sessions in Philadelphia they were to go on the circuit in the counties twice each

---

[67] *Charter and Laws of Pennsylvania, 1682-1700,* pp. 346-51, 406.
[68] Ibid., pp. 388-90, 404-05.
[69] Ibid., pp. 392-93.
[70] Ibid., pp. 390-92.
[71] Ibid., p. 406.

year, and that no appeal could be taken to the Crown from the
general verdict of the supreme court.[72]

2. The Criminal Codes of Provincial Pennsylvania

*A. General Historical Background for an Interpretation of the
Criminal Codes of Provincial Pennsylvania*

In order to form a critical estimate of the nature and development of the criminal codes of provincial Pennsylvania it is essential
to review briefly the general status of criminal jurisprudence in
the last quarter of the seventeenth century. Two tendencies stand
out conspicuously—an extreme severity in the penalties prescribed
and the almost exclusive employment of some form of corporal
punishment as the prevailing mode of executing the penalty imposed.
A much larger number of crimes was then specified as capital
offenses than is the case at the present time, though the situation
was not so bad as it became in England a century later, when
between two hundred and fifty and three hundred crimes were
branded as capital. In the case of crimes not capital, some form
of corporal punishment milder than death was usually inflicted.
Whipping, branding, mutilating, confinement in the stocks or
pillory and "ducking" were among the more popular of these forms
of punishment. At this same time the practise was beginning of
banishing offenders to the colonial districts, which became so popular in the eighteenth century and in the first half of the nineteenth.
Until the outbreak of the Revolutionary War the American colonies
were the main receptacle for the banished criminals of England,[73]
but after 1776 they were superseded by Australia. In view of
these modes of inflicting punishment for crimes, it readily becomes
apparent that there would be little need for the modern prison
system. At the time, the jails were used chiefly for the detention
of those accused of crime who were awaiting their trial, and the
majority of those confined in the prisons of the time were debtors
and political and religious offenders.[74]

At the close of the seventeenth century the barbarous English
criminal code was in force in varying degrees in all of the English
colonies in America, with the sole exception of the Quaker colonies

---

[72] *Charter and Laws of Pennsylvania, 1682-1700,* pp. 407-09.
[73] For the effect of this practice in Pennsylvania see below, pp. 48ff.
[74] F. H. Wines, *Punishment and Reformation,* Chaps. V-VI, George Ives,
A History of Penal Methods, Chapter I. Maurice Parmelee, *Criminology,*
pp. 357-72. J. F. Stephen, *A History of the Criminal Law of England.*

of West Jersey and Pennsylvania. The American adaptation of the code of the mother country was never so extreme as the English code. The notorious "Blue Laws" of Connecticut, adopted in 1642 and 1650, provided for but fourteen capital crimes, and the Hempstead Code of 1664, which was later introduced into Pennsylvania in the Duke of York's laws, enumerated eleven capital offenses.[75] Though these American Puritan codes compare very favorably with the practice of the mother country, they present an unenviable contrast to the mild and humane Quaker codes of West Jersey and Pennsylvania. In the former only treason and murder were capital offenses, and in the latter murder alone was punishable by death.[76] While the Quaker codes did not long remain in force in either colony, it is probable that the influence of these Quaker laws and theories did more than anything else to promote that movement for the liberalizing and humanizing of the criminal codes in this country, which began immediately after the Revolution and spread from Philadelphia throughout the states.[77] This Quaker influence from the beginning operated mainly along two related lines of reform—the reduction of the number of capital crimes and the substitution of imprisonment at hard labor for corporal punishment as the most satisfactory penalty to be imposed for the commission of crimes other than capital.[78]

Looking at their development in the large, the criminal codes of provincial Pennsylvania may be said to have passed through three major transformations. The prevalent criminal procedure of England and the Puritan colonies was introduced in the Hempstead or Duke of York's laws, which were promulgated by Governor Andros on September 25, 1676. These laws were superseded by the Quaker code, which was enacted at the Chester Assembly on December 7, 1682, and with subsequent additions remained in force until May 31, 1718. At this time the Quakers sacrificed their humane criminal code in order to obtain the right of affirmation in judicial procedure, and by the act of 1718 the English and Puritan practices were reintroduced and remained the basis of the criminal procedure of the province, not being abolished until the state began the revision of its criminal code by the act of September 15, 1786.[79]

---

[75] *The Public Records of the Colony of Connecticut*, Vol. I, pp. 509ff. *The Charter and Laws of Pennsylvania, 1682-1700*, pp. 14-15.
[76] Leaming and Spicer, *The Grants, Concessions and Original Constitutions of the Province of New Jersey*, pp. 382-411. *Charter and Laws*, pp. 107ff.
[77] Wines, op. cit., pp. 142ff., 147, 344.
[78] Ibid.
[79] Shepherd, op. cit., p. 389. Bolles, op. cit., pp. 258-59. Richard Vaux, *Brief Sketch of the Origin and History of the State Penitentiary for the Eastern District of Pennsylvania*, Philadelphia, 1872, p. 8.

B. The Original Criminal Code of 1676

On September 25, 1676, Governor Edmund Andros promulgated the laws of the Duke of York by an executive ordinance and thereby made them applicable to Pennsylvania.[80] These laws had been compiled under the Duke's authority to be applied in the government of the territory he had conquered from the Dutch. They were described as having been "collected out of the several laws now in force in his Majesty's American Colonies and Plantations and digested into one volume for the public use of the territories in America under the government of his Royal Highness, James, Duke of York and Albany." They were first promulgated on March 1, 1664, at Hempstead, Long Island, and the criminal code contained therein is usually referred to as the "Hempstead Code." [81] The propinquity of Long Island to the New Haven Colony, the intercommunication between the two colonies, and the resemblance between the wording as well as the content of the two codes, would incline one to the belief that the Hempstead Code was taken more or less directly from the codes of 1642 and 1650 enacted for the New Haven colony.[82] The following portion of the laws applied to the list of capital crimes:

"1. If any person within this Government shall by direct, expressed, impious or presumptious ways, deny the true God and His attributes, he shall be put to death.

"2. If any person shall commit any wilful and premeditated murder he shall be put to death.

"3. If any person slayeth another with a sword or dagger who hath no weapon to defend himself, he shall be put to death.

"4. If any man shall slay, or cause another to be slain by lying in wait privily for him or by poisoning or any other such wicked conspiracy, he shall be put to death.

"5. If any man or woman shall lie with any beast or brute creature by carnal copulation they shall be put to death, and the beast shall be burned.

"6. If any man lieth with mankind as he lieth with a woman, they shall be put to death, unless the one party were forced or be under fourteen years of age, in which case he shall be punished at the discretion of the Court of Assizes.

"7. If any person forcibly stealeth or carrieth away any mankind, he shall be put to death.

---

[80] *Charter and Laws of Pennsylvania, 1682-1700,* Historical Notes, pp. 455ff.
[81] Ibid.
[82] H. E. Barnes, *A History of the Penal, Reformatory, and Correctional Institutions of New Jersey,* pp. 27-8, 341-42.

"8. If any man bear false witness maliciously and on purpose to take away a man's life, he shall be put to death.

"9. If any man shall traitorously deny his Majesty's right and titles to his Crowns and Dominions, or shall raise armies to resist his authority, he shall be put to death.

"10. If any man shall treacherously conspire or publicly attempt to invade or surprise any town or towns, fort or forts, within this Government, he shall be put to death.

"11. If any child or children, above sixteen years of age, and of sufficient understanding, shall smite their natural father or mother, unless thereunto provoked and forced for their self-protection from death or maiming, at the complaint of said father and mother, and not otherwise, there being sufficient witnesses thereof, that child or those children so offending shall be put to death." [83]   (3)

Lesser punishments were provided for other crimes and misdemeanors. Fornication was punishable by fine, corporal punishment or marriage at the discretion of the court. Forgery was to be punished by the pillory, double damages to the injured persons, and disability from again giving evidence in court. The penalty imposed for arson was death or full satisfaction to the injured party, at the pleasure of the court. Excessive drinking was penalized by fine, the stocks or both. Lying and speaking false news was to be punished by fine, whipping and the stocks. As to burglary and robbery, it was provided that the penalty for the first offense was to be branding, for the second, branding and whipping, and for the third, death. Adultery was punishable by corporal punishment, fine or imprisonment. Minor punishments were also provided for such petty offenses as disturbing church meeting, disobeying parents and the like.[84] There were also included sundry laws regulating the treatment of such civil offenses as would be likely to arise in a primitive agricultural society. These were not widely different from those provided in the Levitical code or the Code of Hammurabi.[85] The code abounds in humorous enactments of which the following section of the law regulating the conduct of the inns of the time is a fair sample. This provided that:

"Every person licensed to keep an Ordinary shall always be provided of strong and wholesome beer, of four bushels of malt, at the least to a hogshead, which he shall not sell at above two pence the quart under the penalty of twenty shillings, for the first offence, forty shillings for the second, and loss of his license. It is permitted to sell beer out of doors at a penny the ale quart or under.

---

[83] *Charter and Laws of Pennsylvania, 1682-1700,* pp. 14-5.
[84] Ibid., pp. 18, 27-8, 62-3.
[85] Ibid., pp. 15-7.

"No licensed person shall suffer any to drink excessively or at unseasonable hours after nine of the clock at night in or about any of their houses upon penalty of two shillings six pence for every offense if complaint and proof be made thereof." [86]

Petty offenses were dealt with in the town courts constituted by the constable and two or more of the overseers. The more serious offenses, with the exception of capital crimes, came under the jurisdiction of the court of quarter sessions. Here trial was by a jury of not more than seven or less than six, and a majority verdict was binding in all cases. The capital crimes were tried by the court of assizes. Here a jury of twelve was usual and the verdict had to be unanimous.[87] Minor punishments were inflicted by the constables of the towns or by other specially appointed persons, but the execution of capital offenses rested with the sheriff.[88]

C. The Quaker Criminal Codes of 1682 to 1718

The provisions of the laws of the Duke of York were superseded by those adopted by Penn's first assembly, which was held at Chester on December 4-7, 1682. Here were adopted the sixty-one chapters of what was known as "The Great Law or Body of Laws" of the province of Pennsylvania.[89] This contained the original Quaker criminal code of Pennsylvania and marked out clearly the wide differences between Quaker practices and theories and those of the Puritans in the other colonies and of the mother country. This code can scarcely be appreciated without a brief examination of the intellectual and sociological background of Quaker jurisprudence.

The ideas and customs of the Quakers furnish the best explanation of the nature and content of their criminal code.[90] Mr. Applegarth in his interesting study—*The Quakers in Pennsylvania*—has summarized the more important of their customs and ideas which went so far to shape their legislation. The Quakers evidenced an almost puritanical asceticism and austerity in their mode of life, though they were not so cruel and vindictive as were the Puritans in punishing deviations from group regulations. All forms of sensuality were particularly repugnant to the Quakers, and they

---

[86] *Charter and Laws of Pennsylvania, 1682-1700*, p. 30.
[87] Ibid., pp. 11, 21-2, 33-4, 44, 50, 62.
50, 62.
[88] Ibid., pp. 21, 50, 456.
[89] Ibid., pp. 107ff. and Historical Notes, pp. 465-82.
[90] See Isaac Sharpless, *A Quaker Experiment in Government*, pp. 21-46; *Quakerism and Politics*, pp. 202-20.

were especially careful to provide a strict legal regulation of sexual morality. Next to sexual laxity, profanity received the greatest amount of condemnation by the Quakers and their laws repressing "prophane swearing" and cursing are humorously explicit and thoroughgoing. Gambling was also regarded as a serious offense, and in this category were included many games and amusements now considered quite harmless. Drunkenness was considered a most deplorable vice which they tried to repress with strict regulations, and smoking was regarded as only one degree less serious than drinking. Dueling, with its shedding of blood, was, naturally, forbidden by the Quakers. Again they were opposed to the theater and public amusements and made their introduction and patronage punishable offenses. The Quakers did not rely merely upon legal regulation to secure a high degree of public morality, but resorted to an almost Calvinistic type of inquisitorial supervision over the morality of private citizens. It is stated upon good authority that one of the more prominent of the early governors of the province was in the habit of going through the inns of Philadelphia each night before he retired in order to disperse the hangers-on who might have delayed their home-going after the "unseemly hour of nine o'clcok of the night." [91] Finally, it should be noted that the aversion of the Quakers to unusual cruelty, suffering and the shedding of blood, led them to substitute imprisonment for the death penalty, in all cases except murder, and for the more barbarous types of corporal punishment.[92]

Though the "Great Law" was submitted by the proprietor to the assembly for its sanction, it was not seriously altered and it may be regarded as representing Penn's ideal of a criminal code.[93] The law opened with the declaration, very unusual for the time, which proclaimed that liberty of conscience and freedom of worship should be guaranteed to all who acknowledged the existence and attributes of the one true God.[94] This eliminated at the outset from the province of Pennsylvania the long category of religious offenses which marred the criminal jurisprudence of most of the other colonies at the time, as well as that of all the European countries.

In the main, crimes of violence against the person were punished by imprisonment at hard labor in the "house of correction." For assaulting a parent the child was to be confined in the house of

---

[91] Albert C. Applegarth, *The Quakers in Pennsylvania, Johns Hopkins University Studies in Historical and Political Science,* Vol. X, Numbers VIII-IX, pp. 5-49.

[92] Bolles, op. cit., p. 256.

[93] *Charter and Laws of Pennsylvania, 1682-1700,* pp. 99-104, 477ff.

[94] Ibid., pp. 107-08.

correction during the pleasure of the parent.[95] Assaulting a magistrate was punished by fine and by one month's confinement in the house of correction.[96] If a servant assaulted a master he was to be punished at the discretion of two justices of the peace.[97] In view of the fact that a very large proportion of the population of provincial Pennsylvania was made up of indentured servants, this enactment was of very considerable significance. Assault and battery constituted a breach of the peace and was to be punished "according to the nature and circumstances of the fact." [98] Dueling was penalized by a fine of five pounds or three months' imprisonment.[99] Rioting was accounted an act of violence and was punished accordingly.[100] Neither murder nor manslaughter was included in the crimes and penalties enumerated in the "Great Law," but their punishment was provided for in the supplement to the original code, which was enacted by the assembly in March, 1683. Here is declared that manslaughter should be punished according to the nature and circumstance of the act, and it was decreed with respect to murder that "if any person within this province or territories thereof shall wilfully or premeditately kill another person, or wilfully or premeditately be the cause of, or accessory to, the death of any person, such person shall, according to the law of God, suffer death." [101] Murder, then, was the only capital crime in the Quaker criminal code of Pennsylvania.

In defining the crimes against property and prescribing the punishments therefor, it was decreed that arson should be punished by rendering double satisfaction to the injured party, imprisonment for one year and by receiving such corporal punishment as the court should see fit to impose.[102] Breaking, entering and theft of goods was punishable by fourfold restitution and three months' imprisonment. If the offender was not able to make restitution he was to be imprisoned for seven years.[103] Forcible entry into the possessions of another was regarded as a breach of the peace and was punishable accordingly at the discretion of the court.[104] Lands and goods of "theeves and fellons" were liable to confiscation in order to render satisfaction to injured parties, and, if they possessed

---

[95] *Charter and Laws of Pennsylvania, 1682-1700*, p. 113.
[96] Ibid.
[97] Ibid.
[98] Ibid., pp. 113-14.
[99] Ibid., p. 114.
[100] Ibid., p. 113.
[101] Ibid., p. 144.
[102] Ibid., p. 112.
[103] Ibid.
[104] Ibid., pp. 112-13.

no property, such offenders were to be set at work in the workhouse until satisfaction was rendered.[105]

The longest list of crimes and penalties related to offenses against
public morality. Especially severe were the penalties imposed for
the sexual "crimes." The punishment imposed for "defiling the
marriage bed" was whipping and one year's imprisonment for
the first offense and life imprisonment for the second.[106] Incest
was punished by forfeiture of half one's estate and one year's
imprisonment for the first offense and life imprisonment for the
second.[107] Sodomy and bestiality were penalized by forfeiture of
one-third of the offender's estate and six months' imprisonment
for the first offense and life imprisonment for the second.[108] Rape
was punishable by forfeiture of one-third of the offender's estate
and one year's imprisonment for first offense and life imprisonment for a repetition of the offense.[109] Even the first offense of
bigamy was to be punished by life imprisonment.[110] The penalty
for fornication was not provided in the code of 1682, but in the
additions made in March, 1683, it was provided that fornication
should be punished by "enjoining marriage, or fine, or corporal
punishment, or all or any of these at the discretion of the county
court." [111] The various types of profanity were all penalized by a
fine of five shillings or five days' imprisonment at hard labor, on
a bread and water diet.[112]

The first offense of drunkenness was to be punished by a fine
of five shillings or by five days' imprisonment at hard labor on
bread and water. All subsequent offenses were punishable by a
doubling of the penalty for the previous offense.[113] Those inn-
keepers or others who allowed drunkenness to go on at their houses
were to receive the same punishment as the drunkard.[114] It was
also provided that "if any person shall drink healths, which may
provoke people to unnecessary and excessive drinking" he should
be punished by a fine of five shillings and the pledger of the health
likewise.[115] In spite of these restrictions on excessive drinking
cheap beer was assured by the provision that "all strong beer and

---

[105] *Charter and Laws of Pennsylvania, 1682-1700,* p. 112.
[106] Ibid., pp. 109-10.
[107] Ibid., p. 110.
[108] Ibid.
[109] Ibid.
[110] Ibid., pp. 110-11.
[111] Ibid., p. 145.
[112] Ibid., pp. 108-09.
[113] Ibid., p. 111.
[114] Ibid.
[115] Ibid.

ale made of barley malt shall be sold for not above two pennies Sterling for a full Winchester quart." [116] It was further decreed that whereas selling liquor to Indians tended "to make the poor natives worse, and not better for their coming among them, which is a heinous offence to God, and a reproach to the blessed name of Christ, and His holy religion," any one convicted of so-doing was to be fined five pounds.[117] No law against smoking was enacted in 1682, but in 1696 it was provided that any one detected smoking in the streets by day or night was to be fined twelve pence and the fines were to be used in buying apparatus for fire protection.[118]

The Quaker prejudice against games and theaters appears in the decree that "whosoever shall introduce into this province, or frequent such rude and riotous sports and practices as prizes, stage-plays, masques, revels, bull-baitings, and such like" shall be regarded as peace breakers to be fined at least twenty shillings or to suffer ten days' imprisonment at hard labor.[119] It was further provided that "if any person be convicted of playing at cards, dice, lotteries, or such like enticing, vain, and evil sports and games, such persons shall pay five shillings or suffer five days' imprisonment in the house of correction." [120] Suitable punishment, consisting of fine or imprisonment, was also provided for lying, sedition, speaking slightingly of magistrates, scandalous reporting and scolding, bribery and extortion.[121]

The wide reliance upon imprisonment as a mode of punishment is evident throughout the separate enactments of this code, and it was an epoch-making departure in criminal procedure. Excepting only the closely related Quaker colony of West Jersey, this code of 1682 in Pennsylvania unquestionably marks the first instance in the history of criminal jurisprudence in which imprisonment at hard labor was prescribed as a punishment for a majority of the acts which were branded as crimes by the community.[122]

The legal regulations for the adjustment of civil actions and disputes were not extensively included in this first code of 1682, but were embraced in the act of March, 1683.[123]

In addition to the court system, which has been analyzed above, the law of 1682 made the following provisions regarding procedure

---

[116] *Charter and Laws of Pennsylvania, 1682-1700,* pp. 115-16.
[117] Ibid., pp. 111-12.
[118] Ibid., p. 260.
[119] Ibid., p. 114.
[120] Ibid.
[121] Ibid., pp. 114-17.
[122] Barnes, op. cit., p. 351.
[123] *Charter and Laws,* pp. 127ff.

in criminal cases. The testimony of two witnesses was required to establish proof in any case. Perjury was punished by the penalty which the accused did receive or might have received, satisfaction to the wronged party, exposure as a false witness and disability from further right to testify in the courts of the province. Trials were to be by jury. In criminal cases the grand jury was composed of twenty-four, of which twelve must declare the accused guilty. Forty-eight jurors were to be impaneled for the trial jury, from which twelve were to be selected for the trial, unless fewer than that number remained after "reasonable challenges had been admitted." In that case a new panel had to be enrolled.[124]

While there were many additions and some changes in details, yet when looked at from the broad standpoint of sociology and jurisprudence, this Quaker code of 1682 may be said to have persisted as the basis of criminal procedure in the province until 1718.[125] Though Penn was suspended from power between 1692 and 1694, Governor Fletcher, who was appointed to take his place, permitted the reenactment of an almost identical code in June, 1693.[126] It was again confirmed by the act of November 27, 1700.[127] Though this law was repealed by the Crown, it was reenacted on January 12, 1706, and remained in force until 1718.[128] The general tendency, however, in these successive acts was to increase the severity of the penalties and to introduce the more barbarous types of corporal punishment, such as branding, which had not appeared in the code of 1683. Terms of imprisonment became longer and, though the death penalty was not inflicted on white inhabitants for any crime except murder until 1718, it was executed on negroes after 1700 if they were found guilty of murder, rape, buggery and burglary.[129] By thus widening the application of the death penalty to what was regarded by them as an inferior race, the provincial authorities accustomed themselves to its extension to their own kind a few years later. After a careful investigation of the changes in the

---

[124] *Charter and Laws of Pennsylvania, 1682-1700,* pp. 116-17. What was probably the first, and perhaps the only, instance of a jury of women in the American colonies occurred in Delaware County in 1689. An unusual circumstance called it into existence. A young woman was on trial for "carnal intercourse" and a jury of women was called to discover whether or not she was pregnant. They reported "that they can not find she is, neither be they sure she is not." Punishment was, accordingly, delayed. George Smith, *A History of Delaware County,* p. 174.
[125] Bolles, pp. 257-58. Shepherd, p. 388.
[126] *Charter and Laws,* pp. 192-220. Shepherd, pp. 276-77.
[127] *The Statutes at Large of Pennsylvania, 1682-1700,* compiled by Mitchell and Flanders, Vol. II, pp. 3ff.
[128] Ibid., pp. 171ff.
[129] Ibid., Vol. II, pp. 79, 235.

penalties inflicted and in the degree of punishment prescribed in
the period between 1682 and 1718, one is less likely than before
to accept the popular conception that there was a total break with
precedents in criminal jurisprudence in the law of 1718.[130] While
the Quaker theories did prevail down to that date in a majority
of cases, there can be no doubt that the transition to the English
and Puritan system was being prepared for in the two previous
decades.

D. The Reestablishment of the Anglican and Puritan Codes, 1718

The act of May 31, 1718, which brought the English criminal
code into operation in Pennsylvania, was the product of the peculiar
Quaker aversion to taking an oath and was one phase of the struggle
between the Anglicans and Quakers. Down to the beginning of
the reign of George I in 1714, the Quakers had normally enjoyed
the right of affirmation, but in 1715 an act was passed by Parliament which forbade affirmation as a qualification in criminal procedure and this act was extended in its application to the colonies.
Governor Gookin was determined to carry out the royal decree,
but the provincial officers rebelled against it, and the administration
of justice in Pennsylvania was disrupted.[131] Doctor Bolles thus
summarizes the dispute:

"This construction, which was maintained by the governor, and
shut out many from their offices, and even from the protection of
the law, threw the Province into confusion. The governor refused
to administer the affirmation as a qualification for office; the judges
refused to sit in criminal cases; the administration of justice was
suspended, and two atrocious murderers remained in jail three years
without trial. The Assembly was alarmed; but it resolutely asserted
the rights of the people, and at length Gookin was recalled." [132]

Governor Keith, who succeeded Gookin, advised the assembly
that the best method of inducing the Crown to grant the right of
affirmation would be to adopt the English criminal code. This
advice was accepted, and David Lloyd, the chief justice of the
supreme court, was delegated to draw up a bill which would embody
the criminal laws of England. His work was accepted and the
bill became law on May 31, 1718.[133] A more perfect example of

---

[130] For a somewhat different view see Bolles, p. 258.
[131] Shepherd, op. cit., pp. 361-67. Root, op. cit., pp. 248ff.
[132] Bolles, op. cit., p. 257.
[133] Shepherd, pp. 388-89; Bolles, pp. 255-57; Root, op. cit., pp. 248-53.

the proverbial tendency to "strain at a gnat and swallow the camel" could scarcely be found, and the incident proves that the Quakers could scarcely claim entire freedom from the weakness of so many religious sects in being more concerned with an empty form than with a great moral principle and a notable social reform. For the sake of indulging a sectarian whim they were at the time willing to sacrifice one of their greatest contributions to civilization and human progress. By a strange coincidence Penn died in the same year that his advanced criminal jurisprudence was being uprooted. Professor Shepherd has made the following pertinent comment on this point:

"Indeed, there seems a melancholy significance about the fact that, as the life of William Penn, whose legislation marked by justice tempered with mercy, has been the admiration of the civilized world, was slowly ebbing away, his cherished ideals of humanitarianism were being ruthlessly destroyed and replaced by the gloomy severity of the Middle Ages." [134]

The intent and purpose of the new criminal code was stated in the following words:

"Whereas it is a settled point, that the common law is the birth-right of English subjects, so it ought to be their rule in British dominions; but acts of Parliament have been adjudged not to extend to these plantations, unless they are particularly named in such acts.

"Now forasmuch as some persons have been encouraged to transgress certain statutes against capital crimes, and other enormities, because those statutes have not hitherto been fully extended to this province.

"Therefore, lest there should be any further failure in that behalf, may it please the Governor that it be enacted. . . ." [135]

Though the right of affirmation was guaranteed, this concession was much more than offset by thorough acquiescence in the barbarous severity of the criminal code of England and of the Puritans in other American colonies. The new code was even more rigorous than that contained in the Duke of York's laws promulgated in 1676. Herein twelve offenses had been designated as capital, while in the code of 1718 no less than thirteen crimes were declared to be capital. The list included the various degrees of treason, murder, manslaughter by stabbing, serious maiming, highway rob-

---

Charter and Laws of Pennsylvania, 1682-1700, pp. 371-82. *Statutes at Large of Pennsylvania*, Vol. III, pp. 199-221.

[134] Shepherd, op. cit., p. 389.

[135] *Charter and Laws of Pennsylvania, 1682-1700*, p. 371.

bery, burglary, arson, sodomy, buggery, rape, concealing the death of a bastard child, advising the killing of such a child and witchcraft. Larceny was the only felony which was not made a capital crime. This was made punishable by restitution, fine, whipping and imprisonment.[136] Counterfeiting of paper money and gold and silver coin was made a capital crime by the laws of September 21, 1756, and February 21, 1767,[137] and with this addition, the sanguinary criminal code remained in existence until after the close of the provincial period, when a reforming era was initiated by the act of September 15, 1786.[138] The practise of whipping, branding and mutilation for the punishment of lesser crimes, which was already growing up by 1718, was continued with general uniformity throughout the period. In addition to the greater severity of the punishments which became the rule after 1718, it should be noted that the penalties imposed were such that there was little need for such penal institutions as were adapted to the substitution of imprisonment for corporal punishment. There is, accordingly, no difficulty in understanding why the "common gaol" rather than the workhouse became the typical penal institution of provincial Pennsylvania in the eighteenth century.[139] Mr. J. F. Watson, in his interesting compilation of provincial customs originally published in 1830, offers the following observations upon the barbarous modes of punishment which prevailed down to the Revolutionary period:

"These barbarous measures of punishment were not in accordance with the spirit and feelings of our own forefathers, who early aimed at commuting work and confinement for crime; but the parent country, familiar with its sanguinary code, always revoked the laws formed upon our schemes of reformation. These punishments therefore generally prevailed till the time of our self-government, when measures were speedily taken, first by societies of citizens, and afterwards by the Legislature to introduce those reforms into prison discipline which have made our city and state to be celebrated for its early 'Penitentiary System.' "[140]

E.   *The Administration of Justice under the Provincial Codes*

An account of the methods of administering "justice" under these

---

[136] *Charter and Laws of Pennsylvania, 1682-1700,* pp. 372-82.
[137] *Statutes at Large of Pennsylvania,* Vol. V, pp. 247-48. Vol. VII, p. 91.
[138] Ibid., Vol. XII, pp. 280-90.
[139] See below, pp 55ff. Futhey and Cope assert that after 1718 in Chester County, which may be taken as typical of the eastern part of the state, whipping was the conventional punishment for all crimes other than capital. *History of Chester County,* p. 406.
[140] J. F. Watson, *Annals of Philadelphia,* Revised and enlarged by W. P. Hazard, 1898, Vol. I, pp. 361-62. Cf. Bolles, op. cit., pp. 258-59.

provincial codes is, fortunately, preserved for present-day students in Mr. Watson's work. The following citation from his compendium of information regarding the manners and customs of colonial Philadelphia reproduces the significant passages dealing with "primitive courts and trials" and "crimes and punishments:" [141]

"We have been so long happily delivered from the former exhibitions of the pillory, whipping post, ducking-stool, wheelbarrow-men, and even hanging itself, that it may serve to show the aspect of quite another age, to expose the facts in the days of our forefathers, as derived from the presentments of grand juries, trials in the Mayor's court, or from the Gazettes, to-wit:

"Year 1685—John Rambo is indicted, and gives Peter and Gunner Rambo securities in £500 for his appearance, to answer an indictment preferred by Peter Cock of Kiphah (all Swedish I think) for his having had criminal intercourse with his daughter, Bridget. The witness testified that about the time of Christmas, 1684, the said John Rambo came at midnight to the house of her father, and by pulling off a plank of the house, on the loft, near the chamber, he jumped down to the floor, and directly after got into the bed wherein said Bridget and her two sisters (aged 16 and 19) were also lying, saying he was resolved to be the husband of Bridget (even as his brother had before taken another sister) and must therefore lie there. Whereupon, there being a crowded place, the two sisters, with strange submission, withdrew and lay upon the floor all night in a cold December! The court, after the verdict of the jury, adjudged John Rambo to marry Bridget before she be delivered, or then maintain the child. Both to be fined £10 each. This Bridget was sister to Lassey Cock—a name before mentioned in Penn's council, and was a Justice of the Peace. Afterwards said Rambo was fined £150 for noncompliance. Some may wonder who and where are now the descendants of this disputed love! The name of Rambo is still among us; but the last of the whole blood of that name was Jonas Rambo, a good man, of Upper Merion, who died at the same farm held by his family 140 years.[142]

"The court about this time appointed justices, constables, road overseers, etc., from time to time. William Orion is fined five shillings for being twice drunk.

"The Grand Jury present Joseph Knight, for suffering drunkenness and evil orders in his cave and several drinking houses to debauch persons are also presented. They present also the want of a prison, also the want of a convenient road from Schuylkill ferry to Darby. They present the County Attorney, Samuel Herset, for

---

[141] Mr. Watson's arrangement of the material has been slightly altered in order to preserve a chronological order of presentation.

[142] The Rambo and Cock families were among the most prominent in early Pennsylvania.

not securing a robber in fetters when committed to him. They present the want of a bridge in the road at the north end of the town (meaning at Poole's). They present all caves by the water-side as unfit for houses of entertainment, and as giving many an occasion there to forestall the market.

"John Moon is fined £20 and his servant, Martha Williams £10 for fornication, and to be obliged to be married before the delivery of the child. William Penn had a servant of this name, who settled in Bucks County—a Friend.

"I have seen a pamphlet of 19 pages, printed by William Bradford at Philadelphia in 1691-92, containing 'the first case of this nature happening in this part of the country before'—the whole published under the sanction of the clerk of the court, Samuel Hedge. It elucidates several facts of local interest; it is entitled 'Blood will out, or an Example of Justice in the Tryal, Confession and Execution of Thomas Lutherland, who murthered John Clark, at Philadelphia, Trader—Tried and Executed at Salem, W. J., the 23 Feb. 1691.' The whole points in the trial are too long to be given in this place; but the facts and proceedings, of an unusual character, are preserved in my MS. Annals, in the Historical Society, pages 194 to 196. All the jury took their averment. The 'clerk' asketh: 'Art thou guilty?' He answers: 'Not of the murther, but of the felony.' When first apprehended, he was confronted with the corpse and bid to touch it, which he did, saying, 'If I have murthered he will bleed afresh, and saying, poor innocent man, why should I destroy him—if I hurt him I wish the earth may open and swallow me up!'

"Bold and hardened as he thus appeared, and although he had no direct witness against him, he betrayed himself, by answering questions, into so many contradictions concerning himself at the time of the murder, that he got confused, and finally came to open and general confession, saying the deceased was in his own little vessel, alone by the creek side, when he passed a rope round his neck in his cabin, telling him I would not destroy him, whilst he said, I think you intend to choke me. I then asked him if he had got some money, and he said he had some wampum, a piece-of-eight and some double bits. He cryed—spare my life and take all; but I pulled both ends of the rope together, whilst he cryed, Lord have mercy upon my soul, repeatedly, even till he was dead. It does not appear that there was any attorney or pleadings in behalf of the prisoner; but the court had someone as 'King's Attorney.' When he demanded judgement after the verdict of guilty, the court was much perplexed to pass sentence of death, they being only Justices of the Peace; but as there were 'no superior courts in the province,' the Cororner's Inquest, the jury, and the most part of the country then present, joined in a written petition to the court to give their sentence which was thereupon done accordingly, and in five days afterwards he was executed, a penitent, &c.

"Year 1700—Lewd men and women and disorderly drinking houses are very often presented. Elizabeth Glann is presented for fornication with Peter Packonet. She is fined £10, or to be lashed 21 strokes. Nothing is said of Packonet! Perhaps he was not then before the court.

"Year 1702—John Simes, ordinary and others, are prosecuted 'for keeping a disorderly house to debauch the youth.'—John Smith was disguised in women's clothes walking the streets openly, and going from house to house, against the laws of God and this province, to the staining of holy profession, and against the law of nature.—Edward James, a like offender, at an unreasonable time of night.—Dorothy, wife of Richard Canterill, is indicted also for being masked in men's clothes, walking and dancing in the house of said John Simes, at ten o'clock at night.—Sarah Stiver, wife of John Stiver, was also at the same house, dressed in men's clothes, and walked the streets, and went from house to house, to the encouragement of vice,' &c.—the house was in Front street. Probably there was no further attempt at 'Masquerade Ball' from that time till about 14 years ago, when some foreigner publicly proposed to introduce them at his dining room. It was promptly suppressed by an act of the Legislature, got up, before the night of intended execution, by John Sargent, Esq. It was then supposed for a while that the steady habits of our citizens would have frowned down any further attempt; but the inroads of luxury have since succeeded to evade the force of law by getting through two 'Fancy Balls,' so called, without molestation, and even without any exposure by themselves of their rare enactments in 'monstrous novelty and strange disguise.' We have heard, however, it was a strange medley of strange personages and habiliments.

"1702—George Robinson, butcher, is indicted as a common swearer and drunkard, 'for swearing three oaths in the market place, and for uttering two very bad curses.'

"They afterwards present the same George Robinson for 'uttering a grievous oath, on the 13th of 7 mo. and another on the 10th day of the 8th month.' In those days all cases of drunkenness and profane swearing were punished.

"A riot was committed at Israel Townsend's inn, a sign of the Broad Axe, in Chestnut street (close by Hudson's alley) where they beat the constables with clubs.

"1702—The Grand Jury present, to wit: Sons and servants robbing orchards on the First or Lord's day: the ill consequence of many negroes assembling and acting tumultuously on the same day; the loss of sheep by unnecessary quantity of dogs; the evil of having so many hay and reed stacks in the yards of city houses in case of fires; the great annoyance, daily occurring, of butchers killing their meat in the street, (at the market-place probably) and leaving their blood and offals there.

"1703—The Grand Jury present Henry Brooks, the Queen's Collector at the Hore-kills, (Lewistown) and three others, for raising a great disturbance and riot in the city at the dead of night. They present all houses and persons individually known to play at cards publicly, and they give the names of all the persons so concerned. They present nine persons at one time, for selling strong drink without license. Three barbers are presented for trimming people on First-day. John Walker is presented for using Sassafras street as a rope-walk for the last year; and John Jones, Alderman, is presented for making encroachments on Mulberry street, by setting up therein a great reed stack, and making a close fence about the same. These Grand Juries, almost all of them affirm—very few swear.

"1704—1st of 7 mo.—The Grand Jury present some of the young gentry, for an assault on James Wood, constable, and James Dough, watch, for making a riot at the inn of Enoch Story by night— (in Combe's alley.) The names were William Penn, jun. (Proprietary's son), John Finny, the sheriff, Thomas Gray, scrivener, and Joseph Ralph. (*Quondam infidel*, and friend of Benjamin Franklin!) It is stated that young Penn called for pistols to pistol them, &c. Their host, Story, was also of their party.

"1705—They present Thomas Docherty, barber, for trimming, about three weeks ago, on the first day of the week.

"In the year 1705, men were fined (by law) 20 shillings for labouring on the Sabbath-day, and 10 shillings for being found tippling in a tavern on that day.

"The same year (1705) there was made an act against fornication and adultery. For the latter, the parties received 21 lashes and hard labour for one year, or pay £50 fine, (the injured party had a right of divorce) and for a second offence seven years imprisonment. For fornication, 21 lashes or pay £10 fine each. Severe laws! as the lecherous would judge now! At that time men were fined 12 pence for smoking on the streets! Think of this, ye moderns!

"1715—The Grand Jury find 35 true bills against unlicensed taverns, in one session.

"1717—Women are publicly whipt for having an illegitimate child; and poor runaway apprentices and others, who are whipt, are charged six shillings for the unwelcome service.

"1718—William Wright, merchant, is presented for publicly and maliciously declaring aloud that our Savior was a bastard.

"1720—Edward and Martha Hunt, man and wife, are sentenced to death for making and passing counterfeit dollars. It is said to be the first case in which death was inflicted in the colony for a like offence.

"1721—Nicholas Gaulau, (a foreigner, by his name) 'by colour of his art, as a butcher, did with his breath and wind, blow up the meat of his calf, whereby the meat was made unwholesome to the human body.' He was fined thirteen shillings and four pence for introducing this odious practice—still known among some of us.

"1729—Charles Calaghan was convicted of intent to ravish a child of 10 years—he was whipt round the town at the cart's tail and received 35 lashes. Another man, at the same time received 21 lashes for stealing a saddle.

"Several executions occasionally occur, as mentioned in the Gazettes. Prouse and Mitchell, who were to be executed together, were reprieved under the gallows.

"1730—G. Jones, and one Glasgow, an Indian, stood an hour in the pillory, at the cart's tail—both for assaults, with intent to ravish—the one, a girl of six years of age. Margaret Cash is also whipt for stealing.

"I find it remarked, that the number of criminal offences occur from the great emigration of evil persons, who bought their passage by servitude.

"1731—At New Castle, Catharine Bevan is ordered to be burned alive, for the murder of her husband; and Peter Murphy, the servant who assisted her, to be hanged. It was designed to strangle her dead by the previous hanging over the fire, and before it could reach her; but the fire 'broke out in a stream directly on the rope round her neck, and burnt off instantly, so that she fell alive into the flames, and was seen to struggle therein!' A shocking spectacle for our country!

"1733—December—There was the greatest number of felons arraigned for crimes, ever known in Philadelphia, at one Quarter Sessions. Thirteen men and women were convicted of grand larceny, and sentenced to be whipt.

"1738—Three negro men were hung for poisoning sundry persons in Jersey. They said they had poisoned Judge William Trent, the founder of Trenton, among that number—but when he died, none were then suspected. A lad of five years of age, who had heard much of their hanging, took it into his head to make some imitations, and actually hung himself to death from the stake of a fence!

"A Negro man of Robert Hooper's, Esq., of Rocky Hill, in Somerset, New Jersey, was executed by fire, for having killed the child of his overseer, and firing his master's barn.

"1743—A black man, brought up to the whipping-post to be whipt, took out his knife and cut his throat before the crowd, so that he died immediately—at Philadelphia.

"1750-51—About this time, a great deal of hanging occurs. They hang for house-breaking, horse-stealing, and counterfeiting. It seems that imported criminals swell the list, and many evil persons come out as redemptioners. This remark is made, to wit: 'When we see our papers filled so often with accounts of the most audacious robberies, the most cruel murders, and other villanies, perpetrated by convicts from Europe—what will become of our posterity! In what could Britain injure us more, than by emptying her jails on us! What must we think of those merchants, who, for the sake of a little paltry gain, will be concerned in importing and disposing of these abominable cargoes!' It is probable they got premiums abroad for bringing them out here.

"1759—I observe that the number of criminal offences and executions appears much diminished for some time—so far as the silence of the Gazettes respecting them may be evidence.

"1761—A strange freak seized the minds of some of the young citizens, which was shown 'in several women being stabbed in the streets,' in the evening, 'by some unknown persons.' The terror being great, the Governor offered a reward for their apprehension. The evil was probably magnified according to the terror of the relaters. In time, however, it was so far brought to light as that the Wardens got hold of the facts. The venerable Charles Thomson having been one of those city officers, and acquainted with the facts, ventured to tell them after many years had elapsed and the parties concerned were likely to pass unmolested. It was to the following effect, to wit:

"The insulting of several women in the streets, by cutting their gowns and petticoats with a razor, rendering it dangerous for them to appear therein without protection, as also breaking of knockers and bells, cutting the spouts, &c., was nightly committed, and caused considerable alarm. The soldiers in the barracks were at first blamed for it, but by an arrangement with their commanding officer it was immediately discovered they were not implicated. The Wardens then silently increased the watch more than one half, and soon came across these blades in their depredations. They proved to be the sons and relations of some of the most respectable citizens, and whose parents and friends thought them absent from the city, as at New York, Lancaster, Chester county, &c. By day they lay concealed and slept in the tavern at the south-west corner of Chestnut and Fourth streets, and from thence sallied forth at night to commit their depredations. Robert M. had a brother among them; Anthony W. a son; Doctor A. a son; Mr. W. a brother, &c. In the morning they were carried before the Mayor, appeared penitent, received a very serious lecture, and their friends gave high bail for their good behavior and appearance, and made restitution to all persons who had been injured by them. On this discovery the city instantly became safe and orderly as usual, and the thing was suffered to sleep. I believe they were never prosecuted." [143]

---

[143] J. F. Watson, *The Annals of Philadelphia and Pennsylvania in the Olden Time,* enlarged and revised by W. P. Hazard, 3 Vols. Philadelphia, 1898, Vol. I, pp. 304-11. For further highly interesting and illuminating information concerning criminal jurisprudence and its administration in colonial Pennsylvania consult J. S. Futhey and Gilbert Cope, *A History of Chester County,* pp. 406-11; W. H. H. Davis, *A History of Bucks County,* pp. 723ff.; George Smith, *A History of Delaware County,* pp. 152, 173, 179, 185-86; and J. J. Mombert, *An Authentic History of Lancaster County,* pp. 120ff.

The pettiness of much of the criminal procedure of the colonial period, as well as the Quaker severity in dealing with offenses which irritated their "impurity complex," may be learned from the following description of the method of dealing with fornication in Chester County in the year 1693:

"Some idea may be formed of the mischievously inquisitorial character of Chester county grand juries at this period, from the fact that at one court two newly married couples were made the subjects of presentment because a child was born, in each case, too soon after the marriage. In one case, besides the court charges and a fine of 20s., both parties were sentenced 'to attend at the common whipping post and for the officer to declare their offence to the people;' while in the other case the fine was 50s., but the woman only was subjected to public exposure. This was more wantonly cruel than was inflicted in the former case, and consisted in standing at the common whipping post for one quarter of an hour with a paper on her breast, thus: 'I here stand for an example to all others for committing the most wicked and notorious sin of fornication.' " [144]

Lest one might be inclined to hold that these instances of humorous, but none the less real, barbarism were merely a local product of early Philadelphia, it is worth while to quote briefly from Judge White's description of the manner in which justice was administered in Westmoreland County, in the western part of the province, at the very close of the colonial period and at the time of the formation of the nation. The following passage describes the criminal and judicial procedure in Hannastown, near Greensburg, in 1773 and the following years:

"The first court was held April 6, 1773. At this session a jail was ordered to be erected. It was made of round, unhewn logs, one story high, and had but one small room, where men and women, whites, blacks, and Indians were confined together. The jail was mainly to confine the prisoners until trial, for imprisonment was not generally a part of the sentence after conviction. Punishments were fines, whipping, standing in the pillory or stocks, cropping the ears and branding. The whipping post, which stood in front of the jail, was a stout sapling placed firmly in the ground, with a crosspiece above the head, to which the hands of the culprit were tied, while the lashes were inflicted by the sheriff on his bare back. The pillory consisted of a low platform on which the culprit stood, with uprights supporting a frame with openings in it through which his head and hands projected. At common law

---

[144] George Smith, *A History of Delaware County,* pp. 185-86.

every passer by might cast one stone at the projecting head. The stocks were also a rude framework on which the culprit sat, his legs projecting through the openings in front. When no regular stocks were at hand, the custom was to lift the corner of a rail fence and thrust the legs between the two lower rails.

"At the October sessions of 1773 James Brigland was convicted on two indictments for larceny; on the first, sentenced to pay a fine of twenty shillings, and receive ten lashes at the whipping-post; and on the second, twenty lashes. Luke Picket, for larceny, twenty-one lashes, and Patrick J. Masterson, for the same offence, fifteen lashes. At the January session, 1774, Wm. Howard, for a felony, was sentenced to receive thirty lashes on the bare back, well laid on, and afterwards stand one hour in the pillory. This was the first sentence to the pillory. At every succeeding term of court numerous parties received punishments by whipping, standing in the pillory, branding, etc. At the October sessions, 1775, Elizabeth Smith admitted she had stolen some small articles from James Kincaid to whom she was indentured. She was sentenced to pay a fine, and receive fifteen lashes on the bare back. But Mr. Kincaid complained that he had lost her services for the four days she was in jail, and had been at some expense in prosecuting her; whereupon the court ordered her, to make up said loss, to serve her said master and his assigns two years after the expiration of her indentures. At the April sessions, 1782, James McGill was sentenced to be whipped, stand in the pillory, have his right ear cropt, and be branded in the forehead. At the April sessions, 1783, John Smith, for a felony, was sentenced to pay a fine of twenty pounds, receive thirty-nine lashes on his back, well laid on, stand in the pillory one hour, and have his ears cut off and nailed to the pillory. At the July sessions, 1788, Jane Adamson, a servant of Samuel Sample, had one year added to her indenture for having a bastard child.

"The first person convicted of murder, and hung, west of the mountains, was an Indian of the Delaware tribe, by the name of Mamachtaga. In 1785, in a drunken spree at Pittsburg, he crossed the river to the Allegheny side, nearly opposite Killbuck Island, and killed a white man by the name of Smith. He was tried at Hannastown in the fall of that year, before Chief-Justice McKean. Hugh H. Brackenridge was his counsel. When brought into court, he refused, at first, to plead 'not guilty'; for that, he said, would be a lie; he did kill Smith, but said he was drunk at the time, and did not know what he was doing. The Chief Justice, however, held that drunkenness was no excuse for murder. After his conviction and sentence to death, a little daughter of the jailor fell dangerously ill. He said if they would let him go to the woods he could get some roots that would cure her. He went, got the roots, and they cured her. The day before his execution he asked permission to go to the woods to get some roots to paint his face red, that he might die like a warrior. The jailor went with him, he got the roots, returned to jail, and the next day was executed, painted as a brave warrior. The gallows was a rude structure, with a ladder leading up to the crossbeam, from which the rope was suspended. The sheriff and prisoner ascended the ladder, the rope was tied about his neck, and then the sheriff shoved him off the ladder. The first time the rope broke. The poor Indian, strangled and bewildered, supposed that that was all, and he would then be let go. But the sheriff procured another rope, and he was again compelled to ascend the ladder. This time the majesty of the white man's law was vindicated by the death of the red man, for a crime committed in a frenzy fit, occasioned by whiskey the white man had given him.

"During the trial the Chief Justice and his associate Judge were arrayed in scarlet robes, as was the custom in those days. The grave demeanor and glittering robes of the Judges deeply impressed the poor unlettered son of the forest. He could not believe they were mortals, but regarded them as some divine personages.

"As there was no court-house at Hannastown, the courts were always held in the house of Robert Hanna. Parties, jurors, witnesses, and lawyers were crowded together in a small room, nearly all standing. The Judges occupied common hickory chairs raised on a clapboard bench at one side.

"During the Revolutionary War, while the courts met regularly, but little business was transacted, and the laws were not rigidly enforced. At the October sessions, 1781, only one constable attended, and he was from Pittsburg." [145]

F.   Minor Phases in the Development of Criminal Legislation

In addition to consideration of the technical criminal code in provincial Pennsylvania, there are several other significant developments regarding the legislation touching upon the criminal and allied classes at the time, which are deserving of at least brief analysis at this point. One of them is that which relates to the attempt of the province to offer some check to the notorious practice of sending convicted criminals from England to America, and selling them as servants in lieu of the execution of the sentence. Until the American Revolution, the American colonies were the dumping ground for the worst types of English criminals. As a result of various laws passed from the beginning of the colonizing period down to 1718 transportation was an alternative for all

---

[145] J. W. F. White, "The Judiciary of Allegheny County," in *The Pennsylvania Magazine of History and Biography,* Vol. VII, 1883, pp. 147-49.

sentences more severe than three years' imprisonment. After the Revolution the practice was not abandoned, but a new receiving station was provided in Australia.[146] Doctor F. H. Wines thus describes the system:

"Contracts were made with private persons to convey the transported across the sea; the contractors and their assigns were given the right to their labor during the term of sentence, which they sold to the criminal himself or to his colonial purchaser. Sometimes he was released before he passed the mouth of the river Thames; oftener, on his arrival in Jamacia, Barbardoes, Maryland, or elsewhere on the American coast. For a time four or five hundred were shipped to Maryland annually; others were sent to Virginia. The planters bought them. In effect, they were slaves, for a term of years; and the traffic in convicts was a form of competition with the African slave trade. Reputable American colonists freely expressed their disgust with the system, but it suited the Mother Country, and the practice only ceased with the War of the American Revolution." [147]

Recent students of the problem have concluded that the proportion of indentured servants in Pennsylvania was greater than in any other American colony,[148] though, of course, not many were former convicts. By 1722 the practice had become sufficiently developed so that it was felt to be a menace to the community, and on May fifth of that year the first systematic act was passed penalizing the importation of convicts. It declared:

"Whereas many persons trading into this province have, for lucre and private gain, imported and sold, or disposed of, and daily do import and sell as servants for a term of years, divers persons convicted of heinous crimes, who, soon after their coming into this province, do often run away and leave their master's service and commit many heinous felonies, robberies, thefts, and burglaries, to the great loss of persons purchasing such servants, and the great hurt in general of his Majesty's good subjects residing in, and trading to and from this province . . . ."

it should be enacted that any one importing any person "who hath been convicted of any murder, burglary, rape, sodomy, forgery,

---

[146] F. H. Wines, *Punishment and Reformation,* pp. 162ff.
[147] Ibid., pp. 162-63.
[148] K. F. Geiser, *Redemptioners and Indentured Servants in the Colony and Commonwealth of Pennsylvania.* Doctor Geiser holds that from 1682 to 1708 one-third of the immigrants to Pennsylvania were indentured servants or could trace their ancestry to this class; that from 1708 to 1728 the proportion had increased to one-half; that from 1728 to 1775 they were in a majority; and that from 1775 to 1804 two-thirds of the immigrants were indentured servants and redemptioners.

perjury, or any other felony whatsoever," must pay a duty of five pounds and give fifty pounds security for the good behavior of the imported felon for the following year.[149] A collector of the above duty was appointed.[150] A fine of twenty pounds was decreed if any one imported a felon who was not registered and for the importation of whom the prescribed duty had not been paid.[151] In case a person purchased an unregistered servant without proof of legal importation the servant was to be freed immediately.[152] By an act of the next year it was stipulated that the duties and fines collected on imported servants should be applied to "sinking" the colonial bills of credit.[153] The act of 1722 was superseded by that of February 14, 1730, which retained the same general provisions but added more specific regulations.[154] This act of 1730 was in turn superseded by that of February 3, 1743, but this was repealed by the King in Council in 1746 and the act of 1730 was revived and remained in force until the Revolution.[155] Pennsylvania was not, however, averse to making use of this practice in ridding herself of undesirable convicted criminals. Many instances are recorded where even criminals condemned to death received a remission of their sentence upon the condition that they would leave Pennsylvania and never return. This seems to have been done particularly in the case of those who had been sentenced to death under the severe criminal code of the later colonial period for crimes which contemporary public opinion did not regard as heinous enough to deserve the death penalty.[156]

Another important subject related to the penal legislation of the period was the matter of imprisonment for debt. In this regard the Quakers scarcely exhibited as much relative enlightenment as they did in their criminal jurisprudence. In the additions to the "Great Law" made by the assembly of March, 1683, it was enacted:

"That all persons of known estates, refusing to pay their just debts, if arrested and imprisoned, shall be kept at their own charge, until security be given or satisfaction made; provided no person shall be kept in prison for debt, or fine longer than the second day of the next sessions, after his or her commitment, unless the plain-

---

[149] *The Statutes at Large of Pennsylvania,* Vol. III, pp. 264-65.
[150] Ibid., p. 265.
[151] Ibid.
[152] Ibid., p. 267.
[153] Ibid., pp. 401-02.
[154] Ibid., Vol. IV, pp. 164-71.
[155] Ibid., pp. 360-70.
[156] J. J. Mombert, *An Authoritative History of Lancaster County,* pp. 124-25. J. S. Futhey and Gilbert Cope, *A History of Chester County,* p. 408.

tiff shall make it appear, that the person imprisoned hath some estate that he will not produce; in which case, the court shall examine all persons suspected to be given in the concealing such estate, but if no estate can be found, that the debtor shall satisfy the debt by servitude, as the county court shall order, if desired by the creditor." [157]

The same legislation with respect to debtors was continued in Governor Fletcher's code of June, 1693,[158] and in the law of November 27, 1700.[159] The law of January 12, 1706, placed some specific limitations upon the duration of the servitude which could be exacted for debt. Servitude could not be required of unmarried men over fifty-three years of age and, when under that age, for not more than seven years. In the case of a married man, servitude could not be exacted if the debtor was over forty-six years of age and, when under that age, for not more than five years.[160]

The next important act relating to debtors was that of February 14, 1730, which applied to all cases of indebtedness not exceeding one hundred pounds. The former acts were declared to be a failure and to have worked much hardship without any effective results having been achieved. It was enacted that the debtor should make a sworn statement of the amount of his property and the judge was to assign it, or as much of it as was required, to the creditor. The debtor was then to be discharged unless fraud could be proved or the creditor desired to have him imprisoned. In the latter case it was stipulated that the creditor must pay weekly to the debtor while in prison a sum to be determined by the court, but not to exceed three shillings. In case of any delinquency in this payment the prisoner was to be immediately discharged.[161] The act was amended by that of February 6, 1731, which declared that the act of 1730 should not apply to unmarried men under forty who owed less than twenty pounds.[162] Another amendment was added on February 2, 1765. The maximum amount to which the act of 1730 might apply was raised from one hundred pounds to one hundred and fifty pounds. It was further provided that if the creditor insisted on the imprisonment of the debtor he must pay him weekly five shillings, if the debtor was unmarried, and seven shillings sixpence if he was a man with wife or children.[163]

A more drastic relief measure was deemed necessary and this

[157] *Charter and Laws of Pennsylvania, 1682-1700,* pp. 130-31.
[158] Ibid., p. 200.
[159] *The Statutes at Large of Pennsylvania,* Vol. II, pp. 129-30.
[160] Ibid., p. 250.
[161] Ibid., Vol. IV, pp. 171-75.
[162] Ibid., pp. 211-13.
[163] Ibid., Vol. VI, pp. 392-93.

was realized in the act of February 24, 1770. It was provided that after the debtor had complied with the legal requirements of the act of 1730 and no fraud could be shown, he was to be discharged at once. It was also stated that the debtor could not be reimprisoned for debts incurred before he began the term of imprisonment from which he was discharged.[164] The act of 1770 was slightly amended by that of January 22, 1774, which ordered the trustees of debtors' estates to execute their duty and turn over the estates to the creditors.[165] Finally, the act of August 1, 1776, in celebration of the establishment of the new government, ordered the freeing of all debtors confined in prison.[166] This was only a temporary act of grace and not a permanent abolition of imprisonment for debt. The final abolition of the practice was accomplished by the act of July 12, 1842, which was in part a result of the agitation carried on by the Boston Prison Discipline Society and in part a result of the growth of social and economic democracy during the first half of the nineteenth century.[167]

In concluding the survey of the legislation concerning criminals in provincial Pennsylvania a word should be said about the unusual prevalence of piracy and smuggling in this period. The geographical invitations offered by Pennsylvania to such practices were most attractive, and these were aided by the mild and lax administration of justice and the delinquent provisions for the public defense which were characteristic of the Quaker administration. In addition to these inherent aggravations of the situation, the difficulties imposed upon Pennsylvania in curbing piracy and smuggling were complicated and intensified by the disputes over the authority to deal with matters concerning trade and shipping which were carried on between the province and the mother country. Therefore, it is not surprising to learn that piracy, privateering and smuggling were among the most common and irrepressible of the violations of the peace of the province.[168]

G. Summary of the Criminal Jurisprudence of Colonial Pennsylvania

The outstanding characteristics and tendencies in the development of the criminal codes of provincial Pennsylvania may now be briefly summarized. The earliest phase of criminal procedure

---

[164] *The Statutes at Large of Pennsylvania,* Vol. VII, pp. 347-50.
[165] Ibid., Vol. VIII, pp. 382-85.
[166] Ibid., Vol. IX, p. 6.
[167] Cf. Frank Carlton, "The Abolition of Imprisonment for Debt in the United States," *Yale Review,* Vol. XVII, pp. 339-44. See below, pp. 114ff.
[168] Root, op. cit., pp. 63ff. Shepherd, op. cit., pp. 501ff.

was based upon the criminal code of England as modified through application in the American colonies, particularly in the Puritan colonies of New England. This system, founded upon an extensive array of capital crimes, a wide application of severe corporal punishments and an almost total absence of imprisonment as a mode of punishment, was soon supplanted by the original and humane criminal jurisprudence of the Quakers. This was based primarily upon the substitution of moderate terms of imprisonment at hard labor for the barbarous severity of the earlier corporal punishments and the long list of capital crimes. Owing to the infiltration of non-Quaker elements into Pennsylvania, the resulting increase in the difficulty of controlling the heterogeneous population, and the struggle between the Quakers and the Anglicans over oath and affirmation, the Quakers sacrificed their criminal jurisprudence in order to spare their sectarian tenets. The English and Puritan procedure was restored and remained in force until after the Revolution. Before the close of the eighteenth century, however, the growth of enlightenment and humanity, so powerfully stimulated by the writings of Montesquieu, Beccaria, Blackstone and the French *philosophes,* had begun to permeate even the field of criminal jurisprudence and made it impossible longer to adhere in full to the barbarism of the English and Puritan procedure. The reformers could find no precedents as much in harmony with their principles as the Quaker theories and practices established by Penn and his associates a century earlier. These were, accordingly, gradually revived, and in their second and permanent application became the source from which the modern system of criminal jurisprudence and penal administration has spread throughout the civilized world.

3.   THE PENAL INSTITUTIONS OF PROVINCIAL PENNSYLVANIA

A.   General Historical Setting of the Development of Colonial Penal Institutions in Pennsylvania

The prison, viewed simply as an institution for detaining men against their will, originated in the most remote antiquity. It probably goes back as far as the time of the general practice of cannibalism when future victims were held in stockades to be fattened or to await their turn in contributing the chief course in the menu of their captor.[169] Throughout recorded history one frequently meets with references to prisons used for the confinement of political

---

[169] Cf. P. A. Parsons, *Responsibility for Crime,* pp. 95ff.

and religious offenders,[170] but the prison system of to-day, which is the agency through which imprisonment is made the mode of punishment for the majority of crimes, is an innovation of relatively recent origin.[171] It is quite impossible to fix the exact date of the general beginning of imprisonment as a punishment for crime, and it may, indeed, be seriously doubted if any such date exists, except in a metaphysical sense. All that can be stated with accuracy is that at the beginning of the eighteenth century imprisonment was unusual, except as applied to political and religious offenders and to debtors, though there can be no doubt that it was at that time occasionally employed in the punishment of criminals; and that before the middle of the nineteenth century it was the conventional method of punishing crime in both Europe and America. The eighteenth century was the century of transition from corporal punishment to imprisonment and, though the process of change was most rapid after 1775, there can be no doubt that the general movement was in progress during the entire period.

At the time Penn received his charter from Charles II, there were two institutions in existence, the combination of which later produced the modern prison. These were the jails, or prisons of the time, and the workhouses. The jails or prisons were chiefly used for the detention of those accused of crime pending their trial and for the confinement of debtors and religious and political offenders. They were rarely used for the incarceration of what was regarded as the criminal classes. At each session of the court there occurred what was called a "gaol delivery" and the jail was practically emptied of its inmates, only to be filled again during the interval between the delivery and the next session of the court. Only political and religious offenders, debtors, and the few criminals who had received the rare penalty of imprisonment, remained in the jails or prisons longer than the period which elapsed between successive sessions of the courts. The workhouses, on the other hand, which began to appear about the middle of the sixteenth century, were not for more than two centuries after their origin penal institutions in any sense of the word. They were employed almost solely to repress vagrants and paupers and were not open to the reception of felons.[172]

The great contribution of the West Jersey and Pennsylvania Quakers to the development of modern penology consists in the twofold achievement of substituting imprisonment for corporal

---

[170] Wines, op. cit., pp. 107ff.
[171] Ibid., pp. 117ff.
[172] Ibid., Chap. VI. George Ives, *A History of Penal Methods,* Chap. I.

punishment in the treatment of criminals and of combining the prison and the workhouse. In other words, they originated both the idea of imprisonment as the typical mode of punishing crime, and the doctrine that this imprisonment should not be in idleness but at hard labor. Of the priority of their accomplishment in this regard there can be no doubt. A century later they added the principle that imprisonment at hard labor should be in cellular separation and thus created the modern prison system in its entirety.

In a manner very similar to the situation with respect to the development of the criminal codes in the colonial period, the evolution of penal institutions in provincial Pennsylvania passed through three main stages of evolution. The typical detention jail of contemporary England was provided for in the Duke of York's laws of 1676. This institution was replaced by the Quaker workhouse or house of correction in 1682, and the workhouse remained for about thirty years the basis of the system of penal institutions. After 1718, however, when the criminal code was altered so as to substitute corporal punishment for imprisonment in most instances, the jail reappeared and became the conventional penal institution of the province until the close of the colonial era. Even the few workhouses which remained or were constructed later were not penal institutions, but a part of the system of social relief designed for the repression of vagrants, paupers and unruly servants. But the theory and practice of imprisonment and the workhouse were not lost, and both were speedily revived after the Revolution.

B.   The Legal Basis of the Origin and Organization of the Penal Institutions of Provincial Pennsylvania

The first legislation relative to penal institutions in Pennsylvania occurs in the laws of the Duke of York, promulgated on September 25, 1676. Here it was decreed that:

"Every town shall at their charge provide a pair of stocks for offenders, and a pound for the impounding of cattle; and prisons and pillories are likewise to be provided in these towns where the several courts of sessions are to be holden." [173]

There was thus introduced into the province the conventional English detention jail of the period. It was simply an institution for the "safe-keeping" of accused persons during the interval between meetings of the court of sessions. As has already been pointed out, the penalties imposed by the code of 1676 were almost

[173] *Charter and Laws of Pennsylvania, 1682-1700*, p. 47.

exclusively fine or corporal punishment and there was no need for penal institutions adapted to the permanent imprisonment of criminals. If the provisions of the above clause were carried out, there must have been three of these detention jails or prisons in Pennsylvania from 1676 to 1682, as the court of sessions met at New Castle, Whorekill and Uplands.[174]

From the very beginning of Penn's administration the detention jail was supplanted, in law, at least, by the workhouse or house of correction as the basic penal institution. Even in the laws which Penn and his fellow Quakers had "agreed upon in England" in May, 1682, it was declared that "all prisons shall be workhouses for felons, vagrants, and loose and idle persons; whereof one shall be in every county" and that "all prisons shall be free, as to fees, food, and lodging." [175] It should be noted that under Penn's application and interpretation, the workhouse became a true penal institution no longer limited to the treatment of the destitute and vagrant classes.

The above provisions were enacted with some slight changes as a part of the "Great Law" of December, 1682. Here it was stipulated that:

"All prisons shall be workhouses for felons, thiefs, vagrants, and loose, abusive and idle persons, whereof one shall be in every county.
"Gaolers shall not oppress their prisoners, and all prisons shall be free as to room, and all prisoners shall have liberty to provide themselves bedding, food, and other necessaries, during their imprisonment, except such whose punishment by law, will not admit of that liberty." [176]

The detention jail was not eliminated by this enactment, to be sure, as it had to be retained for holding accused persons for trial.[177] With the single exception of the law of November, 1681, in the neighboring Quaker colony of West Jersey, this act of December, 1682, in Pennsylvania may be regarded as the first instance of the fusion of the workhouse and the prison and the consequent creation

---

[174] Howard, op. cit., pp. 368-70.
[175] *Charter and Laws,* p. 100. It is generally asserted that Penn derived his convictions as to the value of imprisonment and the workhouse system from his early travels in Holland, where he had observed the use of the workhouses as agencies for the repression of pauperism and for the employment of prisoners detained for trial. Richard Vaux, *Brief Sketch of the Origin and History of the State Penitentiary for the Eastern District of Pennsylvania,* p. 28. See also Douglass Campbell, *The Puritan in England, Holland and America.*
[176] *Charter and Laws of Pennsylvania, 1682-1700,* p. 121.
[177] Ibid., p. 120.

of the basis of the modern prison system.[178] The nearest competitor
for chronological priority was Pope Clement XI, who in 1704,
established a combination prison and workhouse at San Michele
in Rome.[179]

In the supplement to the "Great Law" which was enacted by the
assembly in March, 1683, there was a more specific and compulsory
clause relating to the construction of workhouses. It was here
provided:

"That every county within this province of Pennsylvania and
territories thereunto belonging, shall before the last day of the
tenth month, next ensuing, at their own cost and charge, erect, build
or cause to be built in the most convenient place in each county,
respective, a sufficient house, at least twenty foot square, for
restraint, correction, labour, and punishment of all such persons as
shall be thereunto committed by law; and that every county failing
herein shall forfeit and pay forty pounds, to be levied on the goods
and chattels of the inhabitants of such county." [180]

The provisions of the laws of 1682 and 1683 with respect to
workhouses were retained without change in the laws promulgated
by Governor Fletcher in June, 1693.[181] They were also confirmed
and retained without alteration in the laws of November 27, 1700,[182]
and January 12, 1706,[183] with the exception that in 1706 an allowance of two pence per day was made for the support of each
prisoner. It was also stipulated in 1706 that the jails should serve
as workhouses until the latter should be erected. From this provision and from many other sources of evidence it must be concluded
that even before 1718 there had come about a differentiation
between the workhouse and the jail, with the latter the more common institution of the two. When the criminal code was altered
by the act of May 31, 1718, and fines and corporal punishment
were substituted for imprisonment as the typical mode of punishment, the workhouse tended to disappear and where it was retained
to become an institution for repressing vagrants, paupers and incorrigible servants rather than a true penal institution. It seems that
it was in Philadelphia alone that the workhouse was retained
throughout the greater part of the provincial period somewhat
according to the original conception of Penn. As the jail or county

[178] Barnes, op. cit., Vol. II, pp. 34, 351 note.
[179] Wines, op. cit., pp. 121-22.
[180] Charter and Laws of Pennsylvania, 1682-1700, pp. 139-40.
[181] Ibid., pp. 202, 208.
[182] The Statutes at Large of Pennsylvania, Vol. II, pp. 99-100.
[183] Ibid., p. 243.

prison was much the more usual institution and the real basis of the penal system of provincial Pennsylvania from 1718 to 1776, attention will next be directed to the mode of the legal organization of the county jail system.

The first complete organizing law creating a county jail in Pennsylvania was that of March 20, 1725, which decreed that a courthouse and a jail should be erected in Newtown in Bucks County. As this act became the model for all subsequent acts authorizing the erection of county jails, it is worthy of an extended analysis. It was declared that:

"It shall and may be lawful to and for the said Jeremiah Langhorne, William Biles, Joseph Kirkbride, Thomas Watson and Abraham Chapman or any three of them to purchase and take assurance to them and their heirs a piece of land situated in some convenient place in the said township of Newton, in trust and for the use of the said county, and thereon to erect and build or cause to be built, a courthouse and prison sufficient to accommodate the public service of the said county and for the ease and conveniency of the inhabitants.

"For the defraying the charge of purchasing the land, building and erecting the courthouse and prison aforesaid, it shall and may be lawful to and for the commissioners and assessors of the said county or a majority of them, who are hereby required to assess and levy so much money as the said trustees or any three of them shall judge necessary for purchasing the land and finishing the said courthouse and prison: provided always, the sum of money so raised do not exceed three hundred pounds current money of the province." [184]

The method, then, of providing for the erection of a county jail consisted in the appointment of a board of five special commissioners or trustees who were authorized to purchase the required land and estimate the cost of the jail. The sum thus determined was raised in the same manner as any part of the county rate, namely, by the county commissioners and assessors.

The eight remaining acts passed during the provincial period providing for the erection of new county jails were modeled directly after this act of 1725, retaining even the same phraseology. All the subsequent jails erected were those which had to be provided for newly created counties and the act authorizing the building of the jail was uniformly embodied in the general act creating and organizing the administration of the new county. The following acts, passed between 1725 and 1773, provided for the erection of

---

[184] *The Statutes at Large of Pennsylvania*, Vol. IV, pp. 9-10.

a new county jail in a newly created county: Lancaster County by the act of May 10, 1729;[185] York County by an act of August 19, 1749;[186] Cumberland County by an act of January 27, 1750;[187] Berks County by an act of March 11, 1752;[188] Northampton County also by an act of March 11, 1752;[189] Bedford County by an act of March 9, 1771;[190] Northumberland County by an act of March 21, 1772;[191] Westmoreland County by an act of February 26, 1773.[192] The only variations in any of these acts were that in the case of Lancaster County only four trustees were provided for and that Northampton County was allowed four hundred and fifty pounds instead of three hundred pounds with which to build its court-house and jail.[193] Therefore, nine of the eleven counties of provincial Pennsylvania had county jails distinct from the work-house or house of correction. In Philadelphia and Chester Counties it appears that the jail and the workhouse were combined in a single plant.[194]

After the act of January 12, 1706, there was no more legislation concerning workhouses until the act of February 27, 1718, was passed.[195] This act bears much the same relation to the subsequent workhouse acts that the law of March 20, 1725, holds to the later jail legislation. There was a great and fundamental difference, however, between the nature of the workhouse described in the act of 1706 and the type of institution contemplated in that of 1718. The workhouse provided for in the act of 1718 was no longer the Quaker institution for the imprisonment of criminals at hard labor, but was the typical European workhouse for the repression of vagrants and paupers. It was enacted that the work-houses and houses of correction to be erected should be "used and employed for the keeping, correcting, and setting to work of all rogues, vagabonds, or sturdy beggars, and other idle and disorderly persons, who by the laws and usage of Great Britain, or by the laws of this province, are to be kept, corrected, or set to work, in such houses and backsides." [196] While the Quaker sentiment and traditions were strong enough to retain in Philadelphia and to some

---

[185] *The Statutes at Large of Pennsylvania*, Vol. IV, pp. 133-34.
[186] Ibid., Vol. V, pp. 73-6.
[187] Ibid., pp. 90-3.
[188] Ibid., pp. 136-39.
[189] Ibid., pp. 143-46.
[190] Ibid., Vol. VIII, pp. 48-52.
[191] Ibid., pp. 146-49.
[192] Ibid., pp. 316-20.
[193] Ibid., Vol. VI, pp. 276-77.
[194] Ibid., Vol. III, pp. 168-69; Vol. VIII, p. 300.
[195] Ibid., Vol. III, pp. 167-71.
[196] Ibid., p. 168.

extent in Chester County, something of the older organization and function of the workhouse of the late seventeenth century, as established by Penn, there can be no doubt that by 1718 the Quaker system of penal institutions and penal administration had begun to disintegrate, much as their criminal jurisprudence was shattered by the code of March thirty-first of the same year. The year 1718, then, may be taken as the most convenient date for marking the submergence of Quaker jurisprudence and penology and the ascendancy of the English system in the province of Pennsylvania.

The act of February 27, 1718, providing for the erection of workhouses in the provinces declared in its enacting clause:

"Whereas the proprietary and first adventurers in their principal model of this government proposed that for crimes inferior to murder, the punishment might be by way of restitution, fine, imprisonment, and such like; and where the offender proved not of ability to make such satisfaction then he should be kept in prison or a house of correction at hard labor; but no effectual care hath been yet taken to erect such houses, by reason whereof many evildoers escape unpunished, and servants, who, for their neglect and abuses should be kept at work in such houses, are become incorrigible, therefore may it please the governor that it may be enacted. . . ." [197]

To provide for the much needed workhouses, it was enacted that the justices, or a majority of them, meeting in the next quarter sessions after May 1, 1718, might "set down and make orders for building, erecting, or causing to be built and erected or provided, one or more houses of correction and workhouses, with convenient backsides or yards thereunto adjoining, in some convenient places within their several counties or towns corporate." [198] The order of the justices to provide money for the building of the workhouses was to be honored by the county authorities and the sum needed was to be raised as a part of the county rate.[199] It was further specifically enacted that within three years after March 25, 1718, a house of correction or workhouse should be built at Philadelphia in Philadelphia County, at Chester in Chester County, and at Bristol in Bucks County.[200] These prospective workhouses were to be put under the control of "a president, a treasurer and assistants," to be appointed by a majority of the justices of the county assembled

---

[197] *Statutes at Large of Pennsylvania*, Vol. III, p. 167. In spite of the phraseology of this law the workhouses were not employed as penal institutions except in Philadelphia, Bucks and Chester Counties.

[198] Ibid., p. 168.

[199] Ibid.

[200] Ibid., pp. 168-69.

in a quarter session from "the most able and honest inhabitants and freeholders of the said counties." [201] The said president, treasurer and assistants were to constitute a "body politic and corporate in law to all interests and purposes" with all the legal characteristics and power of a corporation.[202] The corporation was to be responsible to the justices of the county, who were to inspect the corporate accounts at each quarter session and punish and dismiss offenders.[203] At least one member of the corporation was "to give punctual and constant attention at the workhouse and house of correction to which they respectively belong." This member of the corporation was to have general charge of the administration of the workhouse and of the discipline of the inmates. He was to present a quarterly report to the justices.[204] The corporation as a whole was to estimate the amount of money needed to operate the workhouse and to present the estimate to the justices who reviewed it and passed it on to the commissioners and assessors to be raised as a part of the county rate.[205] The governing corporation was further empowered to employ such officers as they required to assist them in operating and administering the workhouse, to determine and allow their pay, to remove them for cause and to appoint their successors.[206] The sheriff, constables and all other officers of justice were ordered to give all proper aid and assistance to the corporation.[207] No specific information was contained in the act relative to the type of work on which the inmates were to be engaged, but provision was made for the purchasing of the original stock with which to begin work and for obtaining the future supplies of raw material which would be required.[208]

As has been pointed out above, this act of February 27, 1718, was the general organizing law governing the establishment of workhouses in provincial Pennsylvania until 1767. The next act based upon this precedent was that of March 7, 1746, which was rendered necessary by the failure of Bucks County to carry out the provisions of the act of 1718. It declared that no workhouse had been erected in Bristol, as had been directed in 1718, and author-

---

[201] *The Statutes at Large of Pennsylvania,* Vol. III, p. 169.
[202] Ibid., p. 170.
[203] Ibid., p. 169.
[204] Ibid., p. 170.
[205] Ibid.
[206] Ibid., p. 171. Futhey and Cope, however, state that the first keeper of the Chester County workhouse was appointed by the court of quarter sessions with the consent of the county commissioners and assessors. *A History of Chester County,* p. 411.
[207] *The Statutes at Large of Pennsylvania,* Vol. III, p. 171.
[208] Ibid., p. 170.

ized the burgesses of Bristol to proceed with the establishment of such an institution. Its government was to be the same as that provided for the government of the workhouses created by the act of 1718.[209] An act of March 4, 1763, declared that the County of Lancaster "had suffered most grievously, as well by unruly disobedient servants, as by idle strolling vagrants from divers parts who have taken shelter in that county and borough; and drunkenness, profane swearing, breach of the Sabbath, tumults, and other vices so much prevail that it is not in the power of the magistrates to suppress them and preserve peace and good order, having no house of correction for the punishment of such offenders."[210] To correct these abuses the justices were authorized to provide for the erection of a workhouse and to appoint a corporation to administer it.[211]

The general procedure in erecting workhouses in Pennsylvania was systematized by an act of February 21, 1767, which remained the legal basis for the establishment of such institutions in the state until it was superseded by an act of June 26, 1895. It was provided that if a grand jury at any court of quarter sessions should decide that a new workhouse ought to be erected or an existing one repaired or extended, they should make such recommendation to the justices of the court of quarter sessions and the county commissioners and assessors. If the justices, commissioners and assessors agreed with the recommendation of the grand jury, the money required to erect, extend or repair the workhouse was to be raised as a part of the county rate.[212] The justices of the court of quarter sessions were empowered to appoint "some capable, discreet, and prudent person to be keeper of such workhouse."[213] It was the duty of the keeper to furnish materials for the employment of the inmates, to sell the products, and to turn over the proceeds to the county treasury. The salary of the keeper was to be determined by the justices of the court of quarter sessions.[214] In the workhouse were to be confined all "idle and disorderly persons, rogues and vagabonds."[215]

The last workhouse act of the provincial period was that of February 26, 1773, to erect a "new gaol, workhouse, and house of correction in the city of Philadelphia."[216] It should be noted that

---

[209] *The Statutes at Large of Pennsylvania,* Vol. V, pp. 31-8.
[210] Ibid., Vol. VI, p. 280.
[211] Ibid., pp. 280-82.
[212] Ibid., Vol. VII, p. 86.
[213] Ibid., p. 87.
[214] Ibid.
[215] Ibid.
[216] Ibid., Vol. VIII, pp. 300-04.

this act of 1773 was both a workhouse and a jail act. This is to be accounted for by the fact that in Philadelphia, while the jail and the workhouse occupied separate buildings, they were enclosed by the same wall and constituted a part of the same penal institution.[217] The act stated that, "It has been represented to the Assembly that the gaol and workhouse in the City of Philadelphia are insufficient for the safe custody of the criminals and others committed to the same, and that from the smallness of the lot of ground, the inconveniency of the buildings and inner apartments and the increased number of persons confined therein, the health not only of the said prisoners, but of the inhabitants of the said city is greatly endangered." [218]

To remove these abuses it was enacted that the commissioners of the county of Philadelphia were authorized to raise funds to "purchase a lot of ground in some convenient part of the city and erect thereon a commodious, strong and sufficient gaol, workhouse, and house of correction, with a good yard to each of them, inclosed by walls of a proper height and strength for confining and detaining in safe custody all felons, criminals, and others who shall be committed to the said gaol and workhouse." [219] This act is unusually important in the history of penology, as the new jail and workhouse, which was created as a result, was the famous Walnut Street Jail, in which the first American experiments were conducted with respect to the system of solitary confinement.[220]

Therefore, while every county of provincial Pennsylvania was provided with a county jail, only Philadelphia, Chester, Bucks and Lancaster Counties erected workhouses, and only in the case of those at Philadelphia and Chester is there any reliable evidence that they retained to the slightest degree their original character as penal institutions. The characteristic penal institution of eighteenth century Pennsylvania was the county jail.

C. The Administrative System of the Provincial Penal Institutions

The legal basis of the administrative system of the provincial penal institutions has already been presented in the survey of the organizing laws; a brief summary of this aspect of penal administration will suffice at this point.

With respect to the provincial jails, the general control of the

---

[217] See below, pp. 134ff.
[218] *The Statutes at Large of Pennsylvania*, Vol. VIII, p. 300.
[219] Ibid., p. 301.
[220] See below, pp. 134ff.

physical property was placed in the hands of five trustees and their heirs and assignees. These trustees were named in the general act creating the county. The trustees were entrusted also with the responsibility of keeping up the property and authorizing the raising of the required funds for this purpose. The money was to be raised by the county commissioners and assessors as a part of the county rate.[221] The actual administrative control of the jail was vested in the sheriff, but he usually delegated this function to an undersheriff or a "gaol keeper."[222] The classes of persons received in the jails of provincial Pennsylvania were highly diverse. They included debtors, those accused of all types of crime who were awaiting trial at the regular court session and "gaol delivery," those convicted of capital crimes awaiting execution, and the few convicted criminals that had been sentenced to imprisonment instead of receiving the more usual penalty of some type of brutal corporal punishment. It is quite unnecessary to add that no differentiation was made in the treatment of prisoners on the basis of age, sex, degree of mental stability, or grade of criminality. Roberts Vaux, writing in 1826, thus describes this wholly deplorable and vicious situation which existed fifty years earlier:

"What a spectacle must this abode of guilt and wretchedness have presented, when in one common herd were kept by day and night prisoners of all ages, colors and sexes! No separation was made of the most flagrant offender and convict, from the prisoner who might, perhaps, be falsely suspected of some trifling misdemeanor; none of the old and hardened culprits from the youthful, trembling novice in crime; none even of the fraudulent swindler from the unfortunate and possibly the most estimable debtor; and when intermingled with all these, in one corrupt and corrupting assemblage were to be found the disgusting object of popular contempt, besmeared with filth from the pillory—the unhappy victim of the lash, streaming with blood from the whipping post—the half naked vagrant—the loathsome drunkard—the sick, suffering from various bodily pains, and too often the unaneled malefactor, whose precious hours of probation had been numbered by his earthly judge."[223]

In view of the foregoing description nothing needs to be said about penal discipline in provincial days, for such a thing could

---

[221] *The Statutes at Large of Pennsylvania,* Vol. IV, pp. 9-10, 133-34; V, pp. 73-6, 90-3, 136-39, 143-46; VIII, pp. 48-52, 146-49, 316-20.

[222] Ibid., Vol. IV, pp. 179ff.

[223] *Notices of the Original and Successive Attempts to Improve the Discipline of the Prison at Philadelphia, and to Reform the Criminal Code of Pennsylvania, with a few Observations on the Penitentiary System,* Philadelphia, 1826.

not well exist. The same might be said of penal labor in the provincial jails. Demoralizing idleness was the vicious partner of the corrupting, intermingling and herding of inmates in this unspeakable situation in the colonial jails. The following paragraph summarizes the condition as presented by some of the most eminent of early Pennsylvania jurists in 1828:

"The alteration of the criminal code which took place in 1718, in consequence of the pertinacious attachment of the British government to capital punishments, seems in practice to have restored the dominion of idleness in the interior of our prisons; for although to some minor offences, the punishment of confinement for a short period at hard labor was annexed, yet the concurrent testimony of all who remember its condition, represents the provincial prison of Philadelphia as a scene of profligacy and license, in which all sexes, ages and colors were confounded without classification, without labor, and without restraint." [224]

The customary extortion and other conventional abuses of the jail system were not absent from the jails of provincial Pennsylvania. The sheriffs exacted exorbitant fees from those confined, sometimes even compelling them to live in the sheriff's own house or in taverns and to make such payment for their keep as the sheriff or inkeeper demanded. Within the jail itself the sheriff or "gaol keeper" frequently "oppressed" the inmates by exorbitant charges, by personal favoritism and other well-known means. He often tried to swell his income by establishing a well-equipped bar in the jail, over which he sold liquor to the prisoners, and assured himself of their trade by forbidding them to obtain drink from outside. [225] Wealthy prisoners might readily obtain immunity from the degradation of confinement in the "common gaol" by bribing the sheriff to allow them to live in a tavern or a private house under only the most general surveillance of the officers of the law. To eliminate most of these abuses was the main purpose of the act of February 14, 1730. It was thereby enacted that the sheriff should not take a prisoner to "any tavern, alehouse, or other public victualing or drinking house or to the private house of any sheriff, undersheriff or gaol keeper without the voluntary consent of the person so taken and arrested." [226] The sheriff was further directed to allow any prisoner to "send for and have any beer, ale, victuals or any other necessary food from what place they please; and also to

---

[224] *Report of the Commissioners on the Penal Code, with the Accompanying Documents,* Harrisburg, 1828, p. 12.
[225] J. F. Watson, *Annals of Philadelphia,* enlarged and revised by W. P. Hazard, Vol. III, p. 178.
[226] *The Statutes at Large of Pennsylvania,* Vol. IV, p. 179.

have and use such bedding, linen, and other things as he or she shall think fit." [227] The sheriff was forbidden to sell strong drink in the jail or to allow it to be sold in the jail by others.[228] The sheriff or "gaoler" was forbidden to take any fees except those allowed by law, as determined by the justices of the county. These legal fees were to be displayed in a public place in the jail where they could be easily read by the inmates and citizens.[229] Finally, it was stipulated that the sheriff should not hold office for more than three years in succession, and that after he had held office for three successive years, at least three years must elapse before he could again be qualified to serve.[230] It should be noted that this reform act did not prevent wealthy and prominent delinquents from buying the privilege of confinement outside of the jails. Nor was it successful in preventing the sheriff or "gaoler" from maintaining a bar in the jail. Even as late as 1788, it is stated on the best authority that a well-equipped bar was maintained in the Philadelphia jail.[231] There is no reason for thinking that the act was any more efficacious in entirely eliminating extortion from the administration of the county jail system. Some conception of the brutal treatment of prisoners may be derived from the fact that in 1770 there was one death from starvation in the Philadelphia jail, while in 1772 three prisoners died from the same cause.[232]

A fair idea of the fees paid to the sheriff or jailor for his services in caring for a prisoner in the colonial period may be obtained from the following bill presented by the jailor of Chester County in 1736: [233]

Chester County Dr.
to Nathan Worley,

For maintaining Joseph Bivan from the 13th day of October, 1736, to the 2nd day of July, 1737.

	£	s	d
To Turn Kee fees for every capital crime	0	10	0
To King's allowance 260 days at 2d. per day	2	3	4
To fireing and cloathing for him all winter	2	3	4
Taking four pairs of irons off him when he was to be executed	0	6	0
To a shirt and pair of trousers for him when he was executed—for he was naked	0	10	0
	5	12	8

---

[227] *The Statutes at Large of Pennsylvania,* Vol. IV, p. 180.
[228] Ibid., p. 182.
[229] Ibid., pp. 180-81.
[230] Ibid., p. 183.
[231] *Report of the Commissioners on the Penal Code,* 1828, p. 13.
[232] J. F. Scharf and T. Westcott, *A History of Philadelphia,* Vol. III, p. 1826.
[233] Futhey and Cope, *A History of Chester County,* p. 410.

The standard fee at that time for executing a condemned criminal was five pounds. Incidental expenses at an execution, such as erecting gallows, making a coffin, digging a grave and conducting the funeral amounted to twenty pence.[234]

An act of February 24, 1770, ordered that the sheriff or jailor should be allowed three pence per day for the maintenance of all persons imprisoned after the conviction of any criminal offense. This was to be raised from the county rate and paid to the sheriff.[235]

The authority to establish workhouses was vested in the justices of the court of quarter sessions in each county. They were to estimate the amount of money needed for this purpose and to order the county commissioners and assessors to raise it as a part of the county rate. The general control over each workhouse was vested in a corporation appointed by the justices from the more prominent freeholders of the county. This corporation was to estimate the necessary annual expenses of the operation of the workhouse and submit it to the critical revision of the justices, who were to transmit it to the county commissioners and assessors to be raised in the county rate. The immediate supervision of the institution was vested in one active member of the corporation who was required by law to be present and regulate its administration. The details of the administration were delegated to the officers appointed, paid and dismissed by the corporation.[236] It has been shown above that, at least after 1718, the workhouses were employed almost exclusively for the repression of the vagrants, paupers and disorderly servants and not extensively to receive and punish the criminal classes. In other words, from 1718 to 1790, the workhouses were scarcely a part of the system of penal institutions.[237]

There is no evidence that there was any systematic differentiation in the treatment of the "rogues, vagabonds, sturdy beggars and other idle and disorderly persons" who were admitted to the workhouses. Nor is there any specific information available as to the type of work performed by those confined in the workhouses. One can only reconstruct the possible types of labor from a consideration of the method of employing inmates of the European workhouses of the time and the employment later used in the state penitentiaries. From these "comparative" sources of information it may be supposed that the work varied from the rougher types of manual labor, such as grinding grain, pounding stone, the

---

[234] Futhey and Cope, *A History of Chester County*, p. 410.
[235] *The Statutes at Large of Pennsylvania*, Vol. VII, pp. 346-47.
[236] Ibid., Vol. III, pp. 167-71; Vol. V, pp. 31-8; Vol. VI, p. 280.
[237] Ibid., Vol. III, p. 168.

coarser weaving and spinning, and "cordwaining" or cobbling, to labor which was in no sense productive but was adopted purely for its supposed deterrent value, such as running a tread-mill, turning a friction crank, and carrying heavy weights back and forth across the yard of the workhouse.[238]

D. Descriptive Details Concerning the Provincial Penal Institutions

As the significance of Pennsylvania in the history of penology lies almost entirely in the experiments and advances made in the various institutions located in the city of Philadelphia, it is particularly gratifying that the most complete and specific knowledge is possessed of the successive penal institutions there erected, from the first "cage" of 1682, to the Eastern Penitentiary at Cherry Hill. This information enables the student to reconstruct the record of the entire evolution of modern penal institutions, and of those ideas and practices which constitute the body of modern penal philosophy.[239]

The first record of a penal institution in Pennsylvania is the order of the council, on November 16, 1682, that "William Clayton, one of the Provincial Council, should build a cage against the next council-day, of seven feet long by five feet broad." [240] This was but a temporary expedient, and some time in the interval between 1682 and 1685, Lassey Cock was authorized to build a county jail in Philadelphia at an expense of sixty pounds. That this building was deemed insufficient at the time of its completion is evident from the following action of the provincial authorities:

"At the eighth court 2nd of 7th mo. 1685—The Grand Jury agree, that in lieu of £60 to be paid Lassey Cock, for building of a log house in Second Street intended for a county gaol, he shall have the said log house with the ground it stands on, with the spot of ground adjacent, and a legal title thereto to be procured from the governor with a proportionable lot in Second Street, for which the said county shall satisfy the governor, and shall pay to said Lassey Cock £60 out of the first collected public levy, on consideration, that it doth appear that the said log house cannot be sufficient for the purpose aforesaid intended." [241]

Instead of this structure erected by Mr. Cock, the authorities

---

[238] Cf., Wines, op. cit., pp. 115-18. Ives, op. cit., pp. 188ff. S. and B. Webb, *English Prisons and Local Government*, pp. 92-3, 96-8, 147-57.
[239] The chief source is Watson's *Annals of Philadelphia*, and Scherf and Westcott, *History of Philadelphia*, Vol. III.
[240] Watson, *Annals of Philadelphia*, revised by Hazard, Vol. I, p. 356.
[241] Ibid., pp. 300-01.

rented one side of the residence of Patrick Robinson on the corner
of Second and High Streets to serve as the county jail or prison.
In 1685 the "High Sheriff" announced, "that the hired house of
Patrick Robinson used by him as a prison, was refitting, and that,
with the fetters and chains &c., and his own attendance and
deputies, he hath a sufficient gaol; and if any escapes occurred he
would not blame the county, for want of a gaol, nor the insufficiency
of said house." [242] It appears that the Robinson family lived on
one side of a common entry to the house and that the jail occupied
the other half of the house.[243]

This rented frame building was not regarded as satisfying the
requirements of a good jail or workhouse and in the same year,
1685, the authorities agreed upon the following specifications for
the construction of a new brick "prison":

"The house twenty feet long and fourteen feet wide in the clear,
two stories high,—the upper seven feet, and the under six and a
half feet, of which four feet under ground, with all convenient
lights and doors, and casements,—strong and substantial, with good
brick, lime, sand and stone, as also floors and roofs very substantial;
a partition of brick in the middle through the house, so that there
will be four rooms, four chimneys, and the cock-loft, which will
serve for a prison; and the gaoler may well live in any part of it,
if need be—the whole to cost £140." [244]

The prison, thus described, was not completed, however, until
1695, and in less than a decade it became antiquated. In 1702 the
county grand jury presented "the prison house and prison yard, as
it now stands in the High Street, as a common nuisance.[245] In the
following year the court of quarter sessions appointed a committee
of four to make inquiry and "to report the cost of a new prison
and court house." [246] In spite of annual complaints about the High
Street Prison no practical steps were taken to remedy the situation
until 1717. By that time the need of a new prison had become so
pressing that "sundry persons offered large subscriptions for erecting a new prison at the present site." [247] In the next year the act
of February 27, 1718, provided for the erection of a new jail and
workhouse.[248] In 1723 the new stone prison at the corner of Third

[242] Watson, *Annals of Philadelphia,* Vol. I, p. 356.
[243] Ibid., p. 357.
[244] Ibid., p. 358.
[245] Ibid.
[246] Ibid.
[247] Ibid., p. 359.
[248] *The Statutes at Large of Philadelphia,* Vol. III, pp. 167ff.

and High Streets was completed and the old brick prison on High
Street was sold to "the highest bidder." [249]   Mr. Watson thus
describes the new prison, which served as the jail and workhouse
of Philadelphia until 1780:

"When finished, about the year 1723, the pile consisted of a two-
story stone building, fronting on High Street, for the debtor's jail,
and another two story similar building, fronting on Third Street,
for the criminals, called the workhouse—the latter some distance
from the former, but joined to it by a high wall forming a part
of the yard enclosure. The buildings were of hewn stone; half of
the cellar story was above ground; the roofs were sharply pitched,
and the garrets furnished rooms for prisoners." [250]

After exactly a half-century of service this prison at the corner
of Third and High Streets was deemed no longer adequate for the
needs of the county and city, and the act of February 26, 1773,
authorized the construction of a new jail and workhouse in Philadelphia.[251] The new prison, erected according to the provisions of
this act, was the historic Walnut Street Jail located at the corner
of Walnut and Sixth Streets.[252] It had been completed in part by
1776, when it was turned over to the government as a military
prison. Later it was occupied by the British for the same purpose.
It was finally completed and occupied as a prison in 1780 and an
act of February 28, 1780, ordered the old jail at High and Third
Streets sold.[253]

There is no reason for believing that there was anything in the
other counties so pretentious in prison architecture as the stone
prison of provincial Pennsylvania.[254] All the evidence available
indicates that the jails and workhouses were generally rough frame
buildings, at the best only satisfactory from the standpoint of a
moderately safe and sure detention of the prisoners in custody.
Particularly was this the case with the jails erected in the newer
counties. It is stated that the jail erected in Westmoreland County
in 1773 "was made of round, unhewn logs, one story high, having
but one small room, where men and women, whites, blacks and
Indians were confined together." [255]

---

[249] Watson, *Annals of Philadelphia,* p. 359.
[250] Ibid., pp. 360-61.
[251] *The Statutes at Large of Pennsylvania,* Vol. VIII, p. 300-04.
[252] Watson, *Annals of Philadelphia,* revised by Hazard, Vol. I, p. 361; Vol.
III, pp. 177ff.
[253] *Statutes at Large,* Vol. IX, pp. 255-57; Vol. X, pp. 48-52.
[254] Delaware erected a stone court-house and jail at Chester in 1724. See
Smith's *History of Delaware County,* p. 234.
[255] J. W. F. White, loc. cit., p. 147.

E. Summary of the Development of Provincial Penal Institutions

The outstanding phases of the development of colonial penal institutions in Pennsylvania can be briefly characterized in the following summary. The first type of penal institution provided for in statute was the typical English detention jail of the period, which was employed solely for the detention of those accused of crime pending trial and was emptied at each quarterly "gaol delivery." The stocks, whipping-post, pillory, and branding-iron were the only devices provided for the treatment of convicted criminals. Whether any of these detention jails provided for in laws of 1676 were ever built can not be determined, but as the courts were in session at the period it may be assumed that some provision was made for holding the accused in custody prior to trial.

The second type of penal institution created in the province was the Quaker workhouse, which for the first time brought into combination the jail and the workhouse and made the latter a real penal institution. Apparently, outside of Philadelphia, this reform was primarily statutory rather than actually achieved, and few if any workhouses were built before 1718, after which the workhouse passed from a penal institution into a resumption of its old European characteristics as an institution for the repression of vagrancy and pauperism. Therefore, the county jail was the characteristic penal institution of the colonial period, each of the eleven counties being provided with a jail and but four with workhouses. In the case of the workhouses not more than one or two were employed in any sense as penal institutions. The jails were utilized mainly for detaining those accused of crime and awaiting trial and for the confinement of debtors. Few convicted criminals were confined in the jails, as their sentences were mainly fine or corporal punishment.

The inmates of the jails suffered from the extortion of jailors and from the demoralizing idleness and the corrupting intermingling of all classes, which was an inseparable accompaniment of the system. There was no differentiation in treatment, segregation or confinement provided for the inmates according to age, sex, color, degree of criminality, previous record or mental state, with the slight exception that in Philadelphia some attempt was made to segregate the debtors from the criminals. Finally, the absence of productive labor from the provincial jails made them a complete economic burden, in so far as they were not supported by the fees paid by the inmates. In short, the most conspicuous fact about the colonial period from this standpoint was the almost complete absence of true penal institutions and the hopeless failure of those which existed as reformatory and deterrent institutions.

CHAPTER III

The Origins and Formation of the Pennsylvania System of Prison Administration, 1776 to 1835

I. GENERAL TENDENCIES AND ACHIEVEMENTS [1]

"The Pennsylvania Prison System had its origin in an effort to correct the abuses in the place of incarceration of all classes of violators of law. The common jail, under the colonial government of the Province of Pennsylvania, was a receptacle of every such offender. In the city prison of Philadelphia, located at Market and Third Streets, in 1770, young and old, black and white, men and women, boys and girls were congregated indiscriminately in custody for misconduct, misdeameanor, and crime, either before trial, after conviction, or for want of bail for surety of the peace. It was a moral pest-house." [2]

Richard Vaux, historian of the Eastern Penitentiary, and for many years head of the board of inspectors of the institution, thus described the conditions which gave rise to those reform measures in penal jurisprudence and administration, as a result of which the Pennsylvania system of prison administration was created. It will be the purpose of this chapter to trace in detail the various phases of this process of transition from the juristic and penal barbarism of the later colonial period to the establishment of one of the most important and influential systems of prison administration which has yet been devised. Before proceeding to the detailed analysis of specific advances, a brief survey of the outstanding movements and achievements of the period will be useful in orienting the reader with respect to the subsequent discussion.

The condition of the criminal code and the penal institutions at the close of the colonial period has been sufficiently analyzed so that it may be briefly summarized here merely to indicate by contrast the achievements of the next half-century. In 1775 there was

---

[1] If this chapter seems rather heavily burdened with documents, it is because they constitute some of the most important source material in the whole history of penology and are accessible only in the rare pamphlets possessed by a few of the largest libraries.

[2] Richard Vaux, *The Pennsylvania Prison System,* A Paper Read before the American Philosophical Society, June 20, 1884, p. 3.

little or no imprisonment as a normal punishment for crimes. Felonies were almost exclusively punished by death and the lesser offenses by fines or brutal forms of corporal punishment, such as whipping, branding, mutilating and exposure in the stocks and pillory. There was no unified state prison system. The local county and municipal jails were the typical penal institutions of the period. In them there was no classification or separation of convicts on any basis. No labor was provided. There was no moral nor educational instruction. No attention was given to the possibilities of reforming the offenders. The only aim of criminal jurisprudence and penal procedure was the utter extinction of serious offenders and the deterrence of others by brutal, painful and humiliating penalties.

Fifty years later a radical transformation had been effected. By the provisions of the state constitution of 1776 and acts of September 15, 1786, April 5, 1790, September 23, 1791, April 22, 1794, April 18, 1795, April 4, 1807, and April 23, 1829, the barbarous criminal code of 1718 was replaced by one which for justice, mildness and humanity was almost unique in the civilized world at that time, and which restored Pennsylvania to that position of supremacy in enlightened criminal jurisprudence which it had held under the domination of Penn's laws from 1682 to 1718. The death penalty was abolished for all crimes except murder in the first degree. Fines and imprisonment at hard labor were substituted for the cruel forms of corporal punishment earlier employed in repressing other than capital crimes. The outstanding feature of the change was that the combination of an elimination of most of the capital crimes and of a wide use of imprisonment in the repression of crime, necessitated for the first time the provision of a complete system of penal institutions and a systematic regulation of their administration. The Pennsylvania prison reformers were certainly justified in their statement that "perhaps a more thorough transformation in the character of a penal code, by peaceful legislation, is not recorded in the world's history than that which took place in Pennsylvania during the eighteen years immediately succeeding the Declaration of Independence." [3] The system of penal institutions made necessary by the reform of the penal code was provided for in the above acts and in those of March 27, 1789, April 2, 1803, March 21, 1805, April 4, 1807, February 23, 1809, March 31, 1812, March 13, 1816, March 3, 1818, March 20 and 21, 1821, February 24, 1823, March 15, 1824, March 21, 1825,

---

[3] *Sketch of the Principal Transactions of the Philadelphia Society for Alleviating the Miseries of Public Prisons from Its Origin to the Present Time,* Philadelphia, 1859, p. 5.

March 15, April 1, and April 10, 1826, March 28, 1831, February 27, 1833, and April 14, 1835.

As a result of these acts a state prison system was created along with new and adequate institutions for the reception of all criminals. An elaborate set of rules and regulations was drawn up for the government of these new penitentiaries, which provided for some elementary classification of inmates on the basis of age, sex and crime, and which compelled the separation and the solitary confinement of all prisoners, without any exception. Hard labor was prescribed for all those who were physically able to work, and great emphasis was laid upon the element of reformation, as well as upon deterrence, as the main functions of a complete and well-administered system of penal institutions. Finally, by the acts of March 23, 1826, and March 2, 1827, the first step in that fundamental process of the differentiation of penal institutions on the basis of special classes of inmates was taken by the creation of the Philadelphia House of Refuge, a semi-state institution for the reception and treatment of juvenile delinquents. All of these remarkable changes were accomplished as the result of a well-organized prison reform movement which has rarely been equaled in history for aggressiveness, persistence and enlightened motives. The net product of the period of reform was the Pennsylvania system of prison administration, which in its original form, or in its altered and revised application under the Auburn system, has determined the methods of prison administration for the Western World from 1830 to the present day.[4]

II.   THE FORCES AND AGENCIES WHICH CREATED THE PENNSYLVANIA SYSTEM

1.   EXTERNAL AND INTERNAL CONDITIONS AND DEVELOPMENTS PROMOTING THE REFORM OF THE CRIMINAL CODE AND THE PENAL INSTITUTIONS OF PENNSYLVANIA

A.   The General Historical Background of the Reform Movement

There are two sets of influences which constitute the chief phases of the historical background of prison reform in Pennsylvania, namely, those general forces making for reform and progress of

---

[4] The best contemporary sources of information for the prison reform movement in Pennsylvania from 1786 to 1835 are the works of Roberts Vaux, Caleb Lownes, Robert J. Turnbull and James Mease, which are cited below. A valuable work published since these pages were written is O. F. Lewis, *Development of American Prisons and Prison Customs, 1776-1845.*

all kinds in the eighteenth century, and those specific attempts to reform criminal jurisprudence and penal administration during the same period, which center mainly about the writings and activities of Beccaria, Howard and the Pennsylvania reformers, such as Bradford, Rush, Vaux, Lownes and others.

The ignorance, crudities and barbarism of the "old régime" in Europe were effectively attacked in the writings of the French *philosophes,* such as Montesquieu, Voltaire, Diderot, Turgot and Condorcet, and of their English sympathizers and associates like David Hume, Adam Smith, Tom Paine and Jeremy Bentham. The assault on the old order in the work of these publicists was given concrete and objective form in the French Revolution and its effect upon the other states of Europe. Probably the most important of the doctrines of these writers and of the Revolutionary period was the introduction of rationalism into social and political philosophy and the firm conviction that social progress and advancement was possible through sweeping social reforms carried out according to the dictates of "pure reason." It is obvious that so barbarous and archaic a part of the old order as the current criminal jurisprudence and penal administration of the time could not long remain immune to the growing spirit of progress and enlightenment.[5]

America, in general, and Philadelphia, in particular, were well situated to feel the effect of these new forces. A large number of Frenchmen had been in America during the Revolutionary War, had brought with them many of the ideas of their publicists and had stimulated an American interest in French thought. In addition, many of the more important and influential Americans had been in Europe during the period of the American Revolution and the years immediately following. Philadelphia, as the real center of American civilization and political life during the last quarter of the eighteenth century, was particularly affected by these progressive European developments. Benjamin Franklin had long been a resident of France and was well acquainted with radical French thought. The political leaders who assembled in Philadelphia during the period were all more or less familiar with the advanced political thought of England and France. No other foreign philosopher so influenced the American Constitutional Convention of 1787 as did

---

[5] See John Morley's biographies of Rousseau, Diderot and Voltaire, and his essays on eighteenth-century thought in France in his *Critical Miscellanies;* A. Sorel's biography of Montesquieu; H. Higgs, *The Physiocrats;* J. M. Robertson, *A History of Free Thought;* Leslie Stephens, *History of English Thought in the Eighteenth Century;* and the excellent summary of the writings and thought of this period in Robinson and Beard, *Development of Modern Europe,* Vol. I, pp. 157-82, and *The Cambridge Modern History,* Vol. VIII, Chap. I.

Montesquieu, and his exponents must have been as familiar with his doctrines on the reform of criminal jurisprudence as with his theories of the separation of governmental powers. As the capital of the country during much of the period, Philadelphia received many distinguished foreign visitors, bringing with them the doctrines of their countrymen. Brissot, the Girondist leader in the French Revolution, was among these. Finally, it was to Philadelphia that Jefferson came shortly after his return from France where he had become more familiar with French revolutionary ideas and leaders. All of these conditions combined to make Philadelphia particularly well adapted to the carrying into execution of some of the more radical European programs of social reform.

Powerful and successful attacks were made upon the barbarous and irrational criminal jurisprudence and penal institutions by a group of able and influential writers. The French Publicist, Montesquieu (1689-1755), in his *Persian Letters* and *The Spirit of the Laws,* condemned the barbarous injustice of the French penal code and advocated reforms which would make punishments less severe and more nearly adapted to the specific crimes for which they were imposed. His work attracted and stimulated a more influential writer in the history of the reform of criminal jurisprudence, the Italian, Beccaria (1738-94). His *Crimes and Punishments,* first published in 1764, was probably the most significant single contribution of the eighteenth century to the reform of criminal jurisprudence. He argued powerfully for the need of a more just and accurate method of trial, the necessity for a reduction in the severity of the penalties imposed, a larger use of imprisonment in the punishment of crime and an improvement in the administration of prisons. The greater portion of his work, however, was directed primarily toward securing a reformation of contemporary criminal law.

The English jurist, Blackstone (1723-80), while not violent enough in his criticisms of the old system to please Bentham, condemned the glaring injustices in the unspeakable English criminal code of his day. The multitudinous and diverse reforming interests of Jeremy Bentham (1748-1832), embraced voluminous writings on the reform of both criminal jurisprudence and penal administration.[6] Finally, many of the most important of the doctrines of the reformers were given concrete expression in the French Revolutionary penal code of September 25, 1791, which declared that

---

[6] On Bentham, see W. L. Davidson, *Political Thought in England, the Utilitarians,* pp. 107-13. The best general work is Phillipson, *Three Criminal Law Reformers.*

"penalties should be proportioned to the crimes for which they are inflicted, and that they are intended not merely to punish, but to reform the culprit." All of these developments toward securing a new and more rational and humane criminal jurisprudence were well known to intelligent citizens of Philadelphia.

The first clear anticipations of the modern prison system were the papal prison of San Michele, erected in Rome by Clement XI, about 1704, and the prison at Ghent in Belgium, established by Hippolyte Vilain XIII in 1773. In both of these there was provided some sort of classification and cellular separation of inmates. Labor by the inmates was the rule and reformation was stated to be a chief aim of incarceration. Neither of these prisons attracted much general attention in England or America until their virtues were discovered and reported by the distinguished English prison reformer, John Howard (1726-90). In his travels of inspection between 1773 and 1790 he visited these institutions several times, and his writings contain vivid descriptions of their construction and administration. It was through his writings, well known to Philadelphians, that America gained a knowledge of these advanced institutions and caught the spirit of Howard's labors in the behalf of prison reform.

There is little or no evidence, however, that these institutions in Rome and Ghent directly influenced Pennsylvania penology to an appreciable degree. Their effect seems to have been indirect. Howard's recommendation of their system of administration, as a part of his penal philosophy, induced a number of enterprising and sympathetic English reformers to adopt their principles in English jails and prisons, and the latter became the models followed by the Philadelphia reformers. When, in 1790, the Philadelphia Society for Alleviating the Miseries of Public Prisons desired to influence the legislature of the state in order to secure the adoption of an advanced system of prison administration, their list of successful experiments in the new penology did not include any important reference to Rome or Ghent, but was confined almost entirely to the reforms in new English county prisons, particularly that at Wymondham in Norfolk, erected about 1784 by Sir Thomas Beevor, as a result of the enthusiasm generated by a reading of Howard's writings. In this prison there was provided a separation of sexes and of hardened criminals from first and petty offenders, separate cells for all prisoners at night and for incorrigible prisoners at all times, and a well-equipped workshop for the employment of able-bodied prisoners. [7] Beyond this indirect influence of Howard's

---

[7] *Extracts and Remarks on the Subject of the Punishment and Reformation of Criminals.* Published by Order of the Society Established in Philadelphia for Alleviating the Miseries of Public Prisons, February 25, 1790.

work upon Philadelphia prison reform, ample evidence exists that the Philadelphia reformers were thoroughly conversant with the printed accounts of his travels in the inspection of prisons and with his recommendations of reform based upon these trips. The above-mentioned pamphlet of 1790 contains long extracts from Howard's works which were in accord with the changes urged upon the legislature. Two years earlier, however, the Society had sent Howard the following letter:

"Philadelphia, January 14, 1788.

"To John Howard.

"The Society for Alleviating the Miseries of Public Prisons, in the city of Philadelphia, beg leave to forward to you a copy of their constitution, and to request, at the same time, such communications from you upon the subject of their institution, as may favour their designs.

"The Society heartily concur with the friends of humanity in Europe, in expressing their obligations to you for having rendered the miserable tenants of prisons the objects of more general attention and compassion, and for having pointed out some of the means of not only alleviating their miseries, but of preventing those crimes and misfortunes which are the causes of them.

"With sincere wishes that your useful life may be prolonged, and that you may enjoy the pleasure of seeing the success of your labours in the cause of humanity, in every part of the globe, we are, with great respect and esteem, your sincere friends and well wishers.

"Signed by order of the Society.

"William White, President." [8]

This letter, written less than a year after the formation of the society, would seem to indicate that even in its origin it was powerfully stimulated by Howard's work. Besides the influence of Howard's work, it is evident that Jeremy Bentham's *Panopticon* and its voluminous appendices, published following 1787, had some effect upon prison reform in Pennsylvania. The Western Penitentiary of Pennsylvania, authorized by the law of 1818, is one of the few institutions which was modeled to some degree after Bentham's ingenious plan for perfect prison structure.[9]

Finally, in concluding this summary of the historical background of early prison reform in Philadelphia, the fact must not be forgotten that Pennsylvania, alone of all the states, was fortunate

---

[8] Roberts Vaux, *Notices of the Original and Successive Attempts to Improve the Discipline of the Prison at Philadelphia and to Reform the Criminal Code of Pennsylvania*, pp. 24-5.
[9] See below, pp. 138ff.

enough to have had its very origin linked up with the cause of judicial and penal reform. While the laws passed from 1718 to 1775 were usually about as far as possible from Penn's actual program, the memory of his purposes was kept alive in the enacting clauses. Therefore, when a reform of the criminal code and penal administration became necessary, the movement was rendered respectable and "safe" through its association with the venerable name of the founder of the province. Only those who have had personal experience in social reform can fully appreciate the significance of this situation in breaking down popular prejudice and lessening the inertia in the public mind.

B. Circumstances in Philadelphia Promoting the Cause of Prison Reform 1776-1835

The local conditions which stimulated the movement for prison reform in Philadelphia are implicit in the above discussions of conditions in that city's criminal law and penal institutions at the close of the colonial period, and of the general forces making for social reform in general and prison reform in particular. A city which had been founded in part upon traditions of radical reform in criminal law and penal administration had allowed the earlier practices to be superseded by the conventional barbarism and stupidity of the time in regard to the treatment of the criminal classes. As a result of more than a half-century of such conditions, the penal institutions had reached so deplorable a state that reform would probably have been inevitable in any community. Facing this situation was a community in better touch with the reforming movements in Europe than any other municipality in America, with at least half of its population composed of a religious group founded on the doctrines and practices of humanity and social reform, and with a past which made judicial and penal reform as honorable as it was desirable. In view of this combination of circumstances, it is not difficult to understand why Philadelphia became the most active locality in prison reform in America and the center from which the reforming movement radiated throughout the United States for more than a half-century. As is the case with all great reform movements, juristic and penal reform in Pennsylvania had its origin and main impulses from sources outside of the regular public organs of society. It is to the multitudinous activities of this voluntary reforming society that attention will now be directed.

2. The Philadelphia Society for Alleviating the Miseries of Public Prisons

A. The Origin and Antecedents of the Society

The antecedents of the Philadelphia Society for Alleviating the Miseries of Public Prisons go back to the ideals and practices of the founders of the province and to the reform movements of the eighteenth century. Such was its general background; it had no direct predecessor, as it was the first of the great prison reform societies.[10]

The beginnings of private prison reform movements in Pennsylvania are generally associated with the name of Richard Wistar, a member of the Society of Friends, who, just prior to the outbreak of the Revolutionary War, was attracted by the abject misery of the inmates of the provincial jail and had soup prepared at his own house and taken and distributed among the inmates of the jail.[11] Others became interested in the situation and, on February 7, 1776, there was formed The Philadelphia Society for Assisting Distressed Prisoners, the parent society of The Philadelphia Society for Alleviating the Miseries of Public Prisons and of The Pennsylvania Prison Society.[12] This society had an existence of only nineteen months when it was broken up by the British occupation of Philadelphia. Of its work no official record remains. If one may believe the statement made a century later, without any evidence as to the sources of information, the society was organized to carry on more effectively the work of actual relief of prisoners which had been begun by Mr. Wistar. It is said that members of the society went from house to house with wheelbarrows gathering food and clothing for the convicts. In view of the fact that definite knowledge exists that there were several deaths from starvation in the jail in the period from 1770 to 1776 and that the inmates

---

[10] The other early prison reform societies in the order of their formation are *The London Society for the Improvement of Prison Discipline,* 1815; *The Royal Prison Society of France,* 1819; *The Boston Prison Discipline Society,* 1824; and *The Prison Association of New York,* 1845.

[11] Roberts Vaux, *Notices,* pp. 8-9. There were frequent instances of starvation in the jail at this period.

[12] Ibid., p. 9. *Sketch of the Principal Transactions of the Philadelphia Society for Alleviating the Miseries of Public Prisons,* Philadelphia, 1859, p. 3. The managers of this original society were Joseph Allen, Christopher Marshall, Christopher Ludwick, Isaac Howell, Richard Wells, Benjamin Shoemaker, Joseph Paschall, Benjamin Marshall, Joseph Stansbury, Benjamin Poultney, Richard Humphreys, Samuel Sansom and Thomas Moore. (The last named was treasurer of the society.) *Sketch of Principal Transactions,* p. 3.

were in many cases almost entirely without clothing or bedding, there seems to be little reason for doubting that the purpose and activity of the society centered about improving the physical comforts of the prisoners.[13] The only official notice of its activities which has been preserved is the following account of the termination of its existence:

"The British army having entered the city of Philadelphia in September, 1777, and possessed themselves of the public jails, no further service could be rendered, nor was any election held this month, for the appointment of new managers, so that the Philadelphia Society for Assisting Distressed Prisoners, was dissolved during this memorable period.

"Signed, Richard Wells, Secretary."[14]

Immediately after the peace of 1783 a number of prominent citizens of Philadelphia, led by Benjamin Franklin, Benjamin Rush, William Bradford and Caleb Lownes, organized a movement for the reform of the barbarous criminal code of 1718, which was still in force. Doctor Rush went as far as to advocate the total abolition of the death penalty. Their efforts resulted in the law of September 15, 1786, which substituted for the death penalty, in the case of some of the lesser felonies, "continued hard labor, publicly and disgracefully imposed."[15] The results of this reforming law were not so satisfactory as was anticipated, while the public exposure of the convicts in their labor brought their distressing condition before the attention of a larger number of persons than could have been the case when secluded in the gloomy High Street and Walnut Street Jails.[16] The continued evils of the penal administration, together with this added publicity given to these deplorable conditions, prompted the formation of The Philadelphia Society for Alleviating the Miseries of Public Prisons in 1787.[17] This society, the first of the great modern prison reform societies, was organized on Tuesday, May 8, 1787, in the German School House on Cherry

[13] *The Pennsylvania Journal of Prison Discipline and Philanthropy*, 1887, pp. 24-5.

[14] Roberts Vaux, *Notices*, p. 9. *Sketch of Principal Transactions*, p. 3.

[15] Caleb Lownes, *An Account of the Alteration and Present State of the Penal Laws of Pennsylvania*, pp. 5-6. *Statutes at Large*, Vol. XII, pp. 280-81.

[16] Lownes, op. cit.; *Report of the Commissioners on the Penal Code*, 1828, p. 13; Richard Vaux, *A Brief Sketch of the Origin and History of the State Penitentiary for the Eastern District of Pennsylvania*, p. 11.

[17] Richard Vaux, op. cit., pp. 8-12. The name was changed to that of the Pennsylvania Prison Society, in 1886.

Street.[18] The fundamental impulses, conceptions and purposes of the society are set forth in the preamble of the constitution:

" 'I was in prison and ye came unto me.
. . . . And the King shall answer and say unto them, verily I say unto you, inasmuch as ye have done it unto one of the least of these my brethren, ye have done it unto me.'
"Matthew xxv: 36, 40.

"When we consider that the obligations of benevolence, which are founded on the precepts and example of the Author of Christianity, are not canceled by the follies or crimes of our fellow creatures; and when we reflect upon the miseries which penury, hunger, cold, unnecessary severity, unwholesome apartments, and guilt (the usual attendants of prisons) involve with them: it becomes us to extend our compassion to that part of mankind, who are subjects of these miseries. By the aids of humanity, their undue and illegal sufferings may be prevented; the links which should bind the whole family of mankind together, under all circumstances, be preserved unbroken; and such degrees and modes of punishment may be discovered and suggested, as may, instead of continuing habits of vice, become the means of restoring our fellow creatures to virtue and happiness. From a conviction of the truth and obligation of these principles, the subscribers have associated themselves under the title of THE PHILADELPHIA SOCIETY FOR ALLEVIATING THE MISERIES OF PUBLIC PRISONS." [19]

The remainder of the constitution of the society relates to its official organization and only the sixth article is worthy of special notice. This describes the nature and duties of the so-called "Acting Committee," in which was vested wide authority and which, apparently, constituted the body which carried on the real work of the

---

[18] Roberts Vaux, *Notices,* p. 10. *Sketch of Principal Transactions,* pp. 3-4. The original members of the society were Francis Bailey, John Baker, Gerardus Clarkson, Tench Coxe, George Duffield, Samuel P. Griffitts, Henry Helmuth, Thomas Harrison, Joseph James, John Jones, John Kaighn, George Krebs, Thomas Lloyd, Caleb Lownes, Charles Marshall, Joseph Moore, John Morris, Thomas Morrison, John Olden, Thomas Parkinson, Isaac Parrish, Jonathan Penrose, Zachariah Poulson, James Reynolds, Thomas Rogers, William Rogers, Benjamin Rush, Lawrence Seckel, William Shippen, Jacob Shoemaker, John Swanwick, Richard Wells, William White, James Whiteall, Thomas Wistar, Benjamin Wynkoop and William Zane. *Sketch of Principal Transactions,* pp. 3-4 and notes. A complete list of all members to 1830 is given in *The Constitution of The Philadelphia Society for Alleviating the Miseries of Public Prisons,* 1830, pp. 6-10. *The Philadelphia Journal of Prison Discipline and Philanthropy,* 1887, pp. 76-92, gives the members from 1787 to 1887.

[19] This is reproduced in Roberts Vaux, *Notices,* pp. 10-1; and in Richard Vaux, *Brief Sketch of the Eastern Penitentiary,* p. 9. Printed copies of the constitution were distributed at various periods between 1787 and 1830.

society. It was specified that "The Acting Committee shall consist of the President, two Vice-Presidents, two Secretaries, two Counsellors, Treasurer, and six other members, three of whom to go off at the meetings in the months called January and July. They shall visit the Prisons at least once a month, inquire into the circumstances of the Prisoners, and report such abuses as they shall discover, to the proper officers appointed to remedy them. They shall examine the influence of confinement or punishment upon the morals of the Prisoners. They may draw upon the Treasurer for such sums of money as may be necessary. They shall keep regular minutes of their proceedings, to be read at the Quarterly Meeting of the Society."

While the importance of a precedent should not be underestimated, there seems no reason for doubting that the society of 1787 would have originated without the example of the organization of 1776. Only one member of the older society belonged to the second association, namely, Mr. Richard Wells, and the latter had a far wider program than the former. While still interested in eliminating some of the physical suffering of the prisoners, it was primarily concerned with a thoroughgoing reformation of the whole system of criminal jurisprudence and penal administration, which would cause the incidental evils and sufferings of the old system to disappear with the abolition of the causes for their existence.[20]

B. The Early Composition and Membership of the Philadelphia Society for Alleviating the Miseries of Public Prisons

On account of the similarity between the aims and principles of the Philadelphia Society for Alleviating the Miseries of Public Prisons and the juristic and penological theories of the Quakers, and because of the fact that some of the most active members of the prison society were members of the Society of Friends, it has been customary, even for writers of great authority, to represent the Society for Alleviating the Miseries of Public Prisons as identical with the Society of Friends.[21] As a matter of fact, however, it

---

[20] Sketch of Principal Transactions, p. 3 and note. The Pennsylvania Journal of Prison Discipline and Philanthropy, 1887, p. 26. Caleb Lownes, An Account of the Alteration and Present State of the Penal Laws of Pennsylvania, Containing also an Account of the Gaol and Penitentiary House of Philadelphia and the Interior Management Thereof, Philadelphia, 1792, pp. 6-7. The page references are to the Boston reprint of 1799.
[21] Cf. F. H. Wines, Punishment and Reformation, pp. 142, 147; and Frank Sanborn, Special Report on Prisons and Prison Discipline Made under the Authority of the State Board of Charities, Boston, 1865, p. 7. Beaumont and DeTocqueville present the same view.

is impossible to identify more than one hundred and thirty-six out of a total of three hundred and forty members in the crucial period from 1787 to 1830 as being also affiliated with the Society of Friends.[22] The president of the society during the first forty-nine years of its existence was William White, Bishop of the Protestant Episcopal Church of Philadelphia.[23] These facts, however, are in themselves no reflection upon the Society of Friends, nor do they detract in any manner from the degree to which society is indebted to the Friends for their services to juristic and penal reform. Rather, they are a testimonial to the Quaker element in Pennsylvania, and the reform movement was both a triumph and a vindication of Quaker principles. When they became interested in prison reform the Episcopalians were compelled, in the period following 1787, to accept those Quaker conceptions and practices that they had spurned with contempt seventy years before. On the whole, then, it is not inaccurate in a general sense to regard those reforms which constituted the new penal code and the Pennsylvania system of prison administration as fundamentally the product of a Quaker movement.

The ideas and theories of the reformers were wholly in harmony with Quaker precedents, even if they were to some slight degree affected by the contemporary reform currents in Europe; solitary confinement was the only element which needed to be added to Penn's juridical and penal practices in order to constitute the Pennsylvania system as it was known after 1830; the Quaker antecedents in the early provincial days were most important in making the reform movement "respectable" and in lessening popular prejudice; finally, Roberts Vaux and his son Richard, both Quakers, were for three-quarters of a century the most active members of the prison society in the cause of prison reform, in general, and in the exposition and defense of the Pennsylvania system, in particular.[24] Nor should it be forgotten that there were many eminent and respectable citizens of Philadelphia, such as William Bradford, who, while not formally members of the prison reform

---

[22] In this task of identifying the Quaker members of the prison reform society the writer has received courteous and invaluable assistance from L. Beardsley, the Librarian of the Friends' Historical Library of Swarthmore College.

[23] *The Pennsylvania Journal of Prison Discipline and Philanthropy,* Vol. II, Number 1, 1846, pp. 1-6.

[24] *The Pennsylvania Journal of Prison Discipline and Philanthropy,* Vol. II, Number 2, 1846, pp. 109-22. Roberts Vaux (1786-1836), historian, educator, philanthropist and penologist. Richard Vaux (1816-95), educator, politician, and penologist.

society, were active in the cause of prison reform and cooperated with the society on all occasions.[25]

C. The Work of the Society in Advancing the Cause of Reform in Criminal Jurisprudence and Prison Administration, 1787 to 1835

While it is true that the impetus to reform came from many sources and there were many influential reformers not directly connected with the society, it is equally undeniable that there was no important reform legislation which was not secured in large part because of the efforts of the society. Therefore, a study of the work of the Philadelphia Society for Alleviating the Miseries of Public Prisons is little less than a survey of prison reform in Pennsylvania.

The first recorded activity of the society was the introduction in, 1787, of religious services into the Walnut Street Jail. The keeper of the jail did all in his power to prevent the innovation and gave a sullen consent only on the written command of the sheriff of the county. The prisoners were assembled in a long column in the jail yard. A cannon was placed beside the improvised pulpit and a gunner stood by with a lighted match ready to fire into the mass of convicts at any sight of a riot. In spite of this unfavorable setting, the first sermon was delivered by Doctor William Rogers, a member of the society, with considerable effectiveness and very little disturbance. It is authoritatively asserted that this was the first religious service ever conducted in an American penal institution.[26]

As the society came into existence exactly when the effects of the operation of the law of September 15, 1786, were first becoming perceptible, it was but natural that the first systematic campaign of the society should be directed against the evils which were revealed. Roberts Vaux thus describes the situation as it existed in the year 1787:

"The law of 1786, although in many respects less sanguinary than the former enactments, contained some provisions, the execution

---

[25] It is stated, *Pennsylvania Journal of Prison Discipline and Philanthropy*, January, 1887, p. 8, that Benjamin Franklin was a signer of the constitution of the Philadelphia Society for Alleviating the Miseries of Public Prisons. His name appears as a member in August, 1787.

[26] Roberts Vaux, *Notices*, pp. 14-7. *The Pennsylvania Journal of Prison Discipline and Philanthropy*, Vol. II, Number 1, pp. 1-6. An interesting and probably not inaccurate attempt of an artist to reproduce this scene is to be found as a frontispiece to the Supplement to Number 49 of the *Journal of Prison Discipline and Philanthropy*, 1910.

of which led to the most injurious consequences. It directed that a certain description of convicts should be employed in cleaning the streets of the city and repairing the roads in the neighborhood; and authorized the keeper of the jail to shave the heads of the prisoners, and otherwise to distinguish them by an infamous dress. In this very objectionable manner they were brought before the public. The sport of the idle and the vicious, they often became incensed, and naturally took violent revenge upon the aggressors. To prevent them from retorting injuries still allowed to be inflicted, they were encumbered with iron collars and chains, to which bomb-shells were attached, to be dragged along while they performed their degrading service, under the eyes of keepers armed with swords, blunderbusses, and other weapons of destruction. These measures begot in the minds of the criminals and those who witnessed them, disrespect for the laws executed with so much cruelty, and did not fail to excite the early notice of the society." [27]

A committee of the society was immediately appointed "to inquire into the effects of the lately enacted penal law upon the criminals, now at work in our streets, and also its influence on society." [28] The result of this inquiry was the following memorial of January, 1788, to the general assembly, the first public recommendation of the society.[29] It will be noted that its chief recommendations were "more private or even solitary labour," separation of hardened criminals from first offenders, segregation of the different sexes and the "prohibition of spirituous liquor among the criminals." The following is the text of this first memorial:

"To the Representatives of the Freemen of the Commonwealth of Pennsylvania, in General Assembly met.

"The Representation and Petition of the subscribers, citizens of Pennsylvania.

"Your petitioners have viewed with pleasure the act of a former Assembly, for the reforming of the penal laws of the state, by rendering them 'less sanguinary and more proportionate to crimes,' and though your petitioners conceive that the good ends thereby intended, have not hitherto been fully answered, yet they presume to suggest that the mode of punishment adopted in the 'act for amending the penal laws,' will be more likely to answer the desired purpose, by means of some amendments; a few of which your petitioners beg leave to lay before the house.

"The punishment of criminals by 'hard labour publicly and dis-gracefully imposed,' as indicated in the preamble to the law, your

---

[27] Roberts Vaux, *Notices*, pp. 21-2. Cf. Lownes, op. cit., pp. 5-6; *Report of the Commissioners on the Penal Code*, 1828, p. 13.

[28] Roberts Vaux, *Notices*, p. 22.

[29] *Sketch of Principal Transactions*, p. 6.

petitioners wish the house would be pleased to revise, being fully convinced that punishment *by more private or even solitary labour,* would more successfully tend to reclaim the unhappy objects, as it might be conducted more steadily and uniformly, and the kind and portion of labour better adapted to the different abilities of the criminals; the evils of familiarizing young minds to vicious characters would be removed, and the opportunities of begging money would be prevented; for although the criminals are forbid to have money in their possession, yet no penalty is inflicted on persons furnishing them therewith.

"Your petitioners also wish to recommend to the attention of the house the very great importance of a separation of the sexes in the public prisons—and that some more effectual provision be made for the prohibition of spirituous liquor amongst the criminals, the use of which tends to lessen the true sense of their situation, and prevents those useful reflections which might be produced by solitary labour and strict temperance.

"Your petitioners therefore respectfully request the house will be pleased to take the penal law under their consideration, and make such provision thereon as may more effectually answer the good and humane purposes thereby originally intended." [30]

The legislature's attention and interest were attracted by this preliminary statement of defects and remedies and, on November 20, 1788, the supreme executive council sent a "minute" to a special meeting of the society asking more specific detailed information on the subject. In answer to this request, the society prepared its long memorial of December 15, 1788. This gave an account of the labors of the society in the Philadelphia jail; set forth the notorious defects of the jail administration with respect to food, clothing, bedding, excessive use of alcoholic drinks, the herding of all classes of criminals and debtors and the evils of the system of public labor of the convicts; and concluded with its recommendations of separation of debtors from criminals, segregation of the sexes, total abolition of use of liquor in the jail, and, most important of all, "solitary confinement to hard labour." This is the first recorded recommendation of what became the basic principle of the Pennsylvania system of prison administration and discipline.[31] The exact text of this epoch-making memorial follows:

"In consequence of a minute of the Supreme Executive Council 20th November, 1788, laid before a special meeting of the Society for alleviating the miseries of Public Prisons, a committee was

---

[30] Reproduced in Roberts Vaux, *Notices,* pp. 22-3.
[31] Roberts Vaux, *Notices,* pp. 26-30. *Sketch of Principal Transactions,* pp. 6-7. Richard Vaux, *Brief Sketch of the Eastern Penitentiary,* pp. 12-4.

appointed to take the said minute into consideration, and to give such information to Council as the nature of the minute requires, which committee, having several times met, agree to make the following representation:

"That in the article of clothing few complaints arise respecting the condemned criminals, but amongst the greater number confined in prison previous to trial, there frequently happen cases of great want, many of the prisoners being destitute of shirts and stockings and warm covering, partly owing to the length of time before trial, and partly to the easy access, by various means, to spirituous liquors, for which their clothes are disposed of. Clothing distributed by the society to the apparently most destitute, has, in many instances, been quickly exchanged for rum. No provision being made by law for relieving these distressed objects, or for preventing the abuses of charitable donations, it is at present an evil without a remedy, though it is conceived that a kind of prison dress might be adopted by law, and as easily preserved from sale as those of the convicts.

"In the article of diet an allowance is made by law to the working criminals, and no complaints have come to the knowledge of the society on that head. To those who are committed for trial, the half of a four-penny loaf only is daily allowed, but no provision is made for persons who are committed as witnesses, amongst whom cases of great distress have appeared to the society. A stranger, accidently present at the commission of a criminal action, but without friends to enter security for his appearance as witness, is committed to jail, for the benefit of the community, and suffers more than the actual criminal, and what adds greatly to his grievance, he is afterwards detained for his fees;—and whilst on this subject, the committee would wish to suggest the very great hardship of a prisoner's being detained for his fees after being legally acquitted of the crime for which he had been committed.

"In cases where women are imprisoned, having a child, or children, at the breast, they have only the allowance of a single person, except what arises from the casual supplies of charity, to which the society have contributed, by a distribution to the most necessitous of both sexes, of upward of one hundred gallons of soup weekly during the last winter and spring.

"With respect to lodging, it appears that no provision of any kind is made by law, the prisoners lying promiscuously on the floor, unless supplied by their friends. In some jails in England, mentioned by the humane Howard, they are accommodated with strong cribs, and supplied, at stated times, with clean straw. On the first institution of the society, in their visits to the jail, they found that men and women had general intercourse with each other, and it was afterwards discovered that they were locked up together in their rooms at night; but through the remonstrances of the committee on the impropriety of the practice, the women were, at length, removed into a different part of the prison—the apparent consequence of which was, that from the number of about thirty or forty, at first, in confinement, they have been reduced to four or five; for it was said to be a common practice for the women to procure themselves to be arrested for fictitious debts, in order to gain admission among the men—a constant and steady adherence to this mode of separation, the committee are of opinion, will be of great utility. The present mode of burning fuel in the rooms, in open chimneys, with the very scanty allowance, subjects the unhappy prisoners to great misery, in the severity of winters; if stoves could be introduced, this might be, in some measure, abated.

"The minute of the council calls for information of the quantity of spirits consumed in the jail—but it is not in the power of the committee to give a satisfactory answer on this head. The visiting committee were once informed that twenty gallons had been introduced in one day, at the time the prison keeper stopped selling, on account of the prosecution and fine imposed. Since that time, the visiting committee have never had reason to believe that the prisoners have met with any difficulty in purchasing spirits at the bar; and the debtors have frequently complained that they would not have liberty to buy liquors at any other place, but were obliged to pay in the jail half a dollar for a quart, and eight pence for a gill. To obtain money to purchase spirits, great irregularities, and even outrages, are committed by the prisoners, by not only selling their own clothes, but forcibly stripping others on their first admission in jail, which, though a custom of long standing, by the name of garnish, is oftentimes productive of great subsequent sufferings.

"In reply to the general query respecting the mode of conducting the business of the jail, the committee beg leave to remark that there are three great evils which call for attention, viz: the mixture of the sexes—the use of spirituous liquors—and the indiscriminate confinement of debtors and persons committed for criminal offences.

"The first during the temporary separation, had an evident beneficial effect, as already remarked: how far the practice is steadily continued, is not in the power of the committee to ascertain, as the regular attendance of the visiting committee has been, for some time, withheld, on account of some discouragement and obstacles they met with; but, from the experience they have had, they are fully convinced that it is both practicable and beneficial.

"The sale of spirituous liquors has ever appeared to the visiting committee as greatly contributing to the enormities prevailing amongst the prisoners. If it was practicable to put a total stop to the resort of visitors to the criminals, many of the evils complained of might be remedied; for, there is too much reason to believe, that an improper correspondence and intercourse is held between dishonest people out of the jail and the confined criminals, and that schemes of robbery and concealment are there concerted. The laws hitherto in force against selling spirituous liquors in jail, are either eluded, or the penalty too small to prevent the practice.

"During the many visits paid in the jail by the committee of the society, they could not pass by unnoticed the frequency of many of the criminals intermixing with the debtors, and having the free use of that part of the jail originally appropriated solely for the debtors—of which many of the debtors complained, and at times conceived their lives were endangered. Some of them have informed the committee that they would have given useful information respecting the introduction of liquors, &c. but were deterred from a fear of the criminals, and were not without apprehension that they might give offence to the prison keeper, and induce him to treat them with severity. Particular cases have come to the knowledge of the committee, where debtors, by mixing with the criminals, have formed connexions which ultimately led to their being convicts themselves. There is too much reason to believe that numerous connexions have been formed in this way, to the total ruin of many unfortunate prisoners, who have been compelled to associate with men of infamous morals. But even where this unhappy consequence hath not ensued, it proves a situation of pain and distress to the feeling mind, and often subjects the innocent prisoner to personal abuse and loss of property. Under this head it may be proper to remark, that children, both in the jail and workhouse, are frequently suffered to remain with their parents, whereby they are initiated, in early life, to scenes of debauchery, dishonesty, and wickedness of every kind.

"The female convicts are at present kept in the workhouse, where, for want of proper apartments, they are allowed to associate with girls and young women, confined therein by their masters and mistresses, for sale, or temporary punishment, by which dangerous intercourse many unhappy creatures, who were perhaps only confined by the caprice of their owners, are gradually seduced from their original innocence.

"A large portion of the jail is at present unoccupied, or in the use of the prison keeper and his family, so that the necessary separations might be easily provided for.

"Respecting the employment of the convicts, the committee are of opinion, that on inquiry it will appear that a large portion of their time is unemployed, and that the committee have been informed by the prison keeper, that it was deemed a greater punishment to be detained in the prison than to work in the streets, and that in some cases he prevented their going out to work, alleging that they were too desperate to be in the street, which seems strongly to indicate the necessity of providing solitary labour in the prison. On the whole, as a matter of the utmost moment to the well-being, safety, and peace of society, as well as of the greatest importance to the criminals, the committee think it their duty to declare, that from a long and steady attention to the real practical state, as well as the theory of prisons, they are unanimously of opinion, that *solitary confinement to hard labour,* and a total abstinence from spirituous liquors, will prove the most effectual means of reforming these unhappy creatures, and that many evils might be prevented by keeping the debtors from the necessity of associating with those who are committed for trial, as well as by a constant separation of the sexes.

[Signed]

WILLIAM WHITE,	JOHN CONNELLY,
R WELLS,	JAMES COOPER,
B. WYNKOOP,	CALEB LOWNES,
THOMAS WISTAR,	BENJAMIN THAW,
S. P. GRIFFITTS,	T. HARRISON,
JOHN KAIGHN,	WILLIAM LIPPINCOTT,
WILLIAM ROGERS,	GEORGE DUFFIELD.
C. MARSHALL,	

"Philadelphia, December 15, 1788.

"Endorsed,
"Delivered the 16th, at the Council Chamber. Present, Samuel Miles and R. Willing." [32]

The effect of the memorial of December, 1788, was sweeping. The law of March 27, 1789, enacted all of the chief recommendations of the memorial.[33] The society was further requested to aid the general assembly in preparing a bill which would provide for a thorough reconstruction of the prison system and a systematic revision of the criminal code.[34] In addition to this specific cooperation with the legislature, the society considered it wise to make the minds of the members of the assembly more susceptible to the aims of the reformers by publishing a pamphlet entitled *Extracts and Remarks on the Subject of Punishment and Reformation of Criminals,* five hundred copies of which were distributed among members of the legislature and other public officers.[35] The chief purpose of the pamphlet was to allay the fear that the proposed reforms in Pennsylvania would not prove workable or economical. A considerable collection of extracts from letters and prison regulations was reproduced, which demonstrated the success of the very measures proposed for Pennsylvania which already had been put into practice in a number of recently reformed English county jails or prisons. It was contended that experience had shown that imprisonment at hard labor was profitable even in England "where

[32] Roberts Vaux, *Notices,* pp. 26-30.
[33] *The Statutes at Large of Pennsylvania,* Vol. XIII, pp. 243-51.
[34] Roberts Vaux, *Notices,* p. 31. *Sketch of Principal Transactions,* p. 8.
[35] *Sketch of Principal Transactions,* p. 8.

labor is cheaper and provisions much dearer than in the United States." [36]

Most of the proofs of the success of the new system were drawn from the experience of Sir Thomas Beevor in the newly constructed prison at Wymondham in Norfolk, which had been erected as a result of the inspiration derived from a reading of John Howard's *State of Prisons*.[37] In this "model" jail were to be seen in actual successful operation all of the new principles which it was hoped might be introduced into Pennsylvania. Cells were provided to keep the different types of offenders separate and the sexes were segregated in different parts of the building. Separate cells were provided for each prisoner "in which they sleep, and when necessary, work the whole day alone." [38] This solitary confinement was said by Sir Thomas to be more effective than whipping and "that part of their punishment from which reformation is chiefly expected." [39] This new system was found effective in every way. By providing hard labor for all on six days of every week, it was found that many prisoners earned more than double the cost of their maintenance.[40] As a reformative agency the results were not less satisfactory. It had not yet been found necessary to punish any inmates by confinement in irons.[41] The deterrent effects of the system were also alleged to be most gratifying. The judges on the circuit reported that never in their experience had there been so few commitments to jail.[42]

The Pennsylvania society declared that exactly what was needed at home was to follow this English example and "make our prisons penitentiary houses and places of correction." [43] They pointed to the fact that the success of the Norfolk jail had led to its being imitated in other English jails. The remainder of the pamphlet was chiefly devoted to quotations from Howard's printed works as substantiating the following reform principles, which the society desired to introduce in Pennsylvania: "That reformation hath become

---

[36] *Extracts and Remarks on the Subject of Punishment and Reformation of Criminals*, Philadelphia, February 25, 1790, pp. 4-5. It is interesting to note that the economic argument for the superiority of a system of prison discipline was later branded as sordid when used against the Pennsylvania system by adherents of the Auburn system.

[37] *Extracts and Remarks on the Subject of Punishment and Reformation of Criminals*, p. 4.

[38] Ibid., p. 5.

[39] Ibid., pp. 5ff.

[40] Ibid., pp. 11-2.

[41] Ibid., p. 12.

[42] Ibid., p. 13.

[43] Ibid., p. 14. An exact return to Penn's provisions of a century earlier.

a principal object with the magistracy and rulers";[44] that murder, arson and burglary should be the only capital crimes;[45] that drunkenness is the chief cause of crime;[46] that solitary cells, ten feet high, ten feet long and eight feet wide furnish the best mode of confining convicts;[47] that where labor is consistently provided for prisoners they are able to defray the expense of incarceration.[48] From the whole pamphlet the society arrived at the following conclusion and recommendation:

"From the foregoing extracts we learn that the miseries of the unfortunate prisoner have become subjects of deep investigation in Europe and that by an observance of wholesome rules, gaols may prove the happy means of reformation, and that the criminals instead of being a burden may be transformed into serviceable members of the community. Under these impressions the Society established in the city of Philadelphia for alleviating the miseries of public Prisons, wish to present the subject to the Legislature of Pennsylvania, hoping that the penal laws of the state may be so modelled as to promote reformation in the criminal and safety to the people."[49]

The results of these multifarious activities of the society from 1788 to 1790 appear in the famous law, passed on April 5, 1790, which marks the legal origin of the Pennsylvania system of prison administration.[50] It provided for a revision of the penal code which went further than the revision of 1786 in substituting imprisonment at hard labor for the punishment of crimes; directed the separation of witnesses and debtors from convicts, and the proper segregation of the sexes; and ordered the erection of a block of cells in the yard of the Walnut Street Jail for the solitary confinement of the "more hardened and atrocious offenders."

From 1790 to 1801 the activities of the society centered mainly in urging the further reform of the criminal code; in attempting to improve the condition of debtors in the jail; in opposing extortion in the fee system in the jail; in recommending and offering to pay for a system of "instruction in useful knowledge" in the jail; and in watching the operation of the new criminal code

---

[44] *Extracts and Remarks on the Subject of Punishment and Reformation of Criminals*, pp. 15, 21-2.
[45] Ibid., p. 20.
[46] Ibid., p. 21.
[47] Ibid., p. 19.
[48] Ibid., pp. 18-9.
[49] Ibid., p. 23.
[50] *The Statutes at Large of Pennsylvania*, Vol. XIII, pp. 511-28.

and penal system and reporting delinquency in its administration.[51] The results appear in the law of September 23, 1791, abolishing the death penalty for witchcraft;[52] the law of April 4, 1792, putting the keeper of the debtors' apartment in the jail on a salary rather than on a fee basis;[53] the act of April 22, 1794, abolishing the death penalty for all crimes except murder in the first degree;[54] and the laws of April 15, 1795, and February 15, 1799, extending and perpetuating the criminal and penal codes of 1790 and 1794.[55]

By the end of the first decade of the operation of the new criminal code and penal system so great a degree of laxity had developed in the administrative system that it destroyed the benefits of the newer practices, which had proved very successful immediately after 1790.[56] Accordingly, on December 14, 1801, the society addressed the following memorial to the legislature asking for a strict enforcement of the new system:

"To the Senate and House of Representatives of the Commonwealth of Pennsylvania: The Memorial of the Philadelphia Society for alleviating the miseries of Public Prisons,

"Respectfully Represents:

"That your Memorialists have contemplated with pleasure the progress made by former legislatures in preventing crimes, and reforming criminals, and, encouraged by the ready attention heretofore shown to their applications, are emboldened to call the notice of the legislature to the present state of our Prisons.

"When the reform was made in our penal laws in the year 1790, although the principles were plainly laid down, yet it was not expected that the practical part could be suddenly or completely effected. It was then in some degree a matter of experiment. An experiment, however, though imperfectly made, which has not only increased our internal security, but has been so far approved of as to be adopted in several of our sister states.

"Being ourselves fully convinced of the propriety both of these principles and this practice, we now wish briefly to solicit your attention to a most essential part of this humane and rational plan for preventing crimes and reforming criminals. Ever since the

---

[51] Roberts Vaux, *Notices,* pp. 31-6. *Sketch of Principal Transactions,* pp. 8-11. Albert H. Votaw, "The Pennsylvania Prison Society," in Supplement to Number 49 of the *Journal of Prison Discipline and Philanthropy,* 1910, pp. 5-6.

[52] *The Statutes at Large of Pennsylvania,* Vol. XIV, pp. 128ff.

[53] Ibid., p. 268.

[54] Ibid., Vol. XV, pp. 174-81.

[55] Ibid., pp. 355ff. Vol. XVI, pp. 176-79.

[56] *A Statistical View of the Operation of the Penal Code of Pennsylvania, to Which Is Added a View of the Present State of the Penitentiary and Prison of the City of Philadelphia,* Philadelphia, 1817, pp. 4-5. Lownes, op. cit., pp. 12-3, 19ff.

present establishment of the Prisons we have wished to make the fair experiment of solitude and labour on the convicts. Every year's experience has shown us, that in the present state of the Prison, such an attempt, however desirable, is impracticable.

"We are therefore induced to request that you will devise such means as may appear to you most adequate, to separate the convicts from all other descriptions of prisoners, in order that a full opportunity of trying the effects of solitude and labour may be afforded.

"Signed by direction of the Society.

"WILLIAM WHITE, President.

"Philadelphia, 12th mo. 14, 1801." [57]

Two years more of observation, however, led the society to conclude that the architectural limitations of the old Walnut Street Jail were in large degree responsible for the degeneration of the administrative mechanism of the prison system, and they sent to the legislature, in 1803, a memorial urging the building of a new prison in Philadelphia. In this address they were joined by the inspectors of the Walnut Street Jail.[58]

"To the Senate and House of Representatives of Pennsylvania: The Memorial of the Philadelphia Society for alleviating the miseries of Public Prisons, and of the Inspectors of the Prison of the City and County of Philadelphia.

"Respectfully Represents:

"That in reforming the penal laws of this state the legislature of Pennsylvania contemplated the reclaiming of criminals, as well as preventing crimes; and with this view, adopted the mode of punishing criminals by solitary confinement at hard labour, under such regulations as appeared best calculated to impress strongly on the minds of the convicts, the connexion of suffering with the transgression of the laws. At the time of this reform, the jail of the city and county of Philadelphia, was considered as sufficiently large to carry this benevolent design of the legislature into effect, and to leave suitable room for the confinement of vagrants, prisoners for trial, &c. A period of more than twelve years has elapsed since this reform came into operation, and in the course of that time the number of prisoners of various descriptions has increased to such a degree, owing to the jail of Philadelphia being by law the general place of custody for all the convicts of the state, and likewise to the substitution of long periods of confinement instead of capital punishment, that the said prison is no longer capable of containing them in such a way as to answer the intention of the legislature. The number of vagrants, &c. has so much

---

[57] Roberts Vaux, *Notices,* pp. 36-7.
[58] Ibid., p. 37.

increased, that it is a matter of great difficulty to keep them in order, and impracticable to keep them regularly at labour. The prisoners who are detained for trial, run-away servants and apprentices, are through necessity confined in the same apartment with the vagrants, and the intercourse between such persons crowded together may easily be conceived to be most destructive to the morals of the whole, insomuch that when they are released from prison they are likely to come out intimately acquainted with the arts of villainy, and combined with an extensive association of persons of similar character to make depredations on the public. The great number of vagrants, untried prisoners, &c. produces hurtful effects on the convicts, as the latter are, for want of room, obliged to be kept in too large numbers in one apartment, by which the amelioration of their morals is either prevented or greatly impeded, the keeping of them attended with greater hazard; and they have more opportunity of laying plans of escape; their labour is rendered less productive than it might be, and the idea of solitude is nearly obliterated.

"The health of the city is much endangered by having so many people crowded together in one house. Notwithstanding the great attention to cleanliness, the jail fever made its appearance there during the last winter. Whether under the present arrangements, it will be practicable to prevent its breaking out again, and in case of such an event, extending its effects beyond the prison walls, it is impossible to determine.

"Another house or set of buildings appears to be necessary, where the vagrants might be suitably classed and compelled to hard labour. In such proper apartments these prisoners might, under suitable regulations, be kept at labour so productive as might at least defray the expense of their keeping or maintenance: this, to the idle and disorderly would be such an object of terror, that the number of them would probably soon be lessened.

"By such an arrangement also, the prisoners for trial, servants, and apprentices, could be suitably classed and taken care of, without being made necessary companions of abandoned characters; which is unavoidable in the present state of the prison; whilst the convicts, by having the whole of the present building alloted to them, could be subdivided into smaller classes—more effectually secluded from any confederacy with those out of doors—more easily managed, and have a fairer chance of improving their morals; and while their minds would have fewer objects to distract them, they might become more docile; and while their labour would be rendered more productive, they would be confirmed in those habits of industry which are calculated to render them useful, both to themselves and society.

     *   *   *   *   *

"Placed as we are, in a situation to observe the salutary effects of solitude and labour, in preventing crimes and reforming criminals, we trust you will, as heretofore, receive our application with indulgence, and therefore again respectfully submit to your consideration, the propriety of granting another building, for the purpose of making such separation amongst the prisoners as the nature and wants of this truly benevolent system require." [59]

As a result of this memorial, an act was passed on April 2, 1803, authorizing the raising of money for the erection of a new prison on Arch Street.[60] This was not opened, however, until 1817, and then it was used until 1823, solely for the detention of debtors.[61] Not until the Eastern Penitentiary was opened at Cherry Hill on October 25, 1829, was any systematic provision made for relieving the ridiculous and demoralizing overcrowding of the Walnut Street Jail.

During the years 1809 to 1811, the society made a beginning at the establishment of a library in the Walnut Street Jail, but it would seem from the following report of the library committee that only Bibles were included in the first literary equipment of a Pennsylvania penal institution:

"Bibles and Testaments have been furnished, and some of the prisoners seem inclined to peruse them; it is hoped benefit has resulted from the measure, but the committee is not prepared to give an opinion, as to the utility of introducing any other books." [62]

By 1816 the overcrowding of the Walnut Street Jail had become so serious that the society prepared a pamphlet entitled, *A Statistical View of the Operation of the Penal Code of Pennsylvania, to Which Is Added a View of the Present State of the Penitentiary and Prison of Philadelphia*. The pamphlet, aside from statistical information relative to convictions, was devoted to pointing out the "melancholy and striking contrast" between the "happy effect" of the system, as early administered, and the deplorable situation in 1816, as a result of overcrowding the Walnut Street Jail, which had not been enlarged since 1795, and had become so deficient in housing facilities for the increased number of convicts that from thirty to forty prisoners were normally locked up for the night in a room eighteen feet square.[63] While there is no doubt that this memorial may have had some effect in hastening the opening of the Arch Street Prison for debtors in the following year, the society

---

[59] Roberts Vaux, *Notices*, pp. 37-9.
[60] *Laws of the Commonwealth of Pennsylvania*, 1803, republished under the authority of the Legislature by John Bioren, pp. 87-8.
[61] *Acts of the General Assembly*, 1815-16, pp. 125-27. *The Pennsylvania Journal of Prison Discipline and Philanthropy*, Vol. I, Number 1, 1845, p. 7.
[62] Roberts Vaux, *Notices*, pp. 39-40.
[63] Pamphlet cited, pp. 3-6.

became convinced that the system of sending all the more serious types of prisoners from the entire state to the county prison of Philadelphia was no longer wise or tolerable, owing to the increasing population of the state and the failure to expand the prison plant in proportion. Consequently, in 1818, they sent their first memorial to the legislature urging the erection of state penitentiaries. This was the beginning of the agitation that led to the erection of the Eastern and Western State Penitentiaries:

"To the Senate and House of Representatives, &c.
        The Memorial, &c.
"Respectfully Showeth:
"That in the year 1787, an association was formed by a number of the inhabitants of Philadelphia, for the purpose of lessening the evils and miseries of prisons, and of promoting an amelioration of the penal laws of this state, under the title of 'The Philadelphia Society for alleviating the miseries of Public Prisons,' which society have continued their attention to the subject until the present time, and have the satisfaction, in common with their fellow citizens, of witnessing considerable improvement in the management of the prison in this city. But the progress of which, they apprehend, is obstructed, and many other evils experienced by the necessity of crowding into that establishment great numbers of convicts from all parts of this populous state. They therefore respectfully request the legislature to consider the propriety and expediency of erecting penitentiaries in suitable parts of the state, for the more effectual employment and separation of the prisoners, and of proving the efficacy of solitude on the morals of those unhappy objects.
        "Signed on behalf of the Society.
                WILLIAM WHITE,
                THOMAS WISTAR,
                SAMUEL P. GRIFFITTS,
                JOSEPH CRUKSHANK." [64]

It was due in large part to this memorial of 1818 that an act was passed on March 3, 1818, appropriating sixty thousand dollars for building a penitentiary at Allegheny on the principle of solitary confinement. This same act authorized, but did not command, the sale of the Walnut Street Jail, the removal of the prisoners to the Arch Street Prison, and the erection of a new penitentiary in Philadelphia from the proceeds of the sale of the Walnut Street plant.[65] As no definite action was taken on this authorization of 1818 with respect to building a new penitentiary in Philadelphia, the society came forward with the following final memorial of 1821,

---

[64] Roberts Vaux, *Notices,* p. 41.
[65] *Acts of the General Assembly,* 1817-18, pp. 138-40.

which succeeded in securing the passage of the act of March 20, 1821, appropriating one hundred thousand dollars for the erection of a state penitentiary in the county of Philadelphia capable of receiving two hundred and fifty convicts.[66]

"To the Senate and House of Representatives of the Commonwealth of Pennsylvania, in General Assembly met.

"The Memorial of the Philadelphia Society for alleviating the Miseries of Public Prisons,

"Respectfully Represents,

"That it is now nearly forty years since some of your Memorialists associated for the purpose of alleviating the miseries of public prisons, as well as for procuring the melioration of the penal code of Pennsylvania, as far as these effects might be produced through their influence.

"In the performance of the duties which they believed to be required of them by the dictates of Christian benevolence, and the obligations of humanity, they investigated the conduct and regulations of the jail, and likewise the effects of those degrading and sanguinary punishments, which were at that period inflicted by the laws of this Commonwealth. The result of these examinations was a full conviction, that not only the police of the prison was faulty, but the penalties of the law were such as to frustrate the great ends of punishment, by rendering offenders inimical, instead of restoring them to usefulness in society.

"With these impressions alterations in the modes of punishment and improvements in prison discipline were from time to time recommended to the Legislature, by whose authority many changes were adopted, and many defects remedied.

"These reforms, from the nature of existing circumstances, were, however, of comparatively limited extent, but as far as the trial could be made, beneficial consequences were experienced.

"Neighboring states, and remote nations, directed their attention to these efforts, and in many instances, adopted the principles which had influenced the conduct of Pennsylvania.

"At the time of making the change in our penal code, substituting solitude and hard labour, for sanguinary punishments, the experiment was begun in the county jail of Philadelphia, rather than the execution of the laws should be deferred to a distant period, when a suitable prison might be erected. Under all the inconveniences then subsisting, the effects produced were such as to warrant a belief that the plan could answer the most sanguine wishes of its friends, if it could be properly tried. But the construction of that prison, and its crowded condition, being the only penitentiary used

---

[66] *Acts of the General Assembly,* 1820-21, pp. 94-7. Roberts Vaux, *Notices,* pp. 45-6. *Sketch of Principal Transactions,* pp. 12-3. Richard Vaux, *Brief Sketch of the Eastern Penitentiary,* pp. 18-9.

for all the convicts of the state, leave but slender hopes of the accomplishment of the humane intentions of the Legislature.

"Your Memorialists believe, that they discover in the recent measures of the Commonwealth, a promise, which will fulfill the designs of benevolence in this respect. The edifice now in progress at Pittsburgh for the reception of prisoners, constructed upon a plan adapted to strict solitary confinement, will go far towards accomplishing this great purpose; and your Memorialists are induced to hope, that the same enlightened policy which dictated the erection of a state prison in the western, will provide for the establishment of a similar one in the eastern part of the state.

"Reasons of the most serious and substantial nature might be urged to show the absolute necessity which exists for a penitentiary in the city and county of Philadelphia, whether we regard the security of society, or the restoration of the offenders against its laws. It will not be necessary here to recite the alarming proofs which might be adduced in support of their opinions, but refer to the documents herewith furnished, which exhibit the actual condition of the prison.

"Your Memorialists, therefore, respectfully request, that you will be pleased to take the subject under your serious consideration, and if you judge it right, to pass a law, for the erection of a penitentiary for the eastern district of the state, in which the benefits of solitude and hard labour may be fairly and effectually proved.

"Signed by order and on behalf of the Society.
WILLIAM WHITE, President.
WILLIAM ROGERS, Vice President.
THOMAS WISTAR,　　do
NICHOLAS COLLIN,
SAMUEL POWEL GRIFFITTS,
JOSEPH REED,
ROBERTS VAUX.

Attest.
Caleb Cresson, Secretary." [67]

The confidence reposed by the legislature in the information and achievements of the society is shown by the fact that a majority of the board of commissioners named in the act to supervise the building of the penitentiary were members of the prison society. [68]

In spite of all their labors in this direction, however, the society came very near to losing the opportunity of testing their penological principles, based upon the fundamental doctrine of solitary confine-

---

[67] Roberts Vaux, *Notices,* pp. 43-5.
[68] The members of this board were Thomas Wistar, Samuel P. Griffitts, Peter Miercken, George N. Baker, Thomas Bradford, Jr., John Bacon, Caleb Carmalt, Samuel R. Wood, Thomas Sparks, James Thackera and Daniel H. Miller.

ment at hard labor. By a resolution of March 23, 1826, the legislature appointed Charles Shaler, Edward King and T. J. Wharton as commissioners to revise the penal code. [69] They were directed to carry out the revision according to the system of imprisonment at hard labor with solitary confinement.[70] While engaged on their labors they came under the influence of Louis Dwight, Secretary of the Boston Prison Discipline Society, and the most zealous and energetic supporter of the Auburn system of prison administration based upon congregate workshops and separation at night.[71] As a result of Mr. Dwight's advocacy of the Auburn system, and the favorable impression of it derived from a personal visit and study by the commissioners, the latter recommended in their report that the new penitentiaries at Allegheny and Philadelphia be altered in construction, so that they might be administered according to the Auburn plan.[72] The Philadelphia Society for Alleviating the Miseries of Public Prisons became alarmed at the prospect of losing the benefit of all their labors in behalf of the system of solitary confinement, and they sent one of their members, Mr. Samuel R. Wood, to labor with the chairman of the judiciary committee of the legislature. Mr. Wood's arguments were sufficiently effective, so that when the law of April 23, 1829, was passed, finally establishing the system of penal administration for Pennsylvania, it provided for solitary confinement at hard labor.[73]

As soon as the new state prison system was established, the society renewed the agitation for the abandonment of the Walnut Street Jail and the building of a new county jail in Philadelphia. In this they were in part successful. A new county prison, known as the Moyamensing Prison, was erected, but its construction was not wholly in accordance with the principle of solitary confinement.[74]

Not only did the society labor strenuously in this period for the improvement of the prison system, but they also were the first to point out a need for the differentiation of penal and correctional institutions on the basis of the age of the offenders. Accordingly, in 1823, a committee of the society was appointed to investigate

---

[69] *Acts of the General Assembly,* 1825-26, p. 413.
[70] Ibid.
[71] *The Pennsylvania System of Separate Confinement Explained and Defended,* Philadelphia, 1867, Number 2, "Remarks on Cellular Confinement," by William Parker Foulke, pp. 63-4.
[72] Ibid. *Report of the Commissioners on the Penal Code,* 1828, pp. 77-82.
[73] *Laws of the General Assembly,* 1828-9, pp. 341-54. The acts of 1821 and 1829 were drawn up by Roberts Vaux, Thomas Bradford, Jr., and Samuel R. Wood.
[74] *Sketch of Principal Transactions,* p. 15. *The Pennsylvania System of Solitary Confinement Explained and Defended,* 1867, Number 2, p. 9.

as to the need for an institution for juvenile delinquents in Pennsylvania. In 1826, in an able memorial written by Roberts Vaux, the committee reported in favor of the immediate construction of such an institution.[75] With the aid of other enlightened citizens of Philadelphia, the society was able to secure the erection of the Philadelphia House of Refuge in 1828.[76]

In spite of this formidable list of local achievements, the activities of the Philadelphia Society for Alleviating the Miseries of Public Prisons were not limited to the state of Pennsylvania. A knowledge of the prison reform movement which they promoted and advanced had spread throughout the United States and Europe by 1830. The society was early attracted by John Howard's work in Europe and at the fourth meeting of the members they listened to a letter from Doctor Lettsom of London describing Howard's journeys on the Continent in the investigation of prison conditions.[77] The letter of the society to Howard, himself, sent on January 14, 1788, has already been cited. That the compliment was returned is evident from the following statement from Howard:

"Should the plan take place during my life, of establishing a permanent charity under some such title as that at Philadelphia, viz: A Society for Alleviating the Miseries of Public Prisons, and annuities be engrafted thereupon, for the above-mentioned purpose, I would most readily stand at the bottom of a page for five hundred pounds; or if such society shall be instituted within three years after my death, this sum shall be paid out of my estate." [78]

While the Philadelphia society gained an early inspiration from the work of the English reformers, it was not long before the English began to seek advice from the sponsors of prison reform in Pennsylvania. In 1818, Doctor Stephen Lushington of the London Society for the Improvement of Prison Discipline wrote to the Philadelphia society inquiring as to the effect of the new system of solitary confinement with labor.[79] He was answered by President White in a letter which set forth the difficulties under which the system had been compelled to operate, owing to the overcrowded condition of the Walnut Street Prison, and expressed the optimistic hopes of the society with regard to the future, when the new system could be carried out under architectural surround-

---

[75] *Sketch of Principal Transactions,* pp. 13-4.
[76] John Sergeant, *Address at the Dedication of the Philadelphia House of Refuge,* November, 1828.
[77] Roberts Vaux, *Notices,* pp. 18-20.
[78] Ibid., p. 25, note. Lownes, op. cit., p. 6, note.
[79] Vaux, op. cit., p. 42.

The Philadelphia House of Refuge, 1830

ings which would not defeat its fundamental principles. The last paragraph of the letter is worthy of quotation:

"We feel great satisfaction in your exertions in this dignified cause; and hope you will not be discouraged by any partial considerations, from continuing to cooperate with us, in endeavoring to establish the beneficent principle, that the prevention of crime, and the reformation of the offender, is the object of punishment. And whatever may have been the fears and resentments of those times, which produced the too generally prevailing system, of lightly multiplying criminal offences, and of inflicting death, and other odious punishments; let us indulge in the pleasing hope, that this system of ignorance and barbarism will no longer continue to the disgrace of the nations and governments, who are now arrived at the highest state of civilization, and who profess to be actuated by the benign and salutary influences of Christianity." [80]

The list of corresponding members of the society up to 1830 furnishes a valuable means of estimating the extent of the influence of this Pennsylvania society. Among the corresponding members in Europe were such distinguished names in the history of legal and penal reform as Sir Samuel Romilly, Thomas F. Buxton, William Crawford and William Roscoe of England; Henri Grégoire and Charles Lucas of Paris; and Prince Gallitzen of Russia.[81]

The contributions of the society to the growth of prison reform movements in the United States in the half-century following the Revolution can scarcely be exaggerated.

As early as 1794 the society resolved to make its work broader than a local effort in Philadelphia, and "an extensive correspondence was opened and carried on between the society and the executives of several of the states of the union, which tended to diffuse much information relative to its labours, and led to the adoption of reform in the penal laws in other parts of the continent." [82] The effect of this missionary effort is particularly evident in the law of March 26, 1796, passed in New York, reducing the capital crimes from sixteen to two, and providing for the erection of two state prisons.[83] New Jersey also reformed its criminal code by the law

---

[80] Roberts Vaux, *Notices,* pp. 42-3.

[81] *Constitution and Members of the Philadelphia Society for Alleviating the Miseries of Public Prisons,* 1830, p. 10. Roberts Vaux's writings on the Pennsylvania prison reform were well known in Europe in 1830. See Francis Lieber's translation of Beaumont and De Tocqueville's *The Penitentiary System of the United States,* Appendix, p. 288, note.

[82] Roberts Vaux, *Notices,* p. 34.

[83] John L. Sullivan, "Note on the Penitentiary System of New York State," in G. E. Baker's edition of the *Works of William H. Seward,* Vol. II, pp. 173-80.

of March 18, 1796, and directed the erection of a state prison by the law of March 1, 1797.[84]   In 1813 the secretaries of the society were directed to correspond with those in charge of the new system of penitentiary administration in the other states and to make inquiry as to the extent of the progress already made. It was found that some ten states had established improved penitentiary systems with at least moderate success.[85]   There is no reason to doubt that the impulse to reform in each instance came to some extent from the Pennsylvania movement. It is definitely known that before 1825, Maine, Maryland, Massachusetts, New York, New Jersey and Virginia had adopted for trial the Pennsylvania system of solitary confinement.[86]   Especially interesting was the influence of the Pennsylvania system upon New York State, for it can readily be shown that the great contending prison system—the Auburn system—was but the result of an alteration of the attempt of New York to make a thorough and exact application of the Pennsylvania system of solitary confinement.

During the second decade of the nineteenth century there was a wave of imitation, through the eastern states, of the Pennsylvania system of solitary confinement, and New York, in common with others, decided in 1819 to build a block of cells for solitary confinement in the yard of the newly constructed prison at Auburn.[87] In 1820 the New York authorities sent an inquiry to the Philadelphia Society for Alleviating the Miseries of Public Prisons, asking for advice as to the new method of administration.[88]   The society deputed Roberts Vaux to write the reply and he answered, giving the desired information and enjoining the New York reformers to persist in their intentions.[89]   In 1821 the cell block was opened and eighty hardened criminals were locked in separate cells without labor or exercise. By 1823 this procedure had become so detrimental to the physical and mental health of the prisoners thus confined that it was practically abandoned, and in the following year Elam Lynds, the head keeper and John Cray, the head architect, devised the world-famed Auburn Prison system, which

---

[84] William Paterson, *The Laws of the State of New Jersey*, 1800, pp. 208-21. *Acts of the Twenty-first General Assembly*, 1797, pp. 189-90.

[85] Roberts Vaux, *Notices*, p. 40.

[86] *Report of the Commissioners on the Penal Code*, 1828, pp. 42-50. See below, pp. 170ff.

[87] Sullivan, loc. cit.; Frederick C. Pettigrove, "The State Prisons of the United States under Separate and Congregate Systems," in C. R. Henderson, *Penal and Reformatory Institutions*, pp. 27-67.

[88] *Sketch of Principal Transactions*, p. 12.

[89] *Pennsylvania Journal of Prison Discipline and Philanthropy*, Vol. II, Number 2, 1846, p. 116.

consisted of solitary confinement at night and silent but congregate work in a common workshop by day.[90]

III. PROGRESS IN PENAL LEGISLATION 1776-1835

1. THE REFORM OF THE CRIMINAL CODE, 1776-1842

There were two main causes for the reform of the barbarous provincial criminal code when Pennsylvania obtained its independence. The first was the feeling that the code of 1718 was not a native colonial and national product, but that it was the work of a foreign country, forced upon the province by taking advantage of its early religious scruples and divisions. Especially was this the view taken by the Quaker element in Philadelphia and eastern Pennsylvania. Therefore, it was natural that a reaction against the English criminal jurisprudence should be one of the first manifestations of national spirit after 1776. The second chief cause of reform was the growth of enlightenment and criticism abroad. The movement represented by Montesquieu, Voltaire, Diderot, Beccaria, Paine, Bentham and others had affected the leaders of colonial thought in Pennsylvania to such an extent that reform would probably have been inevitable without the strong local impulses which existed at home. This background of the reform of criminal jurisprudence in Pennsylvania has been well summarized by one of the ablest contemporaries of, and participants in, the movement, William Bradford, justice of the Supreme Court of Pennsylvania, Attorney-General of the United States and designer of the reformed Pennsylvania penal codes of 1790 to 1794. Writing in 1793, he thus explained the transformation of the criminal codes of Pennsylvania:

"We perceive, by this detail,[91] that the severity of our criminal law is an exotic plant, and not the native growth of Pennsylvania. It has been endured, but, I believe, has never been a favorite. The religious opinions of many of our citizens were in opposition to it: and, as soon as the principles of Beccaria were disseminated, they found a soil that was prepared to receive them. During our con-

---

[90] Sullivan, loc. cit.; Pettigrove, loc. cit.; G. De Beaumont and A. De Tocqueville, *The Penitentiary System in the United States,* translated by Francis Lieber, Philadelphia, 1833, pp. 3-7.

[91] This passage follows immediately after a sketch of criminal jurisprudence in provincial Pennsylvania. Bradford's death in 1795, at the age of forty, was a great blow to American jurisprudence. His achievements up to that point incline one to surmise that with a normal life he would have displaced Edward Livingston as the greatest of early American legists.

nection with Great Britain no reform was attempted; but, as soon as we separated from her, the public sentiment disclosed itself and this benevolent undertaking was enjoined by the constitutions. This was one of the first fruits of liberty and confirms the remark of Montesquieu, 'That, as freedom advances, the severity of the penal law decreases.' " [92]

It was natural that when the American reaction against English jurisprudence took place in Pennsylvania, it should take the form of a return to the doctrines and practices of Penn. The new state constitution of September 28, 1776, directed a speedy reform of the criminal code along the line of substituting imprisonment for the various types of corporal punishment. It was stated that:

"The penal laws as heretofore used, shall be reformed by the future legislature of the State, as soon as may be, and punishments made in some cases less sanguinary, and in general more proportionate to the crimes.

"To deter more effectually from the commission of crimes, by continued visible punishment of long duration, and to make sanguinary punishments less necessary; houses ought to be provided for punishing by hard labor, those who shall be convicted of crimes not capital; wherein the criminals shall be employed for the benefit of the public, or for reparation of injuries done to private persons. And all persons at proper times shall be admitted to see the prisoners at their labor." [93]

The absorption of attention and energy by the military struggle with England prevented any immediate reform of the criminal code, but on September 15, 1786, an act was passed which aimed to carry out the provisions of the constitution of 1776.[94] The juristic conceptions of the framers of the act were expressed in the following paragraph:

"Whereas, it is the wish of every good government to reclaim rather than to destroy, and it being apprehended that the cause of human corruptions proceed more from the impunity of crimes than from the moderation of punishments, and it having been found by experience that the punishments directed by the laws now in force, as well for capital as for other inferior offences do not answer the principal ends of society in inflicting them, to wit, to correct and reform the offenders, and to produce such strong impression on the minds of others as to deter them from committing

---

[92] William Bradford, *An Enquiry How Far the Punishment of Death Is Necessary in Pennsylvania, With Notes and Illustrations,* Philadelphia, 1793, p. 20. References are to the London reprint of 1795.
[93] *Constitution of 1776,* Chapter II, Sections 38-9.
[94] *The Statutes at Large of Pennsylvania,* Vol. XII, p. 280.

the like offences, which it is conceived may be better effected by continued hard labor, publicly and disgracefully imposed on persons convicted of them, not only in the manner pointed out by the convention, but in streets of cities and towns, and upon the highways of the open country and other public works. . . ." [95]

It was enacted, accordingly, that every person henceforth convicted of robbery, burglary, sodomy or buggery, instead of suffering the death penalty, should forfeit all property to the state and serve a sentence of not to exceed ten years at hard labor in the jail or house of correction in the county or city where the crime was committed. [96] Horse stealing was penalized by full restitution to the owner, the forfeiture of an equal amount to the state and imprisonment at hard labor for a term not to exceed seven years.[97] Simple larceny, over twenty shillings, was to be punished by full restitution, forfeiture of like amount to the state and imprisonment at hard labor for not over three years.[98] Petty larceny, under twenty shillings, was to receive a like punishment, except that the maximum term of imprisonment was limited to one year.[99] It was further decreed that a mother could not be convicted of the murder of a bastard child unless it could be shown that the child was born alive.[100] Finally, any other crimes not capital, in the earlier code, but punishable by "burning in the hand, cutting off the ears, nailing the ear or ears to the pillory, placing in or upon the pillory, whipping or imprisonment for life," should thereafter be punished by imprisonment at hard labor for not more than two years.[101] In this manner there disappeared from the statute books the most brutal and revolting phases of the criminal jurisprudence and procedure of the colonial period, although the death penalty was still retained for some ten crimes.

The important act of April 5, 1790, establishing the Pennsylvania system of imprisonment in solitary confinement, while primarily a law concerned with penal administration, specified the penalties for crimes committed, but this part of the act simply repeated the specifications of the law of September 15, 1786.[102] The act of September 23, 1791, while chiefly devoted to the details of criminal procedure,[103] made some advances with respect to ameliorating the severity

---

[95] *The Statutes at Large of Pennsylvania,* Vol. XII, pp. 280-81.
[96] Ibid., p. 281.
[97] Ibid., pp. 281-82.
[98] Ibid., p. 282.
[99] Ibid.
[100] Ibid., p. 283.
[101] Ibid., p. 283.
[102] Ibid., Vol. XIII, pp. 511-15.
[103] Ibid., Vol. XIV, pp. 128-31.

of the criminal code. It repealed the death penalty for witchcraft,[104] and ordered that there should be no more branding, whipping or imprisonment at hard labor imposed for adultery or fornication. These crimes were to be punished by a fine of not more than fifty pounds and imprisonment for three to twelve months.[105]

The next great step in the progressive reform of the criminal code of Pennsylvania came in an act of April 22, 1794,[106] but before analyzing the contents of this act it will be useful and interesting to examine the chief doctrines of the able and influential pamphlet, published by William Bradford in 1793, on the desirability of reducing the number of capital crimes in Pennsylvania.[107] This work is most important in a number of ways. In the first place, it summarizes and indicates the sources of the doctrines of the jurist who drafted the revised penal code of Pennsylvania, as passed by the legislature during the years 1786 to 1794.[108] In the second place, it was very influential in bringing about the acceptance by the legislature of the law of 1794 reducing the category of capital crimes in Pennsylvania to that of murder in the first degree alone. Finally, as the product of the ablest legal mind in America at the time, it attracted wide attention at home and in Europe, and furnished the reformers with a valuable instrument to assist in their assaults upon the old order in criminal jurisprudence.

Throughout the work, Mr. Bradford gave evidence of the fact that the works of Montesquieu, Beccaria and Blackstone were not only the chief source of his own conviction that the mitigation of the criminal laws was an indispensable and immediate necessity, but that he regarded them as the main inspiration which had produced the newer and more humane conceptions in criminal jurisprudence.[109] At the outset, Mr. Bradford laid down the dictum that the only object of punishment is the prevention of crime.[110] The purpose of the death penalty, then, must be solely to prevent the person executed from the commission of another crime and to deter others from committing crime through fear of death. If these ends can be accomplished by other modes of punishment, then the death

---

[104] *The Statutes at Large of Pennsylvania*, Vol. XIV, p. 132.
[105] Ibid., pp. 133-34.
[106] Ibid., Vol. XV, pp. 174-81.
[107] Bradford, op. cit. References, as above, to London edition of 1795.
[108] The total abolition of the death penalty had been urged by Doctor Benjamin Rush in 1786-87. Roberts Vaux, *Notices*, p. 33. *A Statistical View of the Operation of the Penal Code of Pennsylvania*, 1817, pp. 3-4. *The Pennsylvania Journal of Prison Discipline and Philanthropy*, Vol. II, Number 3, pp. 205-10.
[109] Bradford, op. cit., pp. 3, 49-80.
[110] Ibid., p. 6.

penalty is unjustifiable.[111] Mr. Bradford contended that solitary confinement at hard labor would accomplish all that had been claimed for the death penalty.[112] He showed that history proves that mild penalties do not encourage the commission of crime nor severe penalties deter from criminal action. The example of Rome and England demonstrates this conclusively. Rome never imposed the death penalty except upon slaves, and yet it was much more orderly than England with its unprecedentedly long list of capital crimes.[113] The experience of America has been similar to that of Rome and England.[114]

Mr. Bradford then turned to a scientific examination of the effect of the ameliorating law of September 15, 1786, in Pennsylvania, upon the commission of those crimes which were removed from the list of capital offenses. He concluded that, when all disturbing influences were eliminated, the results revealed the fact that the number of commissions of these crimes was less in the six years after 1786 than in the six years previous to that time.[115] Mr. Bradford stated that he believed that society might safely dispense with the death penalty in the case of all crimes except premeditated murder and high treason, and it might be that, sooner or later, the progress of intelligence would be sufficient, so that capital punishment might be wholly abolished.[116] IIis conclusion is significant:

"The conclusion to which we are led by this enquiry seems to be, that in all cases, except those of high treason and murder, the punishment of death may be safely abolished, and milder penalties advantageously introduced. Such a system of punishments, aided and enforced in the manner I have mentioned, will not only have an auspicious influence on the character, morals, and happiness of the people, but may hasten the period, when, in the progress of civilization, the punishment of death shall cease to be necessary; and the legislature of Pennsylvania, putting the keystone to the arch, may triumph in the completion of their benevolent work.[117]

Mr. Bradford had the satisfaction of seeing his theories enacted into law in the act of April 22, 1794, "for the better preventing of crimes, and for abolishing the punishment of death in certain cases." It was declared that,

"It is the duty of every government to endeavor to reform, rather

---

[111] Bradford, op. cit., pp. 6-7.
[112] Ibid., pp. 7-8.
[113] Ibid., pp. 10ff.
[114] Ibid., p. 9.
[115] Ibid., pp. 20ff.
[116] Ibid., pp. 35ff.
[117] Ibid., p. 46.

than to exterminate offenders, and the punishment of death ought never to be inflicted where it is not absolutely necessary to the public safety.[118]

Accordingly, it was enacted,

"That no crime whatsoever, hereafter committed, except murder in the first degree, shall be punished with death in the State of Pennsylvania." [119]

It was specified that murder in the first degree would be constituted by all premeditated murder and by all murder committed in attempting rape, arson, robbery or burglary. All other types of murder were to constitute murder in the second degree.[120] The death penalty for murder in the first degree was to be inflicted "by hanging by the neck." [121]

In addition to this remarkable reduction of capital crimes, the act provided reduced penalties for the crimes which were eliminated from the list of those punishable by death. The following were the penalties prescribed: *murder in the second degree,* imprisonment of from five to eighteen years; *manslaughter,* imprisonment for from two to ten years, with from six to fourteen years for a second offense; *murder or concealment of the death of a bastard child,* imprisonment up to five years or a fine at the discretion of the court; *high treason,* imprisonment for from six to twelve years; [122] *arson,* imprisonment from five to twelve years; *rape,* imprisonment for from ten to twenty-one years; *malicious maiming,* imprisonment for from two to ten years and a fine up to one thousand dollars, three-fourths of which was to go to the party injured; *counterfeiting,* imprisonment from four to fifteen years and a fine up to one thousand dollars.[123] "Benefit of clergy" was "forever abolished." [124]

It was provided that if a person be convicted a second time of a crime which was capital on September 15, 1786, he should be confined for life in the solitary cells of the Walnut Street Jail, unless the inspectors saw fit to remove him from these cells.[125] The only exception to this rule was in case the second offense was committed

---

[118] *The Statutes at Large of Pennsylvania,* Vol. XV, p. 174.
[119] Ibid.
[120] Ibid., p. 175.
[121] Ibid., p. 180.
[122] The fact that high treason was not made a capital crime may in some degree be explained by the fact that the "Whiskey Rebellion" in Pennsylvania was at its height in 1794.
[123] *The Statutes at Large of Pennsylvania,* Vol. XV, pp. 175-81.
[124] Ibid., p. 177.
[125] Ibid., pp. 178-79.

after escaping or being pardoned; in such instances the penalty for a second commission of the crime was to be imprisonment for twenty-five years.[126] With some minor revisions, especially in the act of April 23, 1829, this law of 1794 remained the basis of the criminal code of Pennsylvania until the systematic revision of the code in 1860.

A slight increase in the severity of the penal code was produced by an act of April 4, 1807. The act of September 15, 1786, had decreed a punishment of not to exceed two years' imprisonment for those crimes, not capital in 1786, but which had been punished by the brutal forms of corporal punishment and by imprisonment for life. This act of April 4, 1807, raised the maximum limit for these crimes to seven years imprisonment, though it specified that this increase should not apply to bigamy, accessory after the fact in a felony, or the reception of stolen goods.[127] From this time until the act of April 23, 1829, there were no important alterations in the criminal code of Pennsylvania.[128]

A resolution of the legislature, passed March 23, 1826, directed the appointment of three commissioners to revise the criminal code of the state.[129] Charles Shaler, Edward King and T. J. Wharton were appointed to perform this important task. They laid their report before the legislature on December 20, 1827.[130] The commission made no attempt at a complete new codification of the criminal law of the state, as they felt that their authorization did not extend to this limit and the time allotted was not sufficient to the completion of so extensive a task.[131] Rather they aimed at "loping off relics of barbarism," giving a better definition of crimes and eliminating obsolete statutes.[132] One of the most original and valuable innovations introduced was the practice of specifying only the maximum sentence and leaving the minimum to the discretion of the court.[133] This procedure was defended with ingenuity and convincingness.[134] In some cases, the commissioners thought it wise to extend the maximum, and their defense of this step is interesting as indicating that the struggle between prison reformers and the conservatism

---

[126] *The Statutes at Large of Pennsylvania*, Vol. XV, p. 179.
[127] *Acts of the General Assembly of Pennsylvania*, 1806-07, p. 134.
[128] For a list of the penal laws of Pennsylvania from 1700 to 1812, see Bioren's edition of the *Laws of the Commonwealth of Pennsylvania*, Vol. V, 1812, Index. pp. 270-72. An able revision of the penal code by Jared Ingersoll, in 1813, was rejected by the legislature.
[129] *Acts of the General Assembly*, 1825-26, p. 413.
[130] *Report of the Commissioners on the Penal Code*, 1828, p. 105.
[131] Ibid., pp. 93-4.
[132] Ibid., pp. 94-5.
[133] Ibid., pp. 98-100.
[134] Ibid.

of the judiciary is not merely an incident of the present day. They stated that,

"In some instances, the punishment allotted to offenses, appears hardly commensurate with the specified crimes, and this, whether we consider these punishments with practical men, as a means of prevention, or consider penitentiaries with some modern theorists, as mere schools of reform." [135]

On the whole, however, the revision was a work of great skill and ability and the failure of the legislature to adopt it was a severe blow to the progress of criminal jurisprudence in Pennsylvania. Not until 1860 was a criminal code provided which attained the level of excellence and modernity reached in the report of 1827. The reason for the failure to adopt the code is a part of the story of the struggle over penitentiary systems. The same commissioners had been directed to draw up rules for the regulation of the new state penitentiaries and they had reported in favor of the Auburn system.[136] This led to the opposition of the Philadelphia Society for Alleviating the Miseries of Public Prisons, and in the three-cornered conflict which ensued between the penal code commissioners, the commissioners charged with building the Eastern Penitentiary, and the prison society, the legislature ended by rejecting the revised penal code as well as the recommendation of the Auburn system.[137]

Instead of the code recommended by the commissioners, the legislature, by an act of April 23, 1829, adopted a revision which was much less thorough and systematic than the commissioners had suggested.[138] It followed the precedent of the code of 1794 in prescribing maximum and minimum penalties for the first offense of the specified crimes, and the recommendation of the commissioners of 1827 in usually prescribing only the maximum penalty for the second conviction. On the whole, the revision, while constituting no departure in juristic doctrine from the code of 1794, did produce a considerable reduction in the length of the term of imprisonment specified for the various crimes. This was, no doubt, due to the optimism at the time with respect to the remarkable reformative virtues of the Pennsylvania system of solitary confinement at hard labor.

In the first place, it was ordered that in all cases where imprison-

---

[135] *Report of the Commissioners on the Penal Code,* 1828, pp. 96-7.
[136] Ibid., pp. 77-82.
[137] *The Pennsylvania Journal of Prison Discipline and Philanthropy,* Vol. I, Number 1, 1845, pp. 8-12.
[138] *Laws of the General Assembly,* 1828-29, pp. 341-54. This code is also reproduced in Richard Vaux's *Brief Sketch of the Eastern Penitentiary,* pp. 36-42.

ment was the penalty imposed this should be carried out in solitary confinement at hard labor.[139] The following penalties were imposed for the crimes enumerated: *high treason,* for the first offense, imprisonment of from three to six years, and for the second offense, imprisonment for not to exceed ten years; *murder in the second degree,* for the first offense, imprisonment of from four to twelve years, and for the second offense, imprisonment for life; *manslaughter,* for the first offense, imprisonment of from two to six years, and for the second offense, imprisonment for from six to twelve years; *mayhem,* for the first offense, imprisonment of from one to seven years, and for the second offense, imprisonment for not to exceed fourteen years; *rape,* for the first offense, imprisonment of from two to twelve years, and for the second offense, imprisonment for life; *sodomy* and *buggery,* for the first offense, imprisonment of from one to five years, and for the second offense, imprisonment for not to exceed ten years; *kidnapping,* for the first offense, imprisonment for from five to twelve years, and for the second offense, imprisonment for twenty-one years; *arson,* for the first offense, imprisonment of from one to ten years, and for the second offense, imprisonment for not to exceed fifteen years; *burglary,* for the first offense, imprisonment of from two to ten years, and for the second offense, imprisonment for not to exceed fifteen years; *robbery,* for the first offense, imprisonment of from one to seven years, and for the second offense, imprisonment for not to exceed twelve years; *horse-stealing,* for the first offense, imprisonment of from one to four years, and for the second offense, imprisonment for not to exceed seven years; *forgery,* for the first offense, imprisonment of from one to seven years, and for the second offense, imprisonment for not to exceed ten years; *perjury,* for the first offense, imprisonment of from one to five years, and for the second offense, imprisonment for not to exceed eight years.[140] It was further specified that for all crimes not enumerated the penalties should remain as prescribed in earlier laws.[141] Such was the relatively mild penal code under which the Pennsylvania system began its complete operation, as it had made its beginnings under the codes of 1786, 1790, and 1794.[142]

The failure of the penal code commissioners of 1828 to provide Pennsylvania with a relatively systematic and enlightened code of

---

[139] *Laws of the General Assembly,* 1828-29, pp. 341-42.
[140] Ibid., pp. 342-44.
[141] Ibid., p. 345.
[142] As the basis of a comparison, see the admirable summary of the criminal codes of the period in the *Fourth Annual Report of the Prison Discipline Society of Boston,* 1829, pp. 31-54.

criminal jurisprudence has already been discussed. It has been shown that the recommendations of the commissioners were rejected primarily because they insisted in attaching to the revised criminal code, as a sort of "rider," a set of provisions directing the adoption of the Auburn system of prison administration. The friends of the Pennsylvania system considered the sacrifice of the newly proposed criminal code less of an evil than the loss of their cherished penological principles and defeated the bill through lobbying with the judiciary committee of the state legislature. Not until 1860 was the ambition of the commissioners realized in the enactment of a new criminal code. In the interval between 1828 and 1860, however, one important advance was made in the modernizing and humanizing of one phase of jurisprudence which was until relatively recent times divided between civil and criminal law, namely, imprisonment for debt.

Throughout the colonial period, many successive attempts had been made to relieve the conditions of "distressed debtors," but the courts never adopted a liberal interpretation of the laws, and imprisonment for debt persisted far down into the period of the commonwealth. One of the most grievous sources of evil revealed in the Walnut Street Jail by the Philadelphia Society for Alleviating the Miseries of Public Prisons was the mode of treating debtors in 1787-1790, and from 1818 to 1835 a separate prison on Arch Street had been set aside for the incarceration of debtors and witnesses. The first important progressive legislation in this sphere was contained in an act of April 4, 1792, which was designed to do away with the evils of the extortionate fee system which had been in vogue down to that time. This act provided that the keeper of the debtors' apartment in the Philadelphia jail was to be granted a fixed salary of five hundred dollars, which was to supersede all fees hitherto allowed to him or his subordinates.[143] The basis of a general bankruptcy act was laid by a law of April 4, 1798, which provided, "That the person of a debtor shall not be liable to imprisonment for debt, after delivering up his estate for the benefit of his creditors, unless he has been guilty of fraud or embezzlement." [144] This liberal act met the fate of its predecessors and imprisonment for debt continued with little change. The first decisive step was taken in an act of February 8, 1819, which commanded that, "No female shall be arrested or imprisoned for, or by reason of any debt contracted after the passing of this act." [145] The degree to which im-

---

[143] *The Statutes at Large of Pennsylvania,* Vol. XIV, pp. 267-69.
[144] Ibid., Vol. XVI, pp. 98-106.
[145] *Acts of the General Assembly,* 1818-19, p. 57.

prisonment for debt persisted may be seen from the fact that on
June 16, 1836, a long and elaborate act was passed defining and
prescribing the civil and criminal procedure in debtors' cases.[146]
The final act abolishing imprisonment for debt in Pennsylvania was
passed on July 12, 1842. In a most fundamental sense, this act
and the many similar ones which were passed throughout the
country in this same general period were, as Professor Carleton
has so well shown, the product of the wave of indignation that
swept over the country and demanded the abolition of this, along
with the many other undemocratic features of American society and
politics. The movement was an incident of the development of the
Jacksonian democracy and of the rise of the organization of the
industrial proletariat.[147]

In a more immediate sense, it was the outgrowth of a vigorous
campaign of invective directed against the antiquated laws on this
point by Louis Dwight in the annual reports of the Boston Prison
Discipline Society, from 1830 to 1845. In no phase of prison reform
was Dwight more active than in agitating for the abolition of imprisonment for debt. In Pennsylvania, his efforts were ably seconded by the Philadelphia Society for Alleviating the Miseries of
Public Prisons, this being about the only field in which they could
work in harmony and agreement with the leader of the Boston
society. The act of 1842, which was entitled, "An Act to Abolish
Imprisonment for Debt and to Punish Fraudulent Debtors," provided that:

"From and after the passage of this act, no person shall be
arrested or imprisoned on any civil process issuing out of any court
of this commonwealth, in any suit or proceeding instituted for the
recovery of any money due upon any judgment or decree founded
upon contract, or due upon any contract, express or implied, or for
the recovery of any damages for the non-performance of any contract, excepting in cases for contempt, to enforce civil remedies,
action for fines or penalties, or on promises to marry, or moneys
collected by any public officer, or for any misconduct or neglect
in office, or in any professional employment, in which cases the
remedies shall remain as heretofore." [148]

---

[146] *Laws of the General Assembly*, 1835-36, pp. 729-41.

[147] Frank Carleton, "The Abolition of Imprisonment for Debt in the United
States," in *The Yale Review*, Vol. XVII, pp. 338-44. Cf. J. R. Commons
(ed.), *A History of Labor in the United States*, Vol. I, pp. 296ff.

[148] *Laws of the General Assembly*, 1842, pp. 339ff. For complete or nearly
complete lists of laws dealing with imprisonment for debt in Pennsylvania,
see *The Statutes at Large*, Vol. IV, pp. 183-84, note, and G. W. Pepper and
W. D. Lewis, *Digest of the Laws of Pennsylvania*, 1896, Vol. I, p. 2313. For
a discussion of the abolition of debt in Pennsylvania, see W. C. Heffner,
The History of Poor Relief Legislation in Pennsylvania, 1682-1913, pp. 202-04.

2. THE CREATION OF A STATE PRISON SYSTEM

The reform of the criminal code in Pennsylvania from 1786 to 1794, by which the death penalty and milder forms of corporal punishment were eliminated and imprisonment substituted, did not bring about the immediate establishment of a state prison system. Rather the attempt was made to use the Philadelphia county and city jail as a substitute for a state prison until by the growth of population and the consequent increase in the numbers of the delinquent classes, the commonwealth was literally crowded out of the jail system and into a system of state penitentiaries.

The first step toward the creation of a state prison system was taken by the act of March 27, 1789. This provided for the alteration of the Walnut Street Jail so that one part could be reserved entirely for felons. This was to be known as the "common prison of the city and county of Philadelphia." It was stipulated that any felon convicted in any part of the state and sentenced to at least twelve months of imprisonment at hard labor might be sent to the prison at Philadelphia. The expenses of operating the Philadelphia prison were to be defrayed by the several counties in proportion to the number of prisoners from each county. In addition, Philadelphia was to receive one hundred pounds annually for the extra expense incurred in maintaining the prison. In case the proceeds of the labor of the prisoners exceeded the expense of their maintenance it was ordered that the surplus should be divided in proportion to the number of prisoners from each county.[149]

One provision of the act of April 5, 1790, ordering imprisonment at hard labor for all except the "more hardened and atrocious offenders," and directing the solitary confinement of this latter class, stated that, as far as possible, the provisions of this act should be extended to the other counties of the state.[150] That this was generally regarded as impracticable may be seen from the section in the same act, allowing the courts of the several counties to send to the Philadelphia jail those convicted in other counties and sentenced to imprisonment at hard labor for more than twelve months. The expense of maintenance was to be met by the county from which the convicts were sent, provided their labor did not defray their expenses.[151]

This process was carried further by the act of April 22, 1794. This directed that all persons in any county, convicted of any

---

[149] *The Statutes at Large of Pennsylvania,* Vol. XIII, pp. 246, 250-51.
[150] Ibid., pp. 523-25.
[151] Ibid., p. 527.

crime, except murder in the first degree, which was a capital crime on September 15, 1786, should be sent to Philadelphia and confined in the solitary cells erected in 1790, for a period of from one-twelfth to one-half of his term of imprisonment.[152] It was further provided that if any person should commit such a crime for a second time, he was to be imprisoned for life in the solitary cells of the Philadelphia prison, though the inspectors could use their discretion in removing him from solitary confinement.[153]

The Walnut Street Prison soon became overcrowded, and an act of April 2, 1803, provided for the erection of a new county prison in Philadelphia.[154] An act of March 31, 1812, appropriated twenty-five thousand dollars for the completion of the new Arch Street Prison, provided that when it was completed the convicts should be transferred from the Walnut Street Jail, and declared that it should then be "considered, deemed and taken to be the exclusive property of this commonwealth." [155] This was the first act contemplating the provision of a state prison in Pennsylvania. It was never carried into execution, however, as the Arch Street Prison was not opened until 1817 and then only for the detention of debtors.[156] The result of the overcrowding of the Walnut Street Prison, and of the failure to provide a larger building, is apparent in the law of March 21, 1805, which declared that the court of any county might retain for punishment in that county any person sentenced to imprisonment at hard labor for a period up to three years.[157]

The first really permanent achievement in the establishment of the state prison system was brought about in the law of March 3, 1818. This appropriated sixty thousand dollars for erecting in Allegheny County a state penitentiary on the principle of solitary confinement. The select and common councils of Pittsburgh were authorized to appoint five competent commissioners to oversee the construction of the building. The plan was to follow that submitted by the legislature by the inspectors of the Philadelphia prison.[158] The act further provided that the inspectors of the prison of the city and county of Philadelphia, with the consent of the mayor, aldermen and citizens of Philadelphia, and of the com-

---

[152] *The Statutes at Large of Pennsylvania,* Vol. XV, pp. 178-79.
[153] Ibid., p. 179.
[154] *Laws of the Commonwealth of Pennsylvania,* Bioren, 1803, pp. 87-8.
[155] Ibid., 1812, p. 370.
[156] *Acts of the General Assembly,* 1815-16, pp. 126-27. *The Pennsylvania Journal of Prison Discipline and Philanthropy,* Vol. I, Number 1, 1845, p. 7.
[157] *Acts of the General Assembly,* 1804-05, pp. 570-71.
[158] Ibid., 1817-18, pp. 138-39.

missioners of the Northern Liberties and the district of Southwark, might sell the plant and site of the Walnut Street Prison
and remove the prisoners to the Arch Street Prison. Thereupon,
with the consent of the above authorities, the inspectors were
authorized to purchase land and erect a new penitentiary at
Philadelphia on the principle of solitary confinement.[159] While
work was begun on the Allegheny Penitentiary, no action was
taken with respect to the authorized construction of a new penitentiary in Philadelphia. This step was taken by an act of March
20, 1821, ordering the erection of a state penitentiary in Philadelphia
on the principle of solitary confinement.[160] These state penitentiaries were duly constructed by a series of appropriations extending
over the period from 1818 to 1835.[161] The act of April 10, 1826,
divided the state into two penitentiary districts, the eastern and the
western, and directed that all convicts from the eastern district be
sent to the Philadelphia Penitentiary and that those from the
western district should be sent to the penitentiary at Allegheny.[162]
These districts and provisions were retained in the systematic act
of April 23, 1829,[163] and with the opening of the Eastern Penitentiary in October, 1829, Pennsylvania was provided with a complete
state prison system.

3.   THE GRADUAL EVOLUTION OF THE PENNSYLVANIA SYSTEM OF SOLITARY CONFINEMENT AT HARD LABOR

As was the case with the establishment of a state prison system
in Pennsylvania, so with the origin of the Pennsylvania system of
prison administration, based upon solitary confinement at hard
labor, the process was a gradual one. The most remote origins of
this system, of course, go back to the time of the workhouses
which Penn ordered to be established in 1682-83.[164] This practice
was revived by the constitution of 1776, which directed the enactment of laws establishing houses of correction for "punishing by
hard labor, those who shall be convicted of crimes not capital." [165]
This provision of the constitution was in part obeyed in the law of
September 15, 1786, directing the punishment by hard labor of
those convicted of robbery, burglary, sodomy or buggery and of

---

[159] *Acts of the General Assembly,* 1817-18, pp. 139-40.
[160] Ibid., 1820-21, pp. 94-7.
[161] The last appropriating act was that of April 14, 1835.
[162] *Acts,* 1825-26, pp. 280-82.
[163] *Laws of the General Assembly,* 1828-29, pp. 341-54.
[164] *Charter and Laws of Pennsylvania,* 1682-1700, pp. 121-39.
[165] *Constitution of 1776,* Chapter II, section 39.

those convicted of crimes previously punishable by the more brutal forms of corporal punishment. Some attempt was also made in the law to prevent the promiscuous association of all types of convicts. It was commanded "that the keepers aforesaid shall endeavor as much as in them lies to separate as well those who are confined to labor within doors, as those who shall be employed without in such manner as that the old and hardened offenders be prevented from mixing with and thereby contaminating and eradicating the remaining seeds of virtue and goodness in the young and unwary, and the men from an improper intercourse with the women." All contemporary reports of the condition of the jail, however, from 1786 to 1790, indicate that these directions were very imperfectly executed.[166]

The first serious attempt to provide for some degree of separation of criminals in Pennsylvania is to be found in the law of March 27, 1789. This act provided that a special department of the Walnut Street Jail should be fitted up to be occupied by those felons sentenced to imprisonment at hard labor. It was directed that in this part of the jail "cells, sheds and other suitable buildings are to be constructed for the purpose of separating, confining and keeping employed at hard labor all felons sentenced to hard labor and confinement." These were to be properly walled up and secured "to prevent all communication among the said felons and with the persons abroad." [167]

The provisions of the act of 1789 were immediately superseded by those of the more general act of April 5, 1790, which is usually taken to mark the legal origin of the Pennsylvania system. The enacting clause stated that the laws of 1786 to 1789 "have in some degree failed of success from the exposure of the offenders employed at hard labor to the public view and from the communication with each other not being sufficiently restrained within the places of confinement; and it is hoped that the addition of unremitted solitude to laborious employment, as far as it can be effected, will contribute as much to reform as to deter." [168]

To carry this conception into execution it was enacted:

"That the Commissioners for the County of Philadelphia, with the approbation of the Mayor and two of the Aldermen of the City of Philadelphia, and two of the Justices of the Court of Quarter Sessions, for the County of Philadelphia, shall, as soon as con-

---

[166] *The Statutes at Large of Pennsylvania*, Vol. XII, pp. 280-90. Lownes, op. cit., pp. 5-8.
[167] Ibid., Vol. XIII, p. 245.
[168] Ibid., p. 511.

veniently may be, cause a suitable number of cells to be constructed in the yard of the gaol of the said county, each of which
cells shall be six feet in width, eight feet in length, and nine feet
in height, and shall be constructed with brick or stone, upon such
plan as will best prevent danger from fire; and the said cells shall
be separated from the common yard by walls of such height, as,
without unnecessary exclusion of air and light, will prevent all
external communication, for the purpose of confining therein the
more hardened and atrocious offenders, who, by the act entitled
'An Act for amending the penal laws of this State,' have been sentenced to hard labour for a term of years, or who shall be sentenced
thereto by virtue of this act." [169]

Following out these provisions, thirty-six cells were erected,
twenty-four for men and twelve for women.[170] It is evident that
it was the intention of the law that those confined in the solitary
cells should be set at work, but all contemporary reports agree that
such action was never taken and that complete idleness was the
invariable rule. [171]

Not only was this early attempt to establish the Pennsylvania
system abortive and unsuccessful because of the failure systematically to provide labor for those in the separate cells, but it also broke
down because of the insufficiency of the cells erected. It was not
long after 1790 before there were many more felons sentenced to
solitary confinement than there were cells provided to receive them.
As a consequence, they had to be put in the congregate department
of the prison with the other offenders. In addition, so crowded
did the Walnut Street Jail become that it was necessary to put
more than one convict in the solitary cells, the cells being large
enough to house two convicts without any difficulty. In spite of
the law, therefore, it seems that there have been few penal institutions in modern times which were further removed from the application of solitary confinement than was the Walnut Street Jail from
1800 to 1829. In 1816 it was customary to lock up forty prisoners
at night in a room eighteen feet square, and the degree of separation by day was little better. The commissioners on the reform
of the penal code, in 1826, were told that at one time fifty-three
prisoners had been confined in a room twenty feet long and eighteen
feet wide. The only way in which the administration of the jail from
1800 to 1829 could be regarded as an improvement over that of

---

[169] *The Statutes at Large of Pennsylvania,* Vol. XIII, p. 515.
[170] Lownes, op. cit., pp. 9-11. *Report of the Commissioners on the Penal
Code,* 1828, p. 170.
[171] Robert J. Turnbull, *A Visit to the Philadelphia Prison,* etc., 1796, pp.
55-8. Cf. Wines, *Punishment and Reformation,* pp. 146-47.

1780-90 was that, in spite of the ridiculous herding together of the male convicts, the women and boys were separated from the men.[172]

The failure of the law of 1790 to secure the solitary confinement of those so sentenced was legally remedied by the acts of March 3, 1818, and March 20, 1821, which provided for the erection of the Western and Eastern Penitentiaries. It was here definitely stipulated that both penitentiaries should be constructed according to the principle of solitary confinement, but no provisions were made for the employment of the convicts.[173] It was only out of the struggles of 1826 to 1829 that the Pennsylvania system was finally established. The commissioners on the penal code, while directed to report a governing law for the new penitentiaries according to the principle of solitary confinement at hard labor, deviated from their instructions and reported in favor of the Auburn system of congregate workshops. The board of commissioners for the erection of the Eastern Penitentiary recommended solitary confinement without labor. By taking advantage of this deadlock among the public authorities, the Philadelphia Society for Alleviating the Miseries of Public Prisons was able to induce the legislature to enact into law its fundamental program in penal administration— solitary confinement at hard labor.[174] This was finally and definitely prescribed in the law of April 23, 1829.[175]

4. THE ADMINISTRATION AND DISCIPLINE OF THE PENAL INSTITUTIONS

A. The Controlling Authorities

It will be remembered that during the colonial period the administrative control of the jail was vested in the sheriff of the county and that the expense of maintaining the jail was levied and raised as a part of the county rate.[176] This arrangement was followed in Pennsylvania immediately after the attaining of independence. Owing to the greatly increased burdens of administering the Phila-

[172] *A Statistical View of the Operation of the Penal Code of Pennsylvania,* 1817, pp. 3-6. *Memorials of the Philadelphia Society for Alleviating the Miseries of Public Prisons,* 1801 to 1821, cited above. *Report of the Commissioners on the Penal Code,* 1828, pp. 16-8, 170-71.
[173] *Acts of the General Assembly,* 1817-18, pp. 138-40; Ibid., 1820-21, pp. 94-7.
[174] *The Pennsylvania Journal of Prison Discipline and Philanthropy,* Vol. I, Number 1, 1845, pp. 8-11.
[175] *Laws of the General Assembly,* 1828-29, pp. 341-54.
[176] See above, pp. 63ff.

delphia jail after the laws of 1786, 1789 and 1790 had brought about a great accession to the number of prisoners in the city and county jail on Walnut Street, it became necessary to relieve the sheriff of this duty and to create a new controlling body—a board of inspectors. After more than a quarter of a century of experimentation with this type of controlling agency in the jail of Philadelphia, it became the model upon which was based the organization of the board of control of the state penitentiaries in 1826 and 1829.

The first step was taken in the law of March 27, 1789. It was herein decreed that the mayor and aldermen of Philadelphia were to appoint annually six "suitable and discreet" persons to serve as inspectors of the county jail or prison.[177] The duties of these inspectors were: to secure the proper stock of raw material for the prison workhouse; to sell the products of the workhouse and apply the receipts to the expenses of the institution; to investigate the conduct and management of the keeper and to report this to the mayor and aldermen; and to report to the same authorities all needed repairs to the prison buildings.[178] The mayor and aldermen were also to appoint annually a keeper of the prison.[179] The duties of this official were specified to be: the care and custody of the prisoners; the supervision of the work of the prisoners; the execution of the scheme of separation of the prisoners provided for in other sections of the law; the prevention of the entry of other than legally qualified visitors; the exclusion of spirituous liquors, except that which the inspectors might admit in case of sickness; the punishment and reward of the prisoners as might be necessary; and the preservation of proper discipline and cleanliness.[180] The keeper, with the consent of the mayor and aldermen, was authorized to appoint the necessary number of deputies, for whose conduct he was responsible.[181] The keeper was to be paid a suitable salary, and an allowance for his deputies and was to receive a commission of ten per cent. on all prison products sold by the inspectors. Neither he nor his deputies was to accept any fees other than the salary and allowance named.[182] In this way the obnoxious and oppressive fee system was abolished.

The law of 1789 had scarcely gone into operation when it was replaced by an act of April 5, 1790. This decreed that the mayor of Philadelphia, two aldermen and two justices of the peace should

---

[177] *The Statutes at Large of Pennsylvania*, Vol. XIII, p. 246.
[178] Ibid., pp. 246-47.
[179] Ibid., p. 247.
[180] Ibid., p. 247.
[181] Ibid., pp. 247-48
[182] Ibid., p. 248.

appoint semi-annually, on the first Monday in November and May, six prison inspectors.[183] These inspectors were to meet quarterly and appoint two acting inspectors who were to visit and inspect the jail once each week. The inspectors were to make such regulations for the government of the jail as might be approved by the mayor and recorder, and when so approved, the keeper was compelled to execute them under pain of fine and removal.[184] The keeper of the jail was to be appointed by the mayor, aldermen and justices for a term of one year. He was to be paid a fixed salary and to receive a commission of five per cent. on all sales of prison-made products. He was required to give a bond of five hundred pounds guaranteeing the faithful performance of his duties by himself and his deputies. He was authorized to appoint his required deputies and assistants with the consent of the mayor, aldermen and justices.[185] As far as possible, these provisions were, with the necessary local variations, to be made state-wide in their application. In counties other than Philadelphia, the sheriff, with the consent of the justices of the quarter sessions, was to appoint the keeper and under-keepers of the jail. Their removal was made the prerogative of the court of quarter sessions of the county, or of the supreme court justices when on their circuit duties.[186] This act of 1790, with subsequent minor modifications, governed the nature and appointment of the controlling officers of Pennsylvania penal institutions until the passage of the systematic acts of 1826 and 1829 regulating the government of the new state penitentiaries.

The act of April 18, 1795, somewhat extended the powers of the inspectors. They were given full authority to procure all necessary supplies for the convicts and to classify, separate, clothe and employ them. The inspectors were also given sole power to appoint and remove the keeper of the jail, to fix his salary and approve his appointment of deputies.[187] A revision in the mode of choosing the inspectors was brought about in the law of February 23, 1809. It was thereby provided that on the first Monday in May and November the select and common councils of Philadelphia should meet and elect by ballot three prison inspectors. At the same time the commissioners and the select and common councils of the districts of Northern Liberties and Southwark were to meet, and each district was to

---

[183] *The Statutes at Large of Pennsylvania*, Vol. XIII, p. 522.
[184] Ibid., pp. 522-23.
[185] Ibid., pp. 521-22.
[186] Ibid., pp. 524-25. Cf. Allinson and Penrose, *Philadelphia, 1681-1887*, pp. 110-12.
[187] *The Statutes at Large of Pennsylvania*, Vol. XV, pp. 355-56.

elect two prison inspectors. The inspectors thus selected were to constitute the board of inspectors of the Philadelphia prison.[188]

The first provision for the appointment of the controlling authorities of the new state penitentiaries was contained in the act of April 10, 1826, describing the governing board of the Western Penitentiary. It was directed that the penitentiary should be governed by a board of nine inspectors chosen annually in the following manner. Three were to be chosen from the citizens of Pittsburgh by the select and common councils of that city; three were to be chosen by the commissioners of Allegheny County from citizens of Ross Township; and three were to be elected by the justices of the court of quarter sessions from the general body of citizens of Allegheny County. Their powers and duties were to be identical with those of the inspectors of the prison of the city and county of Philadelphia.[189] This act was soon superseded by the general act of April 23, 1829, establishing the governmental and administrative system for both of the new state penitentiaries.

The act of 1829 provided that:

"The penitentiaries aforesaid shall be respectively managed by a board of inspectors, consisting of five taxable citizens of Pennsylvania, who shall be appointed as follows: The judges of the supreme court of the state shall at the first term of any supreme court, which shall be held in any of the districts of the state after the passage of this act, appoint five taxable citizens residing in the city of Pittsburg, or county of, Allegheny, who shall be inspectors of the Western State Penitentiary, to serve for two years; and five taxable citizens residing in the city or county of Philadelphia, who shall be inspectors of the Eastern State Penitentiary, to serve for two years, and until their successors shall be appointed; and in case of any vacancy occasioned by death, resignation, refusal to serve, or otherwise, the same shall be supplied by the said judges, as soon as conveniently may be.[190]

The governing board, thus created, still controls the state penitentiaries of Pennsylvania, though the act of March 27, 1874, took the power of appointing the inspectors from the judges of the supreme court and gave it to the governor of the state.[191] On account of the historical importance of the Pennsylvania system of prison administration and the long duration of the application of the act of 1829, its provisions regarding the officers of the penitentiaries

---

[188] *The Laws of the Commonwealth of Pennsylvania,* 1809, Bioren ed., p. 12.
[189] *Acts of the General Assembly,* 1825-26, pp. 281-82.
[190] *Laws of the General Assembly,* 1828-29, pp. 345-46.
[191] Ibid., 1874, p. 228.

and their duties are of sufficient significance to justify complete reproduction:

"Article I

"Of the Inspectors and Their Duties

"They shall at their first meeting and annually thereafter appoint out of their number a president, secretary and treasurer, and keep regular minutes of their proceedings; they shall hold stated meetings once a month, and adjourned and special meetings whenever necessary; the treasurer shall give bond with sufficient surety in such amount as the inspectors may fix and determine, and shall receive and disburse all moneys belonging to the prison, according to the order of the board; they shall semi-annually appoint a warden, a physician, and clerk for the institution, and shall fix their salaries, as well as those of the under-keepers or overseers, and the persons employed about the prison; they shall serve without any pecuniary compensation, and shall be exempted from military duty, from serving on juries and arbitrations, or as guardians of the poor; they shall visit the Penitentiary at least twice in every week, to see that the duties of the several officers and attendants are performed, to prevent all oppression, peculation, or other abuse or mismanagement of the said institutions; they shall have power, if they on conference find it necessary to make such rules for the internal government of said prison, as may not be inconsistent with, the principles of solitary confinement as set forth and declared by this act.

"They shall attend to the religious instruction of the prisoners and secure a suitable person for this object, who shall be the religious instructor of the prisoners: *Provided,* Their services shall be gratuitous.

"They shall direct the manner in which all raw materials to be manufactured by the convicts in said prisons, and the provisions and other supplies for the prisons shall be purchased, and also the sale of all articles manufactured in said prisons.

"They shall cause accurate accounts to be kept by the clerk, of all expenditures and receipts in the Penitentiaries, which accounts respectively shall be annually examined and settled by the auditors of the County of Allegheny, and of the County of Philadelphia.

"They shall on or before the first day of January in every year, make a report in writing to the legislature, of the state of the Penitentiaries.

"This report shall contain the number of prisoners in confinement, their age, sex, place of nativity, time of commitment, term of imprisonment during the preceding year, noticing also those who have escaped or died, or who were pardoned or discharged, designating the offence for which the commitment was made, and whether for a first or repeated offence, and when and in what court, or by whose order; and in such return the inspectors shall make such observations as to the efficiency of the system of solitary confinement as may be the result of their experience, and give such information as they may deem expedient for making the said institution effectual in the punishment and reformation of offenders.

"They shall have power to examine any person upon oath or affirmation relative to any abuse in the said places of confinement, or matter within the purview of their duties; they shall direct in what manner the rations for the subsistence of the prisoners shall be composed, in conformity with the general directions on that subject hereinafter contained.

"The inspectors in their weekly visits to the several places of confinement shall speak to each person confined therein out of the presence of any of the persons employed therein; shall listen to any complaints that may be made of oppression or ill conduct of the persons so employed, examine into the truth thereof, and proceed therein when the complaint is well founded; and on such visits they shall have the calendar of the prisoners furnished to them by the warden, and see by actual inspection whether all the prisoners named in the said calendar are found in the said prison, in the situation in which by the said calendar they are declared to be.

"A majority of the said inspectors shall constitute a board, and may do any of the acts required of the said inspectors; two of the inspectors shall be a quorum for the weekly visitations hereby directed to be made.

"The warden shall not, nor shall any inspector, without the direction of a majority of the inspectors, sell any article for the use of the said Penitentiaries, or either of them, or of the persons confined therein during their confinement, nor derive any emolument from such purchase or sale, nor shall he, or they or either of them, receive under any pretence whatever from either of the said prisoners, or anyone on his behalf, any sum of money, emolument, or reward whatever, or any article of value, as a gratuity or gift, under the penalty of five hundred dollars fine, to be recovered in the name of the commonwealth, by an action of debt, in any court of record thereof, having jurisdiction of sums of that amount.

"Article II

"Of the Duties of the Warden

"The warden shall reside in the Penitentiary; he shall visit every cell and apartment, and see every prisoner under his care at least once in every day; he shall keep a journal, in which shall be regularly entered the reception, discharge, death, pardon, or escape of any prisoner, and also the complaints that are made, and the punishments that are inflicted for the breach of prison discipline, as they occur; the visits of the inspector and the physician, and all other occurrences of note that concern the state of the prison, except the receipt and expenditures, the account of which is to be kept in the manner hereinafter directed.

"The warden shall appoint the under-keepers, who shall be called overseers, and all necessary servants, and dismiss them whenever he thinks proper, or the board of inspectors direct him so to do.

"He shall report all infractions of the rules to the inspectors, and with the approbation of one of them, may punish the offender, in such manner as shall be directed in the rules to be enacted by the inspectors, concerning the treatment of prisoners.

"He shall not absent himself from the Penitentiary for a night without permission in writing from two of the inspectors.

"He shall not be present when the inspectors make their stated visits to the prisoners under his care, unless thereto required by the inspectors.

"ARTICLE III

"Of the Duty of the Overseers

"It shall be the duty of the overseers to inspect the condition of each prisoner at least three times in every day, to see that his meals are regularly delivered, according to the prison allowance, and to superintend the work of the prisoners.

"They shall give immediate notice to the warden or physician whenever any convict shall complain of such illness as to require medical aid.

"Each overseer shall have a certain number of prisoners assigned to his care.

"He shall make a daily report to the warden of the health and conduct of the prisoners, and a like report to the inspectors when required.

"No overseer shall be present when the warden or inspectors visit the prisoners under his particular care, unless thereto required by the warden or inspectors.

"The overseers shall obey all legal orders given by the warden, and all rules established by the board of inspectors, for the government of the prison.

"All orders to the overseers must be given through or by the warden.

"The overseers shall not be absent themselves from the prison, without permission from the warden.

"No overseer shall receive from any one confined in the Penitentiary, or from any one in behalf of such prisoner, any emolument or reward whatever, or the promise of any, either for services or supplies, or as a gratuity, under the penalty of one hundred dollars and imprisonment for thirty days in the county jail; and when any breach of this article shall come to the knowledge of the warden or inspectors, the overseer or overseers so offending shall be immediately discharged from his office, and prosecuted for the said offence according to law.

"No overseer who shall have been discharged for any offence whatever, shall again be employed.

"Article IV

"Of the Duties of the Physician

"The physician shall visit every prisoner in the prison twice in every week, and oftener, if the state of their health require it, and shall report once in every month to the inspectors.

"He shall attend immediately on notice from the warden that any person is sick.

"He shall examine every prisoner that shall be brought into the Penitentiary, before he shall be confined in his cell.

"Whenever, in the opinion of the physician, any convict in the Penitentiary is so ill as to require removal, the warden shall direct such removal to the infirmary of the institution, and the prisoner shall be kept in the infirmary until the physician shall certify that he may be removed without injury to his health, and he shall then be removed to his cell.

"He shall visit the patients in the infirmary at least once in every day, and he shall give such directions for the health and cleanliness of the prisoners, and, when necessary, as to the alteration of their diet, as he may deem expedient, which the warden shall have executed: *Provided,* They shall not be contrary to the provisions of this law, or inconsistent with the safe custody of the said prisoners; and the directions he may give, whether complied with or not, shall be entered on the journal of the warden, and on his own.

"The physician shall inquire into the mental as well as the bodily state of every prisoner, and when he shall have reason to believe that the mind or body is materially affected by the discipline, treatment, or diet, he shall inform the warden thereof, and shall enter his observation on the journal hereinafter directed to be kept, which shall be an authority for the warden for altering the discipline, treatment, or diet of any prisoner, until the next meeting of the inspectors, who shall inquire into the case, and make orders accordingly.

"The physician shall keep a journal, in which, opposite to the name of each prisoner, shall be entered the state of his health, and if sick, whether in the infirmary or not, together with such remarks as he may deem important, which journal shall be open to the inspection of the warden and inspectors, and the same, together with the return provided for in the first article in this section, shall be laid before the inspectors once in every month, or oftener if called for.

"The prisoners under the care of physician, shall be allowed such diet as he shall direct.

"No prisoner shall be discharged while labouring under a dangerous disease, although entitled to his discharge, unless by his own desire.

"The infirmary shall have a suitable partition between every bed, and no two patients shall occupy the same bed; and the physician and his attendants shall take every precaution in their power to prevent all intercourse between the convicts while in the infirmary. . . .

"ARTICLE IX

"Duties of the Religious Instructor

"It shall be the duty of the Instructor to attend to the moral and religious instruction of the convicts, in such manner as to make their confinement, as far as possible, the means of their reformation, so that when restored to their liberty, they may prove honest, industrious and useful members of society; and the inspectors and officers are enjoined to give every facility to the Instructor, in such measure as he may think necessary to produce so desirable a result, not inconsistent with the rules and discipline of the prison." [192]

B. Administrative and Disciplinary Regulations

When the law of 1786 was passed, introducing imprisonment at hard labor as a punishment for crimes earlier punished by death, branding, whipping and mutilation, some elementary provisions were also made for a system of prison discipline which was now rendered necessary. It was directed that the prisoners were to be lodged, clothed and shaved at the expense of the county. They were to have clothing distinguishing them from ordinary citizens and a "visible mark" on their outer garments so that "they may be marked out to the public note as well while at their ordinary occupations as when attempting to make their escapes." [193] An end was put to the showing of special favors to rich convicts. They were no longer to receive clothing, money or other articles of comfort from outside, nor were they henceforth to be allowed to have

---

[192] *Laws of the General Assembly,* 1828-29, pp. 345ff. These provisions for the government of the state penitentiaries were not altered until the passage of the laws of April 17, 1905, and May 23, 1913. Even these acts were minor revisions rather than an abolition of the original act.

[193] *The Statutes at Large of Pennsylvania,* Vol. XII, p. 284.

servants while in prison.[194] An attempt was made to encourage efforts at reformation through the following enactment:

"And in order to encourage those in whom the love of virtue and the shame of vice is not wholly extinguished to set about a sincere and actual repentance and reformation of life and conduct so as at the expiration of their term of servitude they may become useful members of society. . . ."

the court before whom the person was convicted might "at or before the expiration of their servitude" make inquiry into the prison record of the convict and fully pardon those who had given evidence by their conduct of a "sincere repentance." [195] From what is known of the surroundings of the prisoners at this period, it is safe to believe that the judges were rarely called upon to exercise their pardoning power for this purpose, but it is, nevertheless, not without significance that at this early date there was a crude recognition before the law of the principle of commutation of sentence for good behavior—a practice which did not enter American penology generally until after 1860, when it was imported from the Irish prison system of Sir Walter Crofton, mainly through the efforts of Frank B. Sanborn.[196] Not only was good behavior encouraged, but bad conduct was likewise penalized. It was declared that the keepers of the jails shall have "authority to confine in close durance apart from all society all those who shall refuse to labor, be idle or guilty of any trespass, and during such confinement to withhold from them all sustenance except bread and water, and also to put iron yokes around their necks, chains on their leg or legs or otherwise restrain in irons such as shall be incorrigible or irreclaimable without such severity." [197] The horrible dungeons and heavy irons in the Walnut Street Jail insured a proper severity in the execution of this clause.[198]

More detailed administrative and disciplinary regulations were provided in the act of April 5, 1790. It was ordered that,

"All convicts shall at the public expense of the county during their term of confinement be clothed in habits of coarse materials uniform in color and make and distinguishing them from the good citizens of this commonwealth, and the males shall have their heads

---

[194] *The Statutes at Large of Pennsylvania,* Vol. XII, p. 285.
[195] Ibid., pp. 287-88.
[196] Cf. Frank B. Sanborn, *Special Report on Prisons and Prison Discipline,* Made under the Authority of the Massachusetts Board of State Charities, 1865, pp. 16-33.
[197] *The Statutes at Large of Pennsylvania,* Vol. XII, p. 285.
[198] Cf. *The United States Gazette,* October, 1835.

and beards closely shaven at least once a week and all such offenders shall during the said term be sustained upon bread, Indian meal or other inferior food, at the discretion of the said inspectors and shall be allowed one meal of coarse meat in each week, and shall be kept, as far as may be consistent with their age, sex, health and ability to labor of the hardest and most servile kind in which the work is least liable to be spoiled by ignorance, neglect or obstinacy and where the materials are not easily embezzled or destroyed." [199]

No visitors were to be admitted except the inspectors, employed lawyers, ministers of the gospel and others having a written license signed by two inspectors.[200] The keeper was authorized to punish all forms of infractions of prison rules except serious and murderous assaults. The maximum punishment allowed was confinement of two days in the dungeon on bread and water. He was directed to report all more serious offenses to the inspectors. They were empowered to punish serious offenders by repeated whippings of not more than thirteen lashes at one time, by six days in the dungeon on bread and water, or both.[201] As the penalty for escaping or attempting to escape, a prisoner was to receive such additional imprisonment and corporal punishment as the convicting court should direct.[202] A fine of five pounds was to be imposed for taking any "spirituous or fermented liquors" into the jail.[203]

The disciplinary regulations of the act of 1790 were lightened to some degree by the provisions of an act of April 18, 1795. The specifications of the act of 1790 regarding the type of clothing of convicts, the shaving of their heads and their employment at "labor of the hardest and most servile kind" were repealed.[204] Also the infliction of whippings for infractions of prison discipline was no longer to be allowed. The extreme punishment for such offenses was to be confined in the dungeon on a bread and water diet for ten days, for a first offense and for fifteen days for subsequent offenses.[205]

The above acts governed the regulation of the discipline of the Walnut Street Prison until the act of April 23, 1829, made provision for the treatment of convicts in the new state penitentiaries. The regulations with respect to prison discipline contained in this act were of a very general nature and were by no means systematic

---

[199] *The Statutes at Large of Pennsylvania,* Vol. XIII, pp. 516-17.
[200] Ibid., p. 519.
[201] Ibid., pp. 520-21.
[202] Ibid., p. 526.
[203] Ibid., p. 527.
[204] Ibid., Vol. XV, p. 356.
[205] Ibid., p. 356.

and complete. Large authority was vested in the inspectors and nearly all details of discipline were left to be carried out in the rules of government drawn up by the inspectors. The following regulations were all that were specifically provided for in the law of 1829:

"ARTICLE V

"Of the Treatment of the Prisoners in the Penitentiary

"Each convict sentenced to imprisonment in the Penitentiary, shall, immediately after the sentence shall have been finally pronounced, be conveyed, by the sheriff of the county in which he was condemned, to the Penitentiary.

"On the arrival of a convict, immediate notice shall be given to the physician, who shall examine the state of his or her health; he or she shall then be stripped of his or her clothes, and clothed in the uniform of the prison, in the manner hereinafter provided, being first bathed and cleaned.

"He or she shall then be examined by the clerk and the warden, in the presence of as many of the overseers as can conveniently attend, in order to their becoming acquainted with his or her person and countenance, and his or her name, height, apparent and alleged age, place of nativity, trade, complexion, colour of hair and eyes, and length of his or her feet, to be accurately measured, shall be entered in a book provided for that purpose, together with such other natural or accidental marks, or peculiarity of feature or appearance, as may serve to identify him or her, and if the convict can write, his or her signature shall be written under the said description of his or her person.

"All the effects on the person of the convict, as well as his clothes, shall be taken from him or her, and specially mentioned and preserved under the care of the warden, to be restored to him or her on his or her discharge.

"If the convict is not in such ill health as to require being sent to the infirmary, he or she shall then be conducted to the cell assigned to him or her, numerically designated, by which he or she shall thereafter he known during his or her confinement.

"ARTICLE VI

"Of the Clothing and Diet of the Convicts

"The uniform of the prison for males shall be a jacket and trousers of cloth or other warm stuff for the winter, and lighter materials for the summer, the form and colour shall be determined by the inspectors, and two changes of linen shall be furnished to each prisoner every week.

"No prisoner is to receive anything but the prison allowance.

"No tobacco in any form shall be used by the convicts, and any one who shall supply them with it, or with wine or spirituous or intoxicating fermented liquor, unless by order of the physician, shall be fined ten dollars, and if an officer, be dismissed.

"Article VII

"Of Visitors

"No person who is not an official visitor of the prisons, or who has not a written permission according to such rules as the inspector may adopt as aforesaid, shall be allowed to visit the same; the official visitors are the Governor, Speaker and members of the Senate, the Speaker and members of the House of Representatives, the Secretary of the Commonwealth, the Judges of the Supreme Court, the Attorney-General and his Deputies, the President and Associate Judges of all the Courts in the State, the Mayor and Recorder of the cities of Philadelphia, Lancaster and Pittsburg, Commissioners and Sheriffs of the several counties, and the Acting Committee of the Philadelphia Society for the Alleviation of the Miseries of Public Prisons.

"None but the official visitors can have any communication with the convicts, nor shall any visitor whatever be permitted to deliver to or receive from any of the convicts, any letter or message whatever, or to supply them with any article of any kind under the penalty of one hundred dollars fine, to be recovered as herein before provided for other fines imposed by this act.

"Any visitor who shall discover any abuse, infraction of law, or oppression, shall immediately make the same known to the board of inspectors of the commonwealth, if the inspectors or either of them are implicated.

"Article VIII

"Of the Discharge of the Convicts

"Whenever a convict shall be discharged by the expiration of the term for which he or she was condemned, or by pardon, he or she shall take off the prison uniform, and have the clothes which he or she brought to the prison restored to him or her, together with the other property, if any, that was taken from him or her on his or her commitment, that has not been otherwise disposed of.

"When a prisoner is to be discharged, it shall be the duty of the warden to obtain from him or her, as far as is practicable, his or her former history; what means of literary, moral or religious instruction he or she has enjoyed; what early temptations to crime by wicked associations or otherwise he or she was exposed to; his or her general habits, predominant passions, and prevailing vices, and in what part of the country he or she purposes to fix his or her residence; all of which shall be entered by the clerk in a book to be kept for that purpose, together with his or her name, age, and time of discharge.

"If the inspectors and warden have been satisfied with the morality, industry, and order of his conduct, they shall give him a certificate to that effect, and shall furnish the discharged convict with four dollars to be paid by the state, whereby the temptation immediately to commit offences against society, before employment can be obtained, may be obviated." [206]

It will be noted that the specific directions of the law as to the details of prison administration covered only a part of the whole field of prison discipline. Wide latitude was given to the discretion of the inspectors, who, within the general limitations of the system of solitary confinement, were permitted to determine nearly all of the detailed routine of the administrative system.

IV. THE ARCHITECTURAL HISTORY OF THE BEGINNINGS OF THE PENNSYLVANIA PRISON SYSTEM

1. THE WALNUT STREET JAIL

It was pointed out in the previous chapter that the structure at Market, Third and High Streets, which had served as a jail for Philadelphia from 1723 to 1773, was ordered sold by an act of February 25, 1773.[207] The same act provided for the erection of a "new gaol, workhouse and house of correction in the city of Philadelphia." There was erected, accordingly, the noted, and later notorious, Walnut Street Jail, at the corner of Walnut and Sixth Streets and running back to Prune Street.[208] As early as 1776 it had been occupied by prisoners, but was in that year turned over to the new national government to be used as a military prison.[209] When the British captured the city in 1777 they utilized the structure for the same purpose.[210] Finally, by the act of February 28,

---

[206] *Laws of the General Assembly,* 1828-29, pp. 350ff.
[207] *The Statutes at Large of Pennsylvania,* Vol. VIII, pp. 300-04.
[208] Ibid., Vol. X, p. 50. Lownes, op. cit., pp. 9-11.
[209] *Statutes at Large,* IX, pp. 255-57.
[210] J. T. Scharf and T. Westcott, *A History of Philadelphia,* 1884, Vol. III, pp. 1827-32. This work, Vol. III, pp. 1824-38, furnishes the best sketch available of the development of penal institutions in Philadelphia from 1683-1883.

1780, the property at High and Third Streets was disposed of and the Walnut Street Jail became the permanent county and city prison of Philadelphia.[211]

The Walnut Street Jail was built by Robert Smith, a Philadelphia architect, on land purchased from the proprietors.[212] As originally constructed, it was a typical congregate stone prison in which the prisoners were locked in groups of from twenty to fifty in large cells or rooms twenty feet long and eighteen feet wide. Originally it was used to confine criminals, debtors, accused and vagrants. A gradual process of differentiation later took place. The laws of March 27, 1789, and April 5, 1790, provided for moving the debtors from the convicts' department, on the north or Walnut Street end of the structure, to the workhouse on the south or Prune Street end of the plant.[213] The act of 1790 also ordered the erection of a building in the yard containing separate cells for the solitary confinement of the most "hardened and atrocious offenders." [214] The following description by Caleb Lownes, in 1792, furnishes the best account extant of the physical equipment of the Walnut Street Jail after it had received these alterations and had taken on the essential character and form which it retained until its abandonment in 1835:

"PLAN, CONSTRUCTION, &c. OF THE PRISON

"This place of confinement occupies a lot of 400 feet by 200; on which is erected a large stone building, 184 feet long the north side, two stories high, divided into rooms of equal dimensions, viz. 20 by 18 feet; an entry in the middle of 7½ feet wide, which leads to a hall or passage, extending the length of the building 11½ feet wide, with stairs and windows at each end; the upper story is exactly on the same plan as the lower; the cellars are also on the same plan: there are 8 rooms on each floor, all arched, for the twofold purpose of securing against fire and escapes, with two windows in each room. On the east and west end are two wings extending 90 feet south, two stories high, containing five rooms on the floors of each wing, nearly the size of those in front, but with one window, all arched in the same manner also: The ground floors of these were formerly occupied as places of greater security, upon the general principle of dungeons, but have not been used for some time. On the fourth side is a large stone building, designed for a work-house, where the debtors are now confined. Three hundred feet of the north part of the lot is appropriated to the use

[211] *Statutes at Large*, Vol. X, pp. 48-52.
[212] Scharf and Westcott, op. cit., Vol. III, p. 1827.
[213] *The Statutes at Large of Pennsylvania*, Vol. XIII, pp. 244-45, 523.
[214] Ibid., p. 515.

of the convict prison, and one hundred feet of the fourth part to the debtors. The first is divided into portions for the accommodation of the different classes of prisoners. The women have a court-yard of 90 feet by 32; the vagrants, &c. one of the same dimensions. The penitentiary house, or solitary cells, about 160 feet by 80. Each yard is furnished with pumps, baths, sewers and necessaries: Under the debtor's yard, on the north side, runs a natural water course which is arched, and is a great accommodation.

"DISTRIBUTION OF PRISONERS, AND APPROPRIATION OF THE BUILDING, &c.

"The Men Convicts

"For security and air, are lodged on the second floor of the east wing; one room is occupied by the shoe-makers for a shop; one for the taylors and barber—the rest for lodging rooms.

"The Women Convicts

"Are lodged and employed on the first floor, in the west wing, and have the use of the court-yard already described.

"The Women Vagrants

"Have the upper floor of the west wing—and, occasionally, the use of the women convict's yard.

"Men Vagrants

"Occupy the first floor of the east wing, and have the use of the yard before described.

"SOLITARY CELLS OR PENITENTIARY HOUSE

"This building, directed to be built by the Legislature, was early undertaken, and finished with all possible expedition. It is a plain brick building, three stories high; the first floor is paved with bricks, and is open on the north and south; three arches, running the length and breadth of the building, support the rooms and passages of the house. Each floor is divided into 8 cells, 6 by 8, and 9 feet high, and two passages running through the middle; the passages are about 4 feet wide—have a window at one end, which admits light and air, and a stove in the middle to warm the rooms; each cell has a large leaden pipe, which leads to sewers at the bottom, and which are kept clean by smaller pipes, leading from a cistern, into which, occasionally, is conveyed a sufficient quantity of water. The windows are secured by blinds and wire, to prevent conveyances either in or out. The doors and sashes are so constructed as to admit as much air as the prisoner desires.

"The large yard is occupied by the convicts, to labour and to air themselves in. The yard, in which the solitary cells are built, is occupied as a garden, in which vegetables, for culinary and other purposes, are cultivated. It is managed by some of the orderly convicts." [215]

2. THE ARCH STREET PRISON

When the Walnut Street Jail became antiquated and overcrowded, about the beginning of the nineteenth century, a determined effort was made by the prison reformers of Philadelphia to have a new prison plant erected. An act of April 2, 1803, provided for the sale of unimproved lots in Philadelphia, owned by the state, and ordered that the proceeds should be applied to the building of a new prison on Arch Street.[216] About eighty-five thousand dollars was derived from the sale of lots and, on March 31, 1812, twenty-five thousand dollars in addition was appropriated for the completion of the Arch Street Prison with the view to utilizing it for a state penitentiary.[217] The plant was completed in 1816 and opened early in 1817, but was never used as a prison for criminals. From 1817 to 1823 it was used solely for the detention of debtors and witnesses.[218] By the act of February 24, 1823, it was provided that all accused persons, vagrants, fugitives from justice and disorderly apprentices should be transferred from the Prune Street department of the Walnut Street Jail to the Arch Street Prison.[219] In spite of the fact that considerably more than one hundred thousand dollars was spent on the Arch Street Prison it was never regarded as sufficiently safe and well-constructed to be used as a prison. It is obvious that there was a considerable amount of fraud involved in its erection, as there was later in the building of the Eastern Penitentiary.[220] The following description serves to give some comprehension of the nature of the Arch Street plant, which was never really a prison in the conventional sense of the term:

"The main entrance, offices, keeper's residence, kitchens, and wash-rooms were in the centre front, a building of brick, with basement, and high steps, ascending to the principal story. There

---

[215] *An Account of the Alteration and Present State of the Penal Laws of Pennsylvania*, pp. 9-11.
[216] *The Laws of the Commonwealth of Pennsylvania*, Bioren, 1803, pp. 87-8.
[217] Ibid., 1812, p. 370.
[218] *Acts of the General Assembly*, 1815-16, p. 127.
[219] Ibid., 1822-23, pp. 52-3.
[220] Scharf and Westcott, op. cit., pp. 1832-34.

was a second story, crowned with a pediment, above which rose a small cupola, in which was placed a bell. Back of the central building, the prison rooms extended east and west nearly to Broad and Schuylkill Eighth Streets. They were two stories high, with a basement, and ran out to the small street extending east and west, and there at times the friends of prisoners could hold communication with them. The yards for the use of prisoners were at the northeast and northwest angles of the lot. The main central buildings stood a little back from Arch Street, and were thence continued along that street to Broad and Schuylkill Eighth (Fifteenth) and along the latter to the prison buildings, inclosing them on every side. The structure was never competent for the object for which it was erected, as it was weak and insecure." [221]

3.   THE WESTERN STATE PENITENTIARY

As has already been pointed out, the first state penitentiary provided for in law in Pennsylvania was the Western Penitentiary in Allegheny County. On March 3, 1818, an act was passed appropriating sixty thousand dollars for the erection of a state penitentiary in Allegheny County, which was to be constructed according to a plan submitted to the legislature by the inspectors of the Philadelphia prison. No details of that plan were given in the act, though it was specified that the prison was to be constructed on the principle of solitary confinement. [222] It is not fully known as to exactly what previous structures were studied in drawing up this plan. It was drafted by William Strickland, a distinguished Philadelphia architect. The commissioners in charge of the erection of the Western Penitentiary from 1818 to 1826 were James Ross, Walter Lowrie, David Evans and George Stevenson. The superintendent of construction was Stephen Hills. [223] From a knowledge of the plan, according to which the Western Penitentiary was constructed, and of the sources of information which Mr. Strickland must have had at his disposal, one can reconstruct with some confidence the historical antecedents of the plan of the Western Penitentiary. From his connection with the inspectors of the Philadelphia Prison and with the Philadelphia Society for Alleviating the Miseries of Public Prisons, it is certain that Mr. Strickland was familiar with

---

[221] Scharf and Westcott, op. cit., Vol. III, pp. 1832-33. For a brief history of the Arch Street Prison to 1821, see the *Journal of the Senate,* 1820-21, pp. 331-32, 335.

[222] *Acts of the General Assembly,* 1817-18, pp. 138-40.

[223] *Journal of the Twenty-eighth House,* 1817-18, p. 385; *Senate Journal,* 1818-19, pp. 51-2. The last reference gives full details as to the site of the original Western Penitentiary. Richard Vaux in *The Pennsylvania Prison System,* p. 12, erroneously states that the original plant of the Western Penitentiary was designed by John Haviland.

the general arrangement of the prison at Ghent, which was constructed in part on the cellular plan.[224] From the plan, and the wording of one of the appropriating acts, there can be no doubt that he was also influenced to a very considerable degree by Jeremy Bentham's *Panopticon*.[225] The act of March 21, 1821, appropriated sixty thousand dollars so "as to secure and accomplish a full completion of the outward towers, main building, panopticon cells and culvert, with all other necessary conveniences, so as to be suitable for the reception and solitary confinement of convicts." [226] This would indicate the attempt in some degree to imitate Bentham's ambitious project in prison construction. The plan, on the whole, would indicate the influence of both Ghent and the *Panopticon*. The heavy outside walls were octagonal as at Ghent, while the cells were arranged in a circle around a central observation building, as suggested by Bentham.[227] There was only a general resemblance to Bentham's plan, however, for instead of relatively open cells, with the interior readily visible from the observation building, which Bentham had contemplated, light was almost entirely excluded from the cells of the Pittsburg Penitentiary and access could be had to the cells only through thick iron doors hung on walls three feet thick.[228] The Western Penitentiary was designed, completed and opened according to the administrative plan of solitary confinement without labor.[229] It was a massive stone structure, wholly unsuited for any purpose except a fortress. It may readily be doubted that any fort erected in the western part of the state during the Anglo-French and Anglo-American wars in any way approximated the Western Penitentiary with respect to massive and impregnable construction. It was opened in July, 1826, having been built at a cost to that date of $178,206.00 and provided one hundred and ninety cells, eight by twelve feet, for solitary confinement.[230]

[224] Cf. F. H. Wines, *Punishment and Reformation*, pp. 132-36. Hippolyte Vilain, *Mémoire sur les moyens de corriger les malfaiteurs et les fainéants*, passim.
[225] Jeremy Bentham, *Panopticon or the Inspection House*, 1787, 1792; and *Appendices* to the same, 1793-94. Cf. Wines, op. cit., pp. 140-41, W. L. Davidson, *Political Thought in England, the Utilitarians*, pp. 107-13, and Phillipson, op. cit.
[226] *Acts of the General Assembly*, 1820-21, p. 181.
[227] See the plan in the *Report of the Commissioners on the Penal Code*, op. p. 166 and in the *Eleventh Annual Report of the Prison Discipline Society of Boston*, 1836, pp. 84ff.
[228] *Fifth Annual Report of the Prison Discipline Society of Boston*, 1830, p. 34.
[229] *Report of the Commissioners on the Penal Code*, 1828, pp. 38-9.
[230] Ibid. *Acts of the General Assembly*, 1817-18, pp. 138-40; 1820-21, p. 181; 1823-24, pp. 43-4; 1824-25, p. 45; 1825-26, pp. 161-62. *Journal of the Senate of the Commonwealth of Pennsylvania*, 1827-28, p. 145. When fully completed it contained 226 cells.

It was inevitable that the Western Penitentiary would prove a more or less complete failure. After it had been finished on the principle of solitary confinement without labor, the act of April 23, 1829, provided that both of the state penitentiaries should be operated according to the principle of solitary confinement at hard labor.[231] At first it was thought that no radical alteration would have to be made, but a short experience with the plant demonstrated the fact that it was doomed. The cells were too dark and unhealthy to allow continual solitary confinement of prisoners and they were too small to permit the prisoners to work with any facility. The inspectors of the institution presented the hopelessness of the situation in one of their earliest reports:

"It was unfortunate that the building was first put up and the system of punishment afterwards prescribed. There is, perhaps, no trade or occupation at which a convict could work in any of the cells. Independent of the want of room, in a kind of a vault about 7 feet by 9 in the clear, there is not sufficient light, the only supply being what can reach the culprit after passing through the narrow gratings of a heavy iron door, hung on stone jambs 3 feet thick, after passing through an out door, and across a vestibule 6 feet deep. Constant confinement in these cells is found incompatible with the health of the convicts, and we have found it necessary to permit two or three to be out alternately, which gives an opportunity of intercourse to about twenty, that greatly diminishes the benefit of solitary confinement. The inconveniences and difficulties arising out of the construction of the building are to be ascribed to the circumstances, that, by the 3rd section of the act of March, 1818, the Commissioners were directed to construct the Penitentiary upon the plan exhibited to the Legislature by the inspectors of the city and county of Philadelphia." [232]

In view of these conditions it is a cause of no surprise to learn that on February 27, 1833, it was believed necessary to pass an act directing that the cells of the Western Penitentiary be demolished and rebuilt so as to make possible more healthy quarters for the prisoners and to give better facilities for carrying on the industries of the prison in the individual cells. Sixty thousand dollars were appropriated to carry out this alteration, which was planned and supervised by John Haviland, who had drawn up the plans for the Eastern Penitentiary.[233] Few prison structures have had so short

---

[231] *Report of the Commissioners on the Penal Code,* p. 39. *Laws of the General Assembly,* 1828-29, pp. 341-54.

[232] Report cited, in *Fifth Annual Report of the Prison Discipline Society of Boston,* 1830, p. 34. *Journal of the Fortieth House of Representatives of Pennsylvania,* 1829-30, pp. 634-35.

[233] *Laws of the General Assembly,* 1832-33, p. 55.

and unsuccessful an existence as the Western Penitentiary in its original form.[234]

4. THE EASTERN STATE PENITENTIARY

Far different has been the architectural history of the Eastern Penitentiary, which has been in continual use since 1829, with only minor architectural changes. Pursuant to the act of March 20, 1821, authorizing the construction of the Eastern Penitentiary, a board of eleven commissioners was appointed to purchase a site, select a plan and superintend the construction of the new penitentiary. As finally constituted on December 12, 1821, the board was composed of the following persons: John Bacon, George A. Baker, Thomas Bradford, Jr., Caleb Carmault, Peter Miercken, Daniel H. Miller, Coleman Sellers, Thomas Sparks, James Thackera, Roberts Vaux and Samuel R. Wood.[235] A site of ten acres was purchased for eleven thousand five hundred dollars from the Messrs. Warner. It was located in what was then the outskirts of Philadelphia and, as it had been used as a cherry orchard by its former owners, the site came to be known as "Cherry Hill." From this fact the new penitentiary was conventionally known for years as the "Cherry Hill Penitentiary."[236] The commissioners proceeded to call for plans for the new prison structure and designs were submitted by Charles Loss, Jr., of New York, and by William Strickland, Samuel Webb and John Haviland of Philadelphia. Haviland's plan was selected as that according to which the penitentiary should be constructed.[237]

Assured and final knowledge does not exist as to how far Mr. Haviland's design in this case was a product of his own ingenuity and how far it was consciously modeled after other structures with which he must have been familiar. In its most general aspects Mr. Haviland's plan embraced a combination of the radiating wings

---

[234] For complaints with respect to its ill-planned construction, see *Journal of the Thirty-Seventh House*, 1826-27, Vol. II, pp. 33-5, 331. Ibid., Fortieth House, pp. 634-41. *Journal of the Senate*, 1831-32, Vol. II, pp. 451-55.

[235] Richard Vaux, *A Brief Sketch of the Eastern Penitentiary*, pp. 53-6. *Report of the Commissioners on the Penal Code*, 1828, p. 184.

[236] Richard Vaux, op. cit., pp. 54-5.

[237] Ibid. John Haviland (1793-1852) was probably the most noted architect in the history of penology. He was born in England. In 1815 he met some American engineers while traveling in Russia and was induced by them to come to America. He built the Eastern Penitentiary, the second Western Penitentiary, the New Jersey State Prison at Trenton, the Rhode Island Penitentiary, and many county jails in Pennsylvania and adjoining states. With him was associated Edward Haviland.

or cell-blocks of the Ghent Prison and the central corridor and outside cells of the papal prison of San Michele in Rome. Both of these structures are described with appended drawings in Howard's works, which were at the disposal of, and were doubtless consulted by, Mr. Haviland.[238] Doctor F. H. Wines is convinced that the Ghent Prison was the determining factor in the plan of the Eastern Penitentiary as submitted by Haviland.[239] While there may have been an abject dependence upon these European models, and Mr. Haviland may simply have made minor changes in adapting them to the principles of the Pennsylvania system, there is no reason for assuming that this must have been the case. The possibilities in the construction of the conventional prison plant are so limited that any original architect might well have arrived at the plan of the Eastern Penitentiary in an independent manner. The three possibilities in the general design of the conventional prison are: circular arrangement of the cells, as suggested in the *Panopticon* and carried into execution in the Pittsburg penitentiary; large blocks of inside cells, as in the Auburn Prison; or radiating wings, as at Philadelphia. The cell arrangement is still further limited in its possibilities of variation. There may be outside cells with a central corridor or inside cells with an outside corridor.[240] In view of this principle of "limited possibilities," there is no reason for refusing Mr. Haviland a considerable amount of credit for originality in his design.

The plan of the building, as finally executed, consisted of seven long wings of outside cells radiating from a central office and observation building. Mr. Haviland stated in his description and defense of his plan that this design was selected on account of the superior facilities for observation and ventilation which it presented.[241] The construction was arranged to allow for strict solitary confinement. Each cell was twelve feet long, eight feet wide and ten feet high and was provided with an unroofed exercising yard eighteen feet long.[242] The structure, while not so forbidding in its massive gloominess as the Pittsburg penitentiary, was a heavy solid building intended to strike terror into the minds of offenders and to deter them from the commission of crime. A contemporary and warm supporter of the plan of the new penitentiary thus describes this aspect of its design:

---

[238] F. H. Wines, *Punishment and Reformation,* pp. 132-38.
[239] Ibid., p. 141.
[240] Ibid., pp. 132-49.
[241] *A Description of the Plan for a New Penitentiary,* by John Haviland, Philadelphia, 1824, pp. 3-4.
[242] Ibid., p. 4. See also Richard Vaux, *Brief Sketch,* pp. 69-70.

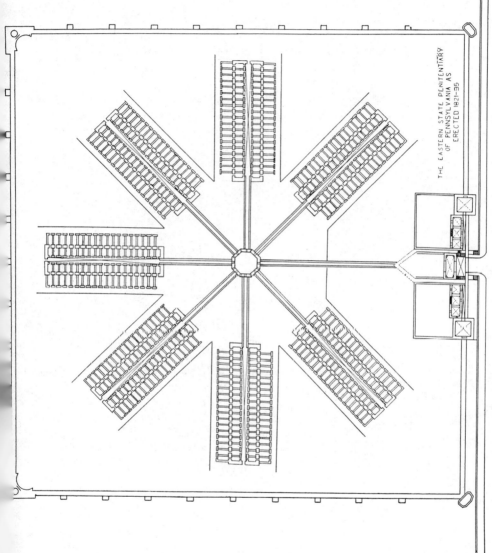

THE EASTERN STATE PENITENTIARY OF PENNSYLVANIA AS ERECTED 1821–35

GROUND PLAN OF THE EASTERN STATE PENITENTIARY, 1829

"Large sums have been expended for the purpose of giving an unusual degree of solidity and durability to every part of this immense structure, which is the most extensive building in the United States. . . . The material with which the edifices are built is a greyish granite, or gneiss, employed in large masses; every room is vaulted and fire-proof. The design and execution impart a grave, severe, and awful character to the external aspect of this building. The effect which it produces on the imagination of every passing spectator is particularly impressive, solemn and instructive." [243]

That a romantic desire to reproduce the architecture of the Middle Ages was quite as important in the design, as it was to find a plan for a conveniently administered structure, is apparent in the following comment by the above authority:

"This penitentiary is the only edifice in this country which is calculated to convey to our citizens the external appearance of those magnificent and picturesque castles of the middles ages, which contribute so eminently to embellish the scenery of Europe." [244]

It has been customary to praise Mr. Haviland for his part in contributing to the evolution of prison architecture. In so far as he powerfully aided the movement for the elimination of the demoralizing congregate prisons that had been common before 1820, the praise is not unmerited. On the other hand, he can scarcely be too much condemned for his influence in fixing the gloomy castle architecture, with its massive, dark and unhealthy construction, upon the prison systems of the United States and Europe. It is probable that no one was more influential in this than Mr. Haviland, and he grew more confirmed in this bent as he grew older. When he was employed ten years later as head architect for a new state prison in New Jersey, even the medieval castle architecture had become too light and airy to suit his taste and he based this structure upon the design of an Egyptian temple.[245] The following extracts from Mr. Haviland's description of his plan furnish a good conception of the chief features of the arrangement and construction of the Eastern Penitentiary:

"These seven blocks of cells which form the body of the design are of the most simple form, being parallelograms which by their disposition possess all the advantages of a polygon figure without

---

[243] George Washington Smith, description reproduced in Richard Vaux, *Brief Sketch*, p. 56.

[244] Richard Vaux, *Brief Sketch*, p. 56.

[245] Mr. Haviland's style of architecture not only determined the arrangement of the Eastern Penitentiary, but also that of the county jails built in Pennsylvania during this period.

the expense attending it. Each building contains 38 cells, twelve feet long, eight feet wide, and ten feet high, with an exercising yard eighteen feet to each. The partition walls between the cells are calculated to be 18 inches in thickness, and their foundation three feet deep; the wall next to the passage is of similar thickness and depth; the exterior wall to be 2 feet 3 inches thick and 4 feet below the level of the yard; in each cell there is a floor of masonry 18 inches in thickness, on which is proposed to be laid long curb-stones, ten inches thick, that extend the whole width of the cells and terminating under the partition wall, which would effectually prevent escape by excavation. The windows are inserted in the barrelled ceiling, and formed by a convex reflector of 8 inches diameter, termed *dead eyes;* This would be found to give ample light to the cells, from a position the best for ventilation and the admission of light, and a desirable one from its being out of the reach of the prisoners climbing up to escape, or to converse from one cell to that of another; this glass is hung up at the apex of a cast iron cone that is securely fixed in the solid masonry of the ceiling, and would be found a cheap and excellent window. A simple bed is provided, that is proposed to be hung against the wall to which it is made to button in the day time, with the bedding enclosed in it, out of the way. It will be understood that the wall next to the passage contains, annexed to each cell, a feeding drawer and peep-hole; the drawer is of cast iron, six inches deep and sixteen inches wide, projecting of sufficient depth into the cell to form, when closed, a table of twelve inches from the surface of the wall on the inside, from which the prisoner will eat his meals. This drawer on the back is intended to be made with a *stop,* that when drawn out by the Keeper in the passage, for the purpose of deposit-ing food, or raiment, closes the aperture behind, and consequently prevents the prisoner seeing the superintendent, or receiving by this opportunity anything but what is intended for him. By this means all the conveniences of a door are embraced, with more security and privacy, and at a considerable less expense than by the introduction of one, which would facilitate the evil of the prisoners conversing from one door to another, and defeat in a great measure the object of solitary confinement.

"A hollow cone of cast iron is fixed securely in the wall, with its apex next the passage, from which small aperture of one-fourth of an inch in diameter, you can command a view of the cell unob-served by the prisoner; a stopper is slid over this peep-hole, and fixed on the outside, so that no person can make use of it but the superintendent. . . .

"A covered way is introduced from each radiating building of cells to the center, for the convenience of superintending the pris-oners, and conveying their food in bad weather; this cheap screen is covered with a shingled roof, and enclosed by weather-boarded sides, in which are inserted windows, and finished with a floor, as may be seen by a reference to the drawings.

"The center building forms a cover for the reservoir; its basement is a general watch-house, and the room over it is a chamber for the accommodation of the under-keepers and watchmen; at the outside of the building on a level with this floor, a platform is designed for the purpose already described, a bell is hung in the roof for the watchmen and domestic purposes of the institution.

"It is of the first importance in a building of this nature that it should be conveniently and securely watched: to effect this the observatory and alarm bell should be in the power of the keeper, commanding the whole prison, and particularly the entrance which should be confined to one aperture—this has been happily effected in the front building, to promote it, the internal buildings of the prison have been as few as possible, and placed so as not to obstruct the sight from the observatory. . . .

"On viewing the elevation of the principal front, it will be seen with what success the designer has attempted to unite a simplicity of style, with that character the nature of the building required, assisted by the walls on each side of the center. The whole front externally has the appearance of an extensive and solid edifice. By this means I have been enabled to give a just and proportional effect to the whole front, that would otherwise look mean, and unfinished without it. . . .

"The exterior wall is estimated at thiry feet high from the level of the ground on the inside, and covered with an inclined coping that projects on the inside four feet, that will frustrate any attempt to climb over it. This wall encloses an area of 650 feet square, in which the cells are disposed." [246]

The act of March 20, 1821, ordered the construction of only two hundred and fifty cells, but this number was increased by an act of March 28, 1831, which provided that,

"The Inspectors of the State Penitentiary for the Eastern District in the County of Philadelphia hereby are authorized and required to construct and erect within the outer walls of the said Penitentiary upon such a plan as they may deem most expedient, buildings which shall contain at least four hundred cells, suitable for the confinement of convicted criminals, in solitary imprisonment, at labor." [247]

The total cost of the structure in its original form, as completed in 1835, was above seven hundred and seventy-five thousand dol-

---

[246] *A Description of the Plan for a New Penitentiary*, by John Haviland, Philadelphia, 1824, 12 pp. passim. See the frontispiece.
[247] *Laws of the General Assembly*, 1830-31, pp. 220-22.

lars.[248] In the legislative investigation of the conduct of the prison officials in 1835 charges were made that there had been serious fraud in the construction of the Eastern Penitentiary, one member of the legislature stating that the work, if done by contract, would not have cost more than half of the actual sum expended.[249] Whether the charges be true or not, it is certain that it was a very expensive structure for the time and that it was much the most elaborate penitentiary plant which had yet been erected in the world. It excited the admiration of visitors from all parts of the United States and Europe and furnished a fitting architectural setting for the famous system of prison discipline which was tried out within its walls.[250]

V.   DEVELOPMENT OF THE ADMINISTRATIVE AND DISCIPLINARY ASPECTS OF THE PENNSYL-VANIA SYSTEM FROM 1776 TO 1835

1.   The Walnut Street Jail

It is scarcely accurate to use the terms "administration" or "discipline" in describing the condition of the Walnut Street Jail before 1786, if not before 1790. With an indiscriminate herding of debtors, criminals, witnesses, vagrants and servants of all ages and sexes;

---

[248]The following were the amounts appropriated for its construction by the legislature from 1821 to 1835:

March 20, 1821	$100,000
March 15, 1824	80,000
March 1, 1825	60,000
March 15, 1826	89,124
April 9, 1827	1,000
April 14, 1828	4,000
April 23, 1829	5,000
April 3, 1830	4,000
March 28, 1831	120,000
February 27, 1833	130,000
April 15, 1834	20,000
April 14, 1835	60,000
Sale of city lots	99,476
Total	$772,600

See Richard Vaux, *Brief Sketch of the Eastern Penitentiary*, p. 63.

[249] *A Concise History of the Eastern Penitentiary of Pennsylvania, together with a Detailed Statement of the Proceedings of the Committee Appointed by the Legislature,* December 6, 1834, by a Member of the Legislature, Philadelphia, 1835, pp. 10-1.

[250] It seems that one of the chief causes for the failure of the structures modeled after the Eastern Penitentiary was that they failed to build the indispensable exercising yards connected with the cells. This was certainly the case with the New Jersey prison erected in 1833-36.

with no attempt to restrain inmates beyond the point of preventing murder—and this not always successful; and with the possibility of obtaining as much liquor as the convict could purchase, either from without or at the bar in the prison, it is highly apparent that such a thing as "prison discipline" could not well have existed. About all that was achieved in prison administration was to prevent the inmates from escaping at will; in other words, the administrative interest centered mainly in preserving a well-guarded periphery to the institution rather than in securing any degree of reformative discipline of inmates. Even this elementary function was scarcely fulfilled, as contemporaries speak of "breaches of the prison wall" and resulting escapes which were "most numerous and alarming."

It was little wonder, then, that the respectable citizens of Philadelphia should have become awakened to the necessity of remedying this indescribable situation and secured the passage of the act of September 15, 1786, which proposed to bring about reform by putting the convicts to work on the streets or in "shops" in the jail. Laudable as were the intentions of the framers of the law, its results were not gratifying, though it seems that the real cause for its failure was the disorderly conduct of bystanders rather than the lack of wisdom in the provisions of the act.[251] Caleb Lownes, an eminent contemporary and one of the promoters of the act of 1786, thus describes its unfortunate operation:

"The directions of the law of 1786, literally complied with, were soon found to be productive of the greatest evils, and had a very opposite effect from that which was contemplated by the framers of the law. The disorders in society, the robberies, burglaries, breaches of the prison, alarms in town and country—the drunkenness, profanity and indecencies of the prisoners in the streets, must be in the memory of most. With these disorders, the number of criminals increased to such a degree, as to alarm the community with fears, that it would be impossible to find a place, either large or strong enough to hold them. The severity of the law and the disgraceful manner of executing it, led to a proportionate degree of depravity and insensibility, and every spark of morality appeared to be destroyed. The keepers were armed with swords, blunderbusses, and other weapons of destruction. The prisoners, secured by cumberous iron collars and chains fixed to bomb shells. Their dress was formed with every mark of disgrace. The old and hardened offender daily in the practice of begging, and insulting the inhabitants—collecting crowds of idle boys and holding them with the most indecent and improper conversation. Thus disgrace-

---

[251] Roberts Vaux, *Notices of the Original and Successive Attempts to Improve the Discipline of the Prison at Philadelphia,* pp. 21-2.

fully treated, and heated with liquor, they meditated and executed plans of escape—and, when at liberty, their distress, disgrace, and fears, prompted them to violent acts to satisfy the immediate demands of nature. Their attacks upon society were known to be desperate and to some they proved fatal." [252]

The condition of the prisoners within the walls was not less distressing than was that of those who were employed on the streets, and the latter, of course, were driven back into the jail structure at night. Contemporary reports reveal the fact that the Walnut Street Jail was at this time nothing more or less than a combined saloon and house of prostitution of the most vicious type. Drink of all sorts was sold at the jail bar and many prostitutes secured their own arrest upon fictitious charges in order that they might ply their trade among the inmates of the jail.[253] The situation of the jail at this time is well summarized in the following paragraph:

"The discipline of the prison was not less remarkably deficient in wisdom and humanity. It will hardly be credited, that so recently as the year 1788, the prison of Philadelphia presented the spectacle of the confinement of debtors with criminals, of honest poverty with the most vile and revolting of crimes, and the indiscriminate intercourse both by day and night of women and men, whether debtors or convicts. Nor was this all; spirituous liquors were sold at a bar, inside of the wall, to all its inmates, and produced, as might be expected, scenes of profligacy and impurity disgraceful to the city of Penn." [254]

The acts of March 27, 1789, and April 5, 1790, ordering a separation of debtors from criminals, a segregation of the sexes, some beginnings of the classification and differentiated treatment of criminals, the prohibition of the use of alcholic liquors within the jail, and the provision of reformative disciplinary regulations by the inspectors, were designed to remove and correct the evils of penal administration as they had existed up to that time.[255]

There are few situations in the history of penal institutions in which all authorities are in so complete agreement as they are with respect to the remarkable transformation wrought in the

[252] Caleb Lownes, *An Account of the Alteration and Present State of the Penal Laws of Pennsylvania*, pp. 5-6.

[253] See the *Memorial of the Philadelphia Society for Alleviating the Miseries of Public Prisons*, 1788, quoted above, pp. 87ff. Lownes, pp. 6-8.

[254] *Report of the Commissioners on the Penal Code*, 1828, p. 13.

[255] *The Statutes at Large of Pennsylvania*, Vol. XIII, pp. 243ff., 511ff.

administration of the Walnut Street Jail by the laws of 1789-90.[256] Caleb Lownes, one of the leaders in the reform movement, states that the essence of the new system was "mild regulations strictly enjoined." [257] It seems that most of the old barbarities were abolished and a wholly new administrative system was introduced which would do credit to many a modern prison. The provisions of the law with respect to classification, segregation, solitary confinement and prohibition of alcoholics have already been described in another place, and attention will be devoted at this point solely to those progressive disciplinary regulations which were devised by the inspectors, most of whom were members of the Philadelphia Society for Alleviating the Miseries of Public Prisons. Caleb Lownes' valuable sketch, written in 1792, just at the time that the new system was thoroughly established and working successfully, constitutes one of the best sources available on the salutary effect of the new system of discipline and administration established after 1790.

The old system of partial starvation for those who could not afford to pay the jail fees and of surfeit and luxury for the rich convicts, was done away with and an ample diet of "coarse and inferior" food was provided for all.[258] An equally beneficial reform

---

[256] Lownes, op. cit., pp. 13ff.; Bradford, *Enquiry*, pp. 20ff.; Roberts Vaux, *Notices*, pp. 32ff.; *Sketch of the Principal Transactions of the Philadelphia Society for Alleviating the Miseries of Public Prisons*, pp. 8ff.; *A Statistical View of the Operation of the Penal Code of Pennsylvania*, 1817, pp. 4ff.; *Report of the Commissioners on the Penal Code*, 1828, pp. 13ff. Robert J. Turnbull, *A Visit to the Philadelphia Prison; Being an Accurate and Particular Account of the Wise and Humane Administration Adopted in Every Part of that Building; Containing also an Account of the Gradual Reformation, and Present Improved State, of the Penal Laws of Pennsylvania*, Philadelphia, 1796.

[257] Lownes, op. cit., p. 12.

[258] Mr. Lownes thus describes the new dietary regulations:
"Sunday—one pound of bread, and one pound of coarse meat made into broth;
Monday—one pound of bread and one quart of potatoes;
Tuesday—one quart of Indian meal made into mush;
Wednesday—one pound of bread and one quart of potatoes;
Thursday—one quart of Indian meal made into mush;
Friday—one pound of bread and one quart of potatoes;
Saturday—one quart of Indian meal made into mush;
A half-pint of molasses to every four prisoners on Tuesday, Thursday and Saturday." pp. 32-3.
"No provisions are allowed besides the prison allowance, except the more laborious part, while orderlies, who are allowed to get some of the heads of sheep from the butchers, at their own expense: this is esteemed an indulgence, and is attended with good effects, both physical and moral. Molasses are experienced to be very salutary to the health of the prisoners, as well as useful in gratifying them with a small luxury. The orderly women are sometimes indulged with tea." p. 14.
The seeming simplicity and monotony of the above diet should not be contrasted with the present-day variety, but with the conventional diet of 1790.

was effected with regard to the clothing of inmates of the jail. Until 1790 they had been covered solely by their own clothing. Contemporary reports indicate that many suffered severely for want of clothing and, when aided by outside gifts, were in the habit of trading the clothing for drink at the bar of the jail.[259] The notorious abuse of "garnish," which prevailed until the establishment of the new system, in 1790, compelled newly admitted prisoners to surrender most of their clothing to the inmates to be given for drink.[260] The abuses growing out of the selling of liquor in the jail were now abolished, and with them the suffering that grew out of the lack of adequate clothing. The inmates were clothed in coarse but comfortable clothing made chiefly by prison labor—a beginning of the "state use" system.[261] The lodging regulations were also greatly improved. Instead of the old practice of sleeping on the floor or on piles of vermin-infested straw, beds and bedding were provided for the first time in the history of Pennsylvania penal institutions.[262]

Besides these physical improvements, other significant advances were made. A physician was engaged to visit the prison at least once each week, and more often, if necessary.[263] Regular Sunday preaching services were held and the convicts were compelled to attend the services in a body.[264] Industry was stimulated by allowing the prisoners the excess product of their labors over and above the cost of maintenance. In some cases this excess had amounted to ten pounds in one year.[265] But the most interesting of all innovations was the modest beginning of a system of rewards and punishments

---

[259] Roberts Vaux, *Notices,* pp. 25-8.

[260] Lownes, op. cit., p. 8. Roberts Vaux, *Notices,* p. 28.

[261] Mr. Lownes describes the clothing provisions in the following manner: "The men are clothed in woolen jackets, waistcoats, and trousers in winter, and linen in summer, shirts, shoes, &c. The orderly prisoners, who by their industry earn a sufficiency for the purpose, are allowed a better suit to attend public worship. The principal objects in their cloathing are usefulness, economy, and decency.

"The women are dressed in plain, short gowns, of woolen in winter, and linen in summer. Most of the cloathing, at present, is spun, wove, and made up in the house, and is designed to be altogether in the future." p. 14.

[262] The following were the chief improvements in lodging facilities: "The prisoners are lodged in beds, with sheets and blankets on bedsteads; the beds are filled with red cedar shavings. We have found this regulation greatly conducive to cleanliness and decency. The former practice of prisoners sleeping in their cloaths, and being crowded together, without any regard to decency, was destructive to the health of the prisoners, and was attended with many other ill consequences, especially where men are collected in the manner they are in prisons." p. 14.

[263] Lownes, op. cit., p. 16.

[264] Ibid., pp. 16-7.

[265] Ibid., pp. 14-5, 20.

for behavior in the prison. The extra allowances of food, clothing and income to industrious and orderly convicts have already been mentioned. In addition to this stimulation of good conduct, an elementary beginning was made toward a system of commutation of sentence for good behavior. Mr. Lownes gives the following description of this early experiment in progressive prison discipline:

"When the present plan was at last attempted, the prisoners were informed that the new system was now to be carried into full effect—that their treatment would depend upon their conduct; and that those who evidenced a disposition that would afford encouragement to the inspectors to believe that they might be restored to their liberty, should be recommended to the governor for a pardon, as soon as circumstances would admit; but if they were convicted again, the law, in its fullest rigour, would be carried into effect against them. A change of conduct was early visible. They were encouraged to labour, and a number were employed at carrying stone, and other laborious work, as the building of the solitary cells. Their good conduct was remarkable. Many were pardoned, and before one year was expired, their behaviour was, almost without exception, decent, orderly, and respectful. This fact is of importance, as it disproves an opinion, that has led to much distress and cruelty, and will, I hope, be an encouragement to those who can feel for this unhappy class of mankind, who have so long been victims to the sad effects of a contrary treatment." [266]

The system inaugurated seems at first to have had a remarkable reformatory and deterrent effect. It is stated that, out of two hundred convicts pardoned for good behavior, only four were returned for reconviction.[267] In two years after the installation of the new system there were only two convictions of burglary and picking pockets in the city of Philadelphia and the number accused of the commission of crimes steadily diminished.[268] The general success of the experiment is well summarized in the following paragraph:

"Such were the means then in the power of the Inspectors, of executing the system in its spirit and design, with the aid of extensive accommodations, and sufficient and suitable labor, that the rooms in the prison, and the prison yard, afforded convenient and ample room for the separation and employment of the convicts; and

---

[266] Lownes, op. cit., p. 13. It can be held with a large degree of accuracy that it required at least a century more for the American prison system to advance far beyond the level of the system of administration established in Philadelphia in 1790.

[267] *A Statistical View of the Operation of the Penal Code of Pennsylvania,* 1817, p. 4.

[268] Ibid.

finally so productive was their labor, that when discharged, considerable balances were found in favor of some, and but few, who had not more or less; that these balances often exceeded ten pounds, and that some of the prisoners appropriated part of their earnings to the support of their families. Such at that time was the happy effect of the system when properly executed." [269]

The most detailed account of the results of this period of reform following 1790 is contained in the account by Robert J. Turnbull of the observations of his visit to the Walnut Street Jail in 1796. He quite agreed with the flattering account given by Caleb Lownes. He found that the inmates were for the most part profitably employed in making cut nails, sawing marble and cutting stone. Their application to these tasks impressed Mr. Turnbull to the extent of his declaring that, "In short, there was such a spirit of industry visible on every side, and such contentment pervaded the countenances of all, that it was with difficulty I divested myself of the idea, that these men surely were not convicts, but accustomed to labor from their infancy." [270] The prisoners were charged for maintenance at the daily rate of one shilling three pence for males and seven pence for females, but were able to earn from two shillings upward. [271] He praised very highly the spotless cleanliness of the institution. [272] A common dining-room was provided for the convicts. [273] There was even introduced the relatively modern practice of making a study of the personal history and criminal record of each prisoner at entry. [274] His description of the nature and administration of the "solitary" department of the institution is especially complete and valuable. There was no work provided for the convicts in the solitary cells. Those sentenced to "solitary confinement at hard labor" were first put in solitary cells with no labor and then later set to work with the other convicts in the congregate workships or in the yard. No furniture of any sort was put in any of the solitary cells and food was brought to the occupants but once each day, in order "that the criminal may be prevented from seeing any person as much as possible." These cells were used chiefly for the worst type of criminals and for violators of the prison rules. There was but one small window

---

[269] *A Statistical View of the Operation of the Penal Code of Pennsylvania,* 1817, pp. 4-5. Cf. *Report of the Commissioners on the Penal Code,* 1828, pp. 14ff.
[270] Robert J. Turnbull, *A Visit to the Philadelphia Prison,* etc., Philadelphia, 1796, p. 6.
[271] Ibid., p. 24.
[272] Ibid., pp. 29-30.
[273] Ibid., pp. 41-2.
[274] Ibid., pp. 49-50.

in each cell and this was arranged, by a series of slanting shutters, so that the inmate "could perceive neither heaven nor earth." [275] So excellent was the discipline among all convicts that the officers exhibited an evident concern lest the convicts be corrupted by over-hearing the profanity of the debtors in their adjoining apartment. No conversation was allowed at any time among any convicts.[276]

As has been the case with so many other promising innovations and experiments in prison reform, the history of the reform movement inaugurated in 1790 is the story of a brilliant success of a bold and original plan in the early years of its operation, and the subsequent progressive deterioration of the system, through the failure of the public authorities to provide the means for continuing the experiment with the same favorable surroundings with which it began. There is general unanimity among contemporary authorities that the main cause for the decline and failure of the promising system of administration installed in the Walnut Street Jail was the overcrowding of that structure and the criminal negligence and procrastination of the state in failing to provide adequate quarters for the increasing delinquent population. The Walnut Street Jail was built according to the needs of the county and city of Philadelphia in 1773.[277] Only slight additions were made following 1790 to adapt it for use as the state prison for the more serious criminals, as well as remaining the county jail for Philadelphia.[278] While these extensions of its capacity were adequate for the delinquent population immediately after 1790, the rapid immigration into the western part of the state at the beginning of the national period made the structure sadly inadequate by 1800.[279] Vigorous efforts on the part of the Philadelphia Society for Alleviating the Miseries of Public Prisons secured the passage of the act of April 2, 1803, ordering the erection of a new prison on Arch Street;[280] but, as has already been pointed out, this was not opened until 1817, and then only as a place of detention for debtors and witnesses.[281] As a result, all systematic discipline and administration was literally crowded out of the Walnut Street Jail. In 1816 no additions had been made to the Walnut Street structure since 1795, while the number of prisoners sentenced to imprisonment in it in 1815 was two hundred and twenty-five, as compared to seventy-

---

[275] Turnbull, op. cit., pp. 55-8.
[276] Ibid., pp. 29, 64.
[277] *The Statutes at Large of Pennsylvania,* Vol. VIII, pp. 300-04.
[278] Caleb Lownes, op. cit., pp. 9-11.
[279] Roberts Vaux, *Notices,* pp. 35-9.
[280] *Laws of the Commonwealth of Pennsylvania,* Bioren, 1803, pp. 87-8.
[281] Scharf and Westcott, op. cit., pp. 1832-34. *Journal of Prison Discipline and Philanthropy,* 1845, p. 7.

two in 1795.[282] This overcrowding, of course, had a cumulative effect in demoralizing the prison discipline. The lack of space in the jail rendered the proper application of the administrative systems impossible and thereby prevented it from exercising its proper reformatory and deterrent functions. This failure, of course, resulted in a greater crowding of the prison through more frequent convictions, and this, in turn, reacted further to demoralize the disciplinary system. As a result of these unfortunate conditions, by 1816 the Walnut Street Jail had returned to about the same level of disciplinary and administrative demoralization that had characterized it before 1790. The only sense in which it was in a better condition in 1816 was that the sexes were now separated, the debtors were removed from the criminals, and spirituous liquors were legally excluded from the jail. The Philadelphia Society for Alleviating the Miseries of Public Prisons thus briefly summarizes the situation as it existed in 1816:

"So many are thus crowded together in so small a space, and so much intermixed, the innocent with the guilty, the young offender and often the disobedient servant or apprentice, with the most experienced and hardened culprit; that the institution already begins to assume, especially as respects untried prisoners, the character of a European prison, and a seminary for every vice, in which the unfortunate being, who commits a first offence, and knows none of the arts of methodized villainy, can scarcely avoid the contamination which leads to extreme depravity, and with which from the insufficiency of the room to form separate accommodations, he must be associated in this confinement." [283]

Another abuse, which both grew out of, and contributed to, the overcrowding of the prison, was the excessive amount of pardoning of convicts after 1800. While the situation was scarcely so bad as it was in New York State, where, from 1812 to 1817, seven hundred and forty of the inmates of the Newgate Prison had been pardoned and seventy-seven served out their sentences,[284] it was serious enough to attract the condemnation of contemporary reform agencies. Doctor James Mease stated in 1828 that from 1799 to 1817 no less than 2,196 convicts had been pardoned in Pennsylvania,

---

[282] *Statistical View of the Operation of the Penal Code*, pp. 5, 13. Cf. James Mease, *Observations on the Penitentiary System and Penal Code of Pennsylvania with Suggestions for their Improvement*, Philadelphia, 1826, pp. 6ff.
[283] *A Statistical View of the Operation of the Penal Code of Pennsylvania*, 1817, pp. 5-6.
[284] J. L. Sullivan, *Note on the Penitentiary System of New York State*, loc. cit.

while the total number sent to the Walnut Street Jail from 1790 to 1816 had been only 2,490.[285] This evil was especially emphasized by the commissioners appointed in 1826 to revise the criminal code. After pointing out the fact "that the flagrant evils of the Philadelphia prison are referrible to the communication which takes place between the convicts by day and night," they stated:

"Other causes have also operated to produce the same result. Among the principal of which is the frequency of pardons, and the system upon which they have of late years been recommended and obtained. The enormous increase in the number of convicts, and the insufficiency of the prison accommodations have, we understand, reduced the inspectors to the necessity of applying, annually, for the pardon of a number of the convicts, to make room for others; and by this means it has happened that the average term of imprisonment actually passed, has been far below the amount inflicted by the sentence of the courts. The operation of a state of things like this, could not be otherwise than mischievous. The frequent changes in the persons of the inhabitants, the occasional enlargement of the most vicious, the abbreviation of the term of punishment of all, would probably, if the discipline of the prison were in other respects perfect, lead to the results we have mentioned; and which have caused the prison of Philadelphia to forfeit the high character it once possessed, and to become a reproach to the city in which it is located, and to the state by whom it ought to be superintended." [286]

After 1816 the condition of the Walnut Street Jail grew even more demoralized and inefficient than before. The only agency making for its improvement—the Philadelphia Society for Alleviating the Miseries of Public Prisons—became convinced that it was hopeless to attempt to effect a permanent reformation of the old prison and it bent all its energies to the establishment and construction of the new state penitentiaries between 1818 and 1829.[287] As a consequence, it is not surprising to learn that in addition to minor abuses, serious riots took place in the prison in 1817, 1819, 1820 and 1821. The outbreak of 1820 came dangerously close to resulting in the escape of the entire convict population.[288] The labors of the Philadelphia Society for Alleviating the Miseries of Public Prisons in condemning the Walnut Street Jail and in securing the

---

[285] James Mease, *Observations on the Penitentiary System and Penal Code of Pennsylvania, with Suggestions for their Improvement,* Philadelphia, 1828, pp. 10-3.
[286] *Report of the Commissioners on the Penal Code,* 1828, pp. 18-9.
[287] Roberts Vaux, *Notices,* pp. 41-6. *Sketches of Principal Transactions,* pp. 11-3.
[288] Scharf and Westcott, pp. 1830-31. Watson, *Annals,* Vol. III, pp. 180-81.

erection of a system of state penitentiaries have already been described. They were joined in this campaign by the inspectors of the Walnut Street Jail. In 1818 the latter sent a memorial to the legislature:

"Mr. G. Evans presented a memorial from the inspectors of the prison of the City and County of Philadelphia, suggesting certain alterations in the penal laws, stating that the said prison at times is crowded to a degree alarming to the health of the prisoners, and the space occupied to be altogether insufficient to class them according to their merits, and to admit solitary confinement; and praying that another prison may be erected, wherein the principle of solitary confinement, in a manner consistent with the health and safe-keeping of the prisoners shall be regularly observed, and to which persons convicted of higher offences shall be sent." [289]

By 1826, when Louis Dwight began to expose the appalling evils in the American prison system in his searching *Reports of the Prison Discipline Society of Boston,* he admitted that no words which could find their way into respectable print were at all adequate to describe the condition of the Walnut Street Jail. No attempt was made in the later years of its existence to reconstruct the system of administration until the historic nuisance was finally replaced by the new Moyamensing County Prison in 1835. The history of the Walnut Street Jail, then, is the record of a conventional late colonial congregate jail or prison, which, after a season of existence as the center of the usual revolting abuses of contemporary jail administration, became temporarily the scene of the first great movement in American prison reform and then entered upon a period of progressive degeneration, until it passed out of existence, nearly half a century later, embodying about as repulsive a system as it had housed in 1785.

2. THE WESTERN STATE PENITENTIARY

While the Pennsylvania system of "Solitary confinement with labour, and instruction in labour, in morals, and in religion," had its partial beginnings in the Walnut Street Jail, following 1790, the vital origins of the systems may be said to date from the establishment of the state penitentiary system, following 1818. Though no one could desire to minimize the historical importance of the Pennsylvania system of prison administration, there is no reason for assigning any original inventive genius to its originators. There are but three

---

[289] *Journal of the House,* 1817-18, p. 163.

possibilities in the situation—complete communication, as in the colonial jails, total separation, as in the theory of the Pennsylvania system, and partial separation, as practiced in the Auburn system. It was natural that, after the revolting abuses of the congregate system had been fully exposed, the pendulum should swing to the other extreme and that there should be a great wave of enthusiasm for complete separation of prisoners in the period from 1800 to 1825. Pennsylvania had been the leader in this new tendency and felt a pride in its diffusion. Moreover, in Pennsylvania there existed the best organized prison reform society on the American continent for more than half a century, which regarded the system of solitary confinement as its particular innovation. As a consequence, it is not difficult to understand why Pennsylvania remained as the classical example of the retention of the extreme tendency to separation, especially after the state had invested more than a million dollars in the physical equipment necessary to carry out this system. The Auburn system, whatever its relative merits, was a more natural and normal development than complete association or complete solitude.

The account of the gradual evolution of the Pennsylvania system from 1790 to 1829 has been given in another section and it will be necessary here simply to give a brief sketch of the beginnings of its operation in the new state penitentiaries. The Western Penitentiary was ready for occupation in July, 1826, and had received twelve convicts by February, 1827.[290] This institution in its earliest state was probably the best example that has ever existed of the solitary system carried to the most vicious extreme. Its massive walls, its dark and silent cells and its lack of exercising yards all combined to give the most complete operation to the effect produced by solitude and gloom. Difficulties were experienced at the outset, even before the law of 1829 ordered the introduction of labor. The need of exercising the prisoners was early apparent and the inspectors urged the building of exercising yards for all cells. As these were not provided, the practice arose of letting out several prisoners in the yard at one time in order to get air and exercise.[291] When the inspectors were ordered to introduce labor into the cells in 1829, their difficulties were still further increased. The cells were too small and dark and it was necessary to carry on all labor, even shoe-making, in common congregate workshops.[292] The necessity of exercise and labor, therefore, caused the partial abandonment

---

[290] *Journal of the Thirty-seventh House of Representatives of the Commonwealth of Pennsylvania*, 1826-27, Vol. II, pp. 33-5, 331, 529-32.

[291] Ibid., p. 530; Ibid., *Fortieth House*, pp. 634-40.

[292] Ibid., pp. 636-40.

of the system of solitary confinement. The inspectors were led, in fact, to express some doubts as to the efficacy of that system.[293] Finally, in their report of 1832, the inspectors confessed that, "constructed as this prison has been it seems next to impossible that that great object, the reformation of its profligate inhabitants, can be largely promoted." [294]

In his report of the same date the warden urged the immediate alteration of the prison structure because "so little has been effected either in a moral, religious or pecuniary point." [295] This complete failure of the administrative system of the Western Penitentiary, as originally constructed, led to the passage of the act of February 27, 1833, ordering the rebuilding of the cells, so as to allow productive labor in individual cells.[296] The Western Penitentiary, then, fulfilled almost none of the requirements of the Pennsylvania system until it was remodeled; its history after that action had been taken belongs to the record of the evolution of penal institutions from 1835 to the present day.

3.   THE EASTERN STATE PENITENTIARY

The early administrative and disciplinary history of the new penitentiary at Philadelphia was quite different from that of the Western Penitentiary. From the outset, commissioners and inspectors, in their public reports, expressed the most optimistic opinions and hopes regarding the operation of the system of solitary confinement. In their report of February 26, 1829, the commissioners in charge of the building of the Eastern Penitentiary thus declared their confidence in the future efficacy of the system of solitary confinement, when carried into execution in the institution which they were about to turn over to the state for occupancy:

"Your commissioners, in closing their report, will take the occasion to remark, that, notwithstanding all that has been written and urged against the adoption of the great principle of separate or solitary confinement of criminals adopted in Pennsylvania almost a half-century ago, and recognized in a most complete manner by the legislature of 1821, which liberally and decidedly expressed their favorable opinion of it, by directing the erection of two state penitentiaries upon that principle, they remain undivided in opinion, and undiminished in their confidence of its ultimate and successful

---

[293] *Journal of the Fortieth House,* pp. 636-37.
[294] *Journal of the Senate,* 1831-32, Vol. II, p. 451.
[295] Ibid., p. 454.
[296] *Laws of the General Assembly,* 1832-33, pp. 55-8.

operation, in meliorating and improving the condition of the unfortunate, misguided beings, upon whom it is intended to operate; and
they trust that Pennsylvania will begin to bring to perfection the
great scheme of reformation which she began, through the means
of the separate confinement of criminals." [297]

The state penitentiary for the eastern district of Pennsylvania
was opened for the reception of convicts on October 25, 1829, and
by January 5, 1830, nine prisoners had been received.[298] Mr. Samuel
R. Wood, a man apparently of the highest qualifications, was
appointed warden. It would have been difficult to have found a
man seemingly better suited to attempt to carry out the Pennsylvania system in a systematic and conscientious manner. He had
long been a member of the Philadelphia Society for Alleviating
the Miseries of Public Prisons; he was a member of the board
of commissioners which built the Eastern Penitentiary; he was
the individual selected by the prison society to lobby with the
chairman of the judiciary committee of the legislature in 1828-29,
in order to secure the final adoption of the Pennsylvania system;
and he had acquired a knowledge of European prison conditions
by a personal visit.[299] The reports of the inspectors and warden,
submitted on the first of January, 1831, are of considerable interest
as indicative of their reactions to the system after the first complete year of its operation. Their enthusiasm appeared to be in no
degree abated. In the following words the inspectors defined the
Pennsylvania system and indicated that it was now able, for the
first time, to demonstrate its efficacy in proper architectural surroundings:

"That system, however imperfectly enforced heretofore, owing to
the faulty construction of our prisons, this board considers to be
briefly this; *solitary confinement at labour, with instruction in
labour, in morals, and in religion.* The noble structure under the
direction of the Board, so honorable to the liberality and philanthropy of the State, has for the first time presented the opportunity of effectually enforcing this mode of punishing and reforming the violators of the laws of society." [300]

The practical application of the system was thus described:

"When a convict first arrives, he is placed in a cell, and left
alone, without work and without any book. His mind can only
operate on itself; generally but a few hours elapse before he peti-

---

[297] Report cited.
[298] *Journal of the Senate*, 1829-30, pp. 467-72.
[299] Ibid., 1830-31, Vol. II, pp. 456-57.
[300] Ibid., p. 458.

tions for something to do and for a Bible. No instance has occurred in which such a petition has been delayed beyond a day or two. If the prisoner have a trade that can be pursued in his cell, he is put to work as a favour; as a reward for good behaviour, and as a favour, a Bible is allowed him. If he has no trade, or one that cannot be pursued in his cell, he is allowed to choose one that can, and he is instructed by one of the overseers, all of whom are master workmen in the trades they respectively superintend and teach. Thus, work and moral and religious books, are regarded and received as favours, and are withheld as punishment." [301]

The industrial situation was reported as highly gratifying, the convicts being moved to exert themselves through the horror of solitary idleness. Since the opening of the prison the convicts had earned something like four hundred dollars more than the expenses of maintenance, exclusive of officers' salaries.[302]

The inspectors expressed great satisfaction with the deterrent effect of the new system of administration. "Great terror," they said, "is known to have been impressed upon the minds of the convict community, by this institution." This was shown by the very small number of prisoners who had been sent to the institution from the populous eastern district. The inspectors held that this was due to the fact that, "the most knowing rogues avoid committing those offenses which would subject them to its discipline." [303]

Warden Wood was particularly impressed with the superior adaptability of the Pennsylvania system to religious instruction:

"In what manner can man be placed, where the words of the gospel would be more impressive than in their situation sitting alone, without seeing or being seen by any human being; nothing to distract their thoughts, or divert them, from the truths delivered to them; alone when they hear, and left alone when the minister has finished, to ponder and reflect." [304]

While the result described by the warden may have been achieved, it is worthy of note that in New Jersey this method of preaching was condemned by prison officials for twenty years, as tending merely to intensify the ordinary soporific effect of the sermons and to encourage the natural impulse to phantasy.

The warden was not less confident of the general virtues of the system:

"In conclusion; I feel bound to say, that every day of my experi-

---

[301] *Journal of the Senate,* 1830-31, Vol. II, p. 456.
[302] Ibid., pp. 461-62.
[303] Ibid., p. 460.
[304] Ibid., p. 465.

ence, only more and more fully convinces me, that separate confinement with labour, and with moral and religious instruction, is the most perfect, and the most beneficial system for the management of convicts known to me—embracing in its details all the advantages, and avoiding most of the evils which are inherent in every other plan." [305]

The reports of the inspectors and the warden for the remainder of this period retain the same vein of exuberant optimism relative to the excellencies of the Pennsylvania system. The only complaints expressed were with respect to the reception of insane prisoners who should have been sent elsewhere, but had been consigned to the penitentiary because of the "disposition of some counties to make use of this prison as a substitute for bedlam;" [306] and with regard to the failure to furnish the prison authorities with enough capital to carry on the prison industries with the maximum amount of efficiency.[307] The report of the inspectors, submitted on January 16, 1833, is especially interesting as indicating the actual working of the reformative principle of the Pennsylvania system, as it appeared to the inspectors:

"We mark, generally, that at first the prisoner indulges in morose or vindictive feelings, and is guilty of turbulent and malicious conduct; but after a few weeks he adopts a more subdued tone, becomes reasonable, and his countenance indicates a more amiable state of mind; is disposed to talk of his past life as one of misery and folly; begins to think that the barrier between him and a good reputation is not impassible; and that there are those in the community, whose prejudices against the condemned are not so strong as to induce the withholding a friendly countenance to his attempts at restoration. In many, the retrospect of life becomes a horrible and loathsome subject of reflection—the sense of shame and feelings of remorse drive them to some source of consolation, and the ordinary means of stifling an actively reproving conscience being denied by reason of their solitariness, the comforts of the Bible and the peace of religion are eagerly sought for." [308]

How little credence, however, can be given to these reports when not checked up by other contemporary comment is well illustrated by the following example. In the winter and spring of 1834-35 a thorough public investigation of the Eastern Penitentiary was conducted, and investigators, inclined to favor the administration, were forced to agree that there existed in the institution:

---

[305] *Journal of the Senate*, 1830-31, Vol. II, p. 466.
[306] Ibid., 1832-33, Vol. II, p. 512.
[307] Ibid., 1833-34, Vol. II, p. 418; 1834-35, Vol. II, p. 473.
[308] Ibid., 1832-33, Vol. II, p. 509.

"First—Frequent misapplication of the public property and public labor to the private advantage of various persons connected with the institution.

"Second—Cruel and unusual punishment inflicted on refractory convicts, resulting in one instance in the death of the sufferer.

"Third—The indulgence in great irregularities and immoralities on the part of those concerned in the management of the institution.

"Fourth—Violation of the laws of the commonwealth, which require the convicts to be kept singly and separately at labor in the cells or work yards." [309]

When one turns to the official reports of the penitentiary for this period, however, no intimation can be found that the system may be called in question. If anything, the reports glow with unusual enthusiasm—a product, no doubt, of what the modern psychiatrist would designate a compensatory reaction. The inspectors, making no reference to the use of the "mad chair," "straight jacket," "iron gag," or the "ducking stool," nor to the death of two insane convicts from the vicious cruelty of the officials, thus expand upon the "humane" characteristics of the Pennsylvania system:

"The Pennsylvania system is emphatically a mild and humane system. Let us look for a moment at the condition of the majority of those who become subject to its regulation. We find them living a hurried and thoughtless life of hourly excitement, and shuddering at the possibility of a pause which could let in (to them the demon) reflection. We see them wanting the ordinary comforts of clothing and cleanliness, without home save that afforded by chance companionship. We find them in the brothel and the gin-shop, giving up to all manner of excesses, indulging in every extreme of vice, self-degraded and brutal. We see them corrupted and corrupting, initiating new candidates in the race of misery and dragging them in their own vortex to a death of infamy and horror. Where do we place them, and how do we treat them? They are taken to the bath and cleansed of outward pollution, they are new-clad in warm and comfortable garments, they are placed in an apartment infinitely superior to what they have been accustomed, they are given employment to enable them to live by their own industry, they are addressed in the language of kindness, interest is shown in their present and future welfare, they are advised and urged to think of their former course and to avoid it, they are lifted gently from their state of humiliation; self-degradation is removed, and

---

[309] *Journal of the Senate*, 1834-35, Vol. II, pp. 512ff. *A Concise History of the Eastern Penitentiary of Pennsylvania, together with a Detailed Statement of the Proceedings of the Committee appointed by the Legislature, December 6, 1834, By a Member of the Legislature*, Philadelphia, 1835.

self-esteem inducted. Pride of character and manliness is inculcated, and they go out of prison unknown as convicts, determined to wrestle for a living in the path of honesty and virtue. Is not this humane?" [310]

Warden Wood, concerning whose conduct the investigation revealed many facts scarcely complimentary, also declared:

"Experience confirms the opinion expressed in former years of the efficacy, the superiority of the Pennsylvania system of prison discipline over all others. This is a pleasing subject of congratulation." [311]

These circumstances, together with many others of a similar nature, must incline one to regard the reports of the inspectors and warden as able special pleading by representatives of vested interests, who had their reputations staked upon the success of the experiment. They must be analyzed with the same critical skepticism as was employed by advocates of the Pennsylvania system in their exposition of the printed documents of adherents of the Auburn system.

VI. PRISON LABOR AND INDUSTRIAL ADMINISTRATION DURING THE PERIOD OF THE FORMATION OF THE PENNSYLVANIA SYSTEM

1. THE WALNUT STREET JAIL

The most tenuous and remote origins of prison labor in Pennsylvania date back to Penn's injunction that "all prisons shall be workhouses,"[312] but it has been already shown that his intentions in this regard never received any systematic execution and that labor in penal institutions was practically non-existent in Pennsylvania in the colonial period.

The more immediate origins of prison employment are to be found in the provision of the constitution of 1776, suggesting that imprisonment at hard labor be utilized in the punishment of all crimes not capital.[313] This exhortation was given legal force by the act of September 15, 1786, ordering the punishment of prisoners by "continued hard labor, publicly and disgracefully

---

[310] *Journal of the Senate,* 1834-35, pp. 467ff.
[311] Ibid., p. 470.
[312] *Charter and Laws of Pennsylvania,* 1676-1700, pp. 100, 121, 139.
[313] *Constitution of 1776,* Chapter II, Section 39.

imposed." [314] According to this act, the prisoners were to be employed in the gaols and workhouses, in the repairing and cleaning of streets and highways, and in "such other hard and laborious work within the county," as the courts should direct.[315] The unfortunate operation of this act has been indicated above, but it seems apparent that the interesting early application of this now frequent type of extra-mural employment of prisoners failed primarily because proper discipline was not enforced upon both prisoners and bystanders.

The failure of the experiment with extra-mural employment led to the passage of the act of March 27, 1789, ordering the employment of convicts in the prison workshops.[316] This act, however, scarcely went into operation when it was superseded by that of April 5, 1790, which provided the general legal regulation of industry in the Walnut Street Jail until it was abandoned in 1835. This act declared that the convicts "shall be kept, as far as may be consistent with their sex, age, health and ability, to labor of the hardest and most servile kind in which the work is least liable to be spoiled by ignorance, neglect or obstinacy and where the materials are not easily embezzled or destroyed." [317] The convicts were to be employed every day except Sunday for eight hours per day in November, December and January; for nine hours in February and October; and for ten hours during the remainder of the year.[318] The keeper, with the consent of two inspectors, was authorized to provide the stock and implements for the labor of the convicts and to make contracts for the sale of the manufactured articles. In addition to his salary, the keeper was to receive a commission of five per cent. on all sales of prison-made goods.[319] The convicts were also to receive a special stimulation to industrial exertion. It was enacted that, "in order to encourage industry as an evidence of reformation," separate accounts should be opened with all prisoners sentenced to hard labor for six months or a longer period. They were to be charged with the cost of their clothing, maintenance and the raw material used in their labor and to be credited with the proceeds of the sale of their manufactured products. If there was any excess over the costs, it was ordered that the prisoners should receive one-half of this "to be laid out in decent raiment for such convicts at their discharge or

---

[314] *The Statutes at Large of Pennsylvania,* Vol. XII, pp. 280-81.
[315] Ibid., p. 284.
[316] Ibid., Vol. XIII, p. 243-51.
[317] Ibid., pp. 516-17.
[318] Ibid., pp. 517-18.
[319] Ibid., pp. 518-19, 521.

otherwise applied to their use and benefit as the said inspectors shall upon such occasions direct." In 1796 the men were charged one shilling three pence and the women seven pence daily. At that time the average daily earning of the male prisoners exceeded two shillings.[320]

This act was slightly amended by that of April 18, 1795, which repealed the section directing that the labor of convicts must be of the "hardest and most servile" kind and also the section which allowed the keeper a percentage on the sale of prison-made goods.[321]

During the period from 1790 to 1835 the most usual occupations of the convicts were nail-making, stone-sawing, shoe-making, weaving and picking and carding wool and hair. The clothing of the prisoners was made by inmates, and this occupied the attention of a large portion of those employed. As no considerable capital was provided for the installation of the public account system, and it was impracticable to lease the labor of prisoners, the industrial and commercial organization was conducted according to the "piece-price" form of the contract system, whereby contractors furnished the raw material and the prisoners were paid so much per foot of stone cut and polished or so much per yard for weaving.[322]

Caleb Lownes presents the following summary of the industrial system at the time when the law of 1790 had first been put into full operation:

"The men are employed according to their abilities and circumstances. The procuring suitable and sufficient employment, was for a considerable time a great difficulty, but there is now a sufficiency of productive and suitable labour for all, and a great number more than are now in the prison.

"The principal employments are, shoe-making, weaving, and tayloring: chipping logwood, grinding plaister of Paris, beating hemp, sawing and polishing marble, swingling flax, picking oakum, wool, cotton and hair; carding wool for hatters, sawing wood, etc.

"The women are employed at heckling, spinning, sewing and washing. . . .

"The law requires, that an account shall be opened with the prisoners, which is done, and they are charged with the costs of prosecution, their diet and cloathing, and credited by their labour, and the balance, if any, is to be given them at discharge, either in money or clothes, at the discretion of the Inspectors, or both—considerable balances have been found in favor of some, and few

---

[320] *The Statutes at Large of Pennsylvania,* Vol. XIII, p. 519. See Robert J. Turnbull, *A Visit to the Philadelphia Prison,* etc., 1796, p. 24.
[321] Ibid., Vol. XV, pp. 356-57.
[322] Lownes, op. cit., pp. 14-5, 20. *Report of the Commissioners on the Penal Code,* 1828, pp. 52, 172-73, 179.

but now have more or less—some balances have been as high as £10, many near it; so that as to their individual expenses, there is not much doubt of their being able to earn as much as will pay all the expense they occasion to the county; and unless the numbers become too few, might be made to contribute towards paying the salaries of the officers of the house. There are men now in the house who appropriate a part of their earnings to the support of their families." [323]

The promising industrial system organized, following 1790, disintegrated along with the general administrative system of which it was a part. As the prison became overcrowded with the increased influx of prisoners from all parts of the state, the limited capacity of the structure led to a continually smaller percentage being employed in a profitable manner, and the general breakdown of the disciplinary system made the labor of those employed less productive. [324] The almost total demoralization of the industrial system of the Walnut Street Jail by the period of the establishment of the state penitentiaries is evident from the passage of the act of February 24, 1823, authorizing the erection in the Walnut Street Jail of that final confession of both intellectual and industrial bankruptcy in penal administration—the treadmill. [325] The wretched condition of prison industry at that time is still further illustrated by the fact that the total product from prison labor did not equal more than eight per cent. of the cost of maintaining and administering the institution from 1823 to 1826. [326]

The industrial situation at the close of the period when the Walnut Street Jail served as the state prison is preserved in the following summary information furnished to the commissioners on the penal code in 1826-27 by the inspectors of the institution. The lack of specific and exact information in reply to the commissioner's questionnaire is a further commentary on the system of industrial administration. The information obtained is valuable, however, as it is about all that is possessed on the subject at the time under discussion:

"The number employed sawing stones varies according to the demand for that kind of labour, and the number of men suited to

---

[323] Lownes, op. cit., pp. 14-5, 20.
[324] *Statistical View of the Operation of the Penal Code of Pennsylvania,* 1817, passim. Roberts Vaux, *Notices,* pp. 35ff. *Journal of the Senate,* 1820-21, pp. 355ff.
[325] *Acts of the General Assembly,* 1822-23, pp. 52-3. Cf. Scharf and Westcott, op. cit., Vol. III, p. 1830. These writers err slightly as to the date of its introduction.
[326] *Report of the Commissioners on the Penal Code,* 1828, pp. 173-79.

it, say from 150 to 200, so also in the weaving and other trades.
The labour of a prisoner in sawing stone is various—according to
the quality of the stone, the strength of the man, the state of the
weather, and the necessity of shifting the stone, from one position
to another, from time to time. Good workmen have sawed 30
feet per week, so with weavers and other trades. An industrious
weaver has in some weeks wove 120 yards. The convicts are not
allowed to work for their own benefit, although if they are industrious and healthy, and as regards stone-cutters, have good weather
and constant employment, they may have a balance to their credit
in the accounts, which are kept according to law with each convict.
Instances have occurred, of considerable sums having been paid
to convicts on their discharge from prison.

"The shoes and wearing apparel are manufactured in the prison
by the convicts, the institution finding the raw materials. Shoes
and a few other articles are manufactured for customers, which
are paid for to the keeper, but we do not manufacture goods for
public or private sale, on prison account. It has been deemed most
profitable to work for others at certain prices for the labour of the
prisoners. By this means we do not require a capital, except what
is employed in tools, &c. . . .

"A statement of the receipts for goods manufactured and sold
cannot be ascertained without an expense of time, labour and
attention, which the actual business of the institution must prevent.

"The employment of the prisoners depends entirely upon the
wants of individuals unconnected with the institution. The inspectors, having no capital as a corporation, do not purchase the raw
material in any case, except what is necessary for convicts' cloathing.
We have no agreements with persons employing the men, which
can justly be construed into a contract. Farming the men out is
not thought of, and it is scarcely practicable, from the nature of
occupations which are carried on. Stone in blocks, from the quarry,
is sent to us to be sawed, for which we receive 18 and 20 cents
per foot. Yarn is sent to be dyed and worked into cloth, for which
we receive six cents per yard; and in no case is there any agreement
but that the prices shall not be raised without due notice." [327]

In addition to those employed in the occupations listed above,
about forty out of the five hundred and ninety-two convicts were
engaged in the domestic service of the prison, for which they were
allowed thirty cents per day.[328] From the schedule of prices for
work performed and the number of convicts confined, taken in
comparison with the actual income from prison labor, it is evident
that not more than from one-seventh to one-tenth of the total popu-

[327] *Report of the Commissioners on the Penal Code,* 1828, pp. 172, 179.
[328] Ibid., p. 179.

lation could have been consistently and uniformly employed in the period of the middle "twenties." The Walnut Street Jail was not less of an industrial failure than an administrative fiasco.

2. THE WESTERN STATE PENITENTIARY

The analysis of the industrial system of the Western Penitentiary during the first decade of its existence must of necessity resemble a catalogue of the serpents of Ireland after the traditional visit of Saint Patrick. The institution was opened in the summer of 1826, on the principle of solitary confinement without labor. It was not until three years later that the law of April 23, 1829, ordered that the original system should be displaced by that of solitary confinement with labor. The limited dimensions of the cells and their darkness made it impossible to carry on any sustained labor in them. Aside from the frequent complaints of the officials with respect to the impossibility of establishing a systematic and productive industrial organization, there exists almost no information with regard to the humble beginnings of industry in the Western Penitentiary. The only references to this subject in the reports state that no work could be carried on in the cells and that it was necessary to assemble the few workmen, for whom employment could be found, in a common workroom,[329] and that the total earnings of all employed in the year 1831 was five hundred and ninety-three dollars.[330] The insurmountable difficulties in realizing an effective industrial system, imposed by the architecture of the structure, was one of the chief causes of the passage of the act of February 27, 1833, ordering the rebuilding of the cells of the Western Penitentiary.[331]

3. THE EASTERN STATE PENITENTIARY

The industrial beginnings of the Eastern Penitentiary were relatively successful. The institution was not opened until six months after the passage of the act of April 23, 1829, ordering the introduction of labor in the administrative system of the new state penitentaries, and the provision of an unusual double-cell arrangement made it possible to carry on labor in isolation without the insuperable architectural difficulties imposed by the original structure at

---

[329] *Journal of the Fortieth House of Representatives,* 1829-30, p. 636.

[330] *Journal of the Senate,* 1831-32, p. 453. The distribution of the total earnings was the following: shoemaking, $244; picking oakum, $340; carpenter work, $1.50; sewing, $7.50.

[331] *Laws of the General Assembly,* 1832-33, pp. 55-8.

Allegheny. The industrial system was very promptly established. On January 5, 1830, the inspectors reported that nine prisoners had been received and all of them had been put to work at once.[332] From the outset, the weaving and dyeing of cloth and shoemaking were the chief industries in the Eastern Penitentiary.[333] The prisoners were said to be unusually industrious because of the desire to escape the pangs of lonesomeness in the solitary cells. From October 25, 1829, to December 1, 1830, the convicts had met all the expenses of maintenance, exclusive of official salaries, and a balance existed of three hundred and ninety-three dollars.[334] A balance over maintenance expenses was also reported for 1831 and 1832, but a loss was declared to exist in 1833 and 1834.[335] The deficit was explained as being due to a general business depression in the country and to the failure of the state to provide enough working capital to maintain the prison industries on the highest level of efficiency.[336]

The commercial organization of the new industrial system was administered according to the "public account" plan, with a slight mixture of the "piece-price" variety of the contract system. The prison authorities purchased the "stock and manufactures" needed and then sold the manufactured product to the contractors. This was done to prevent the "demoralizing contact and intercourse" between contractor's agents and the prisoners, which would have resulted from an application of the true "piece-price" system.[337]

---

[332] *Journal of the Senate*, 1829-30, pp. 467-72.
[333] The industrial distribution of the Eastern Penitentiary down to 1835 was as follows:
"In 1831 there were 87 convicts in custody in the institution; 43 were engaged in weaving and dyeing; 18 in shoemaking; 4 in blacksmithing; 3 in carpentering; 2 in carving; 2 in lockmaking; 2 in wool-packing; and 1 each in carriage-making, tailoring, cooking and washing." *Senate Journal*, 1831-32, Vol. II, p. 447.
"In 1832, with a total of 97 confined, 43 were employed in weaving and dyeing; 32 in shoemaking; 5 as blacksmiths; and 4 as carpenters. The remainder were distributed in sundry minor occupations and in the domestic service." *Senate Journal*, 1832-33, Vol. II, p. 515.
"In 1833 there was a total of 154 convicts confined. Out of this number 59 were occupied in weaving, warping, dyeing and spooling; 52 as shoemakers; and five as carpenters. The rest were distributed as above." *Senate Journal*, 1833-34, Vol. II, p. 418.
"In 1834, with a total of 218 incarcerated, 83 were employed in making shoes; 70 in spinning, dyeing, weaving and dressing; and 6 each as carpenters, blacksmiths and 'sewers.'" *Senate Journal*, 1834-35, Vol. II, p. 473.
[334] *Journal of the Senate*, 1830-31, Vol. II, p. 462.
[335] Ibid., 1831-32, Vol. II, pp. 447-48; 1832-33, Vol. II, p. 515; 1833-34, Vol. II, pp. 415-18; 1834-35, Vol. II, pp. 467-73.
[336] Ibid., 1833-34, Vol. II, p. 418; 1834-35, Vol. II, p. 473.
[337] Ibid., 1830-31, Vol. II, p. 461; 1832-33, Vol. II, p. 515.

VII. THE PENNSYLVANIA SYSTEM IN AMERICAN AND EUROPEAN PENOLOGY

1. THE PENNSYLVANIA SYSTEM IN THE UNITED STATES

The influence of the Pennsylvania system on American penology passed through two main stages, following the general development of the system in Pennsylvania, itself. The first period was marked by the wide imitation of the system of administration established in the Walnut Street Jail in 1790, and the second was characterized by a much more limited adoption of the completely developed Pennsylvania system, as put into operation in the Eastern Penitentiary in 1829.

Philadelphia was the center of prison reform in this country from 1785 to 1825 and it was natural that the type of improvement there initiated should be the model for the other states when they turned their attention to this problem. Therefore, in the period from 1790 to 1830 there was a widely diffused wave of imitation of the system of solitary confinement in the Middle Atlantic and New England States. As in Pennsylvania, the adoption of the principle of solitary confinement in these imitating states was not complete or systematic. They either prescribed solitary confinement only for particularly "hardened and atrocious offenders," or allowed the courts to use their discretion in sentencing those convicted to solitary confinement or to hard labor. Also copying the example of Philadelphia, solitary confinement, when prescribed, was normally imposed for only a portion of the period of imprisonment, and it was usually imposed without labor.

New York was the first state to follow the lead of Pennsylvania. The leaders in this early reform in New York were General Philip Schuyler, Thomas Eddy, Ambrose Spencer and John Jay. The act of March 20, 1796, allowed solitary confinement in the Newgate Penitentiary in New York City, to be erected in accordance with the terms of the act.[338] An act of April 8, 1808, permitted the courts to exercise their discretion in sentencing a convict to solitary confinement or to imprisonment at hard labor.[339] Finally, an act of April 2, 1821, directed that the more hardened offenders be confined in the solitary cells just erected in the Auburn Prison.[340]

---

[338] *Laws of the State of New York,* 1789-96, pp. 674-75.
[339] Ibid., 1808, p. 340.
[340] Ibid., 1821, pp. 216-17.

This experiment proved a disastrous failure, however, and led to the establishment of the Auburn system between 1823 and 1826.[341]

Maryland authorized the introduction of solitary confinement by an act of November, 1809.[342] In 1837 it was provided that this type of punishment should not be imposed for more than one-half nor less than one-twentieth of the total period of imprisonment.[343] In the following year solitary confinement was entirely abolished.[344]

By an act of June 21, 1811, Massachusetts authorized the courts to sentence convicts to hard labor or to solitary confinement.[345] This privilege was not extensively utilized and the new state penitentiary, opened in 1829, was organized on the Auburn system of administration.[346]

Maine, by an act of February 25, 1824, gave the courts the right of using their judgment in deciding whether a convict should be sentenced to solitary confinement or hard labor.[347] The alternative was soon eliminated, however, for an act of February 24, 1827, abolished solitary confinement.[348]

New Jersey authorized the solitary confinement of the worst classes of offenders by an act of May 31, 1820.[349] The innovation did not prove a success and it was abolished by an act of March 7, 1828.[350]

Solitary confinement was first introduced in Virginia by an act of March 9, 1824. It provided for the erection of solitary cells in the state penitentiary and ordered six months of solitary confinement on admission for all convicts sent to the state penitentiary. It might be imposed at intervals thereafter.[351] An act of March 9, 1826, directed that instead of six months of solitary confinement at the beginning of the term, there should be three months at the outset and three months just prior to discharge.[352] An act of March 9, 1833, ordered that solitary confinement should not be inflicted for more than one-twelfth of the sentence nor for more

[341] J. L. Sullivan, *Note on the Penitentiary System of New York State,* loc. cit.

[342] *Laws of the State of Maryland,* edited by Kalty, Harris and Watkins, Vol. IV. Acts of 1809, Chap. 138.

[343] *Laws of 1837,* Chap. 320.

[344] *Laws of 1838,* Chap. 400.

[345] *Laws of the Commonwealth of Massachusetts,* 1811, pp. 418ff.

[346] F. H. Sanborn, *Special Report on Prisons and Prison Discipline,* Boston, 1865, p. 8.

[347] *Public Acts of the State of Maine,* 1824, pp. 1000ff.

[348] Ibid., 1827, p. 1134.

[349] *Laws of New Jersey,* Joseph Justice, 1821, p. 739.

[350] *Acts of the General Assembly of New Jersey,* 1827-28, pp. 212-13.

[351] *Supplement to the Revised Code of the Laws of Virginia,* 1819-33, Richmond, 1833, pp. 293-94.

[352] Ibid., pp. 299-300.

than one month at a time.[353] Finally, the act of March 19, 1850, forbade the solitary confinement of other than refractory, obstinate and insane prisoners.[354]

Such was the diffusion of the early phase of the Pennsylvania system in the eastern United States. It should be noted that, almost without exception, even the solitary confinement of a part of the prison population for a small portion of the total sentence, had been rejected as a failure by the states that had adopted the experiment, and this rejection had in every case except that of Virginia taken place before the opening of the Eastern Penitentiary in 1829. This fact, taken in conjunction with the great popularity of the Auburn system at the time and its able promotion by Louis Dwight, is a sufficient explanation of the remarkable failure of the perfected Pennsylvania system, based on the continual solitary confinement of all prisoners, to attract a favorable following in the United States after 1829. Only two states adopted the elaborate system of prison administration provided for in the act of April 23, 1829, and carried into practical execution in the Eastern Penitentiary after October 25, 1829. Rhode Island opened its new state penitentiary in 1838 on the principle of solitary confinement at hard labor, but relinquished the experiment some six years later.[355]

New Jersey was the only state which made a systematic trial of the Pennsylvania system. It had rejected solitary confinement after the first trial in 1828, and when it was decided to construct a new prison, after the astounding revelations of the investigating committee of 1829-30, the first two committees had reported in favor of the Auburn system.[356] In 1833, however, owing to the influence of the Philadelphia Society for Alleviating the Miseries of Public Prisons, and of the architect, John Haviland, it was finally determined that the new prison should be modeled after the Eastern Penitentiary in architecture and administration, and it was built according to plans submitted by Mr. Haviland.[357] It was abandoned just twenty-five years later by an act of March 18, 1858, providing for the introduction of congregate workshops.[358] Its

---

[353] *Acts of the General Assembly of Virginia*, 1833, p. 18.

[354] Ibid., 1850, p. 15.

[355] E. C. Wines and Theodore Dwight, *Report on the Prisons and Reformatories of the United States and Canada*, 1867, pp. 53-4; *Eighteenth Annual Report of the Prison Discipline Society of Boston*, 1843, pp. 86-9.

[356] *Votes of the Fifty-fourth General Assembly of New Jersey*, 1830, pp. 186-87. Ibid., *Fifty-fifth General Assembly*, 1830-31, pp. 93-4.

[357] Ibid., *Fifty-seventh General Assembly*, 1832-33, pp. 142-53.

[358] *Acts of the Eighty-second Legislature of New Jersey*, 1858, p. 453. See H. E. Barnes, *History of the Penal, Reformatory and Correctional Institutions of New Jersey*, Vol. II, Chap. iii.

failure and abandonment were due to the strange architectural oversight of neglecting to provide exercising yards with the solitary cells, to the demoralization of the administrative system through the interference of party politics, and to the attacks of the prison physician on its detrimental effect on the mental and physical health of the prisoners. Eleven years later solitary confinement was abolished in the Western Penitentiary of Pennsylvania, but it was tenaciously retained in a legal sense in the Eastern Penitentiary until 1913, though it had long before ceased as a part of the practical administrative procedure of the institution.

2. THE PENNSYLVANIA SYSTEM IN EUROPE

If the Pennsylvania system did not meet with the hearty approval of penologists in this country and proved that penal systems, like prophets, are held lightly in their own country, the originators and promoters of the system could take keen satisfaction in the admiration which it received from the most distinguished penologists of Europe.

The interchange of ideas between penal reformers in London and Philadelphia from 1787 to 1820 has already been referred to. The French were scarcely less interested in the movement for the improvement of criminal jurisprudence and penal administration which centered in Philadelphia. As early as 1794, the Duke of Rochefoucauld-Liancourt published a pamphlet in which he praised the reforms effected in Pennsylvania between 1786 and 1793.[359] In 1828, Sir Charles Lucas, writing on the penitentiary systems of Europe and America, called attention to the significant reform movement which had been initiated in Philadelphia.[360] A more signal honor came when France, in 1831, sent two of her most distinguished citizens to make a study of American penal institutions. They were the publicist, Gustave Auguste de Beaumont and the Versailles judge, Alexis de Tocqueville. It was on this visit that De Tocqueville gathered the material for his *Democracy in America,* a work which brought him world-wide fame, while the report on American penitentiaries, mainly the work of De Beaumont, is known only to the few students interested in the historical aspects of penology. Their report on the American prison system is limited mainly to a careful survey and analysis of the rival systems in operation at Auburn and Philadelphia. It is a most calm and

---

[359] *Des Prisons de Philadelphie par in Européen,* Paris, *l'an IV., de la République.*
[360] *Du système pénal et du systéme rèpressif en général.*

judicious document and is not at all marred by partisanship. The Pennsylvania system was held to be more expensive to construct and put in operation, but was regarded as more easily and economically administered. The Auburn system was believed to be cheaper to introduce and better adapted to productive labor, but less readily and successfully administered by the generally mediocre type of officials connected with prison administration.[361] As to the relative efficacy of the two systems in securing the reformation of inmates the authors resort to the following rather curious but keen and subtle bit of penal and social philosophy:

"The Philadelphia system, being that which produces the deepest impressions on the soul of the convict, must effect more reformation than that of Auburn. The latter, however, is perhaps more conformable to the habits of men in society, and on this account effects a greater number of reformations, which might be called 'legal,' inasmuch as they produce the external fulfilment of social obligations.

"If this be so, the Philadelphia system produces more honest men, and that of New York more obedient citizens." [362]

Both systems were regarded as unnecessarily severe:

"To sum up the whole on this point, it must be acknowledged that the penitentiary system in America is severe. While society in the United States gives the example of the most extended liberty, the prisons of the same country offer the spectacle of the most complete despotism." [363]

While the French commissioners were fully appreciative of the admirable advantages of the Pennsylvania system, they inclined to favor the Auburn plan:

"Yet the Auburn system, whose merit in theory is not less incontestable, is, as we have shown above, much cheaper in its execution; it is therefore this system which we should wish to see applied to our prisons, if the question were only to choose between the two." [364]

If the first noted European commissioners to the United States were disposed to recommend the Auburn system, such was not the case with their successors. In 1832 England appointed Mr. William

---

[361] G. de Beaumont and A. de Tocqueville, *On the Penitentiary System in the United States and Its Application in France*, translated from the French with an Introduction, Notes and Additions, by Francis Lieber, Philadelphia, 1833, pp. 19-47. This work, with the addition of Doctor Lieber's notes, is one of the chief sources for the early history of American penology.

[362] Ibid., pp. 59-60.

[363] Beaumont and De Tocqueville, op. cit., p. 47.

[364] Ibid., p. 90.

Crawford, of the London Society for the Improvement of Prison Discipline, as a commissioner to study the systems of penal administration in the United States. His report, submitted in the summer of 1834, was a glowing eulogy of the Pennsylvania system and it led to the erection of the great Pentonville Prison, modeled after the Eastern Penitentiary.[365] This penal institution is important in the history of penology, as it was operated in connection with the Australian transportion system where Captain Alexander Maconochie first put into operation the parole and commutation system, which was later improved by Sir Walter Crofton in Ireland and ultimately became the basis of the Elmira reformatory system.[366]

The Scotch philosopher and psychologist, George Combe (1788-1858), who visited the United States some six years after Mr. Crawford, differed radically from his predecessor and gave his hearty approval to the Auburn system.[367]

The fame of the new American penitentiary system spread beyond France and England, and in 1834 Prussia followed their example by sending Doctor Nicolaus Heinrich Julius (1783-1862), to this country to study its penal institutions. He remained two years and upon his return was a thorough convert to the Pennsylvania system, which, with the aid of German reformers, he succeeded in introducing into Prussia and many other German states.[368]

France was apparently dissatisfied with the results of the investigation of De Beaumont and De Tocqueville, and in 1836 she sent two more commissioners, Frédéric Auguste Demetz and Guillaume Blouet, to make a further study of the problem. While more critical and cautious than Crawford or Julius, they were, however, inclined to favor the Pennsylvania system in a much more decided manner than De Beaumont and De Tocqueville had been disposed to recommend the Auburn plan of administration.[369]

[365] William Crawford, *The Penitentiaries of the United States,* London, 1834, passim. For a critical account of Crawford's mission and its effect, see George Ives, *A History of Penal Methods,* Chaps. v-ix. Mr. Ives says, p. 783, "We may suppose and hope for the sake of his soul, that Mr. Crawford was a commonplace man with little imagination."

[366] Cf. F. H. Wines, *Punishment and Reformation,* Chaps. ix-x.

[367] George Combe, *Notes on the United States of North America,* especially pp. 220-24.

[368] N. H. Julius, *Nord Amerika's Sittliche Zustände nach eigenen Anschauungen in den Jahren 1834, 1835 and 1836,* 2 Vols. Leipzig, 1839; and *Du système pénétentiare américan en 1836,* Rennes, 1837. See the excellent article on Julius in the *Allgemeine Deutsche Biographie,* Vol. XIV, pp. 686-89.

[369] F. A. Demetz and G. Blouet, *Rapports sur les pénétenciers des Etats-unis,* Paris, 1837. Especially pp. 40-6. This report is particularly valuable on account of its elaborate architectural drawings of the American prisons. Blouet was a distinguished French architect, while Demetz was a leading reformer and the founder, at Mettray, of the famous system of agricultural colonies or farms for juvenile delinquents organized on a cottage basis.

These recommendations of the Pennsylvania system by so many distinguished authorities led to its very general adoption in Europe. England adopted it in 1835; Belgium, in 1838; Sweden, in 1840; Hungary, in 1841; France, in 1844; Prussia, about the same time; Denmark, in 1846; Norway, in 1851; Holland, in the same year; while in 1875 France provided for a more extended application of the system through the effect of the investigations of Haussonville from 1872 to 1875.[370] It is true, of course, that in few countries was the adoption as complete as that in Pennsylvania in 1829, but in every case it was sufficient to leave the impress of the "separate" system upon the administration of the penal institutions, and down to the present day the Pennsylvania system dominates the penitentiary system of continental Europe.[371]

3. The Controversy between the Adherents of the Auburn and the Pennsylvania Systems

An adequate account of the bitter controversy that was waged from 1825 to 1860 between the exponents of the rival Pennsylvania and Auburn systems would occupy a large volume in itself, and can only be briefly touched upon here. As has already been seen, the struggle began before either system was thoroughly established. It has already been pointed out that as early as 1826-27 the commissioners who were appointed to devise the system of administration for the new state penitentiaries in Pennsylvania were approached by advocates of the Auburn system and were converted to an advocacy of its adoption. The main conflict was waged between the Prison Discipline Society of Boston, for the Auburn system, and the Philadelphia Society for Alleviating the Miseries of Public Prisons, for the Pennsylvania system. After its organization in 1845, the Prison Society of New York supported the Boston Society in urging the adoption of the Auburn system. The Boston Prison Discipline Society was organized by Louis Dwight (1793-1854).

Dwight had originally prepared for the ministry, but was prevented from preaching by an injury to his lungs in an accident in a chemical laboratory. In 1824 he rode on horseback throughout the

---

[370] Wines, op. cit., pp. 155-56. Dorothea L. Dix, *Remarks on Prisons and Prison Discipline in the United States*, 1845, pp. 78-90. George Sumner, *The Pennsylvania System of Prison Discipline Triumphant in France*, Philadelphia, 1847. The Belgian penologist, Ducpetiaux, was particularly active in urging the adoption of the Pennsylvania system, and Belgium has retained this system more tenaciously than any other European country.
[371] See C. R. Henderson, *Modern Prison Systems*.

eastern part of the country distributing Bibles to prisoners. He was horrified by the appalling abuses in the contemporary prison systems and he determined to devote his life to an improvement of their condition. He organized and directed the Prison Discipline Society of Boston from 1825 until his death in 1854. As secretary of the society he wrote its reports, which are much the best single source for the study of American penology during this period, though they are disfigured by a violent opposition to the Pennsylvania system.[372] He was repeatedly accused of unfairness and dishonesty by members of the Philadelphia Society for Alleviating the Miseries of Public Prisons, but a careful examination of the polemic pamphlets of both parties to the conflict can not fail to impress an impartial reader with the fact that neither was qualified to "cast the first stone." Both were fiercely partisan and both were disgracefully unscrupulous in their use of statistics designed to support their cause or damage their opponents. The only gratifying feature of the controversy was that both systems were so greatly superior to the unspeakable congregate system which they displaced that their competition inevitably worked for the betterment of penal conditions. That Dwight and the Auburn system triumphed was not so much due to superior ability on his part as to the advantages in his position. The Pennsylvania system had been unfairly discredited by the failure of its imperfect application before 1829 and the Auburn system was free from this initial handicap. Furthermore, the Auburn type of administration required less expenditure for introduction and the economic arguments in its favor were, at least superficially, much more attractive than for the Pennsylvania system. Added to these advantages was the superior and more wide-spread organization of the Boston Society throughout the country.[373]

---

[372] See below, pp. 375ff.
[373] The controversy conducted in the reports and publications of these societies can be followed further in the controversial pamphlets which were issued by the exponents of two systems during this period. The following are among the most important.

The Pennsylvania system is upheld and defended in the following articles and pamphlets:

Roberts Vaux, *Letter on the Penitentiary System of Pennsylvania, Addressed to William Roscoe, Esquire,* Philadelphia, 1827; George W. Smith, *A Defence of the Pennsylvania System of the Solitary Confinement of Prisoners,* 1829-1833; Edward Livingston, *Introductory Report to the Code of Prison Discipline,* Philadelphia, 1827; and by the same writer, *Letter on the Pennsylvania System to Roberts Vaux,* 1828; Francis Lieber, *The Penitentiary System of Pennsylvania,* in the Appendix to his translation of Beaumont and De Tocqueville; and by the same author, *A Popular Essay on the Subjects of Penal Law and on Uninterrupted Solitary Confinement at Labor,* Philadelphia, 1838; John Sibley, *A Letter on the Superior Advan-*

In addition to the conflict between these prison reform societies, most of the leaders in the improvement of criminal jurisprudence and penal administration in this country took a decided stand on one side or the other of the controversy. The Pennsylvania system was defended by Roberts Vaux, Edward Livingston, Francis Lieber, Dorothea L. Dix, William Parker Foulke and Richard Vaux. The Auburn plan of administration was warmly favored by DeWitt Clinton, Amos Pillsbury, William H. Seward, E. C. Wines, Theodore W. Dwight, Frank Sanborn and Gideon Haynes. The controversy gradually died out after 1860. With the introduction of a knowledge of the Irish system into the United States, through the efforts of Frank Sanborn and others, about 1865, and its later development into the Elmira reformatory system by 1875, the advocates of both older types of administration soon came to see that they had been supporting a hopelessly crude and elementary penal system and few possessed the audacity or stupidity to prolong the dispute.

It is not the function of the historian to pass judgment on the validity of the assumptions of the Pennsylvania system. The movement of which it was a product was one of the most epoch-making and beneficial in the whole history of prison reform and the aims of its exponents are above criticism. It was, however, from the outset an *a priori* and theological system and scarcely in harmony with sound psychology or criminology. It was, moreover, very one-sided and incomplete. There must be two phases to the operation of any successful prison system, namely, the production of a desire for

---

tages of Solitary Confinement, London, 1838; L. M. Moreau-Christophe, *Emprisonnement individuel,* Paris, 1842; W. H. Suringar, *Considérations sur la réclusion individuelle,* Paris, 1843; *Report of a Minority of the Special Committee of the Boston Prison Discipline Society,* Boston, 1846; F. A. Packard, *A Vindication of the Separate System of Prison Discipline,* Philadelphia, 1839; *An Inquiry into the Alleged Tendency of the Separation of Convicts One from the Other to Produce Death and Derangement,* Philadelphia, 1849; W. P. Foulke, *Remarks on Cellular Separation,* Philadelphia, 1860; *The Pennsylvania System of Separate Confinement Explained and Defended, Philadelphia,* 1867; the many and diverse writings of Richard Vaux from 1850 to 1875.

The Pennsylvania system is condemned in the writings given below: William Roscoe, *A Brief Statement of the Causes which Have Led to the Abandonment of the Celebrated System of Penitentiary Discipline in some of the United States of America,* London, 1826; *The North American Review,* July, 1839, pp. 1-43; also January, 1848; Sir Peter Laurie, *A Letter on the Disadvantages and Extravagance of the Separate System of Prison Discipline,* London, 1848; and by the same author, *"Killing no Murder" or the Effects of Solitary Confinement on Prisoners,* London, 1846; George Combe, *Notes on the United States of North America,* 1838-40, (1841) especially, pp. 220-24; F. C. Gray, *Prison Discipline in America,* 1847; *The Christian Examiner,* March, 1848.

reformation and a provision of a method of training convicts for life in society which will give some assurance that the reformatory impulse may be successfully realized. The reflection and self-examination supposed to be induced by the solitary confinement of the Pennsylvania system might produce a desire to reform, but solitary confinement certainly furnished the poorest conceivable mode of training convicts for a law-abiding existence when discharged. All modern penologists worthy of the name have long ago come to see that convicts can only be trained for social life by sharing in prison some of the duties, responsibilities and penalties which are a part of life in society. Such is the only justification for the introduction of the various types of self-government schemes in modern penal institutions. The Pennsylvania system imposed upon the individual a world removed to the utmost degree from that which he would be called upon to reenter when released. The Pennsylvania system, moreover, will no more square with modern psychology than with present-day criminology and penology. It is now known to be an incontestable fact that protracted and enforced absence from society is highly conducive to the development of abnormal mental traits, and the mid-century arguments written to show that this was not the case are of no more validity than were the attempts to dispute the germ theory of disease by pointing out the fact that many in the past had escaped infection.

VIII. SUMMARY

The foregoing pages have shown that in the introduction into America of that movement for the reform of criminal jurisprudence and penal administration, which had begun with the work of Montesquieu, Beccaria and Howard, Pennsylvania played the leading part. Not only did Philadelphia bring this country into touch with the best products of the movement of reform and enlightenment in Europe in the eighteenth century, but also, by reviving the doctrines and practices of the Quaker founders of the province, it was able to bring to final realization principles of jurisprudence and penology which had existed nearly a century earlier, but had lapsed temporarily because they were too far in advance of the *mores* of the contemporary civilization. By applying the Quaker doctrine that imprisonment should be the basis of punishment and reformation, the Philadelphia reformers first permanently established the fundamental principles of modern criminal jurisprudence, and by adhering to the Quaker proposition that "all prisons should be workhouses" they created the economic foundations of the modern prison system. To this Quaker groundwork in jurisprudence and penology they added their own innovation of the classification, separation and segregation of convicts, and the modern prison system was created. Upon the mechanics of this system was engrafted the epoch-making position in penal philosophy that reformation was the great aim of the treatment of the criminal. However imperfect may have been the system of penal administration whereby this reformation was to be effected, the philosophy was unassailable. Along with these major achievements went the minor accomplishment of removing the revolting abuses of the jail system of the colonial period, connected with the extortionate fee system, the unrestricted sale of liquor, and gross sexual immorality. When the Pennsylvania system was perfected by 1829, Philadelphia was able to repay the penological debt to Europe, which had been accumulating since 1682, by offering for European imitation the most elaborate and complete system of prison administration which had yet been produced. In 1830 Pennsylvania was leading the vanguard of penal reform. The record of its evolution since that time is one of its all-too-tenacious adherence to its original system, until it was left far in the rear through the growth elsewhere of more progressive doctrines and practices, many of which received their vital impulse directly or indirectly from the Pennsylvania reform movement of 1776 to 1835.

CHAPTER IV

DEVELOPMENT OF PENNSYLVANIA PENOLOGY, 1835-1927

I. THE GENERAL LINES OF DEVELOPMENT DURING THIS PERIOD

"IN LOOKING over the Annual Reports made by the Officers of this Institution to the State Legislature for more than thirty years, we find that they have rarely ever omitted to express their entire satisfaction with the workings of the separate system of confinement which Pennsylvania has adopted as her own.

"We are not at this time disposed to controvert the self-complaisant arguments so profusely lavished upon the Legislature from both extremities of the State, in their Annual Reports, as to 'our humane and reformatory' System of Prison discipline.

"We think, however, that it might be well for the Legislature to look at the other side of the question and inquire, whether, in the onward progress of events and in the constant and interesting changes that are always being developed in the world, there might not be a more excellent plan adopted or worked out for the improvement and reformation of this unfortunate people than the one which we have adopted."

Thus wrote the newly appointed board of inspectors of the Western Penitentiary in their annual report for 1866, which is the first instance of which any record has been preserved indicating that the prison officials had become conscious that the renowned system of prison administration created by the previous generation had been challenged by the penological progress of a half-century. Once its sanctity was questioned, however, its passage was rapid. Within three years it had been legally abolished in the Western Penitentiary and, due to the increase in the prison population, had become a fiction in the parent institution at Cherry Hill. Therefore, while the preceding chapter was devoted to an account of the origins of the Pennsylvania system of prison administration, viewed as one of the great steps in advance in the evolution of modern penology, the present chapter will tell the story of how that system gradually disintegrated before the effective pressure of the newer and sounder tendencies and developments in the evolution of penal methods.

181

While the decline of the Pennsylvania system is the central theme of this chapter, its downfall must be viewed from two different standpoints. In the first place, it was legally abandoned in a formal and conscious manner by legislation permitting the congregation of prisoners; and, in the second place, it was in practice gradually and somewhat unconsciously eliminated by changes in population, architecture, administration and industry which were not compatible with solitary confinement. The legal disappearance of the separate system in the Western Penitentiary came as a result of the law of April 8, 1869. In the Eastern Penitentiary, however, while there were never cells enough to allow separate confinement of all the prisoners after 1866, congregation was not legally permissible until the passage of the law of July 7, 1913.

The architectural history of the two state penitentiaries was also considerably divergent during this period. The Eastern Penitentiary has retained its original plant to the present time and has made provision for accommodating the growing population through adding new wings of cells to the structure planned and erected by John Haviland between 1821 and 1835. The Western Penitentiary found it necessary to abandon the original prison after about a half-century of occupation and the laws of March 7, 1873, and June 12, 1878, made provision for the erection of a new plant on the site of the old Western House of Refuge. This location, on the banks of the Ohio River about one mile from the original prison site, proved unhealthy and dangerous on account of floods, fogs and the settling of smoke from adjoining factories. These circumstances led to the law of March 20, 1911, providing for the removal of the Western Penitentiary to a magnificent site in the mountains of Centre County.

Four years later, as a natural outgrowth of a developing sentiment, in favor of a union of the two penitentiaries, the act of June 14, 1915, directed that the new buildings erected on the Centre County site should be constructed on such a scale as to permit the housing of the populations of both the Eastern and the Western Penitentiaries. So much opposition developed to the plan to merge the Eastern and Western Penitentiaries that the plan has now been abandoned. It now appears doubtful if the penitentiary at Riverside in Pittsburgh will be abandoned for some time to come. The Rockview Penitentiary has tended to assume the status of a separate institution for the central part of the state.

The progress in penal methods in Pennsylvania since 1835 has centered mainly around the passage of laws granting commutation of sentence for good behavior; the adoption of a system of classification of prisoners based upon their conduct while incarcerated;

the securing of legislation directing the employment of the indeterminate sentence and parole as valuable adjuncts to the mechanism designed to effect the reformation of prisoners; and the gradual provision of differentiated institutions designed to deal more specifically and scientifically with the various types of individuals embraced within the total delinquent population. Commutation of sentence for good behavior was first legally authorized by an act of May 1, 1861, which was secured mainly through the efforts of the Pennsylvania Society for Alleviating the Miseries of Public Prisons. This law was altered and strengthened by acts of May 21, 1869, and May 11, 1901. The progressive classification of prisoners was first officially recommended in the Western Penitentiary in 1867 and was adopted in the early seventies. This system of classification was not adopted in the Eastern Penitentiary till the close of the first decade of the present century. A preliminary step in the direction of an indeterminate sentence was taken in the revised penal code of March 21, 1860, which provided only the maximum penalties and left the minimum to the discretion of the sentencing court. An avowed indeterminate sentence and parole act was not secured until the passage of the act of May 10, 1909. This tardy provision, however, was not allowed to stand permanently, as it was wholly emasculated by the act of June 19, 1911, and the State of Pennsylvania can not at this late date boast of a true indeterminate sentence act for application to the state penitentiaries.

The process of providing specialized institutions for the treatment of the various classes of delinquents, which was begun by the opening of the Philadelphia House of Refuge in 1828, was continued in the authorization of the establishment of a Western House of Refuge for juvenile delinquents in the city of Allegheny by the act of April 22, 1850. Its removal to Morganza in Washington County was permitted by the act of April 10, 1873, and the institution there established was organized on the "Mettray farm colony" basis with the cottage and family as the units of institutional life and activities. It was formally transferred to the state by the agreement of October 3, 1878. The establishment of an institution designed to deal with a type of delinquents intermediate in age and degree of criminality between those handled in the penitentiaries and in the institutions for juvenile delinquents was contemplated in the acts of June 8, 1881, and April 28, 1887, which resulted in the erection of the Pennsylvania Industrial Reformatory at Huntingdon. A similar institution for women was not legally authorized until the passage of the act of July 25, 1913, creating the State Industrial Home for Women at Muncy, which was completed for occupancy late in 1918.

Supplementary institutions for the treatment of defective types, which were earlier confined in penal institutions or almshouses, have also been provided for since 1835. The establishment of institutions for the care of the idiotic and insane was originally brought about mainly as a result of the agitation begun by Dorothea L. Dix in the late thirties and early forties. The State Hospital for the Insane at Harrisburg was created by the act of March 4, 1841; that at Dixmont by the act of March 18, 1848; and that at Danville by the act of April 13, 1868. Tardy and incomplete provision for the treatment of the criminal insane was supplied by an act of April 11, 1905, establishing the State Hospital for the Criminal Insane at Fairview. Institutions for the feeble-minded and epileptic have been established at Elwyn, by an act of April 7, 1853; at Polk, by the act of June 3, 1893; at Spring City, by the act of May 15, 1903; at Laurelton, by the act of July 25, 1913; and an institution for inebriates was projected in the law of July 25, 1913. A new institution for defective delinquents was provided in 1927.

No phase of the history of the penal institutions of Pennsylvania since 1835 has been more depressing and unsatisfactory than the record of the industrial development in the state penitentiaries. This has been partly a result of general social and economic changes which have rendered the industrial processes, as carried on in the penitentiaries, relatively antiquated and unproductive, but the industrial deficiencies have been due primarily to restrictive legislation, which in Pennsylvania has exhibited to an unusual degree that insanity, stupidity and lack of critical insight or constructive vision which has peculiarly characterized the laws against prison industry throughout the country since the decade of the eighties. From 1835 to 1870 the same general industries and industrial processes were to be found in the state penitentiaries that had characterized their economic organization during the first years of their existence. Weaving, shoemaking, and the making and caning of chairs were the chief productive industries, and they were carried on by the prisoners individually in their cells by the progressively more anachronistic methods of hand manufacture. Not until after the passage of the "state-use" law of 1915 was power-driven machinery introduced as the basis of the industrial processes of the Eastern Penitentiary. Nor was there any notable change in the industries in this institution. Had De Beaumont and De Tocqueville, or Doctor Julius, or Monsieur Demetz returned to Cherry Hill in the year 1910, they would have been able to discover little if any changes in the industrial operations of the institution since the thirties.

In the Western Penitentiary, however, after the law of 1869

permitting the congregation of prisoners had begun to operate, a great change in the industrial activities of the institution took place. Power machinery was introduced on a large scale and there ensued a wide diversification of industries embracing shoemaking, weaving, broom- and brush-making and the manufacture of various types of tinware and heavy hardware. This continued until the laws of 1883 abolishing contract convict labor disrupted the industries of the penitentiary, and the notorious Muehlbronner Act of 1897 completely paralyzed prison industry in Pennsylvania. Down to the period of the seventies the commercial side of the prison industries was organized about a combination of the "public account" system and a modification of the "piece-price" form of the contract system, which provided for a complete institutional control of all prisoners in their industrial operations. This procedure was followed by the Eastern Penitentiary until the passage of the act of June 13, 1883, which abolished the contract system and directed the concentration on the public account and state use plans.

In the Western Penitentiary, as soon as shops could be erected after the passage of the "congregation" law of 1869, the "lease" form of the contract system was adopted, and from the early seventies to 1883 virtually all of the industries of the institution were conducted through the leasing of the prisoners to contractors. The state-use and public-account systems were introduced by the act of 1883 and continued by the act of April 18, 1897. The act of the latter year—the unpardonable Muehlbronner Act—also forbade the employment of more than thirty-five per cent. of the inmates of either penitentiary in productive industry, and also prohibited the use of power-driven machinery. After the passage of this act systematic prison labor in Pennsylvania was, of course, at an end. Even what little could be done to save the industrial system after 1897 was temporarily lost when the act of June 1, 1915, stipulated that the state-use system alone should prevail. The institutions have only recently been able to get readjusted to this type of organization and it is certain that in 1918 the industrial system in the state penitentiaries of Pennsylvania was in a more deplorable and unproductive condition than at any time since 1835. Total idleness is avoided only by the farm and construction work at the new central prison site, and by the feeble beginnings of the Bureau of Restoration in the organization of the penitentiary industries on the state-use plan.

The official attitude of the two state penitentiaries with respect to progressive improvements in prison reform and penal administration varied more widely than any other feature of the history of the institutions during this period. While the Eastern Penitentiary was usually faithfully and efficiently conducted, there can be no doubt that during the last half of the nineteenth century it was the stronghold of penological conservatism and vested interests, and its officials, from inspectors to warden, opposed practically without exception every one of those proposed changes in penal jurisprudence and administration which are to-day viewed as the great achievements in nineteenth-century prison reform. They opposed, among other things, the commutation laws; the "Irish" system of prison administration, based upon the progressive classification of prisoners; the Elmira reformatory system; the indeterminate sentence and parole system; the use of machinery in prison industry; and, above all, the congregation of prisoners for any purpose whatever. The officials of the Western Penitentiary, however, welcomed many of these advances with enthusiasm and adopted without delay such of them as were legally permissible or adapted to penitentiary administration.

But if the Philadelphia penitentiary was the seat of the reactionary forces, such was not the case with the Philadelphia Society for Alleviating the Miseries of Public Prisons. While its membership, to be sure, contained many of the friends of reaction and conservatism, its policy was always dominated by the progressive element, and from 1835 to 1927 it maintained with steady, if variable, success the traditions and reputation which it had established in prison reform from 1787 to 1835. Among the important developments in the improvement of the penal and reformatory institutions of Pennsylvania during this period which were due wholly or in part to the organized efforts of this society may be mentioned: the establishment of a hospital for the insane in the forties; the agitation for a house of correction in Philadelphia County from 1854 to 1870; the original commutation act of 1861; the creation of a State Board of Public Charities in 1869; the establishment of the Huntingdon Reformatory in 1881; and the indeterminate sentence and parole act of 1909. During all this period the society also rendered invaluable assistance in visiting the prisoners in their cells and in aiding them upon discharge—a line of service in which they were for a time imitated by the Allegheny Prison Society in the western part of the state. Finally, they did not exhaust their activities in working for the improvement of the state institutions, but labored effectively for the improvement of the county jails.

II. PENAL LEGISLATION

1. The Reform of the Criminal Code in 1860

By 1858 the anachronisms in the existing penal code and the
confusion resulting from the successive additions to the act of
1829, which had itself been little but an amendment of the codes
of 1790-94, made further acquiescence in the existing penal code
no longer possible, and on April nineteenth of that year the legislature resolved:

"That the Governor of this Commonwealth be and he is hereby
authorized and required to appoint, by and with the advice and
consent of the Senate, three competent citizens, learned in the laws
of this commonwealth, as commissioners to revise, collate and
digest all the acts and statutes relating to or touching the penal
laws of the commonwealth." [1]

The commissioners appointed by Governor W. F. Packer to
carry out his revision of the penal code were John C. Knox,
David Webster and Edward King.[2] Judge King (1794-1873) had
been one of three commissioners on the revision of the penal code
in 1828, and he had the opportunity to put his juristic ideas and
principles into practice after an interval of thirty-two years. It is
generally agreed that the code of 1860 was mainly the work of
Judge King, the most eminent of Pennsylvania authorities on the
law of equity and for years president-judge of the Criminal Court
of Philadelphia County.[3]

Apart from the specific penalties imposed by the code some of
its outstanding features were the following. It was drawn up in
an admirably systematic manner, even if some of the divisions may
have been too logical and artificial, a fault inherent in all attempts
to classify criminal acts. The two most novel and progressive
features of the code were the consistent practice of prescribing
only the maximum penalty for the several offenses and leaving
the minimum to be fixed at the discretion of the sentencing court,
and the courageous abolition of the monstrous and barbarous distinction between grand and petit larceny, which still remains
embalmed in the statute books of many American commonwealths—
a curious but oppressive relic of archaic juristic conceptions.

---

[1] *Laws of the General Assembly*, 1860, p. 392.
[2] "The Revised Penal Code of Pennsylvania," reprinted from *The American
Law Register*, August, 1860, pp. 1-2.
[3] Ibid., loc. cit., pp. 2-3.

The only reactionary anachronism introduced was that contained in the law imposing a penalty for blasphemy. This stipulated:

"If a person shall wilfully, premeditately and despitefully blaspheme, or speak loosely and profanely of Almighty God, Christ Jesus, the Holy Spirit, or the Scriptures of Truth, such person, on conviction thereof, shall be sentenced to pay a fine not exceeding one hundred dollars, and undergo an imprisonment not exceeding three months, or either, at the discretion of the court." [4]

The following were the penalties imposed for the more important crimes. In the field of crimes against the state, *treason* was punished by a fine not exceeding two thousand dollars and imprisonment for a period not to exceed twelve years. *Misprison of treason* was penalized by a fine of not to exceed one thousand dollars and imprisonment for not more than six years.[5]

The following penalties were prescribed for crimes against public morals and decency: *blasphemy,* as above; *sodomy* and *buggery,* a fine of not to exceed one thousand dollars and imprisonment for not more than ten years; *bigamy,* a fine of not more than one thousand dollars and imprisonment for not more than two years; *adultery,* a fine of not more than five hundred dollars and imprisonment for not more than one year; *fornication,* a fine of not more than one hundred dollars; *incest,* a fine up to five hundred dollars and imprisonment for not more than three years.[6]

Crimes against persons were dealt with in the following manner: *murder in the first degree,* "death by hanging by neck"; *murder in the second degree,* imprisonment for not more than twelve years for the first offense and life imprisonment for the second offense; *voluntary manslaughter,* a fine of not more than one thousand dollars and imprisonment for not more than twelve years; *mayhem,* a fine of not more than one thousand dollars and imprisonment for not more than five years; *rape,* a fine of not more than one thousand dollars and imprisonment for not more than fifteen years; *kidnaping,* a fine of not more than two thousand dollars and

---

[4] "The Revised Penal Code of Penna," loc. cit. It is significant that down to the present time all the great revisions of Pennsylvania criminal law have been primarily the work of some one man in each epoch. The enlightened Quaker codes of the late seventeenth century were prepared by William Penn; the notorious code of 1718 was compiled by David Lloyd, though he can not be entirely blamed for its contents; the notable revisions of 1786 to 1794 were the work of William Bradford, Jr., inspired by the spirit of Benjamin Rush; the slightly revised code of 1829 was drawn up by Thomas Bradford, Jr., with the aid and service of Roberts Vaux and S. R. Wood.
[5] Ibid., p. 385.
[6] Ibid., pp. 392-95.

imprisonment for not more than twelve years; *assault and battery,* a fine of not more than one thousand dollars and imprisonment for not more than one year, both or either at the discretion of the court.[7]

The punishments decreed for offenses against personal property were as follows: *robbery,* a fine of not more than one thousand dollars and imprisonment for not more than ten years; *assault to rob,* a fine of not more than one thousand dollars and imprisonment for not more than five years; *larceny,* a fine of not more than five hundred dollars and imprisonment for not more than three years.[8]

The punishment prescribed for offenses against real property follow: *burglary,* a fine of not more than one thousand dollars and imprisonment for not more than ten years; *arson,* without a person in the dwelling house, a fine of not more than two thousand dollars and imprisonment for not more than five years, and with a person in the dwelling house, a fine of not more than four thousand dollars and imprisonment for not more than twenty years.[9]

Finally, with respect to offenses against the coin and forgery, the following penalties were prescribed: *counterfeiting,* a fine of not more than one thousand dollars and imprisonment for not more than five years; *forgery,* the same as for counterfeiting.[10]

The only capital crime, then, in the code of 1860 was murder in the first degree, as in all codes from 1794 to 1860. A revised code of criminal procedure was also prepared by the commissioners and accepted by the legislature.[11] In their long and able report the commissioners presented an elaborate exposition, explanation and defense of their work which was of great assistance in securing its enactment into law.[12]

That the report and the codes were considered of a high order by authoritative contemporary critics is evident from the following comment in one of the leading law reviews of the time:

"The report, as a whole, is a most masterly production, and reflects infinite credit upon the ability, learning, industry, and faithfulness of the Commissioners, and will prove an enduring

---

[7] "The Revised Penal Code of Pennsylvania," loc. cit., pp. 402-08.
[8] Ibid., pp. 408-15.
[9] Ibid., pp. 415-20.
[10] Ibid., pp. 420-25.
[11] Ibid., pp. 427-58.
[12] Ibid., loc. cit., pp. 4ff. The complete documentary sources for this revision are contained in the following: *Report of the Commissioners Appointed to Revise the Penal Code of the Commonwealth of Pennsylvania,* Harrisburg, 1860, p. 129, and *The Penal Laws of Pennsylvania, Passed March 31, 1860,* Harrisburg, 1860, p. 79.

monument to their fame. It is deserving of careful study in all its details, not only by those who are engaged in the practice of criminal law, but by the legislator, and by all who are interested in penal legislation and the entire subject of crimes and punishments. Pennsylvania may now congratulate herself upon possessing a system of penal laws worthy of her advanced civilization, and adapted to the wants of her extended and varied population." [13]

While there is little doubt that the laudatory strain in the above quotation was justified, in view of the relative condition and level of criminal jurisprudence at that time, the progress in the level of criminal law in the last half-century is evident from the following incisive criticism passed upon this code of 1860 by Professor William E. Mikell, Dean of the Law School of the University of Pennsylvania, one of the most eminent of American authorities on criminal jurisprudence, in general, and on the criminal law of Pennsylvania, in particular:

"Perhaps, in the true sense of the term, there is no criminal 'code' in Pennsylvania. The whole body of criminal law has never been reduced to a written code in this state in the sense in which this has been done in some of the States of the Union in which jurisdictions there are no crimes except those specifically prescribed. . . .

"Viewing the code, however, as a whole, there is an utter lack of principle in the grading of crimes as felonies or misdemeanors, either according to the moral heinousness of the offence or the severity of the punishment. . . .

"The work of the commissioners who framed the Code of 1860 shows an utter lack of consistent theory not only of grading the crimes as felonies and misdemeanors, but also in grading the punishment fixed for the various crimes. . . .

"In the case of almost every crime denounced by the code fine and imprisonment are associated. In most cases the penalty provided is fine and imprisonment, in some it is fine or imprisonment. In a few cases imprisonment alone without a fine is prescribed, and in a few others, it is a fine alone without imprisonment. We seek in vain for any principle on which the fine is omitted, where it is omitted; or for a principle on which it is inflicted in addition to imprisonment in some cases, and as an alternative to imprisonment in others. . . .

"The Pennsylvania code has no general section on attempts, but

---

[13] "The Revised Penal Code of Pennsylvania," *loc. cit.*, p. 26. For a list of the criminal laws repealed by the code of 1860, which constitutes a fair index to the previous criminal law of Pennsylvania, see *Laws of the General Assembly*, 1860, pp. 451-58.

in a haphazard manner, in providing for some crimes, provides for the attempt to commit the same, and in some cases has no provision for such attempts. A study of those cases in which provision for punishing the attempt is made, shows an entire absence of any theory or principle in assessing the punishment. . . ." [14]

The criminal code of 1860 has never been systematically revised and remains to the present day the basis of Pennsylvania's criminal jurisprudence. It has been modified by many additions and amendments, but these alterations have contributed rather to greater confusion than to clarity and modernity. Professor Mikell also calls attention to this point:

"The writer has attempted to point out in this paper some of the more glaring and interesting defects in the code. He has by no means exhausted them. There is a great need for a complete revision of the code. It is a jumble of inconsistent theories; a great many sections are badly drawn, others are obsolete; many are inconsistent, many are in conflict; there is much overlapping due to different acts having been passed at different times covering in part the same subject matter, so that it cannot be told whether a given crime should be punished under one section or another prescribing a different punishment." [15]

By 1917 the condition of the penal code of Pennsylvania as regards anachronisms, conflicts and points of confusion had become much like that which existed in 1860, and an act of July 25, 1917, directed the governor to appoint five commissioners to "revise, collate, and digest all the acts and statutes relating to or touching the penal laws of the Commonwealth in such a manner as to render the penal code of Pennsylvania more efficient, clear, and perfect, and the punishments inflicted on crimes more uniform and better adapted to the suppression of crime and the reformation of the offender." [16] Governor Brumbaugh, accordingly, appointed the commissioners and they immediately took up the task of revision which presents an opportunity for constructive and progressive juristic reform unequaled since the days of William Bradford, Jr., as the scientific background of criminal jurisprudence has made more progress since 1860 than it had between the time of Draco and 1860. As a member of the commission charged with the revision, Professor Mikell has given above some notion of the task and at least a slight indication of the promising spirit in which it was

---

[14] *The Journal of Prison Discipline and Philanthropy*, March, 1918, pp. 89-91.
[15] Ibid., p. 92.
[16] *Laws of the General Assembly*, 1917, pp. 1188-89.

attacked.[17] The commissioners appointed drafted a revised code, but the Legislature thus far (June, 1927) has refused to accept their work and bring Pennsylvania criminal jurisprudence up to the level of modern juristic science and penal practice. A new Penal Code Commission and a Crime Commission were created in 1927 and may have better luck that their predecessor.

In any survey of the history of criminal law it is, however, necessary to emphasize the fact that even the progressive and scientific juristic measures advocated by Dean Mikell, and by the members of the American Bar Association who are concerned with the revision of the criminal codes of the country are as much out of harmony with the self-evident and thoroughly established principles of psychology, social science and criminology as the ducking-stool and the pillory. The most advanced criminal code ever proposed by a professional lawyer with any serious hope of its adoption has rested upon assumptions which have been completely repudiated by modern psychological, social and criminal science. Such advanced codes still accept as their fundamental postulate the doctrine that the criminal is a physically and mentally normal individual, and a free moral agent capable at all times of choosing his actions and determining whether he will be a law-abiding citizen or a heinous criminal. All criminals are assumed to be equal before the law, not only with respect to their legal rights but also with regard to their physical and mental capacities and responsibilities.

The law, lawyers and courts are held to be the legitimate agencies for determining and controlling society's methods of dealing with the delinquent classes. It is maintained that it is possible to adjust the penalty to the crime on the basis of the relative assumed damage or challenge to society inherent in the particular act. The major interest and concern of the law and the court remains in the crime rather than the criminal, and the reaction of society in the circumstances is adjusted to the nature of the crime rather than the characteristics and personality of the individual who has committed it. Penalties are held to be adequate to deter from the commission of crime in direct proportion to their severity, irrespective of the personality of the individual punished. Punishment is regarded as primarily and potently reformative in its operation, and after the term of its imposition has expired the individual criminal is viewed as a fit and proper person to resume his position as a free citizen

---

[17] The following commissioners were appointed by Governor Brumbaugh to revise the criminal code: Edwin M. Abbott, William E. Mikell, George C. Bradshaw, Clarence E. Coughlin and Rex N. Mitchell.

in society, irrespective of the fact that the physical or mental causes of his original criminal behavior may have been actually greatly accentuated by the conditions of life during his term in prison. As archaic as the postulates of the most advanced proposed criminal codes are the methods of criminal procedure approved by even many very progressive jurists. The police, district attorney, judge and jury are held to be competent and adequate to the task of determining the guilt of the accused and the treatment to be meted out to him. Likewise, the guilt or innocence of a particular crime with which the defendant is charged is regarded as a much more vital matter than the potential menace of a pathological personality to the community at large. In fact, the question of the commission of the specific crime charged is the only question with which the court concerns itself. And the procedure followed in court is a combination of magic, rhetoric and contradictory and absurd rules of evidence which would bring forth a roar of ribald and contemptuous laughter if they were proposed as the method to be followed in the science laboratories of even a southern Fundamentalist college.

It is necessary for us to come to realize the fact that every dictate of medical and social science unquestionably indicates that lawyers and courts have no more proper function in dealing with criminals (using this term in a scientific sense) than they have in taking full charge of the treatment of mentally defective and insane types—types which were once as much under the sole jurisdiction of lawyers and judges as the criminals are at the present time. As soon as science—natural, biological, medical, psychological and social—comes to be applied to our methods of handling the delinquent classes, it will be seen that the function of criminal law ends with the mere formal legal or judicial supervision of the forms of procedure, comparable to the judicial supervision at present of the processes of committing an alleged insane person to a hospital for the insane and approving his discharge after a cure has been effected. Hence, the improvements in the Pennsylvania penal code recommended by Dean Mikell and his associates appear in the light of modern criminal science as little founded upon the scientific facts in the circumstances as the ordeal, torture and the doctrine of demoniacal possession.

But the day of the operation of scientific criminology is far off, and for the time being the advocates of reform must content themselves with such temporizing with an obsolete structure as Dean Mikell must recommend, and upon the hope of undoing the unwise and unfortunate effects of criminal procedure prior to sentence by such quasi-juristic advances as the indeterminate sentence, parole and probation. By a sane procedure after conviction we may even now do much to offset the evil operation of contemporary criminal jurisprudence and court procedure, though efforts in that direction will be hampered as long as we do not have general facilities for applying probation methods universally to those classes who never should be subjected to the demoralizing influence of penal institutions, and as long as we do not have a real indeterminate sentence law which will enable properly guided prison authorities to retain indefinitely in segregation those delinquent types whose reformation and safe existence in society is impossible or manifestly unlikely.

2. LEGISLATION AFFECTING PRISON ADMINISTRATION

In general there have been no marked changes in the nature of the controlling authorities since the basic act of 1829. To give greater simplicity and uniformity an act was passed on May 10, 1909, which empowered the governor to appoint the three inspectors of the Western Penitenitary who had been appointed by the court of common pleas and the district court of Allegheny County since 1864.[18] From 1909 until the present time the appointment of all the state prison inspectors has been vested in the governor. As to just what form the organization of the controlling authorities of the new Rockview Penitentiary will take, it is impossible to say. Thus far it has been controlled by the same board of inspectors as supervise the Western Penitentiary, the Rockview Penitentiary being still regarded as an adjunct of the Pittsburgh institution. In all probability it will be separated and given a separate board of inspectors.[19]

Down until the creation of the Department of Public Welfare in 1921, only one attempt—and that a rather feeble one—has ever been made to provide a centralized and uniform administration of the penal, reformatory and correctional institutions of the state. This occurred when an act was passed on April 24, 1869, "to create a Board of Public Charities." According to the terms of this act the governor was empowered to appoint five commissioners to serve for a term of five years as a board of public charities. The commissioners were authorized to appoint a general agent and secretary, this officer being intended to carry on the field work and general executive and technical work of the board. The members of the board or their agent were required to visit at least once every

---

[18] *Laws of the General Assembly,* 1909, p. 500.
[19] Some very well informed authorities doubt that the Western Penitentiary will be speedily abandoned.

year all the charitable and correctional institutions in the state which received state aid. They were further directed to send to the legislature a complete annual report setting forth the results of their investigations "with such suggestions as the Board may deem necessary and pertinent." Not only was the board given the authority to recommend necessary changes and reforms, but it was also given a general supervision over all the expenditures of the several penal, reformatory, correctional and charitable institutions of the state. The controlling authorities of all such institutions which received appropriations from the state were required annually to make a report to the general agent of the Board of Public Charities giving the amount of state aid they were requesting for the coming year and setting forth explicitly the purposes for which they proposed to expend the appropriations. Before this budget could go before the legislature it had to be acted upon by the Board of Public Charities and sent to the legislature with a record of the action of the board. To prevent special favoritism or unfair personal interest by members of the board in criticizing the expenditures of the several institutions, it was ordered that no member of the Board of Public Charities should be in any way interested in any contract for building or repairing any institution and that no officer of any of the institutions should be eligible for the office of commissioner or general agent of the Board of Public Charities.[20]

It will be evident from the above analysis of the act that no matter how alert or vigilant the board might be, it could never pass beyond a supervisory and critical capacity, and could never assume any administrative direction or coordination of the several penal, reformatory and correctional institutions. While this original act of 1869 has been amended many times, the alterations down to 1921 have consisted in adding to the membership of the board, giving their action more exactness and authority and allowing an increase in the corps of executive and investigating assistants, but have in no way changed the character of the function and nature of the board.[21] The creation of a prison labor commission by the law of June 1, 1915, might be regarded as a partial step toward giving unified and coordinated administrative control over the penal and allied institutions, inasmuch as this law vested the industrial control of the two state penitentiaries and the state reformatory in the above commission.[22]

---

[20] *Laws of the General Assembly,* 1869, pp. 90-3.

[21] A handy compilation of the several acts relating to the Board of Public Charities giving the status of its legislative sanction to 1921 is to be found in *A Compilation of the Laws Relating to the Board of Public Charities,* Harrisburg, 1916, pp. 13-25.

[22] *Laws of the General Assembly,* 1915, p. 656.

By far the most important act since the original administrative act of 1829 was one passed on the twenty-fifth of May, 1921, creating a Department of Public Welfare and abolishing the Board of Public Charities, the Committee on Lunacy and the Prison Labor Commission. This act is one of the most forward-looking and advanced measures with respect to the centralizing of the public control of the defective, dependent, and delinquent classes in the history of American state legislation on the subject. It wisely put the control of the insane, feeble-minded, criminals and dependent poor in charge of one single governing agency, the Department of Public Welfare. It provided for the creation of a commission of the public welfare, an executive agent; namely, a deputy commissioner, and such other bureaus and agents as were necessary to the organization and execution of the duties of the new department. The more important provisions of this act follow:

"Section 1. Be it enacted, etc., That there is hereby created a Department of Public Welfare, to consist of a Commission of Public Welfare, a Commissioner of Public Welfare, a Deputy Commissioner of Public Welfare, and such bureaus, officers, agents, and employees, as are herein or may hereafter be provided. . . .

"Section 3. The Commission of Public Welfare shall consist of nine members, three of whom, as ex-officio members, shall be the Commissioner of Public Welfare, the Commissioner of Labor and Industry, and the Commissioner of Health, and six of whom shall be appointed by the Governor, by and with the advice and consent of the Senate. Before the first day of September, one thousand nine hundred and twenty-one, the Governor shall appoint three of the said six members of the commission to serve for a period of two years, and three to serve for a period of four years. Thereafter all of said six members shall be appointed for a term of four years. The members of the commission shall serve without compensation, but shall be allowed the expenses necessarily incurred in the performance of their duties.

"Section 4. The Commissioner of Public Welfare shall be appointed by the Governor, by and with the advice and consent of the Senate, for a term of four years. Before entering upon the duties of his office, he shall give a bond to the Commonwealth, in the sum of twenty-five thousand dollars ($25,000), to be approved by the Governor, conditioned for the faithful performance of the duties of his office, and shall take and subscribe the oath prescribed by the Constitution. Vacancies in the office of commissioner shall be filled by the Governor. The commissioner shall receive an annual salary of ten thousand dollars ($10,000), and all expenses necessarily incurred in the discharge of his duties.

"The Deputy Commissioner shall be appointed by the Governor, and shall receive an annual salary of seven thousand five hundred dollars ($7,500).

"Section 5. The commission shall meet, at the State Capitol, at least once every three months, on a date fixed by standing rule, and at any other time and place upon the call of the commissioner. Special meetings may also be had at such times and places as the commission may deem necessary.

"Section 6. It shall be the duty of the commission to advise the commissioner on such matters as he may bring before it or as it may require him to bring before it, and it shall have general supervision over the policies of the department. It shall be the duty of the commissioner to report to the commission, from time to time, the information found upon the examination and visitation hereinafter provided, the measures taken to correct any detrimental conditions in the institutions or places under the supervision of the department, and the result thereof.

"The rules and regulations of the department shall be made by the commissioner, subject to the approval of the commission, and, when so made and approved, shall constitute the duly ordained rules and regulations of the department, and be promulgated and enforced as such.

"The commissioner, with the approval of the commission, shall establish certain bureaus in the department, not to exceed four in number, and apportion to each of them such specific duties as may best promote an efficient administration of the department. One of said bureaus shall be a bureau of mental health to further the prevention and cure of mental diseases. And the head of such bureau shall be a physician specially experienced in mental diseases.

"Subject to the foregoing, all the duties imposed upon, and the powers vested in, the department, shall be exercised and carried out by the commissioner or under his direction.

Section 7. The commissioner, with the approval of the Governor, shall appoint a chief of each bureau. The chiefs of bureaus shall each receive an annual salary of not more than five thousand dollars ($5,000), except the chief of the bureau of mental health, who shall receive a salary of not more than seventy-five hundred dollars ($7,500), and have charge of their respective bureaus, subject to the direction, control, and supervision of the commissioner, and shall perform such duties as he may prescribe.

"The commissioner may appoint such other officers, inspectors, agents, and employees, as the work of the department may require, who shall receive such salary or compensation as the commission may determine. The commissioner may also employ persons having professional of expert knowledge of the matters within the jurisdiction or supervision of the department.

"Section 8. The term "State institutions," as used in this act, shall mean and include all penal, reformatory, or correctional institutions, hospitals for the insane or any other purpose, institutions for feeble-minded, idiotic, or epileptic persons, for the deaf, for inebriates, or for juvenile delinquents, and all charitable institutions whatsoever, within this Commonwealth, maintained in whole or in part by the Commonwealth and whose board of inspectors, managers, trustees, or directors is appointed, in whole or in part, by the Governor or by the Governor by and with the advice and consent of the Senate.

"Section 9. The department shall have supervision over:

"(a) All State institutions as hereinbefore defined.

"(b) All charitable institutions within this Commonwealth which receive aid from the Commonwealth: Provided, however, That the department shall exercise no powers over such charitable institutions, other than those heretofore vested in the Board of Public Charities or the Committee on Lunacy, notwithstanding any language hereinafter used.

"(c) All houses or places within the Commonwealth in which any person of unsound mind is detained, whenever the occupant or owner of the house or person having charge of the lunatic receives any compensation for the custody, control, or attendance, other than as an attendant or nurse, and also of all institutions, houses, or places, in which more than one such person is detained, with or without compensation paid for custody or attendance.

"(d) All county prisons, and all hospitals, almshouses, or poorhouses, maintained by any county, city, borough, township, or poor district of this Commonwealth.

"(e) All institutions, associations, and societies within this Commonwealth, into whose care the custody of delinquent, dependent, or neglected children may be committed, and all houses and places maintained by such institutions, associations, or societies, in which such children may be kept or detained.

"(f) Homes and premises of those in which is conducted the business of receiving, boarding, or keeping infant children under three years of age.

"Section 10. In addition to the foregoing, the department shall also exercise supervision over:

"(a) The administration of any system provided by the Commonwealth for assistance to mothers.

"(b) Any labor or system of labor carried on in the penal, correctional, or reformatory institutions of the State.

"(c) Any system of reparation provided by the Commonwealth for relief from conditions caused by mine-caves, fire, flood, or other casualty, and constituting a menace to public safety and welfare.

"Section 11. It shall be the duty of the department, from time to time, to recommend and bring to the attention of the officers or other persons having the management of the institutions, prisons, almshouses, poor houses, houses, places, associations, or societies, under its supervision as provided in section nine hereof, such standards and methods as may be helpful in the government and administration of such institution, prisons, almshouses, poor houses, houses, places, associations, or societies, and for the betterment of the inmates therein. . . .

"Section 16. All plans for the erection or substantial alteration of any State institutions, county prison, almshouse, poor house, or any building for the care of delinquent children or persons of unsound mind, and all charitable institutions receiving aid from the Commonwealth, shall be submitted to, and approved by, the department; and such buildings shall not be built or such alteration made or contracted for until such approval has first been had and duly filed with those charged with the management of such institution or place. . . .

"Section 31. The Board of Public Charities and the Committee on Lunacy are hereby abolished.

"Section 32. All the powers conferred by law upon the Board of Public Charities or the Committee on Lunacy are hereby vested in and may be exercised by the department.

"Section 33. The Prison Labor Commission, created by the act, approved the first day of June, Anno Domini one thousand nine hundred and fifteen (Pamphlet Laws, six hundred and fifty-six), entitled "An act for the inmates of the Eastern Penitentiary, Western Penitentiary, and the Pennsylvania Industrial Reformatory at Huntingdon, and for such other correctional institutions as shall be hereafter established by the Commonwealth, and making an appropriation therefor," is hereby abolished, but no act or part of any act repealed by the said act creating the Prison Labor Commission shall be hereby revived.

"All the powers conferred upon the Prison Labor Commission are hereby vested in the department."

On June 7, 1923, a general act was passed, reorganizing the executive departments and administration of the State of Pennsylvania, and Article XX of this act continued the Department of Public Welfare, and its departmental administrative and advisory boards and commissions with slightly augmented powers.

The same general continuity has been observed in the nature of the administrative officials of the two state penitentiaries that has been shown to have been the case with the controlling authorities. With a few minor exceptions the administrative direction of the penal institutions is to-day in the hands of the same groups of officials as in 1830, receiving their appointment from the same authorities as provided for in the law of 1829, which was itself based largely on those of 1789 and 1790. The warden, physician and clerk, appointed by the inspectors, have remained as the chief administrative officials of the penitentiaries. There have been only two important additions to this administrative force, namely, a paid moral instructor and a parole officer. A paid moral instructor was provided for the Eastern Penitentiary by a resolution of the legislature of April 16, 1838,[23] and a similar official was added to the administration of the Western Penitentiary by an act of March 25, 1839.[24] Parole officers were necessitated by the indeterminate sentence and parole act of May 10, 1909, and this act authorized the inspectors of each penitentiary to appoint one or more parole officers.[25] The above have been the only important changes in the administrative officials since 1829.

The present legal status of the administration of the state penitentiaries may best be summarized by an analysis of the act of May 23, 1913, which superseded but did not greatly alter the act of April 23, 1829, which had been in operation up to that time. No change was made in the nature or organization of either controlling or administrative authorities. The governor was authorized to appoint five taxable citizens of Philadelphia County as a board of inspectors for the Eastern Penitentiary and five taxable citizens of Allegheny County to serve as a similar governing board for the Western Penitentiary. Their term of appointment was specified as four years and they were to receive no remuneration other than their expenses. The following powers were vested in the board of inspectors: to appoint a warden, chaplain, chief clerk, physician and parole officer; to fix the salaries of all officers and employees in the administrative force of the penitentiary; to make the rules for the government of the institution which were not inconsistent with law; to have charge of the purchase of raw materials and the sale of manufactured articles and of all prison accounts; and to investigate the conduct of employees and hear all complaints connected therewith. The warden was empowered to appoint all subordinates; to dismiss them; and to govern and punish the prisoners in accordance with the rules drawn up by the inspectors.[26]

---

[23] *Laws of the General Assembly*, 1837-38, p. 690.
[24] Ibid., 1838-39, Chap. 66.
[25] Ibid., 1909, p. 498.
[26] Ibid., 1913, pp. 330-33. To save space and to avoid needless repetition, the penal legislation dealing with prison administration and discipline and with prison industry and maintenance will be discussed in connection with those subjects later in this chapter.

III. THE ARCHITECTURAL HISTORY OF THE STATE PENITENTIARIES, 1835-1927

1. THE EASTERN PENITENTIARY

The Eastern Penitentiary, like its great rivals, the Auburn, Wethersfield and Charlestown Prisons, has never left its original plant, and remains to the present day one of the best-preserved examples of the prison architecture of that period when it was passing from the stage of the insecure and rambling county jail to the massive castle-like structures which have characterized penal architecture from the days of John Haviland's avowed reproduction of the medieval citadel to those of the still more inhuman concrete and steel cages, in great corridors of inside cells, which have been so inseparably associated with the more recent products of the savage ingenuity of the prison architects.

The original structure, with its seven radiating wings and five hundred and thirty-two very large outside cells, each with an outside yard, was without doubt the finest and best-constructed example of prison architecture in the world at the time. Its general architectural features were almost beyond criticism, when considered in their relation to the contemporary developments in prison construction. From the beginning, however, the sanitary appliances were deplorably inadequate. These conditions were scathingly criticized in 1849 by Doctor R. A. Given, the enlightened and progressive resident physician from 1844 to 1851.[27] This criticism had the desired results, and in 1851, just before his resignation, Doctor Given was able to present in his report a creditable list of improvements. He revealed at this time the almost unbelievable condition of the sanitary appliances previous to 1851. Before that time there had never been water enough provided to flush the toilets and cess-pipes in the cells oftener than twice in each week, with the result which can best be described in the words of the physician: "I have known the clothes of persons walking through the corridor to become so saturated with the odor that it was perceptible to others even after a walk of some miles in the open air."[28] It is needless to remark that the spiritual forces which the Pennsylvania system was supposed to set in motion must have been considerably handicapped before 1851 by the atmosphere in which they had to operate.

No general changes were made in the plant until 1853, when cell-

---

[27] *Report of the Inspectors of the Eastern Penitentiary*, 1849, pp. 18ff.
[28] Ibid., 1851, p. 32.

blocks one, two and three were remodeled, the cells enlarged, and the total number of cells increased from five hundred and thirty-two to five hundred and sixty.[29] The capacity of the prison continued to be adequate until the close of the year 1866, when, as a result of the general social conditions at the close of the Civil War, the population of the prison increased to five hundred and sixty-nine. By the close of the next year it had increased to six hundred and twenty-six, with a capacity for solitary confinement of only five hundred and sixty. In their report for 1867 the inspectors and warden made a vigorous plea for the erection of additional cells.[30] Opinion at that time, however, was coming to favor the erection of a third state penitentiary in the center of the state, instead of making radical extensions to the existing plants, and the legislature could only be induced to make a small appropriation to extend cell-block number one so as to add twenty more cells. Forty-three thousand dollars were appropriated for this purpose by the act of April 11, 1868, and the cells were occupied in 1871.[31]

The inspectors kept up their agitation for an extension of the Eastern Penitentiary rather than the building of a new institution in an interior county, and they presented a memorial to the legislature urging their point of view on March 11, 1873.[32] The best that they could do at the time, however, was to force a compromise. The legislature appropriated $55,000 by an act of April 18, 1877, and $29,250 by an act of May 18, 1878, for the much needed additions to the Eastern Penitentiary,[33] but at the same time passed the act of June 12, 1878, providing for the establishment of the proposed "middle penitentiary." [34] The extension made possible by the appropriations of 1877 and 1878 were completed for occupancy in 1879. In addition to minor changes it made possible the addition of three new wings of cells, numbers eight, nine and ten, with one hundred and thirty new cells, besides twenty cells added to block three.[35] This gave a total of seven hundred and thirty cells, but the population had increased so rapidly that there were one thousand, one hundred and seventeen prisoners in the Eastern Penitentiary at the close of the year 1879. The next extension of the

[29] Report of the Board of Inspectors of the Eastern Penitentiary, 1853, pp. 21-2.
[30] Ibid., 1867, p. 26.
[31] Laws of the General Assembly, 1868, p. 26. Report of the Board of Inspectors of the Eastern Penitentiary, 1871, p. 9.
[32] Report of the Board of Inspectors of the Eastern Penitentiary, 1872, pp. 33-4.
[33] Laws of the General Assembly, 1877, Chap. 60; 1878, Chap. 98.
[34] Ibid., 1878, p. 180.
[35] Report of the Board of Inspectors of the Eastern Penitentiary, 1878, pp. 41ff.; 1879, p. 61.

capacity of the plant came in 1894 when a new cell block was erected, containing thirty-five cells.[36] The next addition to the old structure was constructed between 1908 and 1911. This was the new twelfth block constructed out of concrete and steel by prison labor. It is, with the possible exception of the newest wings of the Holmesburg Convict Prison, near Philadelphia, the finest example to be found anywhere of the outside cell construction in its latest and most improved form.

The Eastern Penitentiary, then, furnishes a recapitulation in its plant of the entire evolution of a type of prison architecture which intelligent opinion is coming to favor again after a temporary infatuation with the inside cell or steel cage construction. This new block contained one hundred and twenty cells and increased the total capacity of the prison to eight hundred and eighty-five.[37] Even this final extension made no pretention to furnishing enough cells for the separate confinement of all the prisoners, there being fourteen hundred and six prisoners confined on January 1, 1911. In spite of the decision to abandon the institution, a new three-story wing of the Pennsylvania type was opened for occupation at the end of 1926, designed to house two hundred and forty convicts. The architectural situation in the Eastern Penitentiary as respects the housing of prisoners may best be understood by the following citation from several of the annual reports which set forth in a brief manner the architectural details of the twelve cell blocks or wings erected in 1911.[38]

SIZE OF CORRIDORS, ROOMS AND YARDS

First Block—Length, 368 feet; width (corridor) 10 feet; height, 21 feet; number of rooms, 50.
    8 rooms 14   feet long, 17   feet wide, and 11½ feet high.
    42 rooms 16   feet long, 8   feet wide, and 11½ feet high.
Yards— 8 rooms 14½ feet long, 17   feet wide, with wall 11½ feet high.
    42 rooms 14¼ feet long, 8   feet wide, with wall 11½ feet high.
Second Block—Length, 268 feet; width of corridor, 10 feet; height, 21 feet; number of rooms, 38.
    38 rooms 12   feet long, 7½ feet wide, and 14   feet high.
Yards—38 rooms 18   feet long, 8   feet wide, with wall 11½ feet high.
Third Block—Length, 368 feet; width of corridor, 10 feet; height, 19 feet; number of rooms, 40.
    20 rooms 12   feet long, 7½ feet wide, and 14   feet high.
    12 rooms 20   feet long, 8   feet wide, and 14   feet high.
    8 rooms 20   feet long, 17   feet wide, and 14   feet high.
Yards—18 rooms 18   feet long, 18   feet wide, with wall 11½ feet high.

---

[36] *Report of the Board of Inspectors of the Eastern Penitentiary*, 1894, pp. 23ff.
[37] Ibid., 1911, p. 4.
[38] *Annual Report of the Board of Inspectors of the Eastern Penitentiary*, 1892, pp. 23-5; 1911, p. 4.

Fourth Block—Length, 268 feet; width of corridors, 10 feet; height, 33 feet; number of rooms, 100.
 1st floor—50 rooms 15 feet long, 7½ feet wide, and 11 feet high.
 2nd floor—50 rooms 12 feet long, 7½ feet wide, and 12 feet high.
Yards—46 rooms 15 feet long, 8 feet wide, with wall 10½ feet high.

Fifth Block—Length, 362 feet; width of corridors, 10 feet; height, 33 feet; number of rooms, 136.
 1st floor—68 rooms 15 feet long, 7½ feet wide, and 11 feet high.
 2nd floor—68 rooms 12 feet long, 7½ feet wide, and 12 feet high.
Yards—64 rooms 15 feet long, 8 feet wide, with wall 10½ feet high.

Sixth Block—Length, 268 feet; width of corridor, 10 feet; height, 33 feet; number of rooms, 100.
 1st floor—50 rooms 15 feet long, 7½ feet wide, and 11 feet high.
 2nd floor—50 rooms 12 feet long, 7½ feet wide, and 12 feet high.
Yards—46 rooms 15 feet long, 8 feet wide, with wall 10½ feet high.

Seventh Block—Length, 365 feet; width of corridor, 15 feet; height, 38 feet; number of rooms, 136.
 1st floor—68 rooms 16 feet long, 7½ feet wide, and 11 feet high.
 2nd floor—68 rooms 14 feet long, 7½ feet wide, and 22 feet high.
Yards—65 rooms 15 feet long, 8 feet wide, with wall 11 feet high.

Eighth Block—Length, 254 feet; width of corridor, 10 feet; height, 16 feet; number of rooms, 50.
 50 rooms 18 feet long, 8 feet wide, and 12½ feet high.
No Yards.

Ninth Block—Length, 254 feet; width of corridor, 10 feet; height, 16 feet; number of rooms, 50.
 50 rooms 18 feet long, 8 feet wide, and 12½ feet high.
No Yards.

Tenth Block—Length, 306 feet; width of corridor, 10 feet, height, 15 feet; number of rooms, 30.
 30 rooms 18 feet long, 8 feet wide, and 12½ feet high.
No Yards.

Eleventh Block—Number of rooms, 35.
 35 rooms, 16 feet long, 8 feet wide, and 12 feet high.
No Yards.

Twelfth Block—Number of rooms, 120.
 1st floor, 40 rooms.
 2nd floor, 40 rooms.
 3rd floor, 40 rooms.
No Yards.

In addition to the cell wings, the following recent improvements are worthy of brief mention. A new hospital building was erected and a large boiler and engine house in 1901; a store-house in 1905; a new industrial building in 1906; a shop building in 1907; and an emergency hospital in 1908. Still more recently additional shop room has been provided by removing the partitions between the cell yards in the older wings and roofing over the space thus procured. The buildings have been kept in a good state of repair and the antiquated sanitary apparatus has been replaced by modern equipment.[39] The plant appears to be in a condition to furnish a suitable habitat for prisoners for another half-century and is still much superior in spaciousness and comfort to any of the modern American prisons constructed on the steel cage and inside cell block design. From the standpoint of housing the inmates it will, even to-day, rank high among prison structures. There is, however, one defect—a result of historical conditions, which dooms the plant to an early abandonment. While the Eastern Penitentiary was originally constructed well out in the country bordering on the city of Philadelphia, the city has spread until after eighty-eight years it has placed the institution in the midst of a closely built and densely populated district, thereby rendering impossible any proposition to gain more space by extending the walls in some direction. At the same time, the constant accretion of new cell wings and other buildings has filled up almost completely the space available within the walls.[40] These circumstances made it impossible to provide adequate outdoor exercise for the prisoners, and also preclude the possibility of constructing enough shops to occupy the population, now Pennsylvania has been divested of the stupid and short-sighted legislation which has for so long paralyzed its prison industries.

The hopelessness of attempting to retain the Eastern Penitentiary plant permanently as a state penitentiary, in view of the above-mentioned insuperable difficulties, was evident to the progressive reform element, and an act was passed on June 14, 1915, directing that the most famous and historic prison structure in America be abandoned and its occupants be moved to the proposed central penitentiary site in Centre County. This act stated that whereas a large tract of land had been purchased in Centre County for the Western Penitentiary, and this site was located in the central portion of the state and of ample extent to support the inmates of both state penitentiaries, and that whereas "the Eastern Penitentiary is located in a district which has become closely built up, so that the inmates thereof have no opportunity for farming or other healthful outdoor employment, but out of necessity must be kept largely in idleness to their own physical and moral injury; and the combination of the said Eastern Penitentiary and the Western Penitentiary into one institution, under one management, would tend to uniformity and efficiency as well as to great economy in administration," it was accordingly enacted that the plans of the new

[39] The exact cost of the physical plant of the Eastern Penitentiary is difficult to ascertain, but $1,400,000 has been appropriated for buildings.
[40] See the cuts in the *Annual Reports of the Eastern Penitentiary.*

Western Penitentiary be so altered as to permit the erection of an institution of sufficient size to allow the consolidation of the two penitentiaries into what was thereafter to be known as the "Pennsylvania State Penitentiary." [41]

It was originally intended that the new central state prison at Rockview in Centre County should be the joint state prison for both Eastern and Western Pennsylvania, but great opposition developed to this proposal of a union prison, primarily because of the distance to be traveled by relatives in visiting prisoners. As a result, the original act providing for the union of the two institutions in the new plant was never executed. On May 14, 1925, an act was passed creating a commission to investigate and secure a large tract in the eastern part of the state on which to erect a new eastern penitentiary. The new site has been purchased at Graterford in Montgomery County. This means that within a few years the historic plant at Cherry Hill will be abandoned and a new farm site occupied. The sum of $750,000 has been appropriated for the new Eastern Penitentiary.

2. THE WESTERN PENITENTIARY

It will be recalled that the Western Penitentiary was originally erected according to a circular design planned by William Strickland, a Philadelphia architect, and modeled in this respect after Bentham's *Panopticon.* It was also pointed out that this original plant was constructed according to the administrative plan of solitary confinement without labor, and that when labor was introduced by the act of 1829, the cell arrangement was found wholly inadequate and it immediately became necessary to tear down the new prison and erect new cell blocks designed to allow labor in the cells. The new plans were drawn, as it will be remembered, by John Haviland and were modeled after the radiating design of the Eastern Penitentiary, though there were originally but two wings at Allegheny instead of seven, as at Cherry Hill.[42] These wings, containing one hundred and seventy cells, were completed in 1837 and the prison authorities then wisely requested that while the construction tools and machinery "were on the ground" an appropriation should be made for the erection of a new block which would soon be needed.[43] Their suggestion was not heeded, however, and as early as 1841 the prison officials were obliged

---

[41] *Laws of the General Assembly,* 1915, pp. 972-73.

[42] See above, pp. 140ff. No yards were provided for the cells at Allegheny. This proved a serious defect both at Allegheny and at the New Jersey state prison at Trenton.

[43] "Report of the Inspectors," *House Journal,* 1836-37, Vol. II, pp. 411, 438-41.

to begin a decade of petitioning for the erection of another wing
of cells.[44] By 1852 there were one hundred and seventy-four prisoners to be confined in the one hundred and seventy cells and the
inspectors, alarmed lest the separate confinement would have to be
abandoned, made a vigorous and almost pathetic plea for an appropriation to build a new cell block.[45] This time the legislature
responded, and by an act of May 4, 1852, granted twenty-five
thousand dollars for the erection of the long-desired addition.
Wing "C" was immediately erected and provided sixty additional
cells.[46]

The building of the third wing of cells added enough cells to
accommodate the inmates in solitary confinement until the prison
population was increased in an abnormal manner by the economic
and social unrest and confusion incident to the panic of 1857, and
the unsettled conditions preceding the outbreak of the Civil War.
In their report for 1860, the inspectors pointed out the fact that at
the present rate of increase in the prison population the available
cell space would soon be exhausted. They stated that they were
extending the prison walls in order to obtain more yard room and
asked for an appropriation of fifty thousand dollars to increase the
capacity of the plant.[47] The legislature acquiesced and appropriated
forty thousand dollars by an act of April 3, 1860.[48] It was made
none too soon, for the inspectors reported a population of three
hundred and eleven in 1861, with a cell capacity of only two hundred and thirty. They asked for another grant of seventy-five
thousand dollars to complete the proposed extension and began work
on the extension of wing "B."[49] The legislature appropriated fifty
thousand dollars by an act of April 18, 1861.[50] The inspectors, in
their report for 1862, stated that eighty-eight cells were being added
to wing "B" and requested still another appropriation of fifty
thousand dollars to complete this addition and to enlarge wing "C."
They advocated this action on the ground that it was necessary to
anticipate the increase of population which was bound to come as
soon as the war was over. They also expressed their satisfaction
at the installation of gas lights, as the smoke from the adjoining
factories had previously made the cells dark for days at a time.[51]

---

[44] "Report of Inspectors," Senate Journal, 1841, Vol. II, pp. 411, 414; Ibid.,
1842, Vol. II, pp. 51-3.
[45] Ibid., 1852, Vol. II, pp. 578-79.
[46] Ibid., 1853, Vol. II, p. 180; Laws of the General Assembly, 1852, p. 551;
Legislative Documents, 1854, p. 280.
[47] Laws of the General Assembly, 1860, p. 635.
[48] Ibid., 1860, pp. 896-98.
[49] Ibid., 1862, pp. 705-06.
[50] Laws of the General Assembly, 1861, p. 399.
[51] Ibid., 1860, p. 897; 1862, pp. 846-49.

The legislature appropriated thirty-five thousand dollars by an act of April 11, 1862, for the completion of wing "B" and the enlargement of wing "C." [52] The extension of the plant from 1860 to 1864 provided ninety-four additional cells, making a total of three hundred and twenty-four.[53] In their report for 1865 the inspectors pointed out the need for a new hospital building.[54] The report of the inspectors for 1867 proved that their anticipations with respect to the increase of population at the close of the war were not unfounded. At that time there were four hundred and eighty-six prisoners to be confined in the three hundred and twenty-four cells. This indicated the great need of still further additions to the plant.[55] In response to this and later appeals, the legislature appropriated fifteen thousand dollars by an act of April 11, 1868; forty-one thousand five hundred dollars by an act of April 16, 1869; and twenty-five thousand dollars by acts of April 6, 1870, for the erection of a new building containing a female ward, a hospital, dispensary, bathrooms, laundry, library, store-rooms, receiving cells, dungeons and a chapel seating six hundred and fifty.[56] With the exception of a shop building which was necessitated by the law of April 8, 1869, allowing congregate labor, and was erected in 1874, the building of block "D" between 1868 and 1872 constituted the last significant addition to the original plant of the Western Penitentiary. The total cost of the original plant from 1818 to 1874 was six hundred and forty-four thousand dollars.[57]

The first annual report of the secretary and general agent of the new State Board of Public Charities in 1870 gives the best description of the Western Penitentiary just before its abandonment which is available from a contemporary observer. There were three wings of cells, each two stories in height, radiating from a central building. The fourth cell block, erected between 1868 and 1872, and containing the receiving and disciplinary cells, the women's ward, laundry, bathrooms, chapel, hospital and storehouse, was detached from the other buildings and was located parallel to the east wall. The three radiating wings contained three hundred and twenty-four cells and the women's department twenty-four, making a total capacity of three hundred and forty-eight. The radiating cell blocks were constructed of hewn stone and the new detached block of

---

[52] *Laws of the General Assembly,* 1862, p. 462.
[53] Ibid., 1871, p. 1074.
[54] Ibid., 1866, Vol. I, pp. 529, 547.
[55] *Report of the Inspectors,* 1867, pp. 3-4.
[56] *Laws of the General Assembly,* 1868, p. 26; 1869, p. 43; 1870, p. 25. Up to this time the "hospital" had consisted of two small and ill-ventilated rooms directly above the bake-oven.
[57] *Report of the Inspectors,* 1874, p. 16.

brick. The cells on the first story were eleven feet and ten inches high, fifteen feet long, and seven feet and ten inches wide. The cells on the second story were about four feet shorter. The windows on either end of the cells were long narrow slits four inches wide. The prison was heated by steam and its water supply was obtained from the Allegheny River.[58]

The expensive new additions of 1860-1872 had scarcely been finished before an agitation was begun to bring about the abandonment of the plant, which had come to be surrounded by some of the best residential sections of Allegheny as well as by parks. A prison structure was held to be obnoxious in such a community and those opposed to its continuance on the original site were able to muster sufficient strength to secure the passage of the act of March 7, 1873, which marked the first step in the process of its abandonment. This act provided that:

"Whereas, The location of the Western Penitentiary, made over fifty-four years ago, has been included within the corporate limits of the city of Allegheny, and the city parks, and a closely built city surrounds it on all sides;

"And whereas, The said penitentiary is wholly inadequate to the wants of the present time, being entirely too small and improperly arranged to suit the discipline of the present age; therefore,

"Section 1. Be it enacted, &c., That a commission consisting of Hugh S. Flemming, Theodore H. Nevin, Henry M. Long, George D. Riddle, Hugh McNeil, Alfred Slack, James M. Brier, George V. Lawrence, John L. George, John K. Ewing, and Ormsby Phillips, are hereby authorized and empowered to examine, and to report to the Legislature at its present or next session, a suitable site within fifty miles of the city of Allegheny, upon which may be erected new buildings, to be used and occupied as the Western Pennsylvania Penitentiary.

"Section 2. That said commissioners, in their report, shall include the estimates of costs, and other data and matter bearing on the subject of such removal of said Western Penitentiary: Provided, That the State shall be at no expense by the creation of said commission." [59]

The commission handed in a "split" report, the majority favoring the removal, but the minority submitting a vigorous and well-reasoned argument for retaining the existing plant. Their view was also endorsed by the board of inspectors, several of whom were on the commission.[60] Once it had been decided by a majority

[58] Report cited, in *Legislative Documents*, 1871, pp. 1074ff.
[59] *Laws of the General Assembly*, 1873, pp. 38-9.
[60] *Journal of the House*, 1874, pp. 416-17.

vote in the commission that the old plant was to be razed, a long struggle ensued as to the location of the new penitentiary building. An admirable proposal was advanced urging the establishment of the new institution upon a large rural site somewhere in the western part of the state, and this proposition was warmly supported by the earnest and far-sighted reformers of the time, but the local prejudice against removing the institution from the neighborhood of Allegheny and Pittsburgh was too strong to be overcome. The prison must be moved far enough from its original site so as not to deface the landscape in the residential district, but could not be taken beyond the limit of convenient accessibility to the local business interests and the governing and administrative authorities. The outcome of the whole matter was that it was decided to locate the new plant on the site of the old Western House of Refuge on the Ohio River in the city of Allegheny. This site had just been abandoned by the authorities of the House of Refuge because it had been found to be damp, foggy and generally unhealthy and unsanitary, a fact which was well known to the whole community and to none better than to the inspectors of the Western Penitentiary. Yet it was due to the vigorous efforts of the inspectors that this site was selected for the new penitentiary.

Two reasons have been assigned for their action, both of which, no doubt, operated strongly. In the first place, a majority of the board of inspectors resided in a section which would enable them to pass by the House of Refuge site daily on their way back and forth from business in Allegheny and Pittsburgh and would thereby make it most convenient for them to stop when necessary and transact their business as inspectors. This was particularly facilitated as there was a railway station at the House of Refuge site. In the second place, the prison population had greatly increased during the seventies as a result of the financial depression and the old plant was desperately crowded. No active steps had been taken to provide for the erection of the new plant and the inspectors were naturally led to consider the superior availability of the House of Refuge site. Its advantages from the standpoint of providing speedy relief from the congestion in the old prison were well stated by the inspectors in their annual report for 1877. After calling attention to the fact that there were then eight hundred and thirty-one prisoners to be confined in three hundred and forty-eight cells, they said:

"We look around for relief and find that nowhere can it be found so promptly and satisfactorily as in pressing our idea of last year for the appropriation, by the State, of the House of Refuge grounds in the Ninth Ward, Allegheny, not now as an annex to this building, but as the site of a new, enlarged and capacious Western State Penitentiary Building. . . . And to this end we go to the Legislature for authority and means to carry out this project. Much of the labor required to put up this new structure can be performed by the convicts and much of the material required can be removed from time to time from the present building. Working from the start on a thoroughly prepared plan, any desired part of the new edifice may be completed for occupancy at intervals; so that when the whole is done we shall have a building perfect in all its proportions." [61]

Urged on by this double incentive the inspectors made a vigorous fight in the legislature for the selection of the House of Refuge site and secured the passage of the act of June 12, 1878, authorizing the governor to acquire the lands and buildings "recently owned and occupied by the Western Pennsylvania Reform School in the ninth ward of the city of Allegheny." Upon it was to be erected the new penitentiary, and one hundred thousand dollars was appropriated with which to begin work.[62] It is doubtful if a more foolhardy move could have been made, and there have been few instances where the interests of a commonwealth and the welfare of a considerable group of mankind have been more unfortunately sacrificed to personal convenience and immediate opportunism than was the case when this site was decided upon for the new Western Penitentiary. It has become desirable to abandon an expensive plant, costing over two million dollars, though it is still architecturally in perfect condition, because of the dangerously unhealthy nature of the site. But worse than this has been the unspeakable misery to which thousands of men have been subjected since 1881, in the Riverside Penitentiary, from floods, fogs, damp weather, smoke and their train of evil consequences. Before discussing the steps leading to the decision ultimately to abandon the Riverside plant, something must be said of the circumstances connected with its erection.

E. M. Butz was selected as the architect to draw up the plans for the new penitentiary and his summary of the general arrangement of the new structure is of interest because the cell blocks were completed substantially as was originally planned. His description follows:

"F. H. Nevin, Esq., President,

   "Dear Sir:—I herewith present to the Board of Inspectors a

[61] Report of the Inspectors, 1877, pp. 8, 18, 28.
[62] Laws of the General Assembly, 1878, p. 210.

general description of proposed new buildings for the Western Penitentiary of Pennsylvania, Allegheny, Pa.

"The prison building will have a frontage of 1,025 feet, facing the Ohio River, and will be sub-divided as follows, viz.: The rotunda or guard house 90x90 feet from out to out, octagonal shape, located in the center with a wing or cell house 62x467½ feet on each side of same. The office building, Warden's and Deputy Warden's residences, will be placed directly in front of the aforesaid guard house, and central to the entire prison, with a drive-way between said office building and residences, and the prison arranged so that prisoners can be received into the prison direct, without passing through the office building. There will be a wing 62x120 feet, extending from rear of guard house and at right angles with the two wings aforesaid. At the rear of this wing will be placed another wing parallel with main prison 50x150 feet. This wing will be used for kitchen, bakery, store and ware rooms, &c. This will be two stories, each 15 feet high, at each end, where the store and ware rooms are placed, and the kitchen and bakery, which are placed between said store and warerooms, will be one story 30 feet high.

"The guard house or rotunda will be three stories in height. The first story will be 18 feet high, designed to be used for mess-room, the floor being level with main floor of the wings or cell houses on either side, office building in front and wing at rear.

"The second story will be 34 feet high, to be used as guard-room, and is on a level with the third tier of cells in wings aforesaid, the sides of same being open toward the cells, but securely protected with iron gratings. This will allow the guard on duty in the guard-room to see every cell-door in the entire prison, and will also have a full view of all the grounds around the prison. The third story will be 30 feet high, to be used for a hospital, being above the level of the surrounding wings, therefore having abundance of light and ventilation, and well suited for the purpose intended, and will be connected with the cell blocks on either side and with the guard-room below, by means of an elevator and stairways.

"The guard house or rotunda is finished with a dome-shaped roof surmounted with a cupola arranged to contain lantern and reflectors.

"The wings, or cell houses on either side of guard house, are arranged to contain two blocks of cells placed in line five tiers in height, with a ventilating corridor 4½ feet wide between cells, extending the entire length of each block. Each wing or cell-house will contain 540 cells 5x8x8½ feet high in the clear, and 100 cells 7x8x8½ feet high in the clear, making a total of 640 cells in each wing, or 1,280 cells in the entire prison.

"All the cells are arranged with the necessary ventilating ducts, wash basin, &c., complete.

"The entire building will be strictly fire-proof, and will have all modern prison conveniences and improvements.

"Very respectfully, your obt. servant,

"E. M. Butz, Architect." [63]

The north wing of the new penitentiary was the first to be erected and it was completed in 1882. It contained six hundred and forty cells, while eighty cells in the south wing of the old House of Refuge structure were retained for men convicts and another of the old Refuge buildings for the women's department, giving a total cell capacity of seven hundred and fifty. The inspectors appeared to be proud of their work, as will appear from the following extract from their report for 1881-82:

"The structure is as permanent as the everlasting hills which surround it. The material of which it is built is stone, iron and brick. The long stretch of river front secures at all times a healthful breeze, and the unobstructed view in the distance, produces a perspective which ought to commend itself to and unfold the finer feelings of even a convict." [64]

The old prison was not wholly abandoned until 1885, when its grounds were turned over to the city of Allegheny to be used as a park.

The north wing had scarcely been occupied when it was found necessary to begin work on the south wing, as by 1884 there were more prisoners than cells in the new Riverside Penitentiary. Work was begun on the south wing and it was completed in 1892. It was not finished on the scale originally planned, for it contained but five hundred and twenty cells instead of six hundred and forty. This gave a total capacity of eleven hundred and sixty cells for male prisoners, and forty cells for women were provided in one of the remodeled House of Refuge buildings.[65] By 1894, however, the population had again come to be greater than the capacity for separate confinement, but the appeal of the officials for additional extensions was wisely ignored by the legislature.[66]

The prison plant thus built at Riverside between 1878 and 1892 was the most expensive and pretentious prison building which had yet been erected in America. Between 1878 and 1893 one million nine hundred and twelve thousand dollars was appropriated for

[63] *Report of the Inspectors,* 1878, p. 10.

[64] Ibid., 1881-82, p. 7. From 1881 to the present the inspectors of the Western Penitentiary have submitted biennial instead of annual reports.

[65] Ibid., 1883-84, p. 14; 1885-86, pp. 5-6; 1889-90, pp. 7, 16; 1891-92, p. 8.

[66] Ibid., 1893-94, p. 8.

grounds and buildings and the incidental expenses during and since that time have raised the total cost to well over two million dollars.[67] This was about three times the cost of erecting the Cherry Hill institution to 1835, at which time it was the largest and most expensive penitentiary structure in the world. The new Riverside Penitentiary was in 1892 as much the finest example of the inside cell and large cell block design of prison architecture in America as the Cherry Hill plant was of the outside cell and radiating wing type of prison in 1835. In spite of its great cost, however, there were many defects in the new plant entirely aside from its unfortunate environment. In spite of the lavish appropriations for equipment the cells were lighted only by candles up to 1898.[68] Moreover, with the exception of the warden's apartments, the central building and the great cell blocks, none of the new buildings called for in the elaborate plans published with the report of the inspectors for 1883-84 has ever been erected. The shops, hospital building, dining-room, and other buildings for administrative purposes have been provided by utilizing the plant of the Western House of Refuge, very little of which was dismantled after the site was occupied by the penitentiary authorities. The structure has been, thus, a strange mixture of the new and antique. The architectural defects, however, were as nothing compared to the environmental handicaps. The high water in the spring has been a constant menace to the institution and disastrous floods were sustained in 1884, 1902 and 1907, which entailed untold suffering from cold and dampness while the heating plant was disabled during severe weather, at one time as long as three weeks.[69] Again the "sweet breezes," which the inspectors of 1878-82 stated would be wafted from the Ohio River, have consisted during half of the year of dense fogs which settle over the plant each morning and hold and accumulate the smoke from adjoining factories until the institution becomes enveloped in a nocturnal darkness, which makes it impossible for the prisoners to leave their cells until late in the forenoon. Then the dampness of the site has had disastrous effects on the prisoners, especially since 1897, when a large proportion of them have been compelled to remain idle in their cells during a large part of the day on account of the adverse legislation. Finally, the impossibility of introducing agricultural labor has been a serious obstacle in view of the insuperable difficulties in the way

---

[67] The appropriation acts were those of June 12, 1878; June 4, 1879; June 29, 1881; June 28, 1883; June 28, 1885; June 2, 1887; May 25, 1889; June 1, 1891; and May 27, 1893.

[68] *Report of the Inspectors*, 1893-94, p. 10; 1895-96, p. 11.

[69] Cf. Ibid., 1907-08, p. 18.

of developing mechanical industry since prison labor has been paralyzed by the ridiculous Muehlbronner Law of 1897.

In all phases of progress one of the indispensable prerequisites is the ability to view a situation with the mind as free as possible from the influence of the vested interests of the past and this desirable condition is rarely produced except by the infusion of new blood into the ranks of the professional curators of the traditions of the past. This has proved to be as true in prison reform as elsewhere. In Pennsylvania the first radical step in advance came in 1786-87 when the Philadelphia free-thinkers and Quakers joined in disrupting the criminal jurisprudence that had come down from the days of Henry II and earlier, and were later aided by the socially-minded among the more orthodox ecclesiastical bodies. The next important departure was to be seen when a new board of inspectors assumed office in the Western Penitentiary in 1866 and speedily punctured the already venerable myth concerning the perfection and finality of the Pennsylvania system of prison administration. The next development worthy to rank with these dates from the accession of John Francies to the wardenship of the Western Penitentiary in 1909. He speedily grasped the situation and readily understood that the environmental limitations of the Riverside site would prevent the realization of any comprehensive plan of improvement in prison administration, in view of the existing status of prison labor legislation in Pennsylvania. In his first report he made the following vigorous recommendation, which was the first step in what was hoped to be as epoch-making an experiment in the improvement of prison administration in Pennsylvania as the Memorial of the prison reformers in 1787 and its subsequent developments. Mr. Francies wrote at this time:

"In consideration of the large amount of money required to replace the present worn out, dilapidated, inadequate, unsafe and unsanitary buildings now in use and being part of the prison; the smallness of the tract of land to which the institution is confined, its being subject to floods by the Ohio River at certain seasons of the year, the utter impossibility under existing laws to properly employ all the prisoners, thereby working to the detriment of many, mentally, morally and physically, coupled with the fact that the arrangement of the prison itself makes it a modern incubator for turberculosis and other diseases, I unhesitatingly recommend that immediate steps be taken to remove the prison to a location where a sufficient amount of land may be procured at reasonable cost, and buildings erected thereon, so far as possible, by prison labor, that the inmates may in the future be employed in producing their own maintenance, and the counties of this prison district be saved

a large portion of the expense now charged to them and paid into
our treasury for the maintenance of their prisoners." [70]

Acting upon the convictions expressed in this report, Mr. Francies
personally went before the legislature in its next session and secured
the passage of the act of March 30, 1911, directing the removal
of the Western Penitentiary to a rural site, thereby bringing about
the realization of the hopes and ambitions of the enlightened
reformers of the seventies. The necessity for the passage of the
act was ably set forth in the following opening paragraph:

"It appears that the Western Penitentiary is greatly overcrowded,
as well as otherwise inadequate for the purposes for which it is
used, and owing to the construction and location thereof is so
unsanitary that numerous cases of tuberculosis exist among the
prisoners confined therein, as the direct result of their imprisonment; that for the lack of a large tract of land appurtenant to the
said institution, it is impossible, under the existing laws relating
to manufactured products, to keep the inmates sufficiently employed,
by reason whereof a large number thereof become insane and
become permanent charges upon the State; and the said penitentiary
is located in a congested city district, where it is impossible to
extend the buildings and prison yards thereof at any reasonable
cost." [71]

The board of inspectors of the Western Penitentiary were authorized to select a site of not less than fifteen hundred acres in the
western part of the state as a site for the new penitentiary. It was
stipulated that the buildings should be modern, fire-proof and
readily adapted to extension. Their cost was limited to one million
two hundred and fifty thousand dollars. The transfer to the new
site of such convicts as might be needed in construction work was
authorized. Three hundred thousand dollars was appropriated with
which to commence work. [72]

A large tract of land in Centre County, containing over five
thousand acres, was purchased as the site for the new penitentiary
and the work of clearing the ground, excavation and preliminary
construction was immediately started and vigorously prosecuted
by Mr. Francies, who was appointed superintendent of construction
on the new plant, [73] though retaining the position of warden at

---

[70] *Report of the Inspectors*, 1909-10, pp. 15-6.
[71] *Laws of the General Assembly*, 1911, p. 32.
[72] Ibid., pp. 32-4.
[73] From the inception of the work, Mr. Francies had associated with
him as an expert assistant, Mr. James W. Herron, an energetic Pittsburgh
engineer, now the superintendent of the State Reformatory at Huntingdon.

Riverside. Plans were originally made looking forward only to the erection of a new penitentiary for the western district of the state, but the potentialities of the project so impressed the progressive prison reform element in both ends of the state that the above-mentioned act of June 14, 1915, was passed, ordering the consolidation of the two penitentiaries in the completed structure, and a considerable enlargement of the original plans was thereby rendered necessary.[74] It is probable that no better account has been written concerning the early progress on this plant than that submitted by Superintendent Francies at the close of the year 1916:

"By virtue of the unanimous action of the Legislature, and the approval of the Governor of the Commonwealth, a bill providing for the erection of a new penitentiary on a large tract of land in a rural district, that would provide useful and healthful employment for the inmates, became a law on March 30, 1911. The legislation resulted from an exposure of conditions at the old penitentiary at Pittsburgh, which convinced the Legislature and Governor that the prison system then in vogue was faulty throughout, as, because of narrow confines, walled-in seclusion and complete idleness to which a large percentage of the inmates were subjected, moral degradation and physican disintegration were inevitable.

"The matter of selecting a prison site was begun immediately after the passage of the Act. Thirty-three properties were offered for sale to the Board of Inspectors of the Western Penitentiary. Some of the tracts were good, while others were devoid of the necessary natural resources. A tract containing 5,254 acres was selected, 4,318 of which were purchased outright from their owners, and 936 acres obtained from the State Forest Reservation. After the selection was approved by Governor Tener and the Board of Inspectors of the Western Penitentiary, the ground was acquired by the Commonwealth at an average cost of Fifty Dollars ($50.00) per acre.

"Situated at Rockview, in Benner Township, Centre County, six miles southwest of Bellefonte, and an equal distance northwest of State College, on the Bellefonte, Nittany and Lemont Division of the Pennsylvania Railroad, the tract is almost in the exact geographical center of the State, and ideally adapted to agriculture. Approximately 3,000 of the acres purchased are tillable, while the remainder of the tract is extensively timbered, and a goodly portion of the wooded territory, exclusive of that embraced by the domestic water supply shed, may be profitably devoted to cattle raising and fruit growing. The tract contains thirty-four separate parcels of land, most of which were well developed farms, having thereon dwellings, barns and accessory buildings. The property has a front-

---

[74] This plan was abandoned and then reconsidered in legislation of 1927.

age of 4,400 feet along the railroad, which permits of excellent
siding facilities, and also a frontage of 1.1 miles on the Lemont
State Highway, and 1.4 miles on the Bellefonte and Boalsburg Pike.

"As a prison site the property offers many advantages: its healthful atmosphere, natural resources, agricultural features and an
abundant supply of pure mountain water of adequate volume to
provide the Institution for all time to come.

"The topography of the ground, being of an undulatory character, affords natural drainage. The highest elevation on Nittany
Mountain is 2,100 feet and the lowest elevation is 863, at the discharge end of Spring Creek. The average altitude is 1,100 feet
above mean tide at Sandy Hook. The farms purchased for the
prison tract are prolific, and regarded as among the best in central
Pennsylvania. The State Geographical Survey shows that the soil is
adapted to the cultivation of all vegetables and grains peculiar to
the State of Pennsylvania. The tract has rich deposits of sandstone
and hard limestone, and timber sufficient to meet the needs of the
Institution for ages. Three thousand acres are underlaid with the
finest grade of limestone, the depth of which has never been tested,
but has a vertical exposed face of 150 feet along Spring Creek, which
is easy of access. The sandstone has a depth of about 750 feet, and
if applied to building and State purposes would prove a valuable
acquisition to the Commonwealth. . . .

"Shortly after the Governor approved the bill providing for the
erection of the New Western Penitentiary, he appointed the writer
Superintendent of Construction of the new buildings. A corps of
Engineers was immediately assigned to the ground, and surveys
made of the different properties. The titles were carefully examined
by a title and trust company, and the ground was formally taken
over by the Commonwealth. The Board of Inspectors then chose
John T. Windrim of Philadelphia as Architect for the new prison,
and after his appointment Mr. Windrim prepared comprehensive
plans for the proposed new institution, which were signed by Governor Tener, and arrangements made to begin active operations. . . .

"In August, 1912, I personally conducted the first prisoner to
Rockview. This nucleus, a colored man, in a modest way began a
cleaning-up process in an old dwelling, and on September 3rd eight
more inmates were transferred from the old prison to Rockview.
These men, with others who later followed, renovated the Ishler
residence, an old stone farmhouse, thereby establishing the first
temporary prison abode on the tract. Gradually the population at
Rockview increased, and in a short time a prison colony was established. A powerhouse was erected, which supplies heat and light
to the initial group of buildings, which are of a temporary nature.
The buildings of this group were all constructed out of material
obtained by the demolition of old buildings of no practical use, and
located in various inaccessible places on the property. . . .

"The Electrocution-Deputy Warden Building was completed in December, 1914, at which time the ground floor was devoted to dormitories, and a large extra force of prisoners brought from Pittsburgh, when ground was broken for the Dining Hall and Laundry Buildings. The Electrocution Building is of reinforced concrete, two-story, having dimensions of 32 by 230 feet. The ground floor now serves temporarily as prison offices, while the entire upper floor is devoted to cells for condemned murderers, the execution room and the autopsy room. Experts have pronounced the building complete in every detail. The first executions through the agency of electricity took place in the building on February 23rd, 1915.

"The Laundry Building is an imposing structure of reinforced concrete, 30 by 228 feet, was finished on November 10th, 1915, and immediately pressed into service as a temporary abode for prisoners. The Dining Hall, said to be the largest building of its kind in the country, has a seating capacity of 3,000. The building is a splendid example of architecture and concrete workmanship, is 147 by 206 feet, and is connected with the Laundry Building by a tunnel. The Dining Hall is likewise being used temporarily as a dormitory.

"The prisoners at the new prison site have worked untiringly, and not unmindful of the fact that they were building for themselves and future generations of derelicts, a humane abode. And while these wards have labored they have improved in mind and body. More than thirteen hundred (1,300) of them have engaged in the many diversified employments in connection with the erection of the buildings, since 1912. The benefit which they have derived from the labor, the healthful atmospheric conditions, the natural surroundings and the distinct departure from penned-in prison life, from a standpoint of social economy, is incalculable. The monetary saving to the State as a result of their labors is shown in the financial report of the Board of Inspectors, but no approximate inventory of the moral value of the new penitentiary can be made.

"On June 14th, 1915, Your Excellency signed the bill enacted by the Legislature, modifying the plans of the New Western Penitentiary, then in course of construction, for the purpose of providing a State Penitentiary, to supplant the Eastern Penitentiary at Philadelphia and the Western Penitentiary at Pittsburgh. This marked a new epoch in the construction of the institution. In accordance with the provisions of the Act the plans were modified and enlarged. A revised comprehensive plan was approved by Your Excellency on June 29th, 1916.

"As a result of the legislation providing for the modification of the plans for the Institution it was necessary to modify the plans for the Dining Hall then under construction. . . . The building now houses 400 men. The basement was designed for storage, but is now being temporarily devoted to a kitchen and shower baths. . . .

"During the past eighteen months a steam shovel has been in operation, and an industrial railroad outfit has been used to excellent advantage. Eighty thousand cubic yards of limestone excavation have been made. This grading operation has been carried on with great zeal and attention, and the grounds in the vicinity of the permanent buildings are now rapidly assuming their ultimate grades. . . .

"Because of the extensive building activities no thoroughly organized effort could be made along proposed agricultural lines. Notwithstanding this, however, tangible plans to organize and develop the farming industry have been made and put into execution, with the result that we are gradually reaching a self-sustaining basis insofar as grain, garden products and pork are concerned.

"From a small beginning, the tenant farms have been gradually taken over and operated by the prisoners, until in the 1916 season 1,100 acres were farmed by them, and the balance of the land by tenant farmers. . . .

"It can be seen from the foregoing facts that an excellent start has been made toward placing the new Institution on a self-sustaining basis, as regards the food supply.

"Two of the most important individual features contributing to the success of a penal institution, and of lasting benefit to the inmates, are, in my opinion, to give them plenty of good healthful work and proper nourishment. At the new prison site they have the work, and great attention and constant study is given to the food provided for them, that they may have perfectly balanced rations which will build up their physical condition, enabling them to perform their labors without fatigue, thus turning them out better men.

"The inauguration of the new prison system at Rockview has wrought a decided change in the method of dealing with convicts in Pennslyvania. Plenty of outdoor work, in a healthful atmosphere, in the midst of nature, has been conducive to the physical, mental and moral betterment of the wards. . . .

"The prisoners at Rockview are given much latitude. Of the thirteen hundred men transferred to the farm from the Pittsburgh Institution only two have succeeded in making good their escape. In order to provide workmen for the construction work at the new prison site it was necessary to draft many prisoners undergoing long terms. The small percentage of escapes best attests to the merit of the new prison system." [75]

Unfortunately, the original plan for the construction of the new Rockview Penitentiary was adhered to in general principle, and the institution is a magnificent example of the discredited type of con-

---

[75] *Report of the New Western Penitentiary of Pennsylvania from Its Inception to August 31, 1916,* pp. 5-16.

ventional penal cage designed safely to jail convicts rather than to promote their reformation. It was highly regrettable that the dormitory plan could not have been substituted for the most part in the place of the block-and-cell construction. As Mr. Osborne proved, intelligent prison administration can triumph over the greatest handicaps of obsolete and inadequate architectural equipment, but there is no good reason why such architectural obstacles to reformatory prison discipline should be imposed upon enlightened prison officials in the second quarter of the twentieth century. A state may inherit a Sing Sing or an Eastern Penitentiary from an older age, but there is little excuse for fastening an even more repulsive type of structure upon the State of Pennsylvania for another generation. The Rockview Penitentiary is veritably a penological "white elephant." The situation is, of course, mitigated in part by the presence of the great prison farm and the opportunities for extra-mural employment.[76]

IV. THE SYSTEMS OF INDUSTRY AND MAINTENANCE IN THE STATE PENITENTIARIES

1. THE INDUSTRIAL ADMINISTRATION

A. Introductory Review of Prison Industry to 1835

It may prove useful at this point briefly to summarize the main facts involved in the more detailed discussion of the industrial phases of evolution of penal institutions in Pennsylvania in the preceding chapters. It will be remembered that after the law of 1718 had abrogated Penn's system of penal jurisprudence there was little or no labor provided for the inmates of the colonial penal institutions. The laws of 1786, 1789 and 1790, however, following the example of progressive penologists in England, revived the system of imprisonment at hard labor as the typical mode of punishing criminal action and secured in the Walnut Street Jail the first comprehensive application of this system in America. It was shown how these promising beginnings were vitiated by the great increase of criminals in the first quarter of the nineteenth century and the failure to provide adequate buildings for housing and employing them. As a result of these unfortunate circumstances, the industrial system of the Philadelphia jail had been practically destroyed and little if any industrial progress had

---

[76] Cf. A. H. Votaw, *Penal Legislation of 1915 in Pennsylvania,* pp. 13-8.

been made in any other county prison. How precarious a grip on American penology the concept of prison labor had attained by 1820 is apparent from the fact that even in Pennsylvania the laws of 1818 and 1821, ordering the erection of the Western and Eastern Penitentiaries, did not contemplate the introduction of a comprehensive system of industrial operations in either of these proposed institutions. In fact, the Western Penitentiary was originally erected wholly on the plan of solitary confinement without labor and had to be torn down and remodeled as soon as the law of 1829 prescribed labor for the state penitentiaries. Even in the framing of the law of 1829 there was no unanimity among its authors. Thomas Bradford, Jr., opposed the introduction of labor; Samued R. Wood insisted on the adoption of a labor system; and Roberts Vaux, without any great enthusiasm for prison industry, finally joined Mr. Wood and secured the inclusion of solitary confinement at hard labor in the act of 1829.[77] Following out the provisions of this act a system of handicraft industry carried on in separate confinement had been installed in both state penitentiaries by 1836.[78]

B. The Industrial Experience of the Eastern Penitentiary Since 1835

(1) THE NATURE OF THE PRISON INDUSTRIES

In view of the fact that reformation has always been a cardinal principle of the Pennsylvania system of prison administration it was but natural that in their discussion of the purpose of prison labor the authorities should especially stress the reformatory function of industry as a part of the system of penal administration. The value of industry as a factor in effecting reformation was viewed in two aspects. In the first place, it was praised as a preventive agency in that it was supposed to keep the mind of the prisoner occupied to the total exclusion of all "evil" thoughts and reflections. In the second place, it was highly regarded as a positive factor, in that it aimed to provide for the acquisition of a trade and thus to prepare the prisoner for a self-supporting economic existence upon obtaining freedom. The prison authorities of the Eastern Penitentiary not only stressed industry within the prison, but also urged with remarkable vigor and consistency for

---

[77] Richard Vaux, *Sketch of the Origin and History of the Eastern State Penitentiary*, pp. 86-8 and note p. 87. See above, pp. 101, 121.
[78] *Report of the Inspectors of the Eastern Penitentiary, 1835, Senate Journal*, 1835. Ibid., Western Penitentiary, *Senate Journal*, II, pp. 148-51.

fifty years the necessity of a comprehensive system of vocational instruction for all the youth of Pennsylvania, to the end that the economic causes of crime might be uprooted at their source. The great stress laid by the authorities of the Eastern Penitentiary upon the reformatory aspects of prison labor and the slight emphasis placed upon the economic phases as a contribution to maintenance must not, however, be viewed as wholly the product of theoretical ethical convictions. It was rather in part, at least, a defense reaction which developed as a result of the generally unsatisfactory status of the industrial system of the Eastern Penitentiary, when viewed in its economic aspects alone.[79] When, as was the case in a few brief periods, the industries of the Cherry Hill institution were in a relatively prosperous condition the inspectors proudly referred to the fact and pointed to its reduction of maintenance charges. On the other hand, when, as was usually the case, the productivity of the institution was relatively low, as compared with congregate institutions conducted on the contract plan, the authorities invariably found that great virtue resided in the reformatory aspects of prison industry and warmly congratulated themselves upon having escaped the dangerous rapacity of institutions which centered their attention primarily upon material productivity and financial income. But, whatever their dominant motive, one can scarcely fail to commend the attitude of the inspectors in assigning vocational training and reformation priority over material productivity as the great aim of prison industry. One can not, however, agree that the methods pursued by these same authorities in attempting to achieve their end were invariably particularly well-chosen or sagacious.

While general information exists as to the nature of the industrial operations in the Eastern Penitentiary from the period of its establishment, no detailed and consistent statistics were included in the annual reports of the inspectors until the law of May 31, 1844, compelled them to submit a complete statement of all receipts and expenditures.[80] Even after that time no comprehensive figures were given as to the number employed in any given industry. From 1854 to 1871 regular reports were made of the employment of those received, but not of the whole body of prisoners. This seemingly elementary statistical information as to the industrial distri-

---

[79] That the "industrial moderation" of the Eastern Penitentiary did not include the "eight-hour day" is apparent from the statement of the inspectors in their report for 1844, that one of the advantages of the Pennsylvania system consisted in the fact that the lights in the cells enabled the prisoners to work until 9 o'clock at night.

[80] *Laws of the General Assembly*, 1844, p. 585.

bution of the prisoners in the Eastern Penitentiary has never been included in the reports of the institution, though the reports were exceedingly voluminous, page after page being given to irrelevant information which may have been introduced to obscure more vital points which would render the institution liable to criticism. Fortunately, however, after 1872 the reports of the Board of Public Charities provide this essential information which was omitted from the penitentiary reports.

At the outset, weaving and shoemaking were almost the sole industries introduced in the penitentiary, though a few were employed in picking over oakum and wool.[81] The commission which visited the institution in 1839 reported that out of four hundred and seventeen prisoners then confined, one hundred and fifty-five were employed, in weaving and one hundred and forty-eight at shoemaking. Thirty-seven were reported as sick, idle or incapacitated.[82] In his report for 1838 the warden admitted that fewer trades were possible in a system based upon separate confinement than in the great competing system founded on the practice of congregate workshops.[83] In his report for 1849 the physician, Doctor Robert A. Given, condemned the prison industries—shoemaking, weaving and oakum-picking—claiming that from a hygenic standpoint they were purely sedentary occupations which were "proverbially deleterious." [84] The generally unhealthy nature of these industries was intensified by the fact that in the Eastern Penitentiary no physical exercise was possible beyond "roaming" around the microscopic "yards" attached to the individual cells. In 1850 the making of cane seats for chairs supplanted oakum-picking.[85] This became one of the most important of the prison industries in the decade of the seventies and has retained some significance to the present day. During the fifties weaving, shoemaking or "cordwaining," cane-seating and chair-making were the chief prison industries.[86]

In the decade of the Civil War, weaving, which had for thirty years been the most extensive and productive prison industry, began to die out because the progress in mechanical weaving in the outside manufacturing world made the attempt at competition by the hand looms of the penitentiary almost wholly hopeless.[87] Shoe-

---

[81] *Senate Journal,* 1833-34, p. 417.
[82] Ibid., 1838-39, Vol. II, p. 761.
[83] Ibid., p. 433.
[84] *Report of the Inspectors of the Eastern Penitentiary,* 1849, pp. 20-1.
[85] Ibid., 1850, pp. 9-10.
[86] Ibid., 1853, p. 29.
[87] Ibid., 1862, p. 48.

making was extended to compensate for the decline of weaving, and it became much the most important of the industries until it was ousted from this primacy by the manufacture of hosiery in the eighties. By the close of the eighties the great improvement of mechanical devices for the manufacture of shoes put an end to the extensive development of handicraft shoemaking in the penitentiary. Wood-working and chair-making were important industries in the fifties, but died out during the Civil War. They were revived to some degree in the next decade but had disappeared by 1880. Cigar-making (early entered as "segar"-making) was introduced in the decade of the sixties and by 1876 occupied the labor of some ninety men. It gradually declined and disappeared in the nineties, but revived at the beginning of the present century, and on September 4, 1918, furnished employment for eleven men. The making of hosiery, however, has been the chief industry in the Eastern Penitentiary since weaving and shoemaking began to decline to a marked degree during the seventies and eighties. It was introduced in 1874 [88] and by 1879 was engaging the attention of over two hundred prisoners. While it was wholly wiped out as a result of the "panic" of 1893, it was reintroduced in 1902 and remained until 1916 much the most important of the institutional industries. A spasmodic attempt was made in 1903-04 to introduce the making of brushes and mats, but this industry was almost immediately discarded.

Since the period of the industrial depression of 1893, which was followed in Pennsylvania by particularly disastrous laws restricting prison labor, the number of prisoners listed as wholly idle has greatly exceeded those engaged in productive industries. From considerations of both discipline and humanity the prison authorities have in recent years allowed prisoners possessing some degree of artistic mechanical talent to work in their cells at the manufacture of various types of fine hardware and wood-work, the products of which are sold to the public and the proceeds given to the prisoners. This brief review of the nature of the industrial operations in the Eastern Penitentiary since 1835 will serve to show clearly that the industries have always been of a simple nature which would allow execution within the narrow confines of a single cell. Not only were the industries simple and elementary, but being carried on wholly by the handicraft method, they became progressively more antiquated.

From this scanty sketch of the various types of prison industry in the Philadelphia penitentiary attention may be turned to a

---

[88] *Report of the Inspectors of the Eastern Penitentiary*, 1873-74, p. 191.

presentation of such meager statistical information as exists relative to the industrial distribution of the inmates. The first detailed statement of the industrial distribution of the inmates of the Eastern Penitentiary is contained in the report of the legislative investigating commission of 1839: [89]

Weaving	155
Shoemaking	148
Carpentering	4
Blacksmithing	4
Fireman	1
Cooks	2
Baker	1
Turner	1
Gunsmith	1
Cooper	1
Wool-pickers	24
Tailors	2
Last-maker	1
Engineer	1
Apothecary	1
Sewing	20
Jobbing	13
Idle	10
Invalids	12
Sick	15
Total	417

The next complete statement of the industrial distribution of the inmates of the Eastern Penitentiary is found in the report of the inspectors for 1852. In that year the inmates were employed as follows:

Weaving (and spinning)	81
Shoemaking	60
Cane-seating chairs	46
Wood-working and chair-making	19
Blacksmithing	4
Tailoring	4
Miscellaneous work about institution	54
Idle, sick, invalids	15
Total	283

The industrial distribution for the five years from 1855 to 1859 is fairly well indicated by the occupations at which the five hundred and eighty prisoners received in that period were employed during that portion of their imprisonment: [90]

[89] *Senate Journal,* 1838-39, Vol II, p. 761.
[90] *Annual Report of the Eastern Penitentiary,* 1860, p. 20.

Weaving and spinning 163
Shoemaking 162
Cane-seating chairs 137
Chair-making 21
Varnishing 8
Segar-making 4
Boot-crimping 3
Broom-making 3
Burnishing 3
Blacksmithing 1
Domestics 75

Total 580

The industrial situation in the period from the beginning of the
Civil War to the final disruption of prison labor by the Muehlbronner Act of 1897 will be evident from the following tables
giving the number employed in the various occupations which were
of any considerable importance in this generation.[91]

Number engaged in the occupations assigned to the prisoners received in
the Eastern Penitentiary from 1861 to 1872.

Year	Weaving, Spinning	Shoe-making	Wood-working	Cane-seating	Cigar-making	Idle
1861	22	62	5	23		47
1862	6	44	4	34	2	26
1863	4	83	6	43	8	15
1864	6	50	10	46	6	14
1865	4	58	8	93	9	66
1866	54	68	9	98		108
1867	45	93	6	75		54
1868	67	65	1	46		56
1869	51	68	7	74		80
1870	36	90	11	69		80
1871	43	84	6	47		41
1872	52	115	8	31		88

[91] The statistics given are drawn from the reports of the Eastern Penitentiary and from the reports of the Board of Public Charities.

Industrial distribution of the total prison population from 1873 to 1879.

Year	Weaving	Shoe-making	Wood-working	Cane-seating	Jobbing	Cigar-making	Stocking-weaving	Idle
1873	40	121	18	101	88	27		235
1874	40	213	17	119	118	35		184
1875	43	351	40	178	40	64		175
1876	49	297	44	122	80	76		296
1877	55	234	8	59	173	90		235
1878	60	263	1	130	141	44		326
1879	35	330		100	138	50	175	152
1880	62	173		79	158	41	236	154
1881	80	133	2	84	106	12	200	238
1882	35	154		92	117	39	226	223
1883	5	111		84	112	53	271	238
1884	10	107		71	232	25	334	158
1885	10	111	3	10	250	35	335	214
1886	6	111	3	63	213	31	323	155
1887	10	114	3	63	129	27	401	107
1888	10	40	4		130		303	462
1889	10	36	2	40	201	4	308	277
1890	11	52		43	130		319	291
1891	10	44		51	127	10	264	296
1892	7	44		59	75	3	33	766
1893		24		81	124		69	795
1894	11	23			91			1156
1895		36		61	146			1024
1896	10	24		52	101			879
1897	5	32		72	91	5		960

The industrial differentiation in the decade following the operation of the law of 1897 is revealed by the following table showing the occupations which engaged the attention of the prison population.

Year	Weaving	Cane-seating	Jobbing	Cigar-making	Stocking-weaving	Brushes	Mats	Shoe-making	Apprentice	Idle
1898	10	73	60	5				22		908
1899	10	51	53	5				28		896
1900	8	53	54	4				27		716
1901	8	45	47	5				20		770
1902		71	164	7	53			17		630
1903	18	55	270	18	76	78	20	24	213	270
1904	15	62	283	31	196	79		34		386
1905	18	68	428	28	96			33		388
1906	18	71	298	25	98			30		551
1907	18	92	234	17	98			19	142	836
1908	20	98	337	15	114			25	123	692

No statistics are available for the years 1909 to 1911, but some idea of the nature of the prison industries from 1912 to 1916 can be derived from the following statistics relative to the occupation while in prison of those discharged in this period.

Year	Weaving	Cane-seating	Cigar-making	Stocking-weaving	Shoe-making	Idle
1912	6	28	18	151	15	177
1913	9	44	20	210	17	211
1914	7	42	19	204	13	217
1915	11	24	18	208	9	308
1916	11	15	13	117		420

The occupational distribution at the close of the war period is well illustrated by the following list, which gives the situation on September 4, 1918, and may be regarded as typical of the industrial organization at the close of the World War.

Work on Institution Account—Outside
```
    Power house .............................................. 20
    Laundry ................................................... 30
    Storeroom ................................................. 6
    Greenhouse ................................................ 1
    Yard ...................................................... 49
    Blacksmith shop ........................................... 2
    Carpenter shop ............................................ 11
    Machine shop .............................................. 3
    Tinsmith shop ............................................. 4
    Paint shop ................................................ 7
    Plasterers ................................................ 3
    Stone masons .............................................. 1
    Electricians .............................................. 3
    Plumbers and steam fitters ................................ 4
    Bakers .................................................... 17
    Main kitchen .............................................. 14
    Garage .................................................... 2
                                                            ----
        Total .............................................. 177
```
Work on Institution Account—Inside
```
    Runners ................................................... 73
    Clerks .................................................... 3
    Library ................................................... 13
    Printing and binding ...................................... 12
    Nurses and laboratory ..................................... 4
    Diet kitchen .............................................. 6
    School-teachers ........................................... 13
    Weavers ................................................... 17
    Tailors ................................................... 22
    Barbers ................................................... 3
    Special laundry ........................................... 5
                                                            ----
        Total .............................................. 171
```

From preceding page 348
Work on State Use Manufacturing
   Cane-seating 16
   Cigar-making 11
   Shoemaking 42
   Stocking-weaving 38

     Total 107
  Idle 839
  Sick 77

    Grand Total 1371

Down to the year 1918, when the prison labor commission began
to install some power-driven machinery, the industrial operations
of the Eastern Penitentiary were always conducted according to
either the pure handicraft system or hand-propelled machinery.
It began its industrial career in the handicraft stage before the
Industrial Revolution had brought into existence mechanical industry of the large-scale factory type and its governing authorities
never seemed to become awakened to this great transformation or
to the fact that they were lagging a full industrial stage behind
their competitors in the outside world. The archaic and elementary
nature of the industrial operations in the Eastern Penitentiary is
readily apparent in the proud, if somewhat naïve, boast of the
inspectors in 1884 that the total tool and machinery equipment of
the institution did not represent an investment of over six thousand
dollars. The experience of the Eastern Penitentiary, then, was
wholly comparable to the many pathetic cases in the last century
where handicraft artisans maintained a proud but losing and hopeless competition with the irresistible onward march of mechanical
invention and the development of labor-saving machinery. As time
went on and the struggle became palpably disastrous in a financial
sense, the managing authorities developed a defense reaction and
boasted of the fact that they had kept free from the infection of
machinery. Especially did they emphasize the fact that teaching
a handicraft trade to the prisoners was of high educational value,
notwithstanding the fact that it was obvious that such a trade was
doomed in the outside world because of mechanical competition.[92]
A few representative citations from the reports of the inspectors
during the decade of the nineties will serve to illustrate their curious
defense of the economic anachronism contained in the existing
industrial organization and procedure of the Eastern Penitentiary.

"To teach those who have no knowledge of handicraft skill, to

[92] *Annual Report of the Board of Inspectors of the Eastern Penitentiary,*
1868, p. 111; 1884, p. 33; 1892, p. 119; 1893, p. 109; 1896, p. 12.

teach each individual how to use his intelligence and his hands to reach a position in which, on his return to the social position, he may maintain himself by honest work, is surely a reformatory treatment. To accomplish this purpose machinery is not employed in this penitentiary. . . .

"It is believed that labor is an accepted reformatory agency. But that labor should be the labor of the hand, taught to each prisoner, so that it may be to him a certain source of support. To associate persons in congregation in shops where they are engaged in work largely operated by machinery, gives to the prisoner no industrial knowledge. . . .

"Congregate labor with power-driven machinery converts prisons that should be places of punishment and reflection into factories for profit, and makes the Commonwealth a competitor with every honest manufacturer, with the immense advantage of a sure supply of fixed labor, of unlimited capital drawn from taxation, and of absolute indifference for profit, which the honest worker must earn or starve." [93]

It is not difficult to agree with the inspectors as to the therapeutic and reformative value of vocational instruction for prisoners, but it is impossible to admit that this purpose was likely to be accomplished by teaching a handicraft trade which had long been an anachronism in the outside world. The industrial processes in the Eastern Penitentiary, originally sound and sagacious, became as antiquated as the system of discipline and administration, because the governing authorities tenaciously clung to the old order of things and resolutely refused to square their institution with a half-century of mechanical progress and revolutionary transformations of economic methods.

(2) The Relative Productivity of the Prison Industries

The question of the relative productivity of the various forms of industry carried on in the Eastern Penitentiary must be viewed from two standpoints, the financial gain as a whole from each industry and the relative gain in proportion to the number of prisoners engaged in each industry. The latter aspect of the prob-

---

[93] *Annual Report of the Board of Inspectors of the Eastern Penitentiary,* 1892, p. 119; 1893, p. 109; 1896, p. 12. This deprecation of mechanical labor had, to be sure, begun much earlier. In their report for the year 1868 the inspectors remarked that "We have no labor-saving machinery whereby one man is enabled to perform the work of many, and thus increase production, to the disadvantage of honest industry outside, the Inspectors having steadily rejected any proposition to this effect." (p. 111.) At this earlier date their attitude was much more defensible as mechanical industry was less firmly established in the outside world.

lem can be solved by comparing the following statistics regarding the financial revenue from the industries with the tables given above showing the number engaged in the several occupations listed. The statistics contained in the official reports are not strictly comparable by the exact standards of the accountant because of different methods of bookkeeping which were introduced during this long period of nearly a century, but this variability is not sufficient to destroy the historic value of the statistics of prison revenue as illustrating the general trends in the productivity of the industrial operations. From 1835 to 1860 weaving was the most productive industry. In the decade of the Civil War weaving surrendered its primacy to shoemaking and the cane-seating of chairs. In the decade from 1870 to 1880 shoemaking was much the most remunerative prison industry, especially in the late seventies. From 1880 to the period of the industrial depression of 1893 the making of hosiery was not only far the most "paying" industry of the time, but was also much the most remunerative industry in the entire history of the institution. The industrial depression following 1893 dealt hosiery-weaving a hard blow, and from 1893 to 1903 it had to divide first rank in productivity with the cane-seating of chairs. After 1903, however, it tended to revive to a considerable degree and from that time to 1916 it was much more productive than all other forms of prison industry combined.

The productivity of the prison industries was also considerably disturbed by the periodic industrial depressions from 1837 to the present time, but particularly to 1893. The first depression to affect the industries of the Eastern Penitentiary was that of 1837 which seriously disrupted the newly established industrial system, complicated the finances and caused a great accumulation of unsold goods.[94] Twenty years later the panic of 1857 produced a considerable financial loss, not only through the decline of orders for prison-made merchandise, but also on account of the failure of creditors during the panic. The institution also lost a part of its capital fund for manufacturing through the failure of the Bank of Pennsylvania, in which the penitentiary had deposited seven thousand two hundred and fifty-seven dollars.[95] Scarcely had the institution recovered from the stress of 1857-58 when it was again affected by the industrial stagnation caused by the uncertainties of the first year of the Civil War. In 1861 the inspectors pointed

---

[94] *Annual Report of the Inspectors of the Eastern Penitentiary*, 1837, *Senate Journal*, 1837-38, Vol. II, pp. 442, 445.

[95] *Annual Report of the Inspectors of the Eastern Penitentiary*, 1857, pp. 7-10.

out the close relation existing between general business depression
and the state of prison industry:

"The past year has been disastrous to most of those industrial
occupations which prosper in a peaceful condition of public affairs.
This has been produced by the uncertainty attending the investment of capital, the doubt as to the condition of the currency, the
curtailed demand for those products of labor, arising from an
agitation of the principles regulating trade and commerce, depression in general business growing out of the questioned ability to
meet financial liabilities, and the general disarrangement of all
business relations. The labor of the Penitentiary has not been
exempt from the operation of these influences." [96]

After the close of the Civil War there was a slight decline in the
industrial level of the Eastern Penitentiary,[97] but this was insignificant as compared with the effect of the depression following 1873,
when the warden complained that "the unfortunate financial
trouble which has swept over our land has visibly diminished the
sale of our manufactured goods." [98] The depression of 1893 was
the last that affected the prison industries to any degree for the
institution had scarcely recovered from the effects of this blow
when the rash and ill-conceived Muehlbronner Act of 1897 almost
completely destroyed the industrial operations of the state penitentiaries and left little to be disturbed by the depressions of 1907
and 1913-14.

The following table indicates the net earnings or profits of the
industrial operations of the Eastern Penitentiary from 1844, the
first year in which this item was included in the reports, to 1871:

[96] *Annual Report of the Inspectors of the Eastern Penitentiary*, 1861,
pp. 30-1.
[97] Ibid., 1865, pp. 84-5.
[98] Ibid., 1873, p. 192; 1874, p. 191.

Year	Weaving	Shoe-making	Picking Oakum[99]	Wood-working	Black-smithing	Tailoring	Tin-smithing	Jobbing	Cane-seating
1844	$11,740	$4,020	$847	$333	$292	$243	$87		
1845	6,535	4,241	797	431	353	211	72		
1846	8,700	5,675	737	204	305	184	69		
1847	8,167	5,373	678	267	339	192		$60	
1848	7,725	4,873	221	368	97	168	81		
1849	6,189	4,741	219	355	95	247	137		
1850	6,504	4,520	124	79	220	246	91		$351
1851	5,072	5,154	57	881	490	832	73	301	1,309
1852	4,448	2,903	33	1,044	247	220	51	191	1,782
1853	4,637	3,259	12	1,349	296	385	22	219	3,427
1854	6,061	3,892	20	1,858	282	273		195	3,558
1855	5,229	4,320	53	2,089	377	340		141	3,847
1856	6,136	4,176		2,195	414	468		167	2,378
1857	5,889	5,301	13	2,233	328	396	79	102	2,645
1858	5,600	4,718	10	1,254	231	185	51	128	2,635
1859	6,437	6,310	22	1,779	122	166		184	3,485
1860	6,101	4,772	104	1,154	73	306			4,117
1861	3,581	4,698	33	1,271	168	169			2,098
1862	2,383	5,782		1,412	143	131			3,527
1863	1,694	7,132		1,290	173	163		61	3,959
1864	2,100	5,602		1,224	129	149	44	362	4,628
1865	1,915	5,486		1,082	76	232			4,992
1866	4,174	7,164		1,361					8,729
1867	6,618	8,398		1,402	303	208	45	271	9,665
1868	6,592	7,386		1,242	116	169	51	214	9,219
1869	9,575	8,003		2,123		443	40	346	10,730
1870	6,756	7,242		1,914	219	441	30	507	8,891
1871	4,253	8,244		1,999	334	508	42	405	6,547

[99] After 1850, wool-picking instead of oakum-picking.

The following table continues the statistics of net revenue from the industrial operations of the prison in the period from 1873 to 1915.

Year	Weaving	Shoe-making	Wood-working	Black-smithing	Tailoring	Tin-smithing	Jobbing	Cane-seating	Cigar-making	Hosiery
1873	$4,549	$8,534	$5,189	$717	$542	$108	$1,020	$5,305	$866	
1874	2,985	8,137	2,285	1,023	319	50	818	4,678	2,790	
1875	936	8,041	1,172	10	422	3	1,079	3,000	2,825	
1876	3,635	9,795	2,914	214	552	701	1,206	4,176	2,761	
1877	5,414	7,427	2,585	29	511	66	1,128	2,662	3,076	
1878	4,885	7,940	565	114	644		1,493	2,832	3,084	
1879	1,876	15,998	752	56	692		1,723	2,513	3,346	$2,132
1880	1,577	26,866	729	565	644	332	2,751	4,106	5,488	11,924
1881	1,552	19,104	1,061		785		3,008	6,344	5,146	24,875
1882	1,256	13,838	1,438	188	448		2,903	5,952	3,461	19,346
1883	1,462	14,201	1,526	36	462		2,728	7,353	2,922	22,569
1884	1,210	11,059	1,329	235	482		4,339	6,250	5,656	25,772
1885	1,319	9,666	1,225	196	426		4,676	2,425	2,768	31,323
1886	1,749	11,696	1,619	258	512		4,680	3,348	3,099	36,446
1887	1,466	11,547	1,405	267	591		4,829	5,103	1,282	37,167
1888	1,976	12,374	1,350	268	667		2,257	4,904	2,399	34,074
1889	1,188	7,670	1,368	131	545		3,692	2,942	1,884	28,240
1890	1,030	7,928	1,005	118	461		3,999	4,158	885	35,417
1891	903	7,152	944	120	409		4,114	3,503	699	31,525
1892	1,207	8,250	744				3,123	5,092	731	21,970
1893	1,558	6,388	780				2,732	5,981	911	15,639
1894	1,204	5,557	350				2,585	3,527	664	6,386
1895	1,390	3,797	379				2,738	3,601	841	4,996
1896	1,125	3,529	294				2,791	3,889	884	2,812
1897	1,050	2,834	389				2,636	5,190	398	4,839
1898	1,161	2,591	493				2,758	6,478	641	5,471

Year	Weaving	Shoe-making	Wood-working	Black-smithing	Tailoring	Tin-smithing	Jobbing	Cane-seating	Cigar-making	Hosiery
1899	1,282	2,191	427				2,339	5,769	637	8,185
1900	1,681	2,712	338				2,056	5,892	1,374	6,132
1901	1,251	2,079	152				1,118	7,995	761	4,293
1902	1,721	2,271	110				954	7,651	1,403	5,922
1903	1,301	2,228	359				929	7,200	157	3,158
1904	975	2,162			Sewing Rags			5,326	1,947	10,257
1905	1,386		880					2,847	2,473	11,405
1906	1,339	1,244			1,808			2,369	3,051	11,480
1908 [100]	1,786	1,115	123		1,303			1,490	1,705	16,231
1909		1,060			841			1,387	1,358	23,361
1910		1,199			1,761			1,318	2,385	13,529
1911		1,322			1,703			1,261	3,203	12,928
1912		1,396			2,529			1,359	2,756	22,586
1913		1,986			2,562			847	2,567	22,342
1914		2,293			1,746			614	3,356	24,878
1915 [101]		2,076			1,405			621	2,689	36,598

[100] Owing to a change in the dating of the annual reports of the State Board of Charities no statistics are reported for the year 1907.

[101] The new "state-use" law was put in force in 1916 and tended to disrupt the existing industrial system during the period of transition.

(3) THE PREVAILING MODE OF INDUSTRIAL ADMINISTRATION

Any adequate account of the mode of controlling and directing the industrial operations of a state penitentiary from 1835 to 1918 must start from some consideration and understanding of the general nature and problems of convict labor in the country as a whole during this period. While, as has already been made clear, labor was introduced in the newly organized penitentiaries in the quarter of a century following 1790, primarily for its deterrent and reformative virtues and secondarily as a means of partially defraying the cost of maintaining the penal institutions, the real beginning of the expansion and high prosperity of prison labor and industry did not come until the period from 1825 to 1840. In the earlier epoch, sales were difficult because there was no well established connection between the prison shops and the customers in the outside world. With the rise of the "merchant-capitalist," in America, in the period following 1825, this fatal deficiency of the earlier period was remedied and an intermediary was found who was only too glad to furnish raw materials and take the finished product at an agreed-upon rate. The merchant-capitalist usually employed this so-called "piece-price" system of contracting for prison labor, but in many cases carried the process one step further and leased the prisoners during the working day and assumed full control and direction of their labors. The system of contract convict labor, then, was but one incident in the rise of the merchant-capitalist, of which home labor and the sweat-shop were other phases of his attempt to obtain cheap labor.[102]

The origin of this second phase of convict labor in America has been admirably described by Mr. Edward B. Mittelman in the monumental cooperative work on the *History of Labor in the United States,* edited by Professor John R. Commons:

"In his efforts to reduce operating costs, the merchant-capitalist frequently resorted to convict labour. Indeed, it was due largely to his aid that it became possible to carry out successfully the humane plan of setting the prisoners to productive work. Yet humane as this change appeared to the prison reformers of the time, it could not help but exercise a deteriorating influence on the bargaining power of free labourers.

"Close to the end of the eighteenth century, Pennsylvania and New York abolished the death penalty for a large number of crimes

---

[102] John R. Commons et *alii, A History of Labor in the United States,* Vol. I, pp. 101-03; 344ff. The merchant-capitalist had, of course, been the vital element in the English industrial system from 1600 to 1800. See H. D. B. Gibbins, *Industry in England,* pp. 336ff.

as well as many of the forms of punishment which came down from the Middle Ages, like branding, pillorying, etc. As confinement in a penitentiary was substituted, it was provided that the prisoners should be employed at hard labour. Massachusetts followed in 1805, Vermont in 1809, Maryland in 1811, and New Hampshire in 1812.

"While the laws regarding these prisons provided that the convicts be kept at hard labour, none of them was productive. The discipline was poor. The convicts were crowded together in small rooms. During the daytime, and while the prisoners were at work, there was as little supervision as at night. As a rule no shops were built, the prisoners being placed in small groups, probably not more than six, at whatever trade they brought with them, in rooms that might have been used for lodging purposes. Discipline was impossible under such circumstances; they worked, says an anonymous pamphlet on the *Prisons of Philadelphia*, 'under mutual inspection of each other.'

"This was before the merchant-capitalist had made his appearance. There were no customers for the larger output of which the prisons were capable. No master mechanic, working with one or two journeymen, could use the prisons. The result was that the latter had to seek their own market which in fact did not yet exist. The Philadelphia prison operated at an average annual loss of about $30,000, and in New York the state prison during the first twenty-five years of its existence, from 1797 to 1821, inclusive, operated at an average annual loss of $16,919.52.

"With a widened market, however, and the rise of the merchant-capitalist in the late twenties and early thirties, a re-organization in the prisons took place and the modern prison system was launched. Instead of keeping the prisoners crowded together during the night, they were placed in separate cells now provided for them; instead of working them in small shops under 'mutual inspection,' large shops were erected in the prison court yards where supervision and discipline were easy. 'A single overseer,' says the Boston Prison Discipline Society, describing the new shops at the Massachusetts prison, 'really does more to prevent evil communication between one hundred men in this shop, than ten overseers could do to prevent it among the same number in the apartments of the old brick building.' Instead of manufacturing on their own account, the prisoners were now let out to contractors.

"The prison which took the lead in this re-organization was the New York State prison at Auburn. It was begun in 1816 and designed upon the old plan, but in 1819, 'alarmed at the progress of crime, and the condition of the old penitentiaries,' says the report of the Commissioners on the Penal Code of Pennsylvania speaking of prison reform in New York, the legislature authorized an alteration in the plan in consequence of which solitary confinement at night and 'joint' labour during the day were adopted. 'There must be at least one assistant keeper in each mechanic department,' said the keeper of the prison, 'who instructs new convicts, and sees that the old make first-rate work.' At the commencement of the life of this prison, too, 'the agent purchased all raw materials, had them manfactured and sold from a prison store, on account of the state.' But the legislature soon abolished that system and 'directed that no materials beyond a very limited amount should be purchased on account of the state; but that the agent should make contracts for the labour, simply, of convicts, with those who would furnish materials, and dispose of the articles manfactured exclusively on their own account.' In this way, said the keeper, 'great risk and losses are avoided, and much private capital, and personal interest and enterprise, are brought into action, in promoting the active and profitable employment of the convicts.'

"The prison met with success almost from the start. Other states took up the plan and the deficits of the old prisons were soon turned into profits in the new. The New York State prisons at New York and Auburn for the first time became profitable in 1828. Connecticut prisons, too, for the first time became profitable in this year. In 1832 those of Massachusetts became permanently profitable, and in 1835 we learn that Sing Sing, in New York, had a net profit of $28,819.36. The prisons in Maine, New Hampshire, and Vermont were first re-organized during the thirties and wavered between profit and loss.

"According to an estimate made by the Boston Prison Discipline Society, the probable number of persons in prison in the United States, at any one time, in 1833, was 12,260. Based on the nearest census of population (12,866,020 in 1830) this would give 95.2 prisoners to each 100,000 of population. The competition against the free mechanics from this direction would seem insignificant enough, nevertheless the latter felt that the prison system imposed 'an unjust and pernicious tax' on them. 'It is true,' said an address adopted at a convention of mechanics held at Utica, August 20, 1834, 'that mechanics are not called upon to pay money to defray the expenses of the prisoners; but articles manfactured in the prisons are sold in almost every city, town and village, in the State, at prices from 40 to 60 per cent below what the honest mechanic, who supports himself and family, can afford them for; and the consequence is, that hundreds of mechanics are thrown out of employment, and, in many cases, their families are reduced to beggary.' " [103]

While the practice of contracting for the labor or the products of the labor of prisoners became well-nigh universal from 1835 to 1885 or thereabouts, the Eastern Penitentiary remained wholly aloof from this prevailing tendency and the history of its methods of industrial control and administration is chiefly interesting by

---

[103] Mittleman, in Commons, op. cit., Vol. I, pp. 344-47.

way of contrast with the general practice as outlined in the above citation from Mr. Mittelman's analysis. Nor were prisoners ever congregated in shops in the Eastern Penitentiary before 1913. The closest approximation to a shop arrangment that was ever realized at Cherry Hill before this date was the practice, as far as possible, of segregating the various industries by cell groups or wings, so as to have a wing of weavers, a wing of shoemakers, and a wing of chair-makers and cane-seaters.[104] The general and practically universal method of industrial administration in the Eastern Penitentiary was the complete management and supervision of the labor of the convicts by the prison authorities. They purchased the raw materials, supervised the industrial operations, and sold the products in the open market. Only in a few and rare instances did they yield to temptation and make some concessions to the "piece-price" form of the contract system and never have any inmates of the Eastern Penitentiary been leased to contractors. The explanation of this situation must be sought not only in the ethical and penological theories of the governing authorities of the penitentiary, but also in the limitations imposed by the Pennsylvania system of the separate confinement of prisoners. This would not allow congregation in shops, and the extra burdens and difficulties imposed by the necessity of inspecting and directing the labor of hundreds of prisoners in separate cells were greater than the merchant-capitalist cared to assume when almost every other penitentiary in the country welcomed the congregate workshop and the industrial and commercial assistance of the merchant-capitalist contractor.

Partly as the result of a just pride in being free from the undoubted abuses of the congregate-contract system and in part as a defense reaction against the inferior industrial and financial productivity of the Eastern Penitentiary, as compared with the congregate penitentiaries, the inspectors of the Cherry Hill institution took particular pride in declaring their freedom from the octopus of the contract and machinery system and in condemning the latter in vigorous terms.[105] A few representative citations from these reports, most of them written by Richard Vaux, will suffice to make clear the general attitude of the controlling authorities on this point of the ethics and economy of the control of convict labor:

"The labor of convicts here, is not farmed out as in some State Penitentiaries. This course is open to many objections. It is not

---

[104] *Annual Report of the Inspectors of the Eastern Penitentiary,* 1835, *Senate Journal,* 1835-36, Vol. II, p. 326.

[105] See Richard Vaux, *Sketch of the Origin and History of the Eastern Penitentiary,* pp. 124-26, for an attempt to prove the Auburn system less economical than the Pennsylvania system.

perceived that any advantage can result to the prisoner or the institution. The prison authorities, by the operation of this plan, have a divided duty. They are bound to the contractor for the labor he exacts for his *per diem* paid for each convict. This is the most important interest. The care of, and the discipline, and the reformatorial influences which ought to be faithfully exerted for the benefit of the convict, as well as of society, being less palpable when in contrast with revenue, it might most naturally happen that the contractor is favored to the detriment of the convict. . . .

"Conscious of being a convict, associated in common with others like themselves, degraded as far as a knowledge of their condition is participated in by their fellow prisoners can degrade, and feeling that their labor is sold in advance of its performance; an involuntary service exacted during an involuntary servitude; every impulse to reform is crushed, and every effort to regain a lost position in society destroyed. Convicts in congregation may produce a paying productiveness from their prison pursuits, and yet result in the worst economy for the Commonwealth. That State has little to boast of, when it rejoices that its penal institutions are remunerative.[106]

"Taking the best view of this convict labor in its profit-making, self-supporting aspect, it is simply to be thus stated: an individual commits crime, is convicted, his physical capacity to toil is sold to a contractor who becomes the partner of the State in the manufacture of certain products, and from the sale of these products the State gets part of the profit, the contractor a part of the profit; while the outside free laborer is paid as low a price for his free time and capacity, as his employer can afford, to come into competition with the State as a manufacturer. This is called punishment of the convict for his crime.[107]

"It is believed that the congregation of convicts during their incarceration for crime-punishment, and their sale to the highest bidder as human machinery, out of which a profit is to be made, is of far greater evil to society, than society yet fully comprehends.[108]

"This act (of 1883 abolishing contract convict labor in Pennsylvania) does not apply to this State Penitentiary, for the labor of the convicts has never been sold to contractors. In the administration of the discipline here, no one but the regular officers of the prison teaches trades, superintends the labor, or has care of the prisoners. The labor of the prisoners is used only for the manufacture of goods which are sold in the open market, and command from the trades a price, by reason of the care used in securing

---

[106] *Annual Report of the Inspectors of the Eastern Penitentiary,* 1855, pp. 8-9.
[107] Ibid., 1879, p. 76.
[108] Ibid., 1880, p. 7.

the best work. Underselling the market is not permitted, so that no general industry suffers from a reckless competition.[109]

"No contractor is known or recognized, directly or indirectly, as part of the prison management. The labor on goods ordered to be made is, like free labor outside of the prison, furnished as the orders require. The market price is the sole and only criterion for our sales." [110]

Whatever one may think of the validity of these arguments against the contract form of prison labor, it can not be denied that the inspectors presented a fairly complete summary of the conventional arguments against that system, even though they did not wholly justify their own procedure. Not only did the authorities of the Eastern Penitentiary safeguard the interests of the prisoners by excluding contractors from the institution, but they also adopted a liberal policy in stimulating the energy and interest of the prisoners by allowing them a part of the excess of their earnings above the cost of maintenance. As early as 1841 the inspectors stated that such a system was already in operation:

"The practice here is to allot to the prisoner, as soon as he is proficient in the trade he is employed at, a moderate task, estimated at the actual cost of his maintenance. After this is performed, the balance of his labor is credited to him, and the amount paid on his release from prison." [111]

It was further stated that in this year eight hundred and eighty-four dollars had thus been allowed to convicts for overwork. In the report for 1867 the inspectors stated that since 1852 a system had been in operation at Cherry Hill which allowed the prisoners one-half of the excess of their labor product above the cost of their maintenance.[112] Since that time this system has been in continuous operation and has, no doubt, contributed in no small degree to the improvement of industrial operations and morale. The following statistics indicate the amount of money awarded to the convicts as "overwork" allowance since 1852, as far as these amounts have been reported.[113]

---

[109] *Annual Report of the Inspectors of the Eastern Penitentiary,* 1883, p. 103.
[110] Ibid., 1884, p. 33.
[111] Ibid., 1841. *Senate Journal,* 1842, Vol. II, p. 112.
[112] Ibid., 1867, p. 65.
[113] Since the paralyzing of prison industry by the 1897 act, prisoners have also been allowed to work for themselves in their cells.

Year	Number Receiving "overwork" allowance	Amount distributed as credit for overwork.
1852	23	$ 205
1853	150	2,333
1854	202	2,291
1855	177	1,855
1856	190	2,340
1857	197	2,429
1858	174	1,918
1859	199	2,181
1860	183	2,519
1861	129	1,110
1862	175	1,673
1863	212	2,582
1864	188	2,990
1865	192	2,786
1866	239	3,518
1867	311	3,962
1873		3,175
1874		2,121
1875		2,075
1876	173	1,918
1877	292	2,476
1878	339	4,074
1879	481	5,133
1880	741	10,722
1881	787	9,284
1882	815	10,271
1883	655	6,837
1884	755	8,428
1885	761	8,830
1886	808	11,081
1887	781	10,480
1888	540	11,107
1889	426	7,149
1890	584	6,086
1891	309	6,641
1892	280	5,119
1893	286	4,904
1894	333	2,457
1895	333	2,377
1896	175	1,473
1897	238	1,758
1898	238	1,758
1899	185	1,752
1900	121	2,386
1901	102	2,754
1902	165	3,606
1903	177	3,751
1904	400	5,306
1905	296	9,646
1906	not given	10,101

Year	Number Receiving "overwork" allowance	Amount distributed as credit for overwork.
1907	not given	11,498
1908	" "	10,045
1909	" "	12,284
1910	" "	13,084
1911	" "	11,861
1912	" "	12,896
1913	" "	16,134
1914	" "	18,773
1915	" "	19,743
1916	" "	6,343
1917	" "	2,318

(4)   STATE INTERFERENCE WITH PRISON LABOR IN PENNSYLVANIA AND THE ATTITUDE OF THE EASTERN PENITENTIARY

Before taking up the consideration of the interference of the state of Pennsylvania with the labor of convicts it will be necessary to provide a very brief review of the general growth in this country of opposition to convict labor and particularly to convict labor as organized and conducted according to the contract system. In the same way that the rise of contract convict labor was intimately associated with the rise of the merchant-capitalists, so the growth of opposition to contract convict labor was inseparably connected with the development of labor organizations, their struggle to improve the conditions of the laboring classes, and their entry into and influence upon the politics of the state governments in the United States. The opposition of labor to contract convict labor, on the ground that it created an unfair competition with free labor, goes back as far as the first feeble beginnings of labor organization, though this opposition could not become particularly effective until the organization of labor had advanced to a sufficient degree to exert a very considerable influence upon American politics, as it did immediately after the period of the Civil War and Reconstruction. As early as 1823, at the very time when the Auburn system was coming into existence, the mechanics of New York City protested against the alleged menace of convict labor:

"This same year (1823) the mechanics of New York City petitioned the state legislature to abolish the competition of convict labour. Their grievances are summarized in the following passage from a lengthy memorial adopted at a public meeting: 'Your memorialists have seen the convicts imperfectly educated in various trades, hired out to individuals, in some instances at reduced compensation, and in others employed for the benefit of the state, and the products of their labour thrown into market and disposed of at a price very little above the cost of materials of which they were manufactured, to the ruin of free mechanics.' They also proposed that convicts be employed in a state marble quarry." [114]

In 1830 the mechanics of Utica and Brooklyn complained of the competition of convict labor.[115] The industrial depression following 1834 made the competition of prison and free labor unusually apparent to the laborers, and the newly formed "General Trades Union" of New York secured in 1834 the appointment of a legislative committee on prison labor, but this committee failed to recommend the abolition of contract convict labor. The laborers, thereupon, held a great indignation meeting in Tammany Hall on February 24, 1835, condemning the action of the committee.[116] In October of 1835 the above mentioned Union, at its convention in New York City, protested against the prevailing mode of conducting prison labor and demanded the marking of prison-made goods.[117] In March, 1836, the convention of the "National Cooperative Association of Journeymen Cordwainers," meeting at New York City, demanded that officials of their association make an investigation of convict labor and, in case it was found to be a serious menace to free labor, the journeymen were ordered to refuse to work for firms handling prison-made boots and shoes.[118] In Pennsylvania, in 1835, opposition to prison labor, the question of a National Bank, and the agitation for the abolition of imprisonment for debt were made the vital issues in the gubernatorial contest of that year, the laboring element supporting for governor, Congressman Henry A. Muhlenberg who adopted the labor program.[119] In 1842 a secret labor organization, called the "Mechanics' Mutual Protection," was formed in Buffalo, New York, for the explicit purpose of combatting competitive prison labor. It was led by Robert MacFarlane, and by 1847 had fifty locals in New York, Ohio, Michigan, Pennsylvania and Wisconsin.[120] Twenty-two years later the "International Industrial Assembly of North America," was formed in Louisville, Kentucky. This was the beginning of the national federation of labor organizations in America and among its original resolutions was one demanding the opposition to and abolition of, contract convict labor.[121]

[114] J. R. Commons, (ed.) *A History of Labor in the United States,* Vol. I, p. 155.
[115] Ibid., p. 282.
[116] Ibid., pp. 367-70.
[117] Ibid., pp. 431-32.
[118] Ibid., p. 443.
[119] Ibid., pp. 459-60.
[120] Ibid., p. 492.
[121] Ibid., Vol. II, pp. 33-7.

This early opposition to convict labor failed to accomplish any considerable results in the way of eliminating contract labor from prisons because the original labor organizations did not possess enough economic and political strength to force the acceptance of their program upon the state legislatures and because the merchant capitalist maintained his grip upon the manufacturing and commercial world. In the period following the Civil War, however, circumstan ces were greatly altered. The Industrial Revolution had become thoroughly established in the United States, thus creating a much larger industrial proletariat and correspondingly weakening the position of the merchant-capitalist. The greatly increased laboring class began to build up its strong national organizations and had become of sufficient size to command the particular attention and solicitude of ambitious politicians. At this same time when the labor organizations were becoming powerful in both an economic and a political sense there occurred the severe panic and depression of 1873 and the following years, which greatly stimulated the activity of labor organizations in pressing every policy which could possibly improve the deplorable condition of the industrial proletariat. Their old enemy, contract convict labor, was, naturally, a special object of attack. [122] The most powerful labor organization during this period of more successful agitation against convict labor was the "Noble Order of Knights of Labor," founded in Philadelphia in 1869 by Uriah S. Stephens.[123] The depression following 1873 made them especially active. From that time until the end of the eighties they carried on a vigorous campaign for the improvement of labor conditions which embraced a demand for abolition of contract labor. Their political influence was very powerful and in the eighties there was a general wave of legislation in the United States abolishing or limiting contracting for the labor of prisoners.[124] Discredited by their violence and weakened by their loose organization, the "Knights" passed from power in the late eighties and were superseded by the more constructive American Federation of Labor, but the latter organization never made peace with contract convict labor.[125] From 1880 to the present day a steady fight has been kept up by labor and its political lobbyists, agents and allies until at the present time contract convict labor has been abol-

---

[122] Commons, op. cit., Vol. II, pp. 85ff.; R. T. Ely, *The Labor Movement in America,* pp. 75-91; Carroll D. Wright, *An Outline of Practical Sociology,* Part V.

[123] Commons, op. cit., Vol. II, pp. 196ff.; Hollander and Barnett, *Studies in American Trade Unionism,* pp. 353-80.

[124] Commons, op. cit., Vol. II, pp. 243, 351, 462-63, 488-93.

[125] Ibid., pp. 396ff.

ished in more than one-half of the states of the Union. The tendency has been to substitute for the contract system the "public-account" and the "piece-price" systems.[126] The great success which labor has achieved in more recent years in combatting contract convict labor has been due not only to activities of labor organizations, but also to the selfish ambitions of unscrupulous politicians who have not been at all interested in the ethics of systems of prison labor, but have exploited this issue in order to attract the labor vote. On the whole, however, the abolition of the contract system was desirable, but the pendulum tended to swing too far in the direction of state control and the fatal restriction of prison labor, to the detriment of both state and convict and with no corresponding benefit to free labor. In the place of the abuses of "forcing" labor under the contract system there has developed a deplorable tendency toward an expensive and demoralizing idleness. The general problem involved in the modern regulation of convict labor has been admirably and justly stated by the late Carroll D. Wright in the following paragraph:

"In the many investigations which have been made in relation to the prison labour question, few instances have been found where prices have been affected in the least, and rarely a case where wages have been lowered in consequence of the employment of convicts

---

[126] The official government classification and definition of the various types of prison labor follows:

"The Lease System—Under this system the contractors assume entire control of the convicts, including their maintenance and discipline, subject, however, to the regulations fixed by statute. In general, the prisoners are removed from the prisons, and are employed in outdoor labor, such as mining, agriculture, railroad construction, etc., though manfacturing is sometimes carried on. The nature and duration of the employment are within the restrictions of the law fixed by the lease.

"The Contract System—The employment under this system is usually within the prison shops or yards, discipline and control remaining in the hands of the officers, only the labor of the convicts being let to and directed by the contractors for manufacturing purposes. The State usually furnishes shop room and sometimes also provides power and machinery.

"The Piece-Price System—Not only the discipline of the convicts, but the direction of their labor as well, is retained by the State under this system, the contractors furnishing the material to be made up and receiving the finished product, an agreed price per piece being paid for the labor bestowed.

"The Public-Account System—There is no intervention of outside parties under this system, the employment of the convicts being in all respects directed by the State, and the products of their labor being sold for its benefit.

"The State-Use System—This system is similar to the above, except that such articles are produced as will be of service to the State in supplying and maintaining its various institutions, and are appropriated to such use instead of being put on the general market.

"The Public-Works-and-Ways System—Under this system convicts are employed in the construction and repair of public streets, highways, and other public works."

in productive industry. Nevertheless, the moral effect of the supposed competition, and of whatever real competition may have occurred, has been sufficient to create a demand in nearly all the States of the Union for some regulation of the employment of convicts under which competition can be entirely or largely removed, and for the last twenty years or more political platforms have often contained a parodoxial plank demanding that convicts should be employed, not only as a matter of health, but as a source of revenue to the State, but in such a way as to relieve honest industry of competition. It is absolutely impossible to prevent competition if convicts are to be employed in any way whatever. It must be admitted by all sane men that they should be employed and constantly employed upon intelligent labour. The problem, therefore, so far as the economics of the question is concerned, is either to reduce the competition to the lowest point or to manufacture goods in such a way and under such conditions that prices and wages can in no sense be affected. This is the whole of the economic side of the question from the productive point of view." [127]

By a curious irony of fate, Pennsylvania, who was the pioneer in prison labor in the United States, has had the most disastrous experience of any state in this violent reaction against convict labor and toward the enforced idleness of prisoners. For more than twenty years the term "prison labor" has been a misnomer when applied to the penitentiaries of Pennsylvania. Down to the year 1883 the state interfered in no way with the mode of utilizing and administering the labor of prisoners, but since that year it has stepped in to regulate prison labor in a progressively more rigorous manner, until it finally succeeded in well-nigh paralyzing the industrial systems of the state penitentiaries. Professor Louis N. Robinson has well summarized this situation in the following excerpt from his report to the Pennsylvania Legislature in 1915:

"During the period 1676-1883 prison labor developed and expanded. New institutions were established into which the system was introduced. The number of offenders employed under the State was also increased by drafting out of the local jails the long term prisoners and putting them in the penitentiaries. No laws were passed for the purpose of restricting the employment of prison labor in any way. . . .

"Just as the first period 1676-1883 showed the extension of prison labor, the last period emphatically shows a series of checks, curbing the free production of goods within prisons and thereby militating against the choice of occupations because of their value to the delinquent as well as to the State. These restrictions have

---

[127] Carroll D. Wright, *An Outline of Practical Sociology*, pp. 380-81.

applied to: (1) the method of employment (abolition of the contract system); (2) the kind of labor in which the prisoners may
be employed (prohibition of power machinery); and (3) the amount
of goods that may be produced (limitation on the number of
inmates employed)." [128]

The first great victory of the labor element in their struggle
against convict labor in Pennsylvania appeared in the act of June 13,
1883, which abolished contract convict labor in all state and county
penal institutions in Pennsylvania.[129] It was decreed that as soon
as the existing contracts had expired all inmates of state prisons
and reformatory institutions should be employed "in behalf of the
State." [130] They were to be employed for and by the institution in
which they were confined and no more labor was to be hired out
by contract.[131] It was further ordered that convicts were to be paid
wages equal to the amount of their gross earnings, from which
were to be deducted the cost of trial, board, lodging and clothing,
and the balance was to be paid to the dependents of the convicts
or was to go to the convict upon discharge if no dependents
existed.[132] As contract convict labor had never been an integral
part of the industrial system of the Eastern Penitentiary the
inspectors joyfully and proudly declared their immunity from the
operation of this law.[133] They felt no little elation over this point
because the law meant an almost total disruption of the industrial
system of the Western Penitentiary, which had been founded upon
the contract system since 1870.

A further restriction on convict labor was contained in an act
of June 20, 1883, decreeing the marking of all goods made in any
penal institution in the state with the words, "convict made," and
the name of the institution. Only goods made for shipment outside of the state were exempted from the operation of this law.[134]

In 1891 the eight-hour day, which had been so vital an element
in the agitation accompanying the rise of the Knights of Labor and
the American Federation of Labor,[135] was introduced in all the

---

[128] Louis N. Robinson, *Employment and Compensation of Prisoners in
Pennsylvania,* (Report of the Penal Commission, 1915) pp. 59, 63.
[129] *Laws of the General Assembly,* 1883, p. 112.
[130] Ibid.
[131] Ibid.
[132] Ibid. This provision was never enforced.
[133] *Report of the Inspectors of the Eastern Penitentiary,* 1883, p. 103;
1884, p. 333.
[134] *Laws of the General Assembly,* 1883, p. 125.
[135] Commons, op. cit., Vol. II, pp. 375ff.

penal and reformatory institutions of Pennsylvania which were
supported by state appropriations of county taxes.[136]

Prison industry could very well have withstood the restrictions
imposed by the laws of 1883 and 1891, which certainly provided for
the elimination of all possible abuses of convict labor, but neither
politicians nor labor agitators were willing to stop at this point.
The *reductio ad absurdum* of state interference with convict labor
was embodied in the notorious act of April 18, 1897, of which Mr.
Charles A. Muehlbronner had the unenviable distinction of being
the author. This law, probably the most disastrous and ill-conceived
in the whole history of a type of legislation conspicuous for short-
sightedness and a lack of understanding of the deeper problems
involved, ended for the time being all hope of a just and equitable
solution of the problem of convict labor in such a way as to con-
serve the interests of labor, the commonwealth and the prisoners.
The act ordered,

"That, from and after the passage of this Act, no warden, superintendent, or other officer of any State prison, penitentiary, or State
reformatory, having control of the employment of the inmates of
said institution, shall employ more than five per cent of the whole
number of inmates of said institutions in the manufacture of brooms
and brushes and hollow-ware, or ten per cent in the manufacture of
any other kind of goods, wares, articles or things that are manufactured elsewhere in the State except mats and matting, in the
manufacture of which twenty per cent of the whole number of
inmates may be employed: Provided, That this Act shall not apply
to goods manufactured for the use of inmates of such institutions.

"That no machine operated by steam, electricity, hydraulic force,
compressed air, or other power, except machines operated by hand
or foot power, shall be used in any of the said institutions in the
manufacture of any goods, wares, articles or things that are manufactured elsewhere in the State." [137]

As if to make the effect of this law still more pernicious, the
attorney general of the state rendered an opinion that the law
meant that either five, ten or twenty per cent. might be employed,
but never the maximum of thirty-five per cent. of the inmates.[138]

This law enraged even the inspectors of the Eastern Penitentiary,
who had regarded with complacency the passage of the earlier laws
regulating convict labor, having in their annual report for 1896
praised the anti-convict labor laws in the state. In their report for

---

[136] *Laws of the General Assembly,* 1891, p. 100.
[137] Ibid., 1897, pp. 170-71.
[138] *Report of the Inspectors of the Western Penitentiary,* 1897-98, pp. 8-9.

1897 they predicted that the law would mean the end of any effective system of prison industry.[139] In the following year they condemned the restrictive legislation as a general movement. They said, with respect to the general program of restriction:

"The growing tendency here and elsewhere to abolish or restrict labor in penal institutions is to be regretted. There can be no justification for such legislation. It answers no good purpose. It is idle to suggest that it protects outside labor. The output from all the prisoners in the State, if run to the utmost, would be small and could not disturb the labor market to any appreciable extent. It is merely sentiment and cannot stand fair investigation for a moment." [140]

Their comments on the Muehlbronner Act were even more vigorous and pointed:

"There could never be placed on a statute-book more monstrous legislation than this. It is a disgrace to the intelligence of the Nineteenth Century. Every prisoner should be compelled to work— to work hard for eight or ten hours every day. It would produce greater reformation in the character of the prisoners than all other means combined. This Act produces a strange contradiction. Every prisoner sent to the Eastern Penitentiary is condemned by the law to solitary confinement at hard labor, and yet this act forbids putting ninety per centum of those thus sentenced to any labor whatever." [141]

The effect of this unwise act of 1897 was as fatal as the inspectors had predicted. Prison labor became a farce from that time to about 1925 in Pennsylvania. According to the statictics gathered by Doctor Whitin, out of the two thousand nine hundred idle able-bodied male prisoners in the United States in 1909, no less than two thousand and seventy-three were listed from Pennsylvania.[142]

In 1913 there was passed the only liberal act of the period with respect to prison labor, and this was of little consequence because it came after the industrial system of the penitentiaries had been destroyed and affected but one institution. This was the law of July 7, 1913, which stated that "the proper authorities of the Eastern State Penitentiary are authorized, at their discretion, to have any or all of the persons confined in the said penitentiary congregated for the several purposes of worship, labor, learning and

---

[139] *Report of the Inspectors of the Eastern Penitentiary*, 1897, p. 124.
[140] Ibid., 1898, p. 7.
[141] Ibid., 1897, p. 7.
[142] E. Stagg Whitin, *The Caged Man.*

recreation." [143] While this act could have little immediate effect in stimulating industrial activity in the Eastern Penitentiary, it removed a long-standing legal obstacle to an efficient industrial organization of the institution and prepared the way for future legislation designed to regenerate the system of prison labor.

In the period following 1909 a period of reforming zeal in the realm of penology began in Pennsylvania which has been unequaled since the developments from 1786-92 or 1818-29.[144] It was inevitable that the intolerable condition of prison labor and industry should be one of the first matters to engage the attention of all progressive minds interested in prison reform in the state. On July 25, 1913, an act was passed which declared,

"That the Governor is hereby authorized to appoint a commission of seven persons, one of whom shall be a representative of organized labor, one of whom shall be experienced in penology, one of whom shall be a person of skill and experience in making investigations, and four of whom shall be learned in the law, to inquire into the advisability of amending the penal laws of the Commonwealth, so as to provide for the employment of all inmates of all penal institutions, to provide compensation for their labor, and to provide for utilizing the results of such labor in the penal and charitable institutions of this Commonwealth." [145]

The commission which was appointed by the Governor consisted of Edwin M. Abbott, Louis N. Robinson, Patrick Gilday, William D. Grimes, Andrew Hourigan, Robert J. McKenty and Samuel I. Spyker. As secretary and chief investigator for the commission, the work of compiling the report fell largely upon Professor Robinson, who was aided by Mr. Albert H. Votaw of the Pennsylvania Prison Society in an investigation of the labor conditions in the county penal institutions.[146] The commission submitted a brief but encyclopedic report on February 15, 1915. It contained not only a tabular summary of the industrial status of all the penal institutions in Pennsylvania, but also a brief summary of the industrial systems employed in most of the state prison systems in

---

[143] *Laws of the General Assembly,* 1913, p. 708.
[144] See below, pp. 381ff.
[145] *Report of the Penal Commission on the Employment and Compensation of Prisoners,* February 15, 1915, p. 8.
[146] Ibid., pp. 9-13. A. H. Votaw, *Penal Legislation of 1915 in Pennsylvania,* p. 3; Cf. also by the same writer, *The County Prisons of Pennsylvania,* 1914. The committee on legislation of the Pennsylvania Prison Society, of which Rev. Dr. J. F. Ohl was chairman, also submitted a detailed memorandum to the commission which contained a number of constructive recommendations as to possible methods of improving the labor situation in the penal institutions of the state.

the United States. It also presented a brief historical survey of prison industry in Pennsylvania, a critique of existing conditions and a bill embodying the chief reforms deemed necessary in regenerating and reconstructing the long paralyzed industrial organization of the penal institutions of the state. The following criticism of the labor conditions then existing is worthy of quotation, as it sets forth in a lucid manner the absurdities of the situation created by the series of restrictive laws passed following 1883:

"A brief scrutiny of the figures relative to the employment of prisoners in Pennsylvania reveals the fact that detention in idleness is the fate that awaits the majority of convicted criminals in Pennsylvania. Probably no state in the Union has as many idle prisoners as does our own state. The seriousness of this situation can not be over emphasized.

"From the financial point of view no policy could be more silly than that of supporting in idleness the thousands of prisoners which make up the never-ending stream of humanity that pours through our penal institutions. The combined plants represent an enormous outlay of capital, and the annual maintenance cost alone lays a burden of no mean magnitude on the tax-payers of the State. This policy of idleness has no justification either in theory or in fact. It is partly the result of the attempt to eliminate the competition of prison-made goods, and partly the inevitable outcome of our present system of institution for misdemeanants.

"But the financial point of view is by no means the deciding factor. If it could be shown, as in the case of the institution for juvenile delinquents, that the entire time of these unfortunate members of society was spent in ways certain to benefit them physically, mentally and morally to the lasting good of society, no one would object to the size of the bill. Unfortunately, no such rosy picture of our institutions can be accepted as true to the facts. Here and there, exceptional wardens or keepers have tried to do this very thing, but they have been frightfully handicapped by the law or by the nature of the institutions under their charge. Great credit must be given them, but they are the type of men who need not praise but help, which the legislature alone can give.

"What can be said in defense of a system which condemns a man to complete idleness in a cell! No more diabolical punishment could be invented. It is a sentence to gradual dissolution and decay. It means the physical, mental and, in many cases, the moral degeneration of the prisoners. After such a condition has been arrived at, is it any wonder that a prisoner returns to crime and becomes a recidivist. Instead of profiting by the discipline of work, he loses his desire to work and comes to the conclusion that society must owe him a living, a perfectly natural conclusion in view of his experience as a boarder of the state from whom nothing was expected.

"But perhaps the greatest danger in this policy of idleness lies in its effect on family life. Many prisoners have been, prior to their conviction, members of a family group the support of which has rested largely or entirely on their shoulders. Compelled to endure months or perhaps years of inactivity, with no chance to contribute through their effort to the economic welfare of their family group, they must resign themselves to the fate which has overtaken it. Private or public charity must come forward and take up the burden or become an unwilling witness of a disheartening struggle on the part of the remaining members to obtain a livelihood. When the state openly and with intent breaks the economic bond which unites members of a family group, it has no right to criticise the results of this policy which appear in the various forms of desertion, divorce, and laxness in morals. The opportunity to work and the right to the products of his labor ought to be inviolate rights of every prisoner, if not for his sake then for that of his family and for that, above all, of the state." [147]

After a careful historical and analytical study of the situation the commission drew up a series of remedial bills embodying the following recommendations:

"The employment under the State-Use System of the Inmates of the Eastern Penitentiary, the Western Penitentiary and the Pennsylvania Industrial Reformatory at Huntingdon.

"The administrative machinery necessary for the introduction of the State-Use System in these three institutions.

"The purchase of a moderate sized farm to be used in connection with the Eastern Penitentiary.

"An opportunity for the counties to employ the inmates of the jails, workhouses, houses of correction, etc., in the production of goods for the use of county institutions or the inmates thereof.

"The creation of six industrial farms for misdemeanants and the employment and compensation of the inmates.

"A modification of the existing wage system in so far as it applies to the Eastern Penitentiary, the Western Penitentiary and the Huntingdon Reformatory." [148]

Acting on the recommendations of the commission, the legislature passed the act of June 1, 1915, which bore a general resemblance to the act drawn by the commission and was, until after 1921, the governing act for the regulation of prison industry in Pennsylvania. Its terms applied to the two state penitentiaries and the Huntingdon Reformatory. The old limitations as to the percentage of prisoners which might be employed were rendered impo-

---

[147] *Report of the Penal Commission on the Employment and Compensation of Prisoners,* 1915, pp. 63-5.
[148] Ibid., 1915, p. 27.

tent [149] by the introduction of the *state-use* system of industrial administration and by the provision that all inmates physically capable "may be employed for not to exceed eight hours each day, other than Sundays and public holidays." [150] The purposes for which the labor of the prisoners might be utilized were described in the following paragraph:

"Such labor shall be for the purpose of the manufacture and production of supplies for said institutions, or for the Commonwealth or for any county thereof, or for any public institution owned, managed, and controlled by the Commonwealth, or for the preparation and manufacture of building material for the construction or repair of any State institution, or in the work of such construction or repair, or for the purpose of industrial training or instruction, or partly for one and partly for the other of such purposes, or in the manufacture and production of crushed stone, brick, tile, and culvert pipe, or other material suitable for draining roads of the State, or in the preparation of road building and ballasting material." [151]

To supervise the administration of the new industrial system, a *Prison Labor Commission* was created, constituted by one member from the governing boards of the two state penitentiaries and the Huntingdon Reformatory. This commission was vested with full control of the productive labor of the inmates. It was authorized to determine the industries of the several institutions and provide proper and adequate machinery. A fund of seventy-five thousand dollars was provided as working capital at the disposal of the commission. The commission was to have charge of all sales and was ordered to turn the receipts into the above-mentioned manufacturing fund. A complete report of all transactions was to be made monthly to the auditor-general of the state.[152] The inmates of the three institutions concerned by this act were to receive wages, the amount of which was to be determined by the prison labor commission between the specified limits of ten to fifty cents per day. The criteria for determining the amount of wages were the pecuniary value of the labor and "the willingness, industry, and good conduct" of the prisoners.[153]

---

[149] Continued on other than "state-use" manufactures by another act of June 1, 1915.

[150] *Laws of the General Assembly*, 1915, p. 656.

[151] Ibid.

[152] Ibid., 1915, pp. 656-57.

[153] Ibid., p. 658. By an act of June 4, 1915, inmates of county penal institutions were made eligible for work on state and county highways (*Laws of the General Assembly*, pp. 812-14). The proposal of the commission that several industrial farms be created for county prisoners was realized by an act passed in 1917. See A. H. Votaw, *Penal Legislation of 1917 in Pennsylvania*, pp. 3ff.

This act, establishing the state-use system, while constituting a great step in advance, had one fatal defect, namely, that it made the institution of that system optional and imposed no obligations upon public institutions to purchase the products of prison labor. This defect was well summarized by Mr. Albert H. Votaw in the following paragraph, which has proved almost prophetic:

"These laws must be reinforced by additional legislation before they become very effective. There is not any obligation on the part of any prison board to institute these industries. They merely have the privilege of furnishing employment. And unless there is some market to which they may look with reasonable certainty for the disposal of products, there is little or no encouragement to establish these industries. No prison board will be inclined to establish a furniture manufactory unless there shall be a call for the furniture. The Mayor of Buffalo cannot order a desk or a chair for his room unless he has first made requisition on the manager of prison products in the State of New York. If the prisons make what is desired, he is under obligation to purchase from them. If he purchases furniture elsewhere, the controller will not honor the bill unless accompanied by a letter from the sales manager of prison products that such articles are not in stock. We must have some such system in this State before there will be any successful operation of the laws on this subject.[154]

The need for an act compelling all state institutions to buy prison-made products was met quite indirectly but fairly adequately by the act of 1921, creating the Department of Public Welfare which was given control over all the state institutions dealing with the criminal, insane and dependent classes. This required all institutions, as far as possible, to purchase state-made products. On April 7, 1925, an act was passed authorizing the Department of Public Welfare to sell the surplus products of prison industries. The act reads as follows:

"Section 1. Be it enacted, &c., That the Department of Welfare is hereby authorized and empowered to sell to the Government of the United States, including all departments, bureaus, commissions, and other agencies thereof existing under acts of the Congress of the United States; and to the Government of any state or commonwealth of the United States; and to any county, city, borough, township, or other organized sub-division of any state or commonwealth of the United States; and to any institution maintained by, or receiving aid from, any state or commonwealth of the United States, or any organized sub-division thereof, such surplus products

---

[154] Albert H. Votaw, *Penal Legislation of 1915 in Pennsylvania,* pp. 12-3.

manufactured or prepared in the industries established by the Department of Welfare in the Eastern Penitentiary, the Western Penitentiary, the Pennsylvania Industrial Reformatory at Huntingdon, and any other correctional institution of this Commonwealth in which the Department of Welfare has established industries, as are not purchased by this Commonwealth or by any county, city, borough, or township of this Commonwealth, or by any state institution, or by any educational or charitable institution receiving aid from this Commonwealth.

"Section 2. All receipts from the sales of surplus products herein authorized shall be paid into the manufacturing fund, for the uses and purposes of said fund, as provided by law."

Unfortunately, this act does not allow the free and unrestricted sale of surplus products in the open market, which is the one remaining obstacle to a thoroughly efficient system of prison industry in Pennsylvania.

With the establishment and organization of the Department of Welfare the control over prison industry was taken from the discontinued Prison Labor Commission and vested in a branch of the Department of Welfare, known as the Bureau of Restoration. At the present time the warden of each penitentiary simply furnishes a given number of convicts to the Bureau of Restoration at an agreed upon wage per day. The Bureau provides the raw materials and disposes of the manufactured products. In other words, it has full control and supervision of the productive industries of the prison. This represents a great improvement over the old contract system in that the Bureau of Restoration is not only interested in productivity but also is deeply concerned with vocational instruction as a method of assisting in the reformation of criminals.

(5) THE PRESENT CONDITION OF THE INDUSTRIAL SYSTEM OF THE EASTERN PENITENTIARY

The act of June 1, 1915, did not produce the beneficial effects that were hoped for by its framers, primarily because of the fact that no compulsory public customers were provided for prison-made supplies. The commission scarcely began active operations until October, 1917, and then only on a modest scale. About a year later [155] only about one hundred inmates of the Eastern Penitentiary were employed by the prison labor commission, these mainly in the making of shoes and hosiery. As this was considerable less than half the number which was employed in productive industries before

---

[155] September 4, 1918.

1915, it was but natural that the prison authorities came to regard the new system as merely disrupting the old industrial organization without affording any relief from the intolerable and enforced idleness of the prisoners.

Nothing of great significance happened to improve the industrial situation in the Eastern Penitentiary until after the creation of the Department of Public Welfare in 1921. The act creating this supervisory organization made the state-use system obligatory in all purchases by state institutions. Then followed the act of April 7, 1925, partially legalizing the public-account system. Work on farms and public roads had already been relied upon. Hence, from the legal standpoint Pennsylvania can now exploit the four most promising types of industrial operation open to penal institutions: (1) state-use; (2) public-account; (3) public works and ways; and (4) farm work. The Department of Public Welfare under Doctor Ellen C. Potter from 1923 to 1927 made a vigorous effort to alleviate the distressing situation existing in the industrial departments of the state penitentiaries, and at the Eastern Penitentiary she had the enthusiastic coöperation of the new Warden, Colonel John C. Groome. Colonel Groome and the Bureau of Restoration did their best within the difficulties imposed by the limited shop resources of the Eastern Penitentiary, but it is generally agreed that a satisfactory solution of the problem of convict labor and industry in the eastern section of the state will have to await the construction of the new institution and the exploitation of the new prison farm to be operated in connection with it. In 1926 an average of 274 inmates were employed by the Bureau of Restoration in the printing department, shoe shop, hosiery, underwear, weaving and tailoring departments. In the penitentiary shops 102 were employed in the caning shop, 82 in the rag shop and 8 in the cigar shop. Some 250 were employed in individual work of a manufacturing type, while about 350 were engaged in work in connection with the maintenance of the institution. About twenty were employed in an automobile paint and repair shop. Thus 1,079 out of 1,487 convicts were employed.

C. *The Industrial Experience of the Western Penitentiary since 1835*

(1) THE NATURE OF THE PRISON INDUSTRIES

The statistical information upon which any reliable account of the industrial history of the Western Penitentiary must be based is scarcely more satisfactory for the earlier period of its history than that which exists for the Philadelphia institution. This circumstance impressed the visiting committee of the legislature as early as 1837 when it remarked that, "From the confused state of the accounts of the institution, it was impossible for the committee to ascertain the amount of productive labor done by the prisoners, and how near the amount comes to supporting them." [157] From 1835 to 1873 no consistent statistics were included in the annual reports giving the number of inmates employed at the several prison industries. The relative status of these industries has to be gathered from the statistics giving the profits derived from the few trades developed in the institution. Such information exists for most of the years from 1838 to 1873. From 1873 to the present day the reports of the inspectors of the Western Penitentiary have presented all the facts connected with its industrial history in a systematic and thorough way which contrasts in a curious and flattering manner with the total absence of this vital information from the reports of the Eastern Penitentiary.

As was the case in the Eastern Penitentiary, the most important early industries introduced in the Western Penitentiary at Allegheny were shoemaking and weaving. In 1837 the inspectors stated that "shoe-making and weaving are the principal branches of industry contemplated by us in this penitentiary." They explained that their selection was due to the fact that these industries were best adapted to being carried out in the isolation of separate cells.[158] From 1837 to 1870 shoemaking and weaving were the only important industries carried on in the Western Penitentiary, with woodworking, tailoring and oakum-picking as unimportant accessory and spasmodic industries. On the whole, shoemaking was the most important and productive of these two industries until about 1887, when it practically disappeared, owing to the operation of the anti-contract labor laws of 1883. The persistence of shoemaking in the Western Penitentiary presents an interesting topic. Threatened in 1860 by the competition of the expanding shoe industry of New England, especially of Massachusetts,[159] it received a temporary stimulus from the obtaining of government contracts during the Civil War.[160] Shortly after the close of this period shoemaking became the all-important industry in the congregate-contract period from 1870 to 1883. As it was bound up entirely with the contract method of administration, it passed away with that system after the

[157] Report of the Visiting Committee of the Legislature, 1837, p. 54.
[158] Report of the Inspectors of the Western Penitentiary, 1837, Senate Journal, 1836-37, Vol. II. pp. 439-40.
[159] Ibid., 1860, Legislative Documents, 1860, p. 895.
[160] Ibid., 1862, p. 845.

contracts had expired in 1887.[161] Weaving had a period of special prosperity during the decade of the sixties, but died out with the concentration on shoemaking after 1873, and as a result of the deadly competition of outside mechanical weaving with the antiquated hand-looms of the penitentiary.[162] As was the case in the Eastern Penitentiary, it received a new lease of life after 1875 in the form of the weaving of hosiery.

In the period from 1873 to 1887, when the industries of the penitentiary were conducted according to the system of congregation and contracts, shoemaking received a great impetus and was as productive as all other forms of industry combined during this period. Broom-making, which had begun in the sixties, became an important source of income from 1875 onward. Cigar-making was also a uniformly productive industry of considerable significance during this entire period. The making of chains and heavy hardware was a very significant source of revenue in the years from 1879 to 1884. For two years, 1875-77, whip-making was a flourishing industry. From 1887, when the contracts had expired, to 1897, when the fatal Muehlbronner Act was passed, the making of cocoa mats superseded shoemaking as the all-important prison industry.[163] The hosiery industry became very prosperous in the mid-nineties and contested first place with mat-making. Broom-making weathered the 1883 laws and was a consistently productive industry during the whole period. From 1897 to the present time, or at least to 1915, the manufacture of mats, hosiery and brooms has still constituted the vast bulk of the productive industry of the Western Penitentiary, though there has been a considerable decline in all of these owing to the restrictions imposed upon productivity by the law of 1897.

It was a fortunate choice that the inspectors made in 1887 when they selected the manufacture of mats as the substitute for shoemaking. As this industry was given the largest maximum of productivity under the 1897 law, it was possible to continue the existing system of industries after 1897 with the minimum amount of disturbance and curtailment of production. In the last few years, since the state-use system has been in a process of introduction and has caused a temporary disruption of the penitentiary industries, much the most important and remunerative industry carried on by the Western Penitentiary has been the agricultural activities on the large farm in Centre County, which is the site of the new central penitentiary, only recently completed.

---

[161] *Report of the Inspectors of the Western Penitentiary*, 1873, pp. 9, 23-4; 1886-87, pp. 2-3.
[162] Ibid., 1873, pp. 22-4.
[163] Ibid., 1886-87, pp. 2-3.

The report of the legislative investigating commission of 1839 contains no such detailed information concerning the industrial distribution in the Western Penitentiary as was included for the Cherry Hill institution. The only specific information on this point was that, "The prisoners are daily employed in tailoring, shoe-making, weaving, carpenter work, blacksmithing, burnishing silver and oakum picking. All are in solitary confinement." [164] The first definite statement of the industrial distribution of the population of the inmates of the Western Penitentiary after the institution had become thoroughly organized is contained in the first annual report of Mr. Wilmer Worthington, as secretary and general agent of the newly created State Board of Public Charities in 1870. [165] On December 23, 1870, the prison population was thus distributed: [166]

Weaving	185
Shoemaking	90
Cigars and cigar boxes	24
Prison account (domestic)	47
Sick and idle	34

From 1873 onward the annual reports of the inspectors contain a full account of the industrial operations and the industrial distribution. The following table gives the industrial distribution from 1873 to 1887, the period in which the congregate-contract system was in complete operation.

Year	Shoe-shop	Chain-shop	Broom-shop	Cigar-shop	Tin-shop	Marble-shop	Whip-shop	Weaving	Prison Account	Sick and Idle
1873	85									
1874	130		63			46				
1875	162		98	30		10	62	20		
1876	195		90	37	3		53	20	97	
1877	332		47	40	4			25	109	279
1878	285		48	33	10			20	272	175
1879	329	137	56	35	14			14	169	45
1880	289	141	68	47	19				149	41
1881	257	131	65	42	21				157	37
1882	225	111	59	33	22				145	47
1883	232	155	57	60					148	49
1884	327	23	52	69				Mak-	128	148
1885	297		52					ing	140	228
1886	330							Mats	113	49
1887								268		

[164] *Senate Journal,* 1838-39, Vol. II, p. 771.
[165] For some further light on the period before 1870 see the tables of relative productivity given below.
[166] Report cited, in *Legislative Documents,* 1871, p. 1077.

By 1888 the contracts that were allowed to run their course by the act of 1883 had expired and the contract system passed out of existence. The industrial distribution of the population of the Western Penitentiary from this time to the final paralyzing of prison industry by the Muehlbronner Law of 1897 is shown by the following table:

Year	Matting Shop	Hosiery	Broom-Shop	Prison Account	Sick and Idle
1888	412			172	99
1889	428		69	160	92
1890	419		68	207	101
1891	455		74	171	127
1892	494	71	70	153	123
1893	478	176	61	179	124
1894	446	207	128	176	212
1895	468	222	140	198	131
1896	437	245	131	180	112
1897	405	198	107	216	128

The table which follows presents the industrial distribution from 1898 to the period of the World War:

Year	Matting Shop	Hosiery	Broom Shop	Weaving	Day School	Prison Farms	Prison Account	Sick and Idle
1898	190	95	47				267	357
1899	179	87	48		106		273	189
1900	162	81	43		100		296	145
1902	209	89	47				306	59
1904	254	115	46				363	145
1906	257	103	48				404	131
1908	239	143	55				359	545
1910	323	113	56	10			380	174
1912	211	75	48	10			414	168
1914	159	134	45	13			442	158
1916						445	263	404

The industrial distribution at the close of the war period may be gathered from the following statistics setting forth the situation on a typical day—September 10, 1918:

Prison account 265
Employed—Prison Labor Commission 30
    (Matting, 0; brooms, 10; brushes, 2; weaving, 18.)
Sick and idle 425
Prison farms (Centre County).. 529

The history of the technical aspects of the industrial operations of the Western Penitentiary differs radically from that of the other state penitentiary. While the same handicraft system, carried on in separation, that was to be found in the Eastern Penitentiary, persisted in the Allegheny institution down to 1870, a widely different attitude was adopted toward this system from the beginning by the governing authorities. From 1836 to 1860 the warden and inspectors looked on the isolated industrial activities in separate cells as a necessary evil that was essential to preserve the disciplinary and reformatory virtues which were supposed to reside in the Pennsylvania system. Individual labor in separation was never looked on as an economic good in itself, as was the case at Cherry Hill. As early as 1836 both inspectors and warden complained in vigorous terms of the industrial handicap imposed by the absence of shops in which many of the industrial processes could have been carried on with much greater efficiency and with less labor and supervision.[167] From this time to 1860 a general undercurrent of dissatisfaction with the separate industrial system can be detected between the lines of the industrial phases of the annual reports of the authorities. In 1860 the criticism advanced a step farther and was directed not only against the solitary labor, but against the handicraft system. The inspectors had awakened to the great industrial transformation which had taken place in the outside economic world and saw clearly the necessity of bringing the penitentiary industrial system up to the same level of mechanical effectiveness. They pointed out the fact that under the handicraft system of manufacture the execution of the industrial operations in separate cells was more of an inconvenience than a serious handicap, but that the separate system was entirely irreconcilable with the necessary introduction of mechanical methods of manufacture. The immediate adoption of machinery was, moreover, deemed essential to the industrial future of the institution because in the world of free industry machinery had already replaced handicraft methods in weaving and shoemaking, the two main industries of the penitentiary. The inspectors admitted that the Auburn or congregate system was far better adapted to this necessary factory and mechanical type of industrial expansion, but

---

[167] *Annual Report of the Inspectors of the Western Penitentiary,* 1836, in *Senate Journal,* 1835-36, Vol. II, pp. 148-51.

derived some consolation from the claim that it could not be doubted that solitary confinement was more of a reformative agency than congregation.[168]

The report of 1860, then, really sounded the economic doom of solitary confinement and the handicraft system in the Western Penitentiary. In 1866 the inspectors again complained bitterly of the disastrous competition of the New England shoe factories with their boot and shoe industry, still carried on by handicraft methods.[169] The attack upon the old industrial methods was brought out into the open and the issue clearly and sharply drawn by the inspectors in their report for 1867. It was the same group of inspectors that had the year before condemned the Pennsylvania system as a disciplinary proposition. They now attacked its industrial foundations and called for the shop and contract methods of the Auburn system in the following vigorous paragraph:

"If we could work our convicts on the congregate plan, they would all be made available at once, and in this way relieve the counties from the burden of even their partial sustenance. But we have to meet issues as they present themselves to us. These prisoners must be fed and clothed, whether they return remunerative labor or not. Under the circumstances, we get the largest possible amount of work out of the prisoners that is practicable. If the result is unsatisfactory, let it be attributed to the right cause. Discard your cell labor, change your separate system and adopt the congregate, and you will be able to use the muscle and skill of the prisoner much more to the advantage of the Commonwealth." [170]

The law of April 8, 1869, allowed the desired congregation of prisoners for industrial purposes, and by 1873 the congregate shop system was installed. In their report for this year the inspectors praised the new system and declared with assurance that the day was over for handicraft methods in both weaving and shoemaking.[171] A year later the inspectors stated that "the old and unprofitable hand machinery, which has been in use in the prison nearly half a century, has been thrown aside as useless." [172] In 1880 the inspectors said that hand machinery had been discarded even in the manufacture of the clothing of the prisoners, which was now being made on steam propelled looms.[173] By 1880, then, the indus-

---

[168] *Report of the Inspectors of the Western Penitentiary,* 1860, in *Legislative Documents,* 1860, pp. 895-96.
[169] Ibid., 1866, pp. 9-13.
[170] Ibid., 1867, p. 8.
[171] Ibid., 1873, pp. 23-5.
[172] Ibid., 1874, p. 6.
[173] Ibid., 1880, pp. 21-2.

trial revolution in the Western Penitentiary was complete. The handicraft and individual system had been replaced by mechanical industry in congregate shops. The abominable Muehlbronner Act of April 18, 1897, tried to reverse this process of industrial development and to force the industrial operations back one stage. By prohibiting manufacturing machinery other than that propelled by foot or hand power, it attempted a compulsory return to the handicraft and treadmill stage of industrial operations and prison administration.[174] This impossible state of affairs continued until the state-use law of 1915 permitted the return to the modern mechanical methods. It fell short of furnishing complete relief, however, through its failure to provide a market for the increased productivity now possible and also made it impossible for the prison authorities to seek their own markets, as they might have done if the state-use system had been supplemented by the public-account system.[175] These defects, as was pointed out above, were partly remedied from a legal point of view by the laws of 1921 and 1925.

(2)   THE RELATIVE PRODUCTIVITY OF THE PRISON INDUSTRIES

The relative productivity of the prison industries with respect to the provision of revenue to the institution followed closely the industrial distribution of prisoners during the history of the institution. From 1835 to 1865 shoemaking was the most productive industry. It surrendered first place to weaving in the period from 1865 to 1873. In the period from 1873 to 1887, while the contract system was in force, shoemaking was much the most productive industry. From 1879 to 1884 the making of chains became an important industry and produced about one-half as much revenue as shoemaking. Broom-making, in turn, was about one-half as productive as the making of chains. From 1888 to 1915 the making of matting was as distinctly the most productive industry as shoemaking had been from 1873 to 1887. The making of hosiery developed after 1892 and reached the height of its prosperity in 1896, when it contested for first place with mat-making. From that time to the present it has declined, but remained a significant industry until 1915. Broom-making remained a steady source of income throughout this whole period, but was much less productive than the manufacture of hosiery. Since 1915 the sale of farm products has provided the greatest amount of revenue to the Western Penitentiary. The following tables will present a fairly complete summary of

---

[174] See above, pp. 250ff.
[175] See above, pp. 254ff.

the relative productivity of the industries of the Western Penitentiary since 1838:

Income from the Various Penitentiary Industries in the Majority of the Years from 1838 to 1870.

Year	Shoe-making	Weaving	Wood-working	Tailoring	Black-smithing	Picking Oakum	Broom-making	Cigar-making	Merchandise
1838	$3,694	$1,181	$585	$522	$39	$703			$2,762
1839	3,789	3,514	119	325	66	1,255			3,294
1840	5,605	2,324				1,391			3,584
1841	5,205	3,120				1,359			1,534
1842	3,943	3,162				295			1,924
1845	4,978	3,320				147			396
1846	5,392	2,202							1,731
1847	4,975	2,403		533					798
1848	5,285	2,618		328					1,619
1849	5,403	2,538		245					5,098
1850	5,012	2,306		229					476
1852	5,592	1,408		549					4,575
1853	7,153	3,335		543					
1854	5,890	2,388		347					
1856	1,802	2,984	1,030	1,479					
1857	2,460	1,245	1,714						
1860	2,340	2,172							3,208
1861	3,080	2,474							7,431
1862	3,092	2,621							10,684
1863	8,986	10,172							10,809
1864	9,447	8,893							
1865	788	1,257					$122		
1866	2,859	8,951					968		
1867	84	12,242						$1,488	23,248
1868	4,932	12,056						744	18,557
1869	2,171	9,828						704	
1870	2,152	10,062							

The following table sets forth the revenue derived from the industrial operations of the Western Penitentiary from 1873 to 1887, the period in which the congregate-contract system was in operation:

Year	Shoe-shop	Chain-shop	Broom-shop	Whip-shop	Cigar-shop	Tin-shop	Weaving	Structural Iron Shop	Matting-shop
1874	$12,911		$1,501	$3,415	$6,376		$387		
1875	17,317		10,868	7,588	1,991		601		
1876	21,274		10,125	5,085	2,133		2,274		
1877	32,546		6,530		3,216		1,544		
1878	33,556		3,509		2,749		1,635		
1879	35,766	$11,679	6,246		1,577	$194	1,789		
1880	34,129	13,627	6,676		4,623	495	529		
1881	29,034	13,354	7,110		4,138	1,031	538		
1882	28,945	12,769	7,694		4,310	1,769	602		
1883	29,303	15,429	7,915		6,101	2,043	995	$2,816	
1884	36,450	9,887	6,948		7,625	2,060	776	3,560	
1885	41,267		7,008		8,003	2,130	913	3,015	
1886	47,745		2,384			2,596	390		$5,978
1887	36,003						753		16,250

The productivity of the prison industries from 1888 to 1916 is presented in the table which follows: [176]

Year	Matting-shop	Hosiery-shop	Broom-shop	Shoe-shop	Weaving	Agriculture
1888	$27,599			$1,262	$590	
1889	26,920		$3,408	1,027	701	
1890	28,091		7,141	1,412	1,191	
1891	33,186		7,675	984	662	
1892	46,735	$1,168	6,976	1,217	345	
1893	29,156	7,420	7,421	1,273		
1894	28,144	13,648	8,942	1,515		
1895	33,543	19,015	12,409	1,363		
1896	29,056	23,939	13,875	1,568		
1897	31,086	22,011	11,794	1,636		
1898	12,050	12,994	5,797	1,483		
1899	10,554	13,153	4,886	835		
1900	14,753	9,513	4,273	520		
1902	11,636	3,291	4,984	628		
1904	20,700	6,970	5,494	663	1,852	
1906	20,290	3,489	5,691	757	340	
1908	14,777		5,638	1,667	3,021	
1910	29,696	5,191	4,069	1,665	2,910	
1912	20,225	6.076	4,304	1,042	2,098	$1,488
1914	50,103	20,379	2,951	3,712	5,286	10,082
1916				5,510	4,129	16,554

(3)   THE PREVAILING MODE OF INDUSTRIAL ADMINISTRATION IN THE WESTERN PENITENTIARY, 1835-1927

No exact and detailed information exists as to the methods of industrial administration in the Western Penitentiary in the early period, beyond the fact that there was no leasing of the labor of convicts. In their report for 1837 the inspectors stated that the industries were carried on under the full control of prison authorities and that the products were sold to "wholesale customers." [177] The same statement was repeated in the report for 1838 and it was further stated that this sale to "wholesale dealers" was made in

---

[176] The Western Penitentiary was affected by the industrial depressions in the outside world in the same manner as the Eastern Penitentiary. In 1843, 1856, 1866, 1873, 1893, and 1907, the inspectors complained of a decline in productivity due to this cause. See *Reports,* 1844; 1856; 1866, pp. 9-10; 1873, pp. 23-5; 1875, pp. 8-9, 16; 1895-96, p. 10; 1907-08, pp. 17-8.

[177] *Report of the Inspectors of the Western Penitentiary,* 1837, *House Journal,* Vol. II, p. 439.

order to prevent direct competition with "domestic tradesmen." [178] It would, then, seem clear enough that the Western Penitentiary in this early period followed the typical method of disposing of its goods to merchant-capitalists. The only doubtful point is as to whether the goods were disposed of according to the public-account or the piece-price system—whether they were sold to merchant-capitalists through competitive bidding in the open market or whether they were contracted for in advance at a fixed price. Other considerations and external evidence would, however, incline one to believe that the former system was that which was employed in the majority of cases, though there might well have been a mixture of both systems.

With the accession of the new Board of Inspectors in 1866 the war upon the separate system began in both its disciplinary and its economic phases. In their reports in 1866 and 1867 the inspectors called for the adoption of the congregate shops.[179] While they said little or nothing about introducing contract labor, there can be no doubt that this intention was in the back of their minds. The congregate system had from its inception been almost inseparably connected with contract convict labor, and the inspectors could not have been ignorant of this fact. Subsequent events justify the conclusion that they intended to use congregation as a mode of introducing not only the factory, but also the contract system. The act of April 8, 1869, allowed congregation for purposes of labor, and in 1873 and 1874 the hiring of convict labor began in the Western Penitentiary.[180] Eighty-five prisoners were first hired out in 1873 to W. E. Schmertz, a Pittsburgh shoe merchant, at fifty cents per day for the labor of each prisoner.[181] This introduction of the usual form of the contract system was referred to by the inspectors as "the great and crowning feature of our success in the department of labor." [182] In 1874 the inspectors reported a very considerable expansion of the contract system and stated the methods they employed to safeguard the interests of the prisoners.[183] The administration of discipline was wholly retained in the hands of the prison authorities. Hours of labor and allowances for overwork were regulated by the inspectors. No unhealthy or dangerous work was allowed in the new contract system. Finally, the institution reserved the right to take hired convicts from their work for

[178] *Report of the Inspectors of the Western Penitentiary*, 1838, *Senate Journal*, 1837-38, Vol. II, p. 248.

[179] Ibid., 1866, pp. 9ff,; 1867, p. 8.

[180] Ibid., 1873, pp. 23-4.

[181] Ibid., pp. 9, 23-4.

[182] Ibid., p. 9.

[183] Ibid., 1874, pp. 6-7.

purposes of school instruction or advanced classification. The inspectors also set forth in the following paragraph the advantages of the contract system as they appeared from the standpoint of the inspectors:

"The advantages of this system to the state are numerous: There is no capital required to carry on manufacturing business; the responsibility of purchasing raw material and disposing of the manufactured goods is obviated; the fluctuations of trade, decline in prices, carrying over unsold and unsaleable goods, the risks incident to the credit system, and the trouble and expense of hunting up customers and consumers for manufactured work, are all escaped. We supply our daily work and receive our compensation therefor."[184]

In their report for 1879 the inspectors stated their conviction that the contract system, with its superior productivity, far from being a menace to free labor, was really a blessing to the outside laborer. "What a compensation," they said, "to the hard-worked and over-taxed laboring man that he is thus relieved from the necessity of 'grinding out at his mill' the bread that the violators of the law might be compelled to eat in enforced idleness." [185]

Criticism, however, was growing against the contract system on the part of the labor organizations and their political agents, and two years earlier the inspectors had voiced their objections to the proposed substitute for the contract system, the older public-account system. In this report for 1877 they presented the arguments against the public-account system with a comprehensiveness and thoroughness that entitles this criticism to rank with the above cited criticisms of the contract system by the inspectors of the Eastern Penitentiary. Nowhere does the contrast between the two institutions stand out more clearly than in their differing attitudes relative to the virtues of the great contending systems of convict labor. The following were the arguments set forth against the public-account system:

"We object to working on State account for the following reasons:
"1st. The Commonwealth cannot ordinarily become a successful manufacturer. It is impossible to avoid waste and extravagance when there is an exhaustless fund to meet deficiencies.
"2nd. It is an extremely rare occurrence to find any one man, in whom is combined the proper qualifications that would enable him to superintend the mechanical operations of the shop, economically and judiciously purchase the raw material, and wisely and safely dispose of the products, and at the same time to control the

[184] *Report of the Inspectors of the Western Penitentiary,* 1874, pp. 17-8.
[185] Ibid., 1879, p. 11.

disciplinary features of the prison. Either department is sufficient for any one man.

"3rd. The capital required of the State for machinery, stock, &c., to work the different branches of this Institution would be not less than $200,000, and the probability is that it would be exhausted every five or ten years.

"4th. It would require a place of business in the city to dispose of the manufactured goods (thus coming in direct conflict with outside competition), besides requiring a host of salesmen to find customers and a market for the products.

"5th. It would oblige us to run the risk of periodical shrinkage in the value of stock; the wear and tear of machinery, and the constantly recurring losses in bad debts and depreciation in unsold and unsaleable goods.

"6th. On the other hand, by adopting the contract system we avoid all risk of losses in machinery, stock and bad debts, the perplexities of buying, manufacturing and selling, and the unpleasantness of coming in conflict with the outside world engaged in a like business.

"7th. And what is the most important of all, we retain control of 'our convict.' We direct his movements, his labor, his health, his food, his behavior, his prison rights and sanitary regulations. As on a solid rock the Inspectors place themselves upon the contract. They stand between the contractor and the convict; and while, on the one hand they require obedience and faithful labor from the unwilling subject; on the other they insist upon courteous treatment and gentlemanly civility from the contractors and their subordinates." [186]

In spite of the objections of the inspectors to the public-account system and their advocacy of the contract system, the legislature, as has already been pointed out, by the act of June 13, 1883, abolished the contract system and introduced the public-account system. This prevailed until the act of June 1, 1915, introduced the state-use system. The laws passed following March 30, 1911, which have allowed the employment of the inmates of the Western Penitentiary in the erection of the new central penitentiary at Rockview, for all practical purposes introduced the "public-works-and-ways system." The Western Penitentiary has, then, in the history of its systems of industrial administration illustrated all of the great historic modes of controlling and directing convict labor. The great farm which has been purchased and operated at the new site in Centre County also makes it seem certain that the institution will be a pioneer in the new trend toward outside labor and agricultural pursuits as a highly approved method of furnishing healthful

---

[186] *Report of the Inspectors of the Western Penitentiary,* 1877, pp. 9-10.

and remunerative employment for prisoners. We have already made it clear how the acts of 1921 and 1925 strengthened the state-use system by making purchases of prison-made goods obligatory, and in part legalized the public-account system for the sale of the surplus prison-made products.

The Western Penitentiary followed the example of the Eastern in providing an allowance for "overwork" to industrious prisoners, though the period in which this advance to the convicts was made was much shorter than at Cherry Hill. As early as 1837 the inspectors had strongly recommended that each prisoner should be given a part of his earnings when discharged as a means of promoting industry and reformation through allowing the prisoner to "feel the benefit of industry and sobriety." [187] There is no evidence that this recommendation was accepted or that any allowance for overwork was made in the Western Penitentiary until 1870. At that time it was introduced as incidental to the congregate and contract systems. While the Western Penitentiary was more delinquent and tardy in adopting this method of stimulating convict industry than the Philadelphia penitentiary, it was more liberal in its application of the system than the Eastern Penitentiary, in that it allowed the prisoner the total excess of his earnings over the cost of maintenance instead of one-half of the excess as was the case at Philadelphia. The following table presents the amounts awarded to the prisoners for overwork from 1870 to 1888, when the system was abolished upon the termination of the contract system.[188]

Year	Amount	(number of convicts receiving allowance)
1870	$ 992	
1871	629	
1872	513	
1873	1,408	
1874	1,108	
1875	1,653	
1876	2,027	146
1877	2,722	241
1878	2,483	230
1879	4,475	413
1880	7,540	525
1881	14,391	612
1882	11,688	644
1883	17,814	600
1884	19,567	655
1885	16,160	574
1886	17,640	446
1887	15,551	411
1888	6,814	

[187] *Report of the Inspectors of the Western Penitentiary*, 1837, in *House Journal*, 1836-37, Vol. II, p. 440.
[188] The data as to overwork allowances is provided in both the penitentiary reports for this period and in the reports of the Board of Public Charities. See also *Report of the Inspectors of the Western Penitentiary*, 1909-10, pp. 103-04.

It can readily be seen from the above table that the law of 1883 abolishing contract labor was a financial blow to the convicts as well as to the state.

(4) THE ATTITUDE OF THE WESTERN PENITENTIARY TOWARD STATE INTERFERENCE WITH CONVICT LABOR

The governing authorities of the Western Penitentiary have from the first vigorously criticized the attempt of the state to interfere with and regulate the mode of employing convicts. In their report for 1877 the inspectors called attention to the growing criticism of the contract system in the legislature and among the labor elements. Their arguments against the public-account system, which were presented above, were intended as a counter-blast to this tendency.[189] In 1879 the inspectors criticized the current tendency to blame the hard times to contract convict labor. They maintained that the agitation was not conducted so much by honest laborers as by unscrupulous and aspiring politicians who were endeavoring thereby to "nurse" and exploit the labor vote. Their arraignment of these demagogues was especially severe:

"These disaffected non-producers of the country, self-styled leaders of public opinion, mount this hobby of cheap prison labor, and cry out against it as the source of all grievances and the very bane of society."

They cited the noted report of the Massachusetts committee on convict labor as proof that the most careful and impartial investigation of the subject had failed to prove that convict labor offered any serious source of competition with free labor.[190] In their reports from 1883 to 1890 the inspectors bitterly criticized the law of June 13, 1883, abolishing contract convict labor and also condemned the new public-account system as relatively wasteful and non-productive.[191] In 1886 the warden referred to the new conditions imposed by the act of 1883 as nothing more nor less than a retrogressive measure restoring the conditions of 1826. He held that it had caused the institution to lose the benefit of the chief factor in effecting the reformation of the criminal class.[192] In their reports of 1897-98 and 1899-1900 inspectors and warden united in a vigorous condemnation of the detestable Muehlbronner Act of 1897, as well as the vicious interpretation given to the act by the

---

[189] *Report of the Inspectors of the Western Penitentiary,* 1877, pp. 8-10.
[190] Ibid., 1879, pp. 12-3.
[191] Ibid., 1883-84, pp. 11-3; 1885-86, pp. 1-14; 1887-88, pp. 2-5.
[192] Ibid., 1885-86, pp. 13-4.

attorney-general.[193] This criticism continued without any practical effect until 1910, when the newly appointed warden, John Francies, called attention to the impossibility of hoping for any effective industrial system on the Pittsburgh site while the existing restrictive laws were in operation. He urged with success the proposition to move the penitentiary to a new rural site where the convict could be profitably employed in the labor of penitentiary construction and in agricultural pursuits.[194] The governing authorities of the Western Penitentiary, in common with those of the Eastern Penitentiary and the Huntingdon Reformatory, have been somewhat impatient with the lame and halting introduction of the state-use system, as provided for in the law of June 1, 1915. While not unfavorable to the state-use method as such, they have with some justice criticized those half-way measures taken to introduce that system which have merely resulted in the disruption of the existing industrial system without providing any relief from the demoralizing idleness which has prevailed since 1897. The authorities have, however, cooperated with the prison labor commission and the Bureau of Restoration to the fullest extent in the attempt to get the state-use system installed and nowhere has the system of uniform and effective employment of convicts more staunch supporters than in the officials in control of the Western Penitentiary. The act of 1921 creating the Department of Public Welfare, and the acts of May 1, 1923, and April 7, 1925, described elsewhere, have done much to lighten the burdens of a reconstruction of prison industry.

(5)   THE PRESENT CONDITION OF THE INDUSTRIAL SYSTEM OF THE
WESTERN PENITENTIARY

A strange contrast was presented in a survey of the industrial situation in the Western Penitentiary at the end of the war. At the Riverside site in Pittsburgh almost complete idleness prevailed, with the exception of the labor provided by the administrative and domestic routine of the institution. On September 10, 1918, out of seven hundred and twenty convicts at Riverside, but thirty were employed at productive labor for the prison labor commission according to the state-use system. Two hundred and sixty-five were engaged in administrative and domestic labor, a large part of these being so employed out of considerations of humanity to furnish some type of occupation and exercise. Four hundred and twenty-five were listed as sick or idle, over four hundred being idle able-bodied men.

---

[193] *Report of the Inspectors of the Western Penitentiary*, 1897-98, pp. 7-11, 22-23; 1899-1900, pp. 8ff.
[194] Ibid., 1909-10, pp. 15-6.

A more distressing situation could scarcely be imagined, but the legal situation made the prison authorities powerless in the circumstances, though they are among the most severe critics of the conditions. A radically different state of affairs existed at the new prison site at Rockview in Centre County. Here five hundred and twenty-nine convicts were employed [195] in agricultural pursuits on the five-thousand-acre prison farm and in work on the improvement of the grounds of the new penitentiary site, actual construction work having been suspended because of the war. The following table will indicate the industrial pursuits of those at Rockview in 1918:

Domestic service in administration	155
Farm	132
Drivers and barn assistants	47
Grading	45
Canning and preserving plant	41
Repair shops and boiler room	39
Road work	30
Barn work	22
Carpenters	11
Painters	4
Quarry	2

The creation of a Board of Public Welfare, giving it full authority to reconstruct the system of prison industry, has eliminated to a considerable extent some of the worst obstacles to the industrial development in the Pennsylvania penal institutions, and much supplementary legislation since that time has tended to reduce the abuses which have accumulated since 1885.

On April 27, 1925, an important step was taken in advance by authorizing the payment of wages to prisoners under the following conditions:

"Section 1. Be it enacted, &c., That in addition to payments made as provided by law to inmates directly laboring on industries in the Eastern State Penitentiary, the Western State Penitentiary, the Pennsylvania Industrial Reformatory at Huntingdon, and other correctional institutions of the Commonwealth in which the Department of Welfare has established industries, said department is hereby authorized and directed to pay out of the manufacturing fund arising from the sale of the products of the industries established by said department in said State institutions, wages at not more than twenty cents (20c) per day to inmates in said State institutions performing labor of any kind necessary to the proper maintenance of such institutions and the inmates thereof: Provided, That the inmates directly laboring on industries shall first be paid in

[195] September 10, 1918.

full as provided by law: and provided further, That the total paid
to the said inmates directly laboring on industries, and to inmates
performing labor of any kind necessary to the proper maintenance
of said institutions and the inmates thereof, shall not exceed eighty
per cent (80%) of the total net revenue from said industries
established by the Department of Welfare.

"Section 2. The wages herein provided for shall be paid in the
same manner and under the same terms and conditions as the
wages of inmates of said penitentiaries, reformatory, or other correctional institutions directly laboring in such industries as provided by law."

About all of the manufacturing work at the Western Penitentiary
is carried on by the Bureau of Restoration, there being no penitentiary shops as at the Eastern Penitentiary. At the close of 1926
some 266 convicts were employed by the Bureau: 110 in the weaving
department, 80 in the license tag department, 70 in the clothing
department, 3 in the brush department and 3 in the office. The
large number of 658 convicts were employed in the administration
and maintenance of the prison, in order to furnish as much employment as possible. Only 10 were employed in a prison shop—the
novelty woodshop. Some 105 were listed as idle or incapacitated.

The enlightened warden at the Rockview Penitentiary, Mr. J.
O. Stutsman, has done his best to keep his men at work on
productive enterprises, especially the agricultural and preserving
operations of the large prison farm. As compared with the situation in 1917, conditions have been completely revolutionized.

On May 19, 1923, an act was passed, authorizing the employment
of the inmates of the county jails and prisons, which should do
much to relieve the intolerable condition that has existed in this
type of institution in Pennsylvania for many years:

"Section 1. Be it enacted, &c., That all persons sentenced to the
several county jails and prisons, who are physically capable, may be
employed at labor for not to exceed eight hours each day, other
than Sundays and public holidays. Such employment may be in
such character of work and the production of such goods as may
now be manufactured and produced in such jails and prisons, and
may also be for the purpose of the manufacture and production of
supplies for said prisons and jails, or for the preparation and
manufacture of building material for the construction or repair
of the said prisons and jails, or in the manufacture and production
of crushed stone, brick, tile and culvert pipe, or other material
suitable for draining roads, or in the preparation of road building
and ballasting material. . . .

"Section 3. The authorities in charge of any such county jail or prison shall have authority to fix the wages of each prisoner to be employed, and they shall keep an account of all such wages and the amount due each prisoner. Three-fourths of the amount credited to each prisoner, or the entire amount if the prisoner so wishes, shall constitute a fund for the relief of any person or persons dependent upon such prisoner, and shall be paid to such persons, establishing dependency to the satisfaction of the said authorities, at such times as they may prescribe."

D. Brief Summary of Pennsylvania's Experience with Convict Labor

The above summary sketch of the industrial history of the state penitentiaries of Pennsylvania will be sufficient to bring out the chief stages of development and the main problems involved. Probably no other state can present so comprehensive a recapitulation of all the phases of the evolution of prison industry in America as Pennsylvania. Beginning as the originator not only of labor in solitary confinement, but also of the very idea and practice of prison labor, Pennsylvania has since followed all of the leading trends in prison industry in the nineteenth century. In the Eastern Penitentiary was furnished the best example of the persistence of the handicraft stage and the solitary labor plan, which endured almost unimpaired from 1829 to 1913. This is, no doubt, the most perfect illustration of the survival of an original method of prison industry to be found anywhere. In strange contrast with the continuity and conservatism of the Eastern Penitentiary, the Western Penitentiary flirted with nearly all of the prevailing trends in prison industry in the last century. Starting like the Eastern Penitentiary with solitary labor along handicraft methods and conducted commercially by the public-account system, the Pittsburgh institution turned to a complete adoption of the congregate-factory-contract system in the seventies and eighties. In the mid-eighties the public-account system was again brought back, this time with the congregate system. Finally, in the last decade the state-use, public-account and the public-works-and-ways systems have been adopted in part, thus completing all of the possible forms of industrial administration with which it has been possible to experiment.

Not less typical and comprehensive has been Pennsylvania's experience with state interference in the field of prison labor. Beginning with complete freedom for almost exactly a century, there began in the seventies the agitation on the part of labor organizations and political demagogues which resulted by 1897 in the almost complete paralyzing of prison industry. Gradually recovering its better judgment, the state has made a feeble beginning at a lame and halting attempt to make amends for its past mistakes by introducing the state-use, public-account and public-works-and-ways systems of industrial administration, but these were at first so hampered by imperfect legislation that they long remained paper rather than true reform measures.[196] Only since the establishment of the Department of Public Welfare under the direction of Dr. Ellen C. Potter have steps been taken to restore Pennsylvania to a position of leadership in convict industry.

2. THE SYSTEM OF MAINTENANCE IN THE STATE PENITENTIARIES

A. *Legislative Regulations Governing the System of Maintenance*

A review of the systems of maintenance and accounting in the state penitentiaries is interesting as illustrating the continuity from the period of the formation of state penal institutions and the persistence of county independence and autonomy, which was so noticeable in the colonial period. The method of providing support for the state penitentiaries rests in a historical sense upon the act of May 27, 1789. It was therein provided that any prisoners sentenced to more than twelve months' imprisonment in any county in the state might be sent to the Philadelphia Jail on Walnut Street. The cost of maintaining that institution was to be divided between Philadelphia and other counties in proportion to the number of convicts sent from each county. In addition, Philadelphia County was to receive one hundred pounds for the extra expense of administering the Walnut Street Jail. In case the profits from the labor of prisoners exceeded the cost of maintenance, the excess was to be divided among the counties in proportion to the number of their convicts in the institution.[197] This same general arrangement was continued by the act of April 5, 1790.[198] When the two state penitentiary districts were organized in Pennsylvania by the act of April 10, 1826, it was provided that the expense of maintaining the prisoners

---

[196] It may be interesting as a basis of comparison with the Pennsylvania situation to note the status of convict labor in the United States in 1917. In 1914-15 the application of the various "systems" of convict labor ranked as follows: (1) Lease system, 1 state and 950 convicts; (2) contract system, 18 states and 6,981 convicts; (3) piece-price system, 4 states and 1,193 convicts; (4) public-account system, 19 states and 11,807 convicts; (5) state-use system, 35 states and 33,805 convicts; public-works-and-ways, 27 states and 11,063 convicts. Statistics given by F. H. Hankins in *The New International Year Book*, 1917, p. 527.

[197] *The Statutes at Large of Pennsylvania*, Vol. XIII, pp. 246, 250-51.

[198] Ibid., p. 527.

in each district should fall upon the counties in the district.[199]
All earlier regulations, however, were superseded by the act of
April 23, 1829, which has, with only minor modifications, governed
the maintenance systems of the state penitentiaries from 1829 to
the present day.[200] This act was, however, based upon the general
premises and precedents established by those of 1789, 1790 and
1826. The powers and responsibilities of the boards of inspectors,
as established by this act, made these officials the most important
body in control of the procedure of providing for defraying the
expenses of the state penal institutions. The inspectors were given
the power of fixing the salaries of all the administrative officials
of the state prisons and were authorized to control the industrial
operations of these institutions. They had, then, almost complete
original jurisdiction over the methods and operations which would
determine the expense of maintaining the penitentiaries. Until the
passage of the act of 1869 creating the State Board of Public
Charities and that of 1883 beginning state interference with convict labor, the inspectors had almost complete control over the
financial and economic aspects of the administrations of both state
penitentiaries. The following section [201] of this act provided that
the counties should defray the expense of feeding and clothing the
convicts while the salaries should be paid by the state:

"The expenses of maintaining and keeping the convicts in the said
Eastern and Western Penitentiaries, shall be borne by the respective counties in which they shall be convicted, and the said expense
shall be paid to the said Inspectors by orders to be drawn by them
on the Treasurers of the said Counties, who shall accept and pay
the same: Provided Also, That the said orders shall not be presented to the said Treasurers before the first Monday of May in
each and every year: And Provided Also, That the said Inspectors
shall annually, on or before the first Monday of February transmit
by public mail, to the Commissioners of such Counties as may
become indebted for convicts confined in said Penitentiaries, an
account of the expense of keeping and maintaining said convicts,
which account shall be signed by said Inspectors, and be sworn
or affirmed to by them and attested by the Clerk; and it shall be
the duty of said Commissioners, immediately on receipt of said
accounts, to give notice to the Treasurers of their respective Counties of the amount of said accounts, with instructions to collect
and retain monies for the payment of said orders when presented;

---

[199] *Acts of the General Assembly,* 1825-26, pp. 280-81.
[200] *Laws of the General Assembly,* 1828-29, pp. 341ff.; Richard Vaux,
Sketch of the Origin and History of the Eastern Penitentiary, pp. 36-51;
Acts of the Assembly relating to the Eastern Penitentiary, pp. 46-7.
[201] Section 9 of the act of April 23, 1829.

and all salaries of the officers of the said Penitentiaries shall be paid by the State; and it shall be the duty of the Inspectors to transmit to the Auditor General the names of the persons by them appointed, and the salaries agreed to be paid to each of them under the provisions of this Act, which sums shall be paid in the usual manner, by warrants drawn by the Governor upon the Treasurer of the Commonwealth." [202]

While it was not the object of special legislation, it has become a part of fixed precedent that the state, in addition to paying salaries, shall make appropriations for all important alterations and additions to the penitentiary buildings and for all extraordinary and unusual expenditures. This act of 1829 has remained in force to the present day, modified only by unimportant minor legislative amendments. By an act of May 31, 1844, the inspectors were ordered to make their annual reports to the state more specific, so as to include a detailed and itemized account of all receipts and expenditures.[203] This requirement was made still more strict and definite by an act of February 27, 1847. A method of state supervision over the expenditures proposed by the inspectors was provided by the act of April 24, 1869, creating the State Board of Public Charities. This provided that the inspectors "shall annually give notice to the said General Agent (of the above board), on or before the first day of November in each year, of the amount of any application for State aid they may propose to make, and of the several purposes to which said aid, if granted is to be applied." [204] The general agent of the board was directed to examine into these applications for state aid and to transmit his opinions to the board, who were in turn to submit their findings and recommendations to the legislature.[205] This act was amended on May 1, 1913, to compel the inspectors to submit their estimates and application for state aid to the general agent of the board on or before September first of each year.[206]

This method of dividing the cost of maintaining and administering the state penal institutions between the state and the counties differs from the majority of the Eastern States where the county has never had the importance that it has retained in Pennsylvania. In these states the total expense of conducting the penal institutions of the state is normally borne by the state and raised as a part

---

[202] This act was amended in 1833 (Act of February 27, 1833) to read "The expenses of keeping the convicts in the said . . ." thus omitting the word "maintaining."

[203] *Laws of the General Assembly,* 1844, p. 585.

[204] Ibid., 1869, pp. 90ff.

[205] Ibid.

[206] Ibid., 1913, p. 149.

of the state tax. The method in Pennsylvania is, perhaps, more equitable, in that counties pay in proportion to the number of convicts that each sends to the state penitentiary in its district, but this advantage is to some degree offset by the added burdens and confusion of several systems of accounting and by the fact that in cases where the state is for one reason or another delinquent or deficient in its allowances to the penitentiary, the deficiency has to be met by the counties. The system may to some slight extent tend to reduce criminality, in that it sets a financial penalty upon counties which furnish a disproportionate number of convicts. While the state has usually made full appropriations to cover the salaries of officers in the period since the Civil War, such was not always the case before that time. The appropriations for salaries have normally been somewhat below the amount actually paid for this item of penitentiary expense and the deficit has been thrown upon the counties. In some cases the salary appropriation was little more than half of the actual expenditure of the inspectors. A few examples selected at random will illustrate this curious and irritating deviation from the legal regulation and provisions. In the case of the Eastern Penitentiary the salaries paid in 1852 amounted to $14,866, while the state appropriated but $8,000.[207] In 1857 the expenditures for salaries was $15,911, and the appropriation $9,200.[208] In 1862 the salaries totaled $16,387, while but $12,800 was appropriated.[209] Similar instances of deficiencies are not lacking in the experience of the Western Penitentiary. For example, in the period from 1849 to 1852 the total amount of the salaries was $30,757, and the state appropriated only $24,000.[210]

B. Statistics Dealing with the Maintenance Cost of the State Penitentiaries

The following tables will attempt to present a comprehensive summary of the changes in the penitentiary population and in the income and expenditures involved in their maintenance from the period of their establishment, in so far as such statistics are available. It will be noted that years of financial depression in the outside world were doubly disastrous, because they not only reduced the income of the prison from its industries, but also greatly increased the number of convicts to be supported:

---

[207] Report of the Inspectors of the Eastern Penitentiary, 1852, p. 6.
[208] Ibid., 1857, p. 14.
[209] Ibid., 1862, p. 52.
[210] Report of the Inspectors of the Western Penitentiary, 1853, Senate Journal, Vol. 11, p. 181.

(1) THE EASTERN PENITENTIARY AT PHILADELPHIA 1821-1917[211]

Year	Average number of convicts	State appropriations for erection, equipment and repair of buildings	State appropriation for salaries	Gratuities to discharged convicts	Income from prison industry	Subsistence cost, clothing, etc.	Deficit charge to counties
1821		$100,000					
1824		80,000					
1825		60,000					
1826		89,125					
1828		4,000					
1829	9	5,000	$1,000				
1830	32	4,000					
1831	44	120,000					
1832	89						
1833	122	130,000					
1834	180						
1835	267	60,000			$12,530	$17,529	$4,998
1836	360	25,000					9,476
1837	385						5,564
1838	401	10,000					14,043
1839	418						14,623
1840	405						16,730
1841	347						17,860
1842	342						11,027
1843	334		8,000				7,318
1844	360		8,000		17,468	18,180	4,229
1845	319		8,000		12,705	18,529	not given
1846	326		8,000		15,663	19,024	” ”
1847	294		8,000		14,991	19,797	” ”
1848	283		8,000		13,283	18,665	” ”
1849	276		8,000	$666	11,768	16,632	” ”
1850	307		8,000	666	11,950	17,337	” ”
1851	304		8,000	666	13,705	18,359	” ”
1852	280	10,000	8,000	667	16,630	17,875	12,011
1853	271	10,000	8,000		17,802	20,051	9,778
1854	275		8,000		18,794	23,264	12,488
1855	278		9,500		20,655	24,718	12,715
1856	273		8,700	800	17,910	24,034	16,078
1857	334	5,000	9,200		20,518	27,657	15,599
1858	384	1,000	12,895	1,000	18,159	26,664	16,980
1859	380	2,425	12,895		23,466	27,608	12,056
1860	424		12,000		21,107	29,107	10,194
1861	449	15,000	12,800		15,066	27,060	16,764
1862	396	1,750	12,800		17,882	24,815	11,350
1863	358	7,250	12,800		21,493	26,658	9,828
1864	338	12,500	14,800		25,075	34,804	15,530
1865	331	10,150	17,500		22,829	43,956	25,999
1866	510	650	17,800		25,110	51,226	45,809

[211] Owing to lack of uniform bookkeeping in this long period, the following table is variable and incomplete, but it brings out the more important elements and tendencies in the financial history of the system of maintenance.

(Table continued from preceding page)

1867	594	650	17,800		31,892	58,354	48,468
1868	622	45,650	20,000		31,685	60,351	51,309
1869	616	4,350	20,000		35,180	59,568	42,940
1870	622	2,600	20,000		35,363	58,888	53,148
1871	629	6,600	27,000		37,027	65,781	not given
1872	610	6,100	27,000		32,495	76,390	53,460
1873	598	2,000	27,000		23,618	not given	49,449
1874	632	1,500	27,000		22,419	" "	47,162
1875	720				20,317	" "	58,845
1876	866	3,000	53,675		21,571	" "	66,956
1877	1,012	52,000	26,675		26,891	" "	69,153
1878	1,019	31,250	38,000		31,268	" "	55,983
1879	1,075	4,000	77,850		30,135	" "	58,604
1880	1,066				46,970	" "	38,681
1881	1,031	2,000	77,850		49,194	" "	19,799
1882	981				39,638	" "	26,521
1883	1,015	4,000	77,850		38,821	" "	29,292
1884	1,035				41,492	" "	31,087
1885	1,108	3,500	84,104		38,998	" "	33,787
1886	1,123				45,263	" "	28,257
1887	1,096	3,500	77,850		47,260	" "	23,764
1888	1,150				51,541	" "	23,537
1889	1,110		21,500		47,693	" "	33,046
1890	1,055				37,853	" "	45,070
1891	1,041	2,000	94,000		38,939	" "	42,713
1892	1,037				45,505	" "	79,267
1893	1,129	4,000	94,000		29,021	" "	42,599
1894	1,299				18,900	" "	64,000
1895	1,391	4,000	100,000		17,076	" "	71,571
1896	1,400		52,000 [212]	2,780	12,477	" "	81,348
1897	1,231		52,000	3,735	11,326	" "	83,983
1898	1,251		50,963	3,160	11,853	" "	76,443
1899	1,202		53,645	3,375	11,545	" "	77,654
1900	1,149		61,901	3,020	11,719	" "	73,482
1901	1,022		81,950	5,000	10,018	" "	69,327
1902	941		81,950	5,000	8,936	" "	71,948
1903	1,010		86,278	2,670	8,194	" "	78,203
1904	1,005	11,650	65,408	2,750	11,419	" "	89,624
1905	1,132		67,176	2,895	12,122	" "	83,348
1906	1,144		71,060	2,910	11,194	" "	63,889
1907	1,158		82,660	3,130		" "	67,071
1908	1,367	11,729	80,860	2,655	25,240 [213]	" "	86,056
1909	1,539	2,936	86,293	2,590	29,469	" "	88,422
1910	1,460	37,883	95,188	3,915	21,491	" "	98,451
1911	1,368	27,765	100,724	4,170	21,693	" "	94,726
1912	1,381	2,489	101,235	2,615	31,877	" "	95,965
1913	1,501	4,367	110,368	2,715	31,634	" "	99,841
1914	1,550		121,802	4,730	34,070	" "	97,809
1915	1,692	5,822	120,737	3,810	44,631	" "	104,986
1916	1,518		115,204	9,203			171,996
1917	1,424						213,033
1926	1,398				245,142		310,117

[212] Since 1896 this column indicates both salaries and some minor appropriations toward prison equipment, but these additions are negligible.

[213] From 1908 onward the overwork allowance was not deducted from the income from convict labor. The net income can be ascertained by a comparison with the statistics of overwork given above.

(2)   THE WESTERN PENITENTIARY AT PITTSBURGH 1818-1917

Year	Number of convicts remaining at end of year	State appropriations for erection, equipment and repair of buildings	State appropriations for salaries	Gratuities to discharged convicts	Income from prison industry	Subsistence and clothing costs	Deficit charge to counties	Gain exclusive of salaries
1818		$60,000						
1821		60,000						
1824		30,000						
1825		28,921						
1826	10	5,000						
1827	26		$2,000					
1829	62	3,000	2,000					
1830	64	5,000						
1831	68							
1832	90				$593			
1833	106	60,000						
1834	91	20,000						
1835	122	14,400						
1836	111	25,000						
1837	104							
1838	107				6,653			
1839	134	5,000			8,669			
1840	139				11,997	$9,551		$2,446
1841	161				13,001	9,238		3,772
1842	162	5,000			12,050	10,304		1,745
1843	148		5,000					
1844	130		5,000					
1845	130		5,000		10,128	9,475		653
1846	126		8,945		9,667	9,187		480
1847	112		6,315		7,775	7,322		452
1848	115		6,315		10,168	9,020		1,147
1849	123		6,000		9,069	8,241		827
1850	134		6,000	$333	9,184	8,560		624
1851	174		6,000	333				
1852	187	25,000	6,000	750	12,329	11,577		751
1853	201		6,000		11,514	10,662		851
1854	159		6,000		13,399	13,148		250
1855	115	5,000	9,212					
1856	177		9,200	275	6,615	12,773	$6,608	
1857	187	6,270	9,672			10,107	13,628	3,520
1858	218	4,500	10,150	500				
1859	265	15,118	10,150	308				
1860	311	40,000	11,161		11,945	17,169	5,224	
1861	288	50,000	11,161		16,238	20,458	4,219	
1862	234	35,250	12,000		16,257	20,014	2,530	
1863	228		13,200		20,467	20,004		463
1864	204		13,800		41,589	24,582		17,006
1865	259	250	16,030		21,125	18,122		3,002
1866	418	9,250	16,900		12,870	36,999	18,946[214]	

[214] It is obvious that the amount stated as the county charge for the years 1866, 67, 68 and 69 must be somewhat below the actual deficiency. The amounts given in this table are taken from the report of the general agent of the Board of Public Charities. After this date (1869) the amounts given are derived from the reports of the Western Penitentiary.

(Table continued from preceding page)

1867	486	500	20,800		12,599	46,365	27,390
1868	437	17,500	21,150		18,476	49,798	19,912
1869	402	44,800	21,150		17,883	39,266	18,882
1870	375	27,680	22,324		14,590	49,948	42,465
1871	418	6,958	22,400		17,468	50,039	46,686
1872	461	10,450	22,450		15,979	61,487	50,530
1873	443	5,694	24,350		16,545	69,435	59,812
1874	463	20,000	24,350		31,186	50,548	19,302
1875	569	5,850	24,500		46,332	63,871	17,539
1876	727	5,500	25,000		55,022	72,642	17,619
1877	831	500	25,000		58,910	73,688	14,777
1878	823	100,500	35,000		51,827	62,760	10,932
1879	799	222,000	70,000		67,784	78,631	10,846
1880	759				69,957	85,726	15,768
1881	711	588,462			64,260	86,429	22,169
1882	642				63,520	91,153	27,633
1883	701	276,925	70,000		71,357	100,055	28,697
1884	747				69,924	99,948	30,023
1885	733	271,000	70,000		63,687	99,167	35,479
1886	706				62,748	99,321	36,573
1887	697	201,000	70,000		58,173	106,005	47,382
1888	683				32,749	88,324	55,495
1889	749	71,000	70,000		36,487	93,415	56,927
1890	783				42,567	98,126	55,559
1891	827	46,000	70,000		42,629	119,262	72,633
1892	911				59,965	139,232	79,267
1893	1,018	75,800	120,000		47,995	139,089	91,093
1894	1,169				55,002	159,821	104,819
1895	1,159	8,492	120,000		71,059	162,893	91,384
1896	1,105		64,746[215]	2,600	74,401	155,387	80,986
1897	1,054		46,411	3,150	72,305	151,852	79,547
1898	956		63,750	3,290	37,085	133,362	96,277
1899	879		62,617	3,270	33,466	146,791	77,554
1900	827		63,043	2,910	32,486	140,056	75,527
1901	693		64,150	5,000	32,112	116,101	75,631
1902	710		64,150	5,000	23,715	99,605	75,890
1903	848		65,657	2,330	34,625	100,680	66,054
1904	923		77,018	2,730	39,839	102,663	62,823
1905	929		75,425	2,740	30,192	89,761	59,568
1906	943		82,489	3,315	33,317	87,871	54,553
1907	1,122		82,855	3,015	31,516	105,849	74,332
1908	1,341		97,061	3,095	28,084	123,572	95,488
1909	1,261		121,851	3,075	25,810	166,597	140,786
1910	1,056		97,610	4,520	45,158	127,265	82,106
1911	997	7,545	132,308	4,670	38,162	118,891	80,729
1912	926	198,280	122,528	6,160	37,008	125,122	88,114
1913	813	65,754	127,314	6,440	22,141	155,404	133,263
1914	951	92,121	236,071[216]	5,840	17,637	138,315	120,678
1915	1078	188,529	285,243		21,831	171,800	149,974
1916	1,112	223,651	165,062	7,430	8,841	208,795	199,953
1917	1,199						

[215] From 1896 to the present time this column includes appropriations for both salaries and other expenses borne by the state, other than building expenses. The salaries absorbed almost the total appropriation in nearly every year.

[216] In 1914 and 1915 the appropriations other than for salaries as given in this column were unusually heavy. The actual amount appropriated for

(3)   SITUATION FROM 1917 TO 1926

The following tables, compiled by Mr. B. L. Scott of the Bureau of Restoration, for the use of the author, give an adequate impression of the population and expenditures in the state penitentiaries since 1917. The figures for the Western Penitentiary include the inmates and expenses of both the Rockview and the Pittsburgh institutions.

NUMBER IN INSTITUTION AT SPECIFIED DATES

Year	Eastern	Western (including Rockview)
1917	1,434	1,142
1918	1,411	1,223
1919	1,523	1,350
1920	1,557	1,272
1921	1,606	1,470
1922	1,741	1,844
1923	1,674	1,859
1924	1,293	1,659
1925	1,386	1,647
1926	1,487	1,701

NUMBER COMMITTED DURING YEAR

Year	Eastern	Western (including Rockview)
1917	563	472
1918	602	511
1919	674	546
1920	545	400
1921	651	644
1922	737	913
1923	588	680
1924	418	623
1925	532	691
1926	558	597

TOTAL EXPENDITURES DURING YEAR

Year	Eastern	Western (including Rockview)
1917	$374,891	$456,356
1918	456,649	710,651
1919	573,609	779,038
1920	677,587	863,220
1921	534,118	713,191
1922	645,479	812,817
1923	705,834	748,374
1924	640,531	775,859
1925	639,449	926,769
1926	595,667	943,762

salaries in 1914 was $125,196, and in 1915, $177,070. On the whole, though, the figures given in this column indicate very closely the actual growth of the salary list of the institution. This reflects not only the increased number of officials made necessary but the wage increase due to higher cost of living.

The preceding review of the financial history of the state penitentiaries does not present a cheerful picture. In the decade of the forties and in a few years since, the Western Penitentiary earned enough through prison labor slightly to exceed the cost of maintenance exclusive of salaries. With the possible exception of the year 1864, this institution has never equaled through its earnings the combined cost of maintenance and salaries, and since 1864 it has never earned an amount even approximately equal to the maintenance expenses, to say nothing of the ever growing salary list. Never in its history has the Eastern Penitentiary failed to be a burden upon both the state and the counties, never having earned enough in any year to equal the cost of feeding and clothing the convicts. This proves beyond any possible doubt that the Pennsylvania system can make no claim as to any preeminent economic virtues.[217] While the earnings of the Western Penitentiary increased to a notable degree under the congregate system, they did not increase so rapidly as did the cost of maintenance. But without entering into the disputed question of the relative economic standing of the Pennsylvania as compared with the Auburn and Irish systems, it can not be denied that the state penitentiaries of Pennsylvania have been a tremendous burden upon both state and counties, particularly in the period since the Civil War.

No extenuating circumstances or compensations in the way of educational or reformative advantages can be claimed in the way of offsetting this economic load, as is the case with the Huntingdon Reformatory. Except for some very recent innovations in the Western Penitentiary, no attempt has been made to provide vocational instruction, and both convicts and prison authorities have generally united in the contention that the life of disintegrating and enforced idleness leaves the convict worse at discharge than upon reception. Finally, it should be noted that the economic burden imposed by low earnings and a high maintenance cost was never relatively so great as it was at the close of the World War. The chief explanation is, of course, the restrictive labor legislation dealt with above, combined with a great increase in the cost of food and clothing.

Scientific and centralized economy was not introduced into the finances of the Pennsylvania penitentiaries until the Department of

---

[217] See Richard Vaux, *Sketch of the Origin and History of the Eastern Penitentiary,* p. 125, for an attempt to prove the Pennsylvania system more economical than the Auburn system. His effort does not carry conviction, because: (1) he omits the period of the greatest productivity of the Auburn prison; (2) the New York expenditures include salaries; (3) the earnings of the New York prisons were incomparably greater than those of the Pennsylvania penitentiaries in proportion to population.

Public Welfare, following 1923, established a standard system of cost accounting and estimates for all the institutions dealing with the dependent and delinquent classes in Pennsylvania. This reform has greatly reduced the annual deficits.

V.   ADMINISTRATION AND DISCIPLINE IN THE STATE PENITENTIARIES OF PENNSYLVANIA, 1835 TO 1927

1.   The Application of the Pennsylvania System and Its Struggle with the Progress of Penology in the Nineteenth Century

A.   General Tendencies in the Application of the Pennsylvania System

The administrative history of the penal institutions of Pennsylvania is inseparably intertwined with the introduction, the application and the disappearance of the Pennsylvania system. As the last section was concerned with an account of the formation and introduction of the system, so the present describes its practical application; its period of great popularity, especially with foreign observers; its waning prestige, due to the progress of penological concepts and methods in the world at large; and its final disappearance along with most of the other products of early nineteenth-century penology. The passing of the Pennsylvania system in no way involves a necessary conclusion that it was in any way inferior to other systems which were a product of the same period. Some of its fundamental principles—the substitution of imprisonment at hard labor for corporal punishment or confinement in total idleness, and the removal of the convict from indiscriminate and degrading association with his fellow prisoners—constituted some of the greatest advances in the history of penology. It was inevitable, however, that any system which was evolved in a period when there existed none of the modern knowledge of biology, psychology, sociology and anthropology, which is indispensable to any rational and effective solution of the problems of criminology and penology, should sooner or later come to be antiquated and outdistanced by the progress of information in the century that has worked far greater changes in human knowledge than any previous millennium. The best Philadelphia hospital of the year 1790 would now appear exceedingly primitive, and the life of a sick man would be far safer in the hands of a much inferior modern physician than it was under the care of Benjamin Rush. As penology is no less dependent upon the surrounding state and conditions of scientific knowledge than the allied department of general medicine, it need occasion no surprise that what constituted a most advanced system of penology from 1790 to 1840 should appear hopelessly anachronistic by 1890.

It need give rise to no more difficulty in comprehending the unusually extended persistence of this system in Pennsylvania. It has been the custom to assign this to be the excessive perversity and conservatism of the controlling authorities of the two penitentiaries, but such an explanation would betray a most imperfect knowledge of the historic circumstances connected with the problem. In the first place, the early success of the system was a source of great pride to the prison authorities and to Pennsylvanians in general. Civic pride as well as personal convictions made it natural to postpone to the longest possible degree the admission that the system had outlived its usefulness. It was also wholly natural that the weakening should first appear at Pittsburgh in the Western Penitentiary, because this institution had never been regarded as the classic illustration of the Pennsylvania system. With the Eastern Penitentiary the situation was quite different. It was the parent institution of the system. It had a glorious past and a venerable historical reputation and tradition to defend. After 1869 it remained the last representative of the Pennsylvania system in America. Again, Richard Vaux, who dominated the board of inspectors of the Eastern Penitentiary during the forty years which he served as its president, had a firm conviction that the Pennsylvania system was the best system of prison discipline which had yet been devised and he defended the practices of the institution at Cherry Hill from a conscientious sense of duty.[218]

These circumstances alone would serve sufficiently to make clear why the Pennsylvania system persisted so long in the Eastern Penitentiary. In addition to these, however, there was another most important element. It has long been a patent fact among historians that nothing is so effective in strengthening, reviving or perpetuating a system or dogma as to put it on the defensive through violent attacks by exponents of another system or dogma. Such a condition was supplied in a very complete degree by the assaults of Louis Dwight and the Boston Prison Discipline Society upon the Pennsylvania system, in general, and upon the Eastern Penitentiary, in particular.[219] From 1827 until his death in 1853 Dwight rarely

---

[218] See especially his brochure on *The Pennsylvania Prison System, A Paper read before the American Philosophical Society, June 20, 1884.*
[219] See above, pp. 176ff. and below, pp. 375ff.

missed an opportunity to use the annual report of his society as the medium for a bitter criticism of the Pennsylvania system and a eulogy of the Auburn system.[220] After the Boston Prison Discipline Society ended its existence in the fifties, the criticism of the Pennsylvania system was sustained in a milder form by the New York Prison Association and by the exponents of the "Irish" and "Elmira" systems in the period of the sixties and after. These facts should amply suffice to disprove the common assertion that the anachronistic survival of the Pennsylvania system in the Eastern Penitentiary was in any large degree due to unique perversity or conservatism on the part of the governing authorities of the institution. The studies in social psychology, revealing the great significance of the so-called "gregarious instinct" or the "instinct of the herd" in social life,[221] and the original investigations of Freud and his disciples into the field of the psychology of "repression" [222] have been the product of the last generation. Until their appearance there was little reason for believing that the Pennsylvania system was a scientific monstrosity in prison discipline, as well as an economic failure.

B. The Experience of the Eastern Penitentiary in Applying and Abolishing the Pennsylvania System

As a general observation and estimate it may safely be held that the authorities of the Eastern Penitentiary were much better criminologists than penologists. That is, they gave evidence of an appreciation of the fact that criminal conduct has its origin in an unhealthy and abnormal social and economic environment [223] and in a defective personality, but they failed almost entirely to comprehend the fact that the reformation of a criminal involves the

---

[220] *Annual Report of the Prison Discipline Society of Boston*, 1827, pp. 121-28; 1828, pp. 39-47; 1830, pp. 32-3; 1931, p. 75; 1832, p. 54; 1833, pp. 116ff; 1834, p. 60; 1835, pp. 20-2; 1837, pp. 50-4; 1838, pp. 45-57; 1839, pp. 48-53; 1842, p. 62; 1843, pp. 44-103 (this is an especially long and comprehensive attack); 1845, pp. 98ff; 1846, p. 50; 1848, p. 51; 1849, p. 70; 1850, p. 37; 1852, pp. 80ff.

[221] Cf. W. McDougall, *Introduction to Social Psychology;* W. Trotter, *The Instinct of the Herd in Peace and War;* Graham Wallas, *The Great Society;* and especially E. A. Ross, "Association," in the *American Journal of Sociology*, March, 1919, pp. 502ff.

[222] Hitschmann, *Freud's Theories of the Neurosis;* Lay, *Man's Unconscious Conflicts;* Healy, *Mental Conflicts and Misconduct;* White, *Principles of Mental Hygiene*, Chap. V. Cf. H. E. Barnes, *The Repression of Crime*, Chap. VIII.

[223] See especially the *Report of the Inspectors of the Eastern Penitentiary*, 1870, p. 37.

training for a normal adjustment to the social environment and
can not be successful based upon the practice of developing broken
and unoffending hermits. A successful prison system can scarcely
be tested by its ability to turn out Robinson Crusoes, and such
was, at the best, all that the Pennsylvania system could make any
serious pretention to producing. This curious contrast nowhere
appears better than in the annual report of the inspectors for the
years 1873-74. This contained a very able and enlightened statement of the necessity of studying the problems of crime causation
in the abnormalities of the social environment and in the defects of
a faulty biological heredity. From these premises the very unusual
deduction was made that crime was the product of social instincts
and passions and that the only logical method of reforming the
criminal consisted in isolating and desocializing him.[224] Probably
a more accurate brief summary of the psychological weaknesses of
the Pennsylvania system has never been given than the statement
of Mr. Thomas Mott Osborne that "it showed a touching faith
in human nature, although a precious little knowledge of it." [225]

The fundamental character of the Pennsylvania system, as inter-
preted by its exponents passed through three definite stages of
characterization all of which grew naturally out of historic circumstances. In the period from 1790 to 1841, or more specifically from
1829 to 1841, it was designated primarly as the "solitary" system.[226]
In the decade of the thirties, however, the alleged barbarities of
the system of imprisonment in enforced solitude and silence became
the center of the attacks of the opponents of the system, and the
word "solitary" came to be a stigma rather than a mark of special
virtue in penal discipline. To answer this criticism the officials
began in the early forties to emphasize the fact that the distinctive
thing about the Pennsylvania system was the fact of separate confinement and not that of imprisonment in solitude or silence. It
was pointed out that separation did not mean either of these things
and great emphasis was laid upon the alleged facilities of the
convicts to associate and converse with prison officials and official
visitors, while at the same time being prevented from degenerating
association with their fellow convicts.[227] From 1842, then, to the
close of the sixties, the official designation of the Pennsylvania

---

[224] *Report of the Inspectors of the Eastern Penitentiary*, 1873-74, pp.
29-30, 44ff.
[225] T. M. Osborne, *Society and Its Prisons*, pp. 96-104. See also George
Combe, *Remarks on the Principles of Criminal Legislation and the Practice
of Prison Discipline*, London, 1854.
[226] See especially *Senate Journal*, 1830-31, Vol. II, p. 465. See also above,
pp. 120-21.
[227] *Report of the Inspectors of the Eastern Penitentiary*, 1844, pp. 5-6.

type of prison administration was the "separate method of confinement with labor and moral instruction." After 1866, however, it could no longer accurately be described as a system of separation, because from that time onward the lack of cell room forced multiple confinement.[228] To save themselves from inconsistency the inspectors had to cast about for another title descriptive of their system of prison discipline. For this emergency they invented the term, "the individual treatment system." This appellation appears in the report for 1872 [229] and it remained the official designation until the system was legislated out of existence in 1913. In their report for 1879, in reviewing the progress of the Pennsylvania system during a half-century, the inspectors pointed out how the system had originally been known as the "silent" method and next as the "separate" system, "and now, in its matured years, claims to have evolved out of a philosophic application of principles and facts from experience, the truer designation of the individual treatment method of applying punishment for crime." [230]

The following survey of the fate of the Pennsylvania system in the state penitentiaries will follow rather closely the chronological arrangement in order better to bring out the historic changes and trends. It should also, perhaps, be noted that the following discussion relates wholly to the administrative and disciplinary aspects of the application of the system, the legal, architectural and economic phases having already been analyzed.

In their report for 1836 the inspectors set forth the difficulties which had been overcome in the establishment of the Pennsylvania system and rejoiced in their success in making this system one of the landmarks in prison reform: [231]

"Opposed at home by a respectable body of our fellow citizens, who, with views quite as honest, held adverse opinions; its main principles questioned by a commission of our own State, specially instituted to examine the subject; assaulted by the official agent of an influential and indefatigable society of a sister State, because it conflicted with his favorite system; attacked from abroad by persons of high consideration in the moral and political world, who had become endeared to America by their military and other services, the friends of the Pennsylvania system held their course

---

[228] See above, p. 202.

[229] *Report of the Inspectors of the Eastern Penitentiary*, 1872, p. 12.

[230] Ibid., 1879, p. 53. The inspectors erred in designating the first stage that of the "silent" system. This term was in 1830 generally applied to the Auburn system of administration.

[231] *Report of the Inspectors of the Eastern Penitentiary*, 1836; *Senate Journal*, 1836-37, Vol. II, pp. 371-72.

unchecked, and with a steadiness and a perseverance worthy of their cause, made their opinions public sentiment."

That the inspectors did not shrink from regarding their system of prison administration as the special recipient of divine favor is apparent from the following citation from their report for 1837:

"We cannot close this report without our acknowledgements to the Supreme Ruler of the Universe, for His goodness, in crowning our efforts with so much success." [232]

The report of the inspectors for the year 1842 is of particular interest as expressing the optimism of the officials at this time and as defining the workings of the system. In the first place, they stated at length the reasons why the Pennsylvania system should be regarded as a system of salutary separation rather than as one of silence and solitude:

"Although the prisoners are separated from each other, they are not deprived of intercourse with their fellow-men. They are visited during the day by their overseers, when serving them meals, and for the purpose of instruction in their trade or business, or whenever called by a prisoner; by the Warden of the prison as far as possible; by the Moral Instructor in the performance of his duties; and by the visiting members of the Board of Inspectors regularly semi-weekly, and by all the members during each month; besides this superintending care, they are occasionally visited by some one or more of the official visitors recognized by law. Such intercourse with them has a tendency to elevate and reform the character of the prisoners." [233]

Next, the inspectors predicted that with proper aid from the legislature the Pennsylvania system would become a great honor to the state:

"The Inspectors assure the Legislature, that if it be permitted to develop itself fully, under the fostering influence of that policy which has always been extended to it by the Legislature, that the time is not far distant, when the Penitentiary System of our State, will be regarded among the proudest monuments of the wisdom of her people." [234]

Finally, the inspectors made a forceful statement of the reformative virtues of their system:

"The effect of the separate system superinduces reflection, and

---

[232] *Report of the Inspectors of the Eastern Penitentiary*, 1837, *Senate Journal*, 1837-38, Vol. II, p. 443.
[233] Ibid., 1842, pp. 5-6.
[234] Ibid., p. 5.

a retrospect of past life. When the mind is in such a state, it is then that the proper treatment may lead to the happiest results. Show the prisoner that he is cut off from pernicious example; that during his confinement he is not a spectacle for the community; that by improving his condition he has everything to gain; and that he may yet become a good citizen. Elevate his thoughts; improve his mental character; teach him the benefits of a solid reformation; make him feel the necessary consequence of a continuance in evil; give him evidence that there are those who have an interest in his welfare; seek for, and encourage, symptoms evincing a change in his moral organization; bestow on him the means, both mechanical and mental, to resist temptation on his again regaining his liberty; and if in all cases success does not follow such labors, yet in many, inestimable advantages are experienced by the prisoner, and conferred on the public. The inspectors have numerous examples of the happiest consequences flowing from this treatment, upon which alone the Pennsylvania system of prison discipline can be effectually administered." [235]

In the next year the following sharp attack was made upon Louis Dwight and the other critics of the system by the inspectors in their report:

"So long as the Pennsylvania system has been in operation, it has fully satisfied its authors and advocates. It continues to convince unbiased examination; it is superseding rival and opposite modes of punishment; and it will, at last, by the force of facts and experimental operation, in support of its theory, paralyze the efforts of interested opposition, and take the bread from the mouths of mercenary scribblers." [236]

In 1845 the Eastern Penitentiary was honored by a visit from a committee of the Boston Prison Discipline Society and the inspectors evidently believed that they had converted their ancient enemies to the superior reformative features of the Pennsylvania system. They said:

"The Board entertains a hope, that, as our Penitentiary is understood, and the operations of the plan on which it is conducted, examined, the separate confinement of prisoners, will become, not the Pennsylvania, but the American System of Prison Discipline." [237]

The first international prison congress, which was held in Frankfort-on-the-Main in 1845, endorsed the system of solitary confine-

---

[235] *Report of the Inspectors of the Eastern Penitentiary,* 1842, p. 7.
[236] Ibid., 1843, p. 11.
[237] Ibid., 1845, p. 19.

ment as applied to short-term convicts. This enviable distinction gave the inspectors courage to assert that the "superiority of the Pennsylvania over the Auburn system is now a fixed fact—it is beyond cavil, beyond doubt." [238] Their report for 1846 also contained what is perhaps the best official declaration of the principles of the Pennsylvania system:

"These features are—separation of the prisoners from each other at all times—moral and intellectual improvement—honest and persuasive efforts to reform and reclaim the prisoners. Prevention by constant separation from each other of the evil of contamination and the prejudicial influence which must arise from the association of the more or less hardened offenders. The prevention by separation of the acquaintance and knowledge which the community of evil-minded persons obtain of each other by association in the place of punishment. The ability is afforded by the separation of offenders, to individualize the corrective and reformatory treatment best suited to their peculiar characters. The almost certain consequence which results from the separate system, of making these no worse who cannot be made better by the infliction of punishment they undergo. The addition of all improvements which experience and not mere theory suggests in the improvement of the moral and physical condition of the prisoners. These are the principles upon which the Pennsylvania system is based." [239]

In the years 1849 to 1851 there came up for vigorous discussion in the official reports the much debated question as to whether there was any direct correlation between solitary confinement and the development of insanity among convicts. This had been a frequent charge made against the Pennsylvania system by its opponents [240] and had been categorically denied by the prison authorities.[241] From the first, however, one finds in the reports of the inspectors an indication that there was always a troublesome number of insane prisoners in the Eastern Penitentiary, but the inspectors accounted for this on the ground that they were either insane or predisposed to insanity when sentenced.[242] In 1849, however, there appeared in the report of the enlightened physician, Robert A. Given, the first

---

[238] *Report of the Inspectors of the Eastern Penitentiary,* 1846, p. 17.
[239] Ibid.
[240] See *Reports of the Boston Prison Discipline Society,* 1835, pp. 20-2; 1838, pp. 45-7; 1843, pp. 49ff.; 1849, p. 70. *Journal of the Legislative Council of New Jersey,* 1839, pp. 80-3.
[241] See *Report of the Inspectors of the Eastern Penitentiary,* 1843, pp. 32ff.; 1844, pp. 41ff.; 1845, pp. 55ff.
[242] *Report of the Inspectors of the Eastern Penitentiary,* 1835, *Senate Journal,* 1835-36, Vol. II, p. 326; Ibid, 1839, *Senate Journal,* 1840, Vol. II, p. 590.

attack upon solitary confinement from an official source. He urged a greater humanizing of the discipline, especially in the way of bringing the convicts in contact with the outside world through allowing the reception of letters and visits from relatives.[243] In his report for the following year, Doctor Given stated that there could be no doubt of the deleterious effect of solitary confinement upon the "dull-minded," especially when idle.[244] In his report for 1850, Louis Dwight stated that a Canadian penal commission which visited the Eastern Penitentiary found fifty cases of insanity among three hundred inmates.[245]

But the most damaging evidence that appeared to oppose the contention that the discipline of the Eastern Penitentiary did not invite insanity was contained in the annual message of Governor William F. Johnston in 1850. Here he revealed the startling and vital information that the actual amount of insanity in the Eastern Penitentiary had been skilfully reduced through the practice of the inspectors in appealing to the governor to pardon convicts as soon as they had begun to show signs of mental and physical deterioration. Governor Johnston said in part:

"The Eastern and Western Penitentiaries have been conducted with skill and prudence, and in the reformation and security of offenders, society has derived important advantages. It is, however, worthy of serious consideration whether in the adoption of a system of solitary confinement, the severity of the punishment authorized by law does not injuriously affect the mental and physical vigor of the prisoner. The frequent recommendations to the Executive for the pardon of convicts afflicted with ill-health and mental imbecility, would appear to require a modification of the penal laws." [246]

In their report for 1851, the inspectors replied, stating that the real cause of the large percentage of insanity was not the separate system, but the fact that the sentences imposed were too long. They recommended that a revision of the penal code be undertaken with the purpose of reducing the prescribed penalties.[247] Doctor Given, however, had the courage to fix the responsibility where it belonged. He frankly stated that those "lacking in mental vigor" could not safely be kept in continued solitary confinement. He also pointed

---

[243] *Report of the Inspectors of the Eastern Penitentiary*, 1849, p. 27. The forbidding of all contact with the outside world was, perhaps, the outstanding barbarity connected with the Pennsylvania system.
[244] Ibid., 1850, pp. 24-8.
[245] *Report of the Boston Prison Discipline Society*, 1850, p. 37.
[246] *Annual Message of the Governor*, 1850, p. 11.
[247] *Report of the Inspectors of the Eastern Penitentiary*, 1851, p. 13.

out the delinquency of the controlling authorities in not giving sufficient attention to the hygienic and psychotherapeutic aspects of
prison discipline. "A few years ago," he said, "the effects of our
discipline on the health of those subjected to it were entirely unsuspected, its friends being so dazzled by its moral influences as to be
totally blind to its physical and mental evils." [248] The recommendations of the inspectors as to a reduction of penalties was in part
realized in the new penal code of 1860, which specified only the
maximum penalties and left the minimum to the discretion of the
sentencing court.[249] A decade later multiple confinement began
and less prevalence of insanity was reported. The revelations of
1849 and 1851, however, prove beyond any possibility of doubt from
actual experience what modern psychology might safely assume
a priori, namely, that there was an undoubted correlation between
a large amount of induced insanity and the separate system of
imprisonment.

In his report for 1853, the moral instructor presented a very
concise statement of the reformative effects of separate confinement through producing a condition of reflection and penitent
retrospection:

"The utmost that can be claimed for any reformatory system
of punishment, I apprehend, is its predisposing influence to serious
reflection. . . . The power of Divine Grace we know can effect
a change in the heart of any man under any circumstances, and
God always works by means adapted to the end; but so long as
'evil communications corrupt good manners,' the association of evil
men places an almost insuperable obstacle to the moral improvement of the already corrupted. The separation of convicts removes
that obstacle—is favorable to the exercise of serious reflection, gives
vitality to the conscience, and disposes the mind to retrieve the
unhappy failures of the past." [250]

In their report for 1860, in spite of the fact that by this time
every other American state that had adopted the Pennsylvania
system had abandoned it for the congregate system, the inspectors
stated with great assurance that the superiority of the separate
system was no longer open to any doubt:

"Experience has fully supported the theory on which the separate
system of Penitentiary imprisonment was based. It has refuted
all the charges with which it has been assailed. It has demonstrated
its humanitarian, reformatory, discipline. It has proved itself

---

[248] *Report of the Inspectors of the Eastern Penitentiary*, 1851, pp. 24-6.
[249] See above, pp. 187ff.
[250] Ibid., 1853, p. 38.

benevolent and improving. It defiantly asserts itself hostile to neither the moral, mental nor physical constitution. It tests its advantages by individualizing all the applications of its treatment, thus yielding to demands for its adaptation to individuals, rather than the unphilosophic mode of dealing with classes in congregation. Thus has experience spoken. Controversy on this question has long ago been ended." [251]

This report is particularly interesting as it constitutes not only an attack upon the old enemy Auburn system, but also the first assault upon the system of classification which was being successfully applied at this time by Sir Walter Crofton as the basis of his famous "Irish" system of prison discipline. [252] It is often the case with exponents of a particular system of thought or practice that their claims and pretentions vary in inverse ratio with the actual status of their cause. This tendency was well revealed in the inspectors' report for 1862, when, in spite of the rejection of the Pennsylvania system by the United States, they claimed for it all the progress ever made in penal reform up to that time. "It can now be fairly claimed," they said, "that no improvement has been adopted in any country that was not initiated by this Commonwealth, and the wisdom of her law-makers." [253]

In 1868 the inspectors became alarmed at the criticisms of the Pennsylvania system which were being made at this time by the inspectors of the Western Penitentiary and they protested in strong terms against the proposal to introduce the congregate system into the Pittsburgh institution. [254] They also reasserted the excellence of the separate system and denied the criticisms directed against it:

"Appealing, therefore, to past experience, we are justified in unequivocally asserting that the Pennsylvania system of penitentiary discipline understood and properly applied, is not injurious to the health, has no injurious influence on the mind, is neither inhuman nor cruel, that it benefits the convicts, that it protects society, that it tends to strengthen the discharged prisoner in a determination to lead an honest life, that it does not entail on the prisoner the known degradation of his condition, that it prevents the organization of a crime-class in communities, and that if properly administered, it is now the most philosophic and effective sys-

---

[251] *Report of the Inspectors of the Eastern Penitentiary*, 1860, p. 32.
[252] See Mary Carpenter, *Reformatory Prison Discipline as Developed by the Rt. Hon. Sir Walter Crofton in the Irish Convict Prisons*, London, 1872.
[253] *Report of the Inspectors of the Eastern Penitentiary*, 1862, p. 43.
[254] Ibid., 1868, pp. 28-31.

tem for the treatment of crime as an actual condition of persons in all societies." [255]

The inspectors became even more frightened in the following year when the law of 1869 had ordered the introduction of congregation in the Western Penitentiary and had thereby left the Eastern Penitentiary alone as the sole representative of the separate system. They defended the Pennsylvania system at length and urged the Legislature not to commit the fatal error of abolishing this system in the institution at Philadelphia, as well as at Pittsburgh.[256] In 1871 the inspectors made their report a vehicle for a long defense of the Pennsylvania system and a bitter attack on the congregate system. They maintained that there was no possibility of combining the two systems, as the authorities were trying to do at the Western Penitentiary, and held that either one or the other of the systems was wholly good or wholly bad; a compromise would only serve to bring out the worst features of both.[257]

From 1872 to 1879 the most interesting feature in the reports of the inspectors bearing upon the application of the Pennsylvania system was the above mentioned transition in the nomenclature whereby the Pennsylvania system came to be officially designated as the "individual treatment system," instead of the "separate system," this change being forced in order to avoid inconsistency after the lack of adequate cells following 1866 had made separate confinement impossible.[258]

---

[255] *Report of the Inspectors of the Eastern Penitentiary*, 1868, p. 9.
[256] Ibid., 1869, pp. 5ff.
[257] Ibid., 1871, pp. 15ff.
[258] *Report of the Inspectors of the Eastern Penitentiary*, 1872, p. 12; 1873-74, pp. 23ff.; 1879, p. 53. It may be interesting to note in passing that prison administrators of long experience have tended to general agreement that the worst form of associated confinement is the locking of two convicts in one cell; general association being preferred to this practice. This fact shows how little bearing the conditions in the Eastern Penitentiary had upon the merits of the Pennsylvania system after 1870. By 1881 only 435 out of 1025 convicts at Cherry Hill were in solitary confinement. (See *Report of Inspectors*, 1881, pp. 84, 86. By 1893 there were 1,248 prisoners for 720 cells.

It may be of some value at this point to include a reprint of the rules governing the Eastern Penitentiary in 1872. There seems little reason to believe that they differed materially from those in operation after 1829, except that after 1869 violations of disciplinary rules prevented the convict from availing himself of the benefits of the commutation law of 1869.

RULES FOR THE PRISONER
"In each cell there is a printed copy of these Rules:
"You are desired strictly to observe the following Rules established by the Inspectors for your government:
"First.—You must keep your person, cell and utensils clean and in order.
"Second.—You must obey promptly, all directions given to you, either by the Inspectors, Warden or Overseers.

The year 1879 was a notable year in the history of the Pennsylvania system in Pennsylvania for it marked the completion of fifty years of the separate system in the Eastern Penitentiary. The occasion must have appeared rather gloomy because, instead of the Pennsylvania system having become the American system, as was earlier confidently predicted by the inspectors, it had been abandoned everywhere except at Philadelphia and even there it had become obsolete on account of the inadequacy of cell accommodations. In spite of these circumstances, however, the inspectors made their report a long eulogy of the Pennsylvania system, showing its juristic antecedents and quoting from earlier reports to show the great success of the operation of the system.[259] The report of 1879 was also important because it stated that a school had been established for the training of the younger officers of the institution in which the warden and the older deputies gave instruction in the principles of the Pennsylvania system.[260] In one sense this was a laudable departure, in that it would produce a higher degree

---

"*Third.*—You must not make any unnecessary noise, either by singing, whistling, or in any other manner; but in all respects preserve becoming order. You must not try to communicate with your fellow-prisoners in the adjoining cells, either from your own apartment, or during the time you are exercising in your yard.

"*Fourth.*—All surplus food must be placed in the vessel provided for that purpose; and all wastage of materials, or other dirt, must be carefully collected and handed out of the cell, when called for by the Overseer.

"*Fifth.*—You must apply yourself industriously, at whatever employment is assigned you; and when your task is finished, it is recommended that your time be devoted to the proper improvement of your mind, either in reading the books provided for that purpose, or in case you cannot read, in learning to do so.

"*Sixth.*—Should you have any complaint to make against the Overseer having charge of you, make it to the Warden or Inspector—if against the Warden to an Inspector.

"*Seventh.*—Be at all times, in your intercourse with the officers of the Penitentiary, respectful and courteous, and never suffer yourself to be led astray from your duties, by anger or revengeful feelings.

"*Eighth.*—Observe the Sabbath; though you are separated from the world, the day is not the less holy.

"The inspectors desire to treat every prisoner under their charge with humanity and kindness; and they hope that in return, the prisoner will strictly conform to the rules adopted for his government, which are not merely advisory, but are a law to him, especially the third, any violation of which will incur proper punishment.

"*Special Notice.*—Violations of these rules or any part of the discipline of the Institution, will deprive the prisoner of the benefit of the 'Commutation Law'." (From Richard Vaux, *Sketch of the Origin and History of the Eastern Penitentiary*, pp. 99-100.)

[259] *Report of the Inspectors of the Eastern Penitentiary*, 1879, pp. 8ff., 20ff. This report is especially valuable as presenting a good sketch of the history of prison reform in Pennsylvania. It forms the logical supplement to the work of Roberts Vaux on the formation of the Pennsylvania system.

[260] Ibid., pp. 86-8.

of administrative efficiency, but there can be no doubt that, on the other hand, it tended to produce a high degree of conservatism in the prison officials. Before there was any opportunity presented for a promising young officer to introduce any original ideas or innovations he was initiated into the methodology of the old separate system and soon became an advocate of its retention. There is little doubt that this procedure was of very considerable significance in making possible the extraordinary persistence of the old system in the Eastern Penitentiary.

In their report for the year 1880, the inspectors presented a table designed to prove that since multiple imprisonment had begun in 1866 there had developed a much greater tendency toward recidivism. The correlation can not be regarded as established, however, for a number of reasons. In the first place, two convicts were not put into one cell until 1866 and, therefore, the increase of reconvictions immediately following the Civil War can not be regarded as a result of double confinement. In the second place, no considerable increase of reconvictions begins to appear until following 1875, when, as in 1865 to 1867, they are readily accounted for on the ground of the unusual industrial depressions of the period which made it particularly difficult for convicts to find honest self-supporting labor. [261]

By 1889 the inspectors apparently despaired of the inherent effectiveness of the Pennsylvania system on the basis of its own strength and held that divine aid might be necessary to supplement the reformative workings of the system:

"The 'individual treatment' of prisoners is regarded as the most rational method to reach a realization of the hope of reformation. It often fails. The inherent depravity of even the young resists, or fails to receive, the appeals made to them. Discouragement must not follow this failure. There may yet be a seed lodged even in stony ground that will grow. With God all things are possible." [262]

In 1891 the inspectors maintained that the new disciplinary methods which constituted the Elmira Reformatory system had not "yielded any marked benefits," but contended that "great success has attended" the Pennsylvania system. [263] In 1893 they violently condemned the introduction of that progressive legislation in this country which threatened the repose of the Pennsylvania system. A long defense of the value of experience and tradition in penal

---

[261] *Report of the Inspectors of the Eastern Penitentiary,* 1880, p. 23.
[262] Ibid., 1889, p. 108.
[263] Ibid., 1891, p. 33.

administration was appended, which almost rivaled in conservatism the social philosophy of Burke.[264]

After the death of Richard Vaux in 1895 the defense of the Pennsylvania system gradually died out. In 1904 the unusually frank and intelligent report of Warden Byers made it clear that it had long been a physical impossibility to carry out the provision of the law of 1829 imposing the penalty of solitary confinement, even if one were willing to ignore the progress of seventy-five years in penology and attempt to do so. There were in 1904 about four hundred and fifty more prisoners than cells. Warden Byers further proceeded to point out the fact that the existing practice of putting two men in a cell was the worst form of congregation and suggested that it would be far better to lock three convicts in each cell where it was necessary to have more than a single occupant.[265] The law of July 7, 1913, allowing the congregation of the inmates of the Eastern Penitentiary "for the several purposes of worship, labor, learning and recreation" at last terminated the legal existence of the venerable anachronism, after it had ceased its actual existence forty-seven years before.[266]

Some insight into the degree to which the Pennsylvania system had disappeared in practice and tradition before its legal termination may be obtained by the fact that the act of 1913 did not receive the slightest reference or comment in the report of the inspectors or of any of the other officers of the institution, in spite of the fact that from the standpoint of formal legislation it meant the end in America of one of the most important and influential systems of prison discipline ever devised. It was actively defended for thirty years after it had ceased to exist in its pure form, and it lingered along as a legal ghost for nearly twenty years after it had ceased to have any conspicuous apologists. Were De Beaumont and De Tocqueville, William Crawford, Frederic A. Demetz, Doctor Nicolaus Julius, or even Richard Vaux, to visit the Eastern Penitentiary to-day they would doubtless regard themselves as the victims of an optical illusion to behold groups of fifty men assembled in the yard of the prison for purposes of recreation and engaged in practically unrestricted conversation.[267]

It was ordered by the act of June 14, 1923, that adequate exercise

---

[264] *Report of the Inspectors of the Eastern Penitentiary*, 1893, p. 110.
[265] Ibid., 1904, pp. 7ff.
[266] *Laws of the General Assembly*, 1913, p. 708.
[267] Such a condition was observed by the writer in September, 1918. The conduct of the convicts was such that the unprejudiced observer could scarcely withhold his approval of the humane policy and practice which has been introduced by Warden McKenty.

should be provided for convicts in state prisons. The Act reads as follows:

"Section 1. Be it enacted, &c., That every warden, board of prison managers, prison inspectors, or any other person in authority, in charge of any prison or penitentiary, who may or shall have in charge any person confined therein whether such person be a tried or an untried prisoner, shall provide that such person shall have at least two hours daily, physical exercise in the open, weather permitting, and upon such days on which the weather is inclement, such person shall have two hours daily, of physical exercise indoors of such prison or pententiary: Provided, however, The same is safe and practical, and the judges of the several courts are to be the judges thereof.

"Section 2. Such physical exercise is not, under this act, to be taken by any person confined, as hereinbefore defined, within the confines of his cell or room in which he shall be confined.

"Section 3. This act is not to apply to persons confined who are not physically able to take such physical exercise as provided for."

C. The Pennsylvania System in the Western Penitentiary

While the Pennsylvania system was ousted from the Western Penitentiary over forty years before it was legally abolished at Cherry Hill, there can be no doubt that the authorities of the Western Penitentiary between 1835 and 1866 quite outdistanced the Philadelphia officials in florid and adulatory rhetoric invoked in defense of the separate system. In all these laudatory comments the Pennsylvania system was represented as possessing three outstanding virtues: first, forced reflection in solitude; second, the fact that no two prisoners would be able to recognize each other as ex-convicts when discharged; third, the absence of mutual corruption which was alleged to ensue when convicts were allowed to associate freely.[268]

Owing to the confusion incident to the necessity of tearing down the original structure of the Western Penitentiary and building a new one adapted to labor in separate cells, the separate system was not thoroughly and permanently installed until 1838. In their report for this year the inspectors stated that the new penitentiary was completed and that the advantages of the Pennsylvania system

---

[268] See especially the *Annual Report of the Inspectors*, 1847, *Senate Journal*, 1847, Vol. II, pp. 241-42.

"have been nearly, if not fully realized in this prison." [269] The warden noted the severity of the discipline and stated that several ex-convicts, who had served terms in the Auburn Prison and who had later been reconvicted and sent to the Western Penitentiary, informed him that they would prefer to spend two years in the Auburn Prison to one in the Western Penitentiary.[270] By 1839 the officials had become thoroughly convinced of the superiority of the separate system. In the annual report the inspectors maintained that "general health, subordination, industry, docility, and an evident disposition to receive advice and instruction have prevailed through the last year." They further held that this situation was "one of the most striking illustrations of the superiority of the Pennsylvania system over that of any other ever devised for the improvement and reformation of offenders." [271]

After the industrial depression of 1837 the number of convictions in Pennsylvania greatly increased, until in 1842 there were one hundred and sixty-three prisoners confined and only one hundred and seventy available cells. As the legislature had failed to grant the request of the inspectors for an appropriation for a new cell block, the latter became alarmed lest this refusal was indicative of the intention of the legislature to abandon separate confinement. They addressed the following protest against the contemplation of any such action, accompanied by a forceful statement of the valuable features of the Pennsylvania system:

"We feel assured that it is by no means the design of the Legislature to abandon the humane and beneficent policy of Pennsylvania with regard to the treatment of offenders against her laws; from whence so many blessings have already resulted to that unhappy class of individuals. Ages upon ages had come, and gone, before any charitable feeling had been excited, or any compassion aroused for the sufferings of guilt in the heart of even the most benevolent, in any part of the world. The unfading honor, of first introducing into her criminal code, the moral culture and reformation of the guilty, belongs exclusively to Pennsylvania. Higher objects than the mere punishment of the malefactor grace her statute books. With the hand of heaven descending charity, she has combined with her places of penance and punishment, hospitals

---

[269] *Report of the Inspectors of the Western Penitentiary,* 1838, *Senate Journal,* 1837-38, Vol. II, pp. 247-48. It should be remembered that, as was the case with the New Jersey state prison built by John Haviland at Trenton at the same time, 1833-36, the Western Penitentiary was not provided with any exercising yards attached to the cells. This naturally increased the severity of separate confinement.
[270] Ibid., p. 251.
[271] Ibid., 1839, *Senate Journal,* 1838-39, Vol. II, p. 224.

for the treatment of moral diseases—kindness and encouragement, with moral and religious instruction, are uniformly extended to such as evince a disposition to amend their lives, and every incentive to thorough reformation are inseparable objects of her system." [272]

The report of the inspectors for the year 1846 contained an even more eulogistic statement of the virtues of the separate system and was motivated primarily by the recent abolition of that system in the Rhode Island state penitentiary, thus leaving the Pennsylvania system only in New Jersey and Pennsylvania:

"The miserable victim of the law in our day, finds himself, notwithstanding his crimes, an object of the tender care and regard of the state, and of the deepest solicitude of the humane and benevolent around him. They forget not that he is an immortal spirit. That he is still an object of God's regard. The soft and soothing sounds of affection and sympathy, of instruction and prayer, fall upon his ear. Useful and salutary labor, clean and wholesome apartments, a comfortable place to lay his aching head and weary limbs, air and water, ample sustenance, the light of Heaven and the Holy Scriptures to guide his heart to God. Such is the spirit of the Pennsylvania system. It is blessed from on high, and will remain an imperishable memorial of her enlightened beneficence and humane consideration for the guilty inmates of her public prisons, and is now spreading its practical benefits, by similar institutions reared on the basis of her enlightened humanity, not only through sections of our own, but over governments and countries of the old world." [273]

In 1852 the authorities were greatly disturbed over the section of the message of Governor Johnston, which has already been referred to and which set forth the governor's suspicion that solitary confinement was conducive to a decline of physical and mental vigor on the part of the prisoners. Inspectors, warden and physician united in a vigorous attempt to prove that the Pennsylvania system was not injurious to the health of the prisoners.[274] In 1852 the inspectors went so far as to state that "since the first retributive exaction for penal offenses, there has been no device of human legislation so just to the criminal and so pregnant of good consequences to the public." [275] The classical eulogy of the Pennsylvania system was, however, contained in the report of the inspectors for 1854. Here

---

[272] *Report of the Inspectors of the Western Penitentiary,* 1842, *Senate Journal,* 1842, Vol. II, pp. 51-2.
[273] Ibid., 1846, *House Journal,* 1846, Vol. II, p. 162. The architectural arrangements of the Western Penitentiary make it certain that the "light of Heaven" referred to by the inspectors must have been "spiritual" light.
[274] Ibid., 1850, *Senate Journal,* 1850, Vol. II, pp. 608-13.
[275] Ibid., 1852, *Senate Journal,* 1852, Vol. II, p. 577.

they worked themselves into an almost neo-platonic ecstasy in their effort to set forth the many and numerous points of supreme excellence in the Pennsylvania system of prison discipline and administration. This is probably the most extreme and exaggerated praise that the system ever received from its advocates:

"Pennsylvania, the precursor of all her sister States in the present system of prison discipline, has justified its wisdom before the world in the practical results of its successful administration in this institution. Anticipated evils, existing more in speculative humanity and morbid philanthropy than in substantive fact, have failed in their realization. Disease and mental imbecility so confidently predicted as necessarily incident to separate confinement, have resulted in health and intellectual improvement. Depraved tendencies, characteristic of the convict, have been restrained by the absence of vicious association, and in the mild teaching of Christianity, the unhappy criminal finds a solace for an involuntary exile from the comforts of social life. If hungry, he is fed; if naked, he is clothed; if destitute of the first rudiments of education, he is taught to read and write; and if he has never been blessed with a means of livelihood, he is schooled in a mechanical art, which in after life may be to him the source of profit and respectability. Employment is not toil nor labor, weariness. He embraces them with alacrity, as contributing to his moral and mental elevation. They help to fill the zodiac of his time, which would otherwise be spent in unavailing complaint, and fruitless importunity for release. Shut out from a tumultuous world, and separated from those equally guilty with himself, he can indulge his remorse unseen, and find ample opportunity for reflection and reformation. His daily intercourse is with good men, who, in administering to his necessities, animate his crushed hopes, and pour into his ear the oil of joy and consolation. He has abundance of light, air, and warmth; he has good and wholesome food; he has seasonable and comfortable clothing; he has the best of medical attendance; he has books to read, and ink and paper to communicate with his friends at stated periods; and weekly he enjoys the privilege of hearing God's holy word expounded by a faithful and zealous Christian minister.

"Thus provided, and anxiously cared for by the officers of the prison, he is in a better condition than many beyond its walls guiltless of crime. He labors, but it is for his subsistence, like any other member of the community, and by his industry he relieves that community of the burden of his support.

"It is a fact worthy to be remembered by the Legislature, that for the last ten years, not one county sending convicts to the Western Penitentiary has been called upon to contribute a solitary dollar towards their subsistence. Such being the domestic economy of this institution, and such its happy results, we are not required to enter into an elaborate vindication of the principle upon which it is based. The system has disappointed the anticipation of its enemies, and surpassed the confident expectations of its friends, and there, for the present, we leave it." [276]

So animated a panegyric as the above would leave a strong suspicion in the mind of the reader that the system was actually nearing its end. Such proved to be the case. By 1861 there were eighty-one more prisoners than cells, and the strict application of the Pennsylvania system was at an end in the Western Penitentiary.[277] In 1864 a new board of inspectors was appointed. Its members apparently approached the problem of prison discipline from an unprejudiced standpoint and examined the existing situation in a purely objective manner.[278] Within two years they had become convinced that a radical transformation was necessary, and in their report for 1866 presented the following criticism, which was the first formal and systematic attack upon the separate system by the inspectors of either state penitentiary in Pennsylvania:

"In looking over the Annual Reports made by the Officers of this Institution to the State Legislature for more than thirty years, we find that they have rarely ever omitted to express their entire satisfaction with the workings of the separate system of confine-ment which Pennsylvania has adopted as her own.

"We are not at this time disposed to controvert the self-complaisant arguments so profusely lavished upon the Legislature from both extremities of the State, in their Annual Reports, as to our 'humane and reformatory' system of Prison discipline.

"We think, however, that it might be well for the Legislature to look at the other side of this question and inquire, whether, in the onward progress of events and in the constant and interesting changes that are always being developed in the world, there might not be a more excellent plan adopted or worked out for the improvement and reformation of this unfortunate people than the one which we have adopted? As we have made from time to time our frequent visitations to the convict's cell, and have engaged him in conversation and studied his situation, we have often been oppressed with the feeling of despair that seemed to settle upon his face as he would look forward (sometimes through a quarter of a century) to a hopeless future. In his loneliness he broods over his condition, walking his dreary cell in the quiet hours of the night, and during the unemployed moments of the day. No human face

---

[276] *Report of the Inspectors of the Western Penitentiary*, 1854, *Legislative Documents*, 1854, p. 271.

[277] Ibid., 1861, *Legislative Documents*, 1861, pp. 705-06.

[278] The members of this new board of inspectors were: Theodore H. Nevin, James B. Lyon, James Marshall, George R. White, and Robert H. Davis.

visible save that of the Officers and his Keepers, he feels that 'his hand is against every man and every man's hand is against him,' and having no object or interest beyond his own walls to attract his attention or arrest his thoughts, he falls back upon himself and his fancied wrongs, and in sullen anguish preys upon his own vitals!

"Man is formed for society. He cannot well live without it. Ostracize him from the world and his fellow men, and he soon looses his own self-respect, because he feels that he has forfeited that of others.

"We hold these men for their reformation as well as punishment. Would not the successful accomplishment of the former purpose supersede, to a great extent, the necessity for the latter?

"The great problem, which we think is not yet solved, is, *what* is the best mode of accomplishing this end? If those who frame our laws consider that our present System is the most desirable and ought not to be modified or changed, then we would urge upon them the imperative necessity of making provision at once for an increased number of cells in this prison." [279]

There can be no doubt that this statement of the inspectors spelled the doom of the Pennsylvania system in the Western Penitentiary. Without the active support of the controlling authorities it had little chance of permanent survival. They were aided in the campaign for its abolition by the increased population following the close of the Civil War and by the industrial depression of that period. The crowding and the unfavorable financial situation made the legislature more than usually willing to acquiesce in the suggestion of the inspectors that the separate system be abolished.

In their report for the year 1867 the inspectors maintained that the separate system had never prevented communication in the Western Penitentiary. They claimed that conversation was carried on through pipes leading from one cell to adjoining ones and by "telegraphing" on doors. They stated their belief that the best prison system was a combination of the Auburn and Pennsylvania systems, with further utilization of the "Irish" method of classifying prisoners.[280] In 1869 two epoch-making laws were passed in Pennsylvania—one introducing the principle of commutation of sentence for good behavior and the other permitting associated labor in the Western Penitentiary.[281] In their report for this year the inspectors praised the operation of both of these new laws:

---

[279] *Annual Report of the Inspectors of the Western Penitentiary*, 1866, pp. 4-5.
[280] Ibid., 1867, pp. 36-7.
[281] *Laws of the General Assembly*, 1869, pp. 18, 1268.

"The twin laws of 'congregation' and 'commutation,' enacted by the last Legislature and approved by the Governor, have been put in successful operation. Their effects are already noticeable upon the conduct of the prisoners, and their prospective advantage will be felt in all time. . . . The spirit and morale of the prison has changed. The convicts acknowledge a difference and show it." [282]

By 1871 the new system had become established and the inspectors included in their report the following description of its operation, which revealed an entire complacency in the passing of the Pennsylvania system and a complete confidence in the superiority of the new order:

"We have just emerged from a chrysalis or transition stage in the management of this institution. The reach from a rigid solitary system of discipline to the more liberal and enlightened congregate idea, is a tedious and difficult one, especially where public opinion has been educated for a long series of years to the belief that the existing régime is infallible. . . . The public and the prisoner have each sustained us. The cordial endorsements which we have received from those who are interested in the moral reforms of the day, have greatly encouraged and emboldened us in all that we have done; and the thankful recognition of our efforts to benefit them, physically, morally, and religiously, which we are constantly receiving from the convicts, has been reward enough for all our labor and toil." [283]

In 1873 and 1874 the first large congregate shop was completed and opened, and in their report for 1874 the inspectors presented a very vivid description of the benefits conferred upon the individual prisoner by the new methods of labor. This should be compared with the praise of the Pennsylvania system as set forth in the report for 1854, which was quoted above:

"But to the prisoner the advantages of this change are still more apparent. When taken from his solitary cell, his strength is debilitated, his appetite fastidious, his face pale, the color from his cheek gone, and his eye has assumed the incipient appearance of insanity; his incarcerated life has been one of hopeless misanthropy, and often times his physical strength has become prostrated and his mental activity benumbed by the indulgence of vice and sensuality which a solitary life tends greatly to promote.

"Now look at these same men in their places in the workshops. Their manhood and self-respect have returned, their countenances show an intelligent interest in their work, a healthy appetite has returned, the bloom on the cheek has resumed its place, and if

[282] *Report of the Inspectors of the Western Penitentiary*, 1869, pp. 5-6.
[283] Ibid., 1871, pp. 5-6.

one did not *know* that he was in a prison, he could not distinguish these from any similar workmen outside.

"Yet best and most of all is the wholesome discipline which *labor* always brings in its train. There is nothing so promotive of good order as to make an imprisoned man *tired;* his sleep is sweet at night, and he has no time for mischief during the day." [284]

It is interesting to note that the authorities of the Western Penitentiary did not go to the other extreme of abandoning solitary confinement altogether, but retained it for newly admitted convicts and those guilty of insubordination and other forms of misconduct.[285] It was, thus, adapted to that supplementary position to congregation where it has been found of great permanent value to all institutions which have adopted it in this form. The unfortunate thing about the experience of the Pennsylvania system is that it has usually been tried in a form which doomed it to failure, namely, as applied to all inmates continuously, or has been ignored entirely. As utilized by Walter Crofton in his "Irish" system of prison administration for temporary application to newcomers and as a mode of punishment for recalcitrants, it has proved well-nigh indispensable and in this form is likely to have a permanent place in prison administration.[286]

2.   THE MAJOR FEATURES OF THE PROGRESS IN PENAL ADMINISTRATION AND DISCIPLINE SINCE 1835

A.   Introductory Observations

The preceding sections of this chapter are of interest primarily as bearing upon the experience of a modern community in applying the test of a practical experiment to one of the leading prison systems that has been thus far devised. Owing to the fact that this experiment has proved to be a relative failure with respect to its lack of adaptability to the advances made since 1829 in the field of criminology and penology, the subject-matter has little bearing upon a solution of the problems of the future in penal administration. The present section, therefore, differs radically from the preceding one in this respect, being as it is, a record of the introduction of those phases of prison administration which have shown

---

[284] *Report of the Inspectors of the Western Penitentiary,* 1874, pp. 7-8.
[285] Ibid., 1871, p. 8; 1873, p. 6.
[286] The separate system is to-day retained in Pennsylvania only in the Philadelphia County Convict Prison at Holmesburg.

themselves to be of permanent value and have been demonstrated to be the essentials of any plan for the future reconstruction of the methods of dealing with the problem of delinquency. These advances by common consent among penologists are held to be: (1) the commutation of sentence for good behavior; (2) the indeterminate sentence, operated in conjunction with a parole system; (3) the progressive classification of prisoners in accordance with a study of their personal history prior to commitment and their behavior in confinement; (4) the separation of the defective from the delinquent class and a proper specialization in the treatment of both; (5) the careful psychological observation and analysis of the delinquent population; (6) the sterilization or permanent segregation of habitual criminals; (7) the moral, social, vocational and academic education of convicts; (8) the introduction of preventive methods, such as probation, designed to avoid when possible the necessity of the expense and humiliation of imprisonment.[287]

B.   The Commutation of Sentence for Good Behavior

What was probably the earliest instance of the application of the principle of the commutation of the sentence of a prisoner for good behavior appeared in a law, passed in 1817 in the state of New York, and put into operation in the state prison at Auburn. It provided that all prisoners sentenced for five years or less might earn a reduction of one-fourth of their sentence by good behavior and the performance of a stipulated amount of "overwork." This appears, however, to have been regarded quite as much an economic measure as a disciplinary feature and it remained purely a local enactment. It is to the broader development of the principle as an integral factor in the improvement of prison discipline that one must look for the sources from which it came into the practice of the state of Pennsylvania. It is generally held that the first writer to enunciate the doctrine of the commutation of sentence for good

---

[287] In addition to the Pennsylvania documents cited the writer has found most useful in preparing this section: E. C. Wines, *The State of Prisons and Child-saving Institutions;* F. H. Wines, *Punishment and Reformation;* C. R. Henderson, *Penal and Reformatory Institutions;* B. De Quiros, *Modern Theories of Criminality;* J. B. Lindsley, *Prison Discipline and Penal Legislation;* Corinne Bacon, *Prison Reform;* Mary Carpenter, *Reformatory Prison Discipline as Developed by the Rt. Honorable Sir Walter Crofton in the Irish Convict Prisons;* Philip Klein, *Prison Methods in New York State;* E. Stagg Whitin, *The Caged Man,* Dr. Bernard Glueck's article on the Psychiatric Clinic at Sing Sing Prison in the *Mental Hygiene Magazine* for 1918, and the literature surveyed in my *Repression of Crime,* Chap. X.

behavior as a basic principle in the improvement of prison discipline was Archbishop Whatley of Dublin. In 1829 he published a letter in the *London Review* in which he set forth his belief that the definite time sentence should be replaced by one which represented a certain amount of labor to be performed before release and would allow a convict to reduce his sentence by industrious application to assigned tasks. This suggestion was given a practical application with great success by Captain Alexander Maconochie in his reconstruction of the penal discipline at Norfolk Island, an Australian penal colony, in the years following 1840. When, in 1853, Walter Crofton began his epoch-making work in reorganizing the Irish prisons, he adopted as a component part of his celebrated "Irish" system of prison administration the so-called "mark" or commutation system of Maconochie. From Ireland it was introduced into America by the enthusiastic admirers of Crofton's methods, among whom were E. C. Wines, Theodore Dwight, Frank B. Sanborn, Gaylord B. Hubbell and Z. R. Brockway. Though many of the principles of the "Irish" system have since been gradually adopted in this country, the principle of commutation was the first element of this system to be introduced, primarily, no doubt, because it necessitated the least violent and extensive break with traditional administrative methods.

The introduction of the commutation system into the administrative procedure of Pennsylvania was primarily the result of the work of the Philadelphia Society for the Alleviation of the Miseries of Public Prisons. By their agitation and campaign of education the legislature was induced to pass the act of May 1, 1861, which first established the principle of commutation in Pennsylvania.[288] This act directed the wardens of the two state penitentiaries to keep an accurate record of all infractions of the disciplinary rules of the institutions. In case of no violation of these rules a prisoner was to be entitled to the following reduction of his sentence: one day for the first month; three days for the second month; six days for the third month and the remainder of the first year; four days for each month in the second year; an additional day for each month two to ten years; and two additional days above ten years. The wardens were directed to discharge convicts with a certificate of good conduct as soon as they had served out their sentences less the prescribed deductions.[289] The inspectors of both state penitentiaries vigorously opposed this commutation act, in part,

---

[288] *The Journal of Prison Discipline and Philanthropy*, Vol. XVI, October, 1861, Number 4, pp. 170-200. (This reference includes an argument against the system.)
[289] *The Laws of the General Assembly*, 1861, pp. 462-63.

no doubt, because its peculiarly complicated schedule of reductions would require a large amount of additional administrative labor. In their report for 1861 the inspectors of the Eastern Penitentiary sharply condemned the law, their main objection apparently being the additional burden of compiling the individual records, though it is difficult to see how this could have been a serious objection if the Pennsylvania system was, as its exponents claimed, founded primarily upon a careful attention to individual conduct on the part of the prisoners.[290]

Even more outspoken was the criticism of the inspectors of the Western Penitentiary. They maintained that it would make so much extra work that more officials would be required; that it was unconstitutional to take the pardoning power from the governor in such a manner; and that the inspectors would not execute the law in their institution. They further commended the inspectors of the Eastern Penitentiary for their stand with respect to the law.[291] The opposition of the prison authorities and the ruffled pride of the courts were sufficient to procure the declaration by the courts that the commutation law of 1861 was unconstitutional. In their report for 1862 the inspectors of the Western Penitentiary proclaimed their great satisfaction that "the constitution of the Commonwealth had been thus preserved," though their satisfaction could not have been less over the reduction of administrative duties.[292] The friends of prison reform were not discouraged, however, and persisted in their demand for a commutation law until the act of May 21, 1869, was passed. This directed that the wardens of the penitentiaries keep a record of the conduct of all prisoners and stated that if no charges of misconduct stood against the prisoner he was entitled to a reduction of one month for each of the first two years; two months for the third and four year; three months for the fifth to the tenth years; and four months for the period from the tenth year to the time of discharge.[293] As this law was much more liberal than that of 1861, the delay was not entirely fruitless. By this time the new board of inspectors had come into power in the Western Penitentiary and its members were from the first advocates and supporters of the second commutation law.[294] The inspectors of the Eastern Penitentiary, while no longer violent in their criticism of the commutation law, belittled

---

[290] *Report of the Inspectors of the Eastern Penitentiary,* 1861, pp. 36ff. and Appendix, *passim.*
[291] *Legislative Documents,* 1862, pp. 847-48.
[292] *Report of the Inspectors of the Western Penitentiary,* 1862, p. 7.
[293] *Laws of the General Assembly,* 1869, p. 1268.
[294] *Report of the Inspectors of the Western Penitentiary,* 1869, pp. 5-6.

its significance. They maintained that it was but an expedient
devised by administrators of congregate prisons to lessen the difficulty of maintaining discipline in so defective a system. It was
entirely superfluous in so perfect a system as that in operation
in the Eastern Penitentiary.[295] The act of 1869 remained in force
as the basis of the commutation system until the passage of the
act of May 11, 1901, which provided,

"That every convict confined in any State Prison, Penitentiary,
Work House, or County Jail in this State, on a conviction of
felony or misdemeanor, whether male or female, where the term
or terms equal or equals or exceeds one year, exclusive of any
term which may be imposed by the court or by statute as an alternative to the payment of a fine, or term of life imprisonment, may,
if the Governor shall so direct, and with the approval of the Board
of Managers, earn for himself or herself a commutation or diminu-
tion of his or her sentence as follows, namely: Two months for
the first year, three months for the second year, four months for
the third and fourth years, and five months for each subsequent
year. And for each fractional part of a year the said convict may
earn the same rate of commutation as is provided for in the year
in which the said fractional part occurs." [296]

This act was, thus, considerably more generous in its prescribed
reductions than that of 1869. This remained in operation in the
state penitentiaries until the acts of May 10, 1909, and June 19, 1911,
provided for the introduction of the principle of the indeterminate
sentence.[297] It still continues in force in those institutions, such as
the county jails and workhouses, where the indeterminate sentence
law has not been introduced.

C. Indeterminate Sentence and Parole

The principle of commutation, discussed above, was in one sense
a type of indeterminate sentence. It was, however, much too rigid
and definite in its provisions to constitute a true indeterminate
principle. The first application of the principle of an indeterminate
sentence in America, if not in the world, seems to have been in
the New York House of Refuge as provided by a law of 1824.[298]
A very similar practice was introduced into the government of the
Philadelphia House of Refuge which was created in 1826. Here

---

[295] *Report of the Inspectors of the Eastern Penitentiary*, 1870, p. 25.
[296] *Laws of the General Assembly*, 1901, p. 166.
[297] Ibid., 1909, pp. 495ff.; 1911, pp. 1055-59.
[298] *Laws of the State of New York*, 1824, pp. 110-12.

the board of managers was given large discretion in the matter of discharging or indenturing inmates.[299] This application of the indeterminate principle was, however, wholly limited to juvenile institutions and few if any reformers possessed any idea that the principles might be beneficially extended to institutions for adult delinquents. As with the practice of commutation, one has to turn to Europe for the origins of the principle of the indeterminate sentence as applied to adult convicts. It has been stated upon reputable authority that the first comprehensive statement and defense of the theory of the indeterminate sentence was contained in the *Moral Philosophy* of the brilliant if eccentric Scot, George Combe, written about 1835. In 1839 Frederick Hill, inspector of prisons for Scotland, in his report to the secretary of state for home affairs, definitely recommended the introduction of the indeterminate sentence into the prisons of England and Scotland. As far as the writer is aware, it has never been fully determined whether or not Hill obtained the idea of the indeterminate sentence from Combe or as the result of his own experience. But whoever may claim the honor of having first presented the principle, it is doubted by no one that its most effective exponent was Matthew Davenport Hill, the brother of Frederick Hill. Almost from the first it has been agreed that the indeterminate sentence must have as a supplementary principle and practice the system of parole or "ticket-of-leave," as it is known in England. The fundamental value of the parole system in the discharge of prisoners was noted by Jeremy Bentham as early as the close of the eighteenth century. The elaboration of the principle was left, however, to Bonneville De Marsangy of France, who became its great and untiring exponent.

The "twin principles" of the indeterminate sentence and parole were combined by Crofton in his Irish prison system and were introduced into American practice in the famous "Elmira" system, where they were first applied in the treatment of young and relatively petty offenders, though the Cincinnati Prison Congress of 1870 recommended their immediate application in all state penitentiaries. Though it is generally held that the parole and the indeterminate sentence are a fundamental unity in principle and successful practice, their acceptance and progress in America were more or less uneven. The parole system, being less radical in appearance, as a rule came earlier, entering the state prisons of this country rather generally in the decade of the nineties. The indeterminate sentence found no widespread welcome until about 1910,

---

[299] *Acts of the General Assembly of Pennsylvania,* 1825-26, pp. 133ff.

when a campaign for its introduction was waged by the enlightened jurists of the country and by the American Institute of Criminology and Criminal Law. At the present time about half of the states have adopted the indeterminate sentence and something more than half the parole system.

Before taking up the subject of the formal adoption of an indeterminate sentence law in Pennsylvania, it will be interesting briefly to refer to a type of extra-legal indeterminate sentence which prevailed in the state penitentiaries during the middle of the last century, namely, the practice of wholesale pardoning. As early as 1835 the inspectors of the Eastern Penitentiary complained of the excessive use of the pardoning power by the governor and urged that this right should be used only in cases of clearly established innocence.[300] In their report for 1864 the inspectors of the Western Penitentiary presented the summary statistics of the use of the pardoning power in that institution. Since the opening of the institution two thousand and eighty-two convicts had been admitted and no less than four hundred and sixty-three had been pardoned by the governor.[301] In 1867 the inspectors of the same institution stated that this abuse of the pardoning power constituted the most serious obstacle to an effective system of discipline.[302] To how great an extent the inordinate amount of pardoning revealed by these statistics was a result of the importuning of the prisoner and his friends and how far it was the result of the recommendations of the inspectors to prevent physical or mental breakdown in prison, as was charged by Governor Johnston, is a subject for future special investigation. It would seem, then, that a very real, if extra-legal, form of indeterminate sentence existed in Pennsylvania at a very early date, or to put it in another way, that the portion of the sentence actually served was determined, as the inspectors of the Western Penitentiary expressed it, "by the amount of money and the number of friends available to press the suit for a pardon."[303]

Aside from the above-mentioned use of an approximately indeterminate sentence in the House of Refuge following 1826, the first introduction of the principle of the indeterminate sentence in Pennsylvania was contained in the act of April 28, 1887, organizing the government of the Huntingdon Reformatory. This provided a very close approach to the true indeterminate sentence. The only time specification which was allowed in the sentence was that it

---

[300] Report of the Inspectors of the Eastern Penitentiary, 1835, Senate Journal, 1835-36, Vol. II, p. 323.
[301] Report of the Inspectors of the Western Penitentiary, 1864, p. 7.
[302] Ibid., 1867, pp. 5, 37.
[303] Ibid.

could not exceed the maximum prescribed for the crime in the penal code of the state.[304] More than twenty years passed before this principle was extended to the state penitentiaries, even in a temporary and imperfect manner.[305] The interesting steps which led up to the passage of the law of May 10, 1909, introducing the indeterminate sentence in the Pennsylvania penitentiaries, as well as an enumeration of the different individuals and societies instrumental in securing this important reform measure, are well set forth in the following memorandum furnished the writer by Doctor J. F. Ohl, who has for the last fifteen years been an indefatigable worker in the cause of prison reform in Pennsylvania:

"In 1904 the Pennsylvania Prison Society appointed a standing committee on legislation of which the Rev. Dr. J. F. Ohl has from the beginning been the chairman. Sometime between 1904 and 1907 Judge William H. Staake called the attention of Dr. Ohl to the desirability of making the acquaintance of General St. Clair A. Mulholland, then an inspector of the Philadelphia County Prisons, with advanced ideas on penal subjects, and gave him a letter of introduction to the General. Dr. Ohl and General Mulholland at once found that their views on the necessity of many reforms were identical and began to gather information as to methods, experiences and results from every possible source. They carried on an extensive correspondence with Governors, Attorney Generals, Penitentiary Wardens, and other persons interested in prison reform in all the states in which progressive legislation had been enacted and tried. Further, until the General's death in February, 1910, they made a number of trips to Harrisburg to argue bills before the proper committees. The material gathered through correspondence served as a basis for the legislation subsequently proposed, and for a widespread propaganda throughout the State by means of circulars, letters, pamphlets, and leading newspapers.

"In 1907, authorized by the Pennsylvania Prison Society, Dr. Ohl and General Mulholland succeeded in having a joint resolution introduced in the Legislature at Harrisburg providing for the creation of a commission to investigate the condition of the penal, reformatory and correctional institutions of Pennsylvania and to suggest necessary steps in reorganizing the penological concepts and practices of Pennsylvania. This resolution was passed, but was vetoed by Governor Stuart on the ground that there were already too many commissions, that he did not think it wise to add another,

---

[304] *Laws of the General Assembly,* 1887, p. 65.
[305] Probably the most violent and implacable foe of the principle of the indeterminate sentence and parole in Pennsylvania was Warden Cassidy of the Eastern Penitentiary. See the reports of this institution, 1883, p. 80; 1888, pp. 115-16; 1889, pp. 113-14; 1894, p. 161.

and that he deemed it better if those interested in matters of prison reform would come to the Legislature with bills of a more specific nature. Thus it came about that members of the Pennsylvania Prison Society, the Protestant Episcopal City Mission, and the American Society for Visiting Catholic Prisoners, together with State Senator Ernest L. Tustin, met at the residence of Mr. John E. Baird, on the evening of April 24, 1908, to discuss what might be done to start penal reform in this state. The meeting was organized by the election of the Rev. J. F. Ohl as chairman, and Gen. Mulholland as secretary. At this meeting it was unanimously resolved to secure, if possible, at the next meeting of the Legislature (1909), the enactment of a law providing for adult probation, the indeterminate sentence and parole. At the second meeting of this self-constituted committee, held September 14, 1908, at the residence of James E. Gorman, Esqr., the Committee resolved to call itself 'The Pennsylvania Society for the Promotion of Improved Penal Legislation,' with the officers of the Committee respectively as President and Secretary. At a subsequent meeting Mr. John E. Baird was made treasurer, who, not wishing to serve, was succeeded by the Rev. R. Heber Barnes. Meanwhile, the President and Secretary, utilizing to the fullest extent the material they had assembled, prepared the draft of a bill providing for adult probation, the indeterminate sentence and parole, and had the same printed. At a meeting, at Mr. Gorman's residence on December 19, 1908, a sub-committee was appointed with B. Frank Clapp, Esqr., as chairman, to take the draft of this bill into consideration and 'to perfect it so as to embody these ideas.' At this meeting it was also announced that the Pennsylvania Prison Society and the American Society for Visiting Catholic Prisoners would each contribute fifty dollars toward expenses. The bill as finally perfected, chiefly by Mr. Clapp, was introduced at Harrisburg by Senator Tustin, and became known as the Tustin bill. It was passed, received the Governor's signature May 10, 1909, and went into effect June 30, 1909. This act was pronounced 'admirable' by the Committee on Criminal Law Reform in its report at the International Prison Congress of 1910." [306]

The following provisions constitute the essentials of the "Tustin Bill" which refer to the matter of the indeterminate sentence.[307] The general policy and procedure of the new law was set forth in the following paragraph:

---

[306] Adapted and condensed from a manuscript memorandum furnished to the writers by the Rev. Dr. J. F. Ohl. Of course, it should not be forgotten that Chaplain Milligan of the Western Penitentiary had for years vigorously if ineffectively, urged the passage of a thoroughgoing indeterminate sentence and parole act.

[307] Laws of the General Assembly, 1909, pp. 495ff. The provisions of this act relating to probation will be dealt with in another place.

"Whenever any person, convicted in any court of this Commonwealth of any crime shall be sentenced to imprisonment in either the Eastern or Western Penitentiary, the court, instead of pronouncing upon such convict a definite or fixed term of imprisonment, shall pronounce upon such convict a sentence of imprisonment for an indefinite term; stating in such sentence the maximum and minimum limits thereof; fixing as the minimum time of such imprisonment, the term now or hereafter prescribed as the minimum imprisonment for the punishment of such offence; but if there be no minimum time so prescribed, the court shall determine the same, but it shall not exceed one-fourth of the maximum time, and the maximum limit shall be the maximum time now or hereafter prescribed as a penalty for such offence." [308]

Certain exceptions were made to the universal application of this law. It was stipulated that in cases of third convictions of crimes receiving a penitentiary sentence the maximum penalty imposed in every case should be thirty years. Further, it was stated that the benefits of the commutation law of 1901 should not apply to those sentenced under the new indeterminate sentence law. The necessity of creating a parole system, as the indispensable accompaniment of the indeterminate sentence, was recognized. It was provided that the boards of inspectors of the two state penitentiaries should meet monthly and examine the records of prisoners who had served their minimum sentence, and, after reviewing their cases, should recommend to the governor of the state that he release on parole such of these prisoners as the inspectors believed would "live and remain at liberty without violating the law." If the inspectors felt that they could not justly recommend the paroling of any prisoner who had served his minimum sentence, they were directed to forward to the governor in writing their reasons for their action. Before the governor could parole [309] any prisoner recommended to him by the inspectors as eligible for parole, it was necessary that the case should previously be examined by the Board of Pardons, composed of the lieutenant-governor, the secretary of the commonwealth, the attorney-general and the secretary of internal affairs. If they recommended parole the governor was authorized to order such action.[310] It was stipulated that the convict should legally be regarded as on parole to the expiration of the maximum sentence, unless earlier pardoned. In case of a violation of the conditions of the parole the convict was to be required to serve out

---

[308] *Laws of the General Assembly*, 1909, p. 496.
[309] Ibid., p. 498. The same limitations are placed upon the governor's power to exercise the pardoning power in Pennsylvania.
[310] This board rarely or never reverses the judgment of the inspectors.

the unexpired maximum sentence, unless sooner pardoned or paroled. If a paroled prisoner should be convicted of crime while on parole, it was decreed that he should serve both the new sentence and the remainder of the old maximum, without enjoying any privileges of commutation. If, on the other hand, the paroled prisoner gave evidence by his conduct on parole that he had been cured of his criminal propensities, the inspectors might recommend to the governor that the prisoner receive a full pardon. To insure some effective control and supervision of the parole system of each institution the inspectors were directed to appoint one or more parole officers to take charge of the parole machinery of each state penitentiary.

While not a pure indeterminate sentence law, the above statute was one of the most liberal in the history of criminal jurisprudence as applied to a state prison. With its limitation of the minimum to one-fourth of the maximum it made possible the relatively speedy release of the less serious type of convicts or of those who gave evidence of having been improved by their term of incarceration, while the provision of a maximum of thirty years for all types of recidivists enabled the authorities to retain in confinement for practically a life term that most dangerous and clearly marked criminal class. Had it been possible to preserve this act for permanent enforcement Pennsylvania might have again attained to something like the preeminence she enjoyed in liberal criminal jurisprudence in the latter part of the eighteenth century. The new law, however, was bitterly opposed by the more conservative members of the judiciary of the state [311] and was soon emasculated in a way to make its operation much less liberal and effective in all cases, while in some the situation was much more oppressive than the conditions which had existed before the passage of the 1909 act.

In 1911, Mr. Edwin M. Abbott, a Philadelphia criminal lawyer and then a member of the legislature, introduced an amendment to this act which removed the limitation of the minimum sentence to one-fourth of the maximum and made it possible for the judges to fix the minimum at any point which was one day less than the maximum. The thirty-year maximum for recidivists was also abolished, as well as the provision that the maximum sentence must be the maximum provided in the penal code of the state. The amended bill was passed on June nineteenth [312] and its application

---

[311] A number of the more progressive judges, on the other hand, have expressed their emphatic approval of a real indeterminate sentence. See the *Journal of Prison Discipline,* March, 1914, pp. 27-8.

[312] *The Laws of the General Assembly,* 1911, pp. 1055ff.

marked the practical destruction of the principle of the indeterminate sentence in Pennsylvania for the time being. In commenting on the effect of the new law in the *Journal of Prison Discipline* Doctor J. F. Ohl made the following pertinent observations upon the fatal significance of the amendments:

"The act of 1909 was based upon a very careful study of the writings of the most advanced penologists and of the statutes of those progressive states that have introduced the indeterminate sentence and parole with the greatest amount of success. Its viewpoint was that of those who seek the reformation of the wrongdoer, and not of those who still have in their minds the old idea of retributive justice only; it made a break with the old codes, aimed to deal with the man and not with his crime, and had regard to his future rather than to his past. This bill was so amended (in 1911) as virtually to eliminate from it the vital principle underlying the indeterminate sentence and parole. This amendment puts it into the power of the court to fix any minimum below the maximum, instead of a minimum not exceeding one fourth of the maximum; it permits the court to name a lower maximum than the one now prescribed by law for any given offence; and it strikes out the thirty-year clause altogether. The practical effect of these changes is to destroy in great measure the value and efficacy of the indeterminate sentence as a remedial and reformatory measure. In other words, the amendment restores the vicious inequality of sentences, which is always so apt to breed a feeling of injustice and resentment in the one convicted, and which therefore greatly unfits him as a subject for reformatory treatment. It proceeds upon the long-accepted but false assumption that the court can in every case determine the exact degree of culpability and then adjust the punishment accurately to the crime. This is not only absurd, but it is impossible. As the law now stands, we shall again find, as is indeed already the case, that the same court or adjoining courts may, even under practically identical conditions, impose greatly varying sentences, instead of putting all upon whom sentence is passed on an equality and giving all, under identical conditions, an equal chance, as the law originally contemplated. Again, under the amended law the court virtually determines when a prisoner shall be eligible to parole. This is, however, utterly subversive of the theory upon which the indeterminate sentence is based, namely, that parole is to be granted when a prisoner is believed to be fit to be restored to society as a law-abiding citizen. The time when this may be done no court under the sun can fix, but only those who have the prisoner in charge and under observation, and even they may make mistakes." [313]

The operation of the amended act has not been less vicious than

---

[313] *The Journal of Prison Discipline and Philanthropy*, November, 1911, pp. 21-3. His complete remarks have been somewhat condensed.

Doctor Ohl predicted. The grossest inequality of sentences for the same crime exists, and in many cases the minimum sentences have been so high that they have compelled a longer term of imprisonment than would have been necessary under the older commutation system. To be sure, some of the more progressive judges have made a wise use of the almost complete discretionary power which was conferred upon them by the act of 1911 and have been most intelligent and liberal in the use of their sentencing powers, and in their case the amendment has operated to improve the penal practice of the state, but with the vast majority of the judges the amendment has led to a gross abuse of this extensive power bestowed upon the judiciary.[314] Mr. Albert H. Votaw calls attention to the following examples of the severity of the operation of the "indeterminate sentence" law of 1911:

"The court has the power by this law to make the minimum sentence any time at all to within one day of the maximum. A convict whose offence by statute may be punished by an imprisonment of twenty years could have a minimum sentence fixed at any time from one day to nineteen years, eleven months and twenty-nine days. There were four prisoners at the Eastern Penitentiary at the time the last report was made whose maximum was twenty years and whose minimum was the same lacking one day. There were thirty-eight prisoners sentenced to a maximum of twenty years whose minimum was eighteen years or more. According to the old law of commutation for good behavior, every one of these prisoners would have been entitled to freedom on good behavior at the end of twelve years and three months. This law of commutation for satisfactory conduct has been in vogue for fifty years and we have not learned that the judiciary of the State had issued any remonstrance. The number according to the last report whose maximum was twenty years was 86. These under the old law of commutation might be released in 12 years, 3 months. Of these 88, under present law, 55 will remain longer than under commutation. And under present law, 31 may be released earlier than under commutation. It is the inequality of sentences which has produced dissatisfaction." [315]

These instances can be supplemented by many others. Among those received in the Western Penitentiary in 1916 five were given a minimum of six and a maximum of eight years; five a minimum of seven and a maximum of ten; three a minimum of ten and a

---

[314] A study of the sentences imposed between 1911 and 1918 seems to indicate that the judges in the western part of the state have exhibited the greatest degree of liberality in applying the law of 1911.

[315] Albert H. Votaw, *Penal Legislation of 1917 in the Commonwealth of Pennsylvania*, p. 18.

maximum of twelve; five a minimum of ten and a maximum of
thirteen; six a minimum of ten and a maximum of fifteen; four a
minimum of sixteen and a maximum of twenty; five a minimum of
eighteen and a maximum of twenty; and one a minimum of nineteen and a maximum of twenty.[316] Even worse abuses of the sentencing power are revealed by the records of the Eastern Penitentiary. In 1917 there were in that institution thirty-one prisoners
with a minimum sentence of four years and a maximum of five
years; twenty-five with a minimum of five and a maximum of six;
forty-two with a minimum of five and a maximum of seven; fifteen
with a minimum of six and a maximum of seven; eleven with a
minimum of nine and a maximum of ten; fifteen with a minimum
of ten years and a maximum of twelve; twenty with a minimum
of ten and a maximum of fifteen years; fifteen with a minimum
of twelve and a maximum of fifteen; fourteen with a minimum
of fifteen and a maximum of twenty; thirteen with a minimum of
eighteen and a maximum of twenty; thirteen with a minimum of
nineteen and a maximum of twenty; eight with a minimum of
nineteen years and eleven months and a maximum of twenty years;
and one with a minimum of twenty-seven years and a maximum
of twenty-eight.[317]

Of course, it must be granted that in many cases the minimum
should be made as near the maximum sentence as is possible in
order to restrain and keep in custody during the longest possible
period those dangerous recidivists and degenerate criminals who
require and should receive permanent and effective segregation
from society during their entire lifetime, but there is little evidence
that the cases of extreme minimum sentences were scientifically
and systematically applied for this purpose. Little machinery as
yet exists in Pennsylvania which will enable a sentencing judge to
learn with certainty the identity of the incurable criminals. In most
cases the extreme minimum sentences seem to have been arbitrarily
imposed on account of the heinous nature of the crime itself, or
from unusually revolting conditions under which it was committed,
or because of the unfavorable impression created by the prisoner
in the court-room.

Realizing that the 1911 amendments had defeated the real purpose and methods of the indeterminate sentence, the advocates of
the more progressive penology in Pennsylvania, especially the committee on legislation of the Pennsylvania Prison Society, kept up
an enlightened agitation for the restoration of the 1909 law and,

---

[316] *Biennial Report of the Western Penitentiary,* 1916, pp. 49-50.
[317] *Annual Report of the Eastern Penitentiary,* 1917, pp. 54ff.

in 1917, were able to secure the passage of an act achieving this desirable end, but this promising accomplishment was destroyed by Governor Brumbaugh, who, with singular opaqueness to modern thought and practice and want of sympathy with the penological progress of the last half-century, vetoed the bill.[318] The situation up to the year 1918, therefore, remained as it has since 1911.

Though the principle of the indeterminate sentence was thus partially defeated in the state penitentiaries after 1911, it won a victory in another field in 1913. The act of July 25, 1913, providing for the creation of the State Industrial Home for Women, which has since been erected at Muncy, embodied the application of the principle of the indeterminate sentence and parole for all sentenced to the institution. The institution was to receive "any female between sixteen and thirty years of age, upon conviction for, or upon pleading guilty of, the commission of any criminal offense punishable under the laws of the State." The sentence imposed upon such women convicts was to be indeterminate. No minimum was allowed to be specified, while the maximum was to be three years, unless the legal maximum for that crime was more than three years, in which case the legal maximum was to be given. The controlling board was empowered to parole inmates at their discretion and to recommend permanent discharge of inmates to the convicting judges when such action was deemed desirable.[319] The principle of the indeterminate sentence, then, in Pennsylvania was fully recognized and applied in the two reformatory institutions and in the two correctional institutions, while in the state penitentiaries it was formally recognized and practically defeated until 1923.

After much agitation, running over a decade, the friends of reform were finally able to secure the passage of an Indeterminate Sentence Act on June 29, 1923. This amended the act of June 19, 1911, in the following fashion:

"Section 6. Whenever any person, convicted in any court of this Commonwealth of any crime *punishable by imprisonment in a state penitentiary,* shall be sentenced to imprisonment *therefor* in any penitentiary *or other institution* of (the) *this* State, *or in any county or municipal institution,* the court, instead of pronouncing upon such convict a definite or fixed term of imprisonment, shall pronounce upon such convict a sentence of imprisonment for an indefinite term: Stating in such sentence the minimum and maximum limits thereof; and the maximum limit shall never exceed the maxi-

[318] Albert H. Votaw, *Penal Legislation of 1917 in the Commonwealth of Pennsylvania,* pp. 18-9.
[319] *Laws of the General Assembly,* 1913, pp. 1311-19.

mum time now or hereafter prescribed as a penalty for such offense; *and the minimum limit shall never exceed one-half of the maximum sentence prescribed by any court:*

"Provided, *That nothing herein contained shall be construed to derogate from the power of the judges of the courts of quarter sessions and of the courts of oyer and terminer, or other court of record having jurisdiction, of the several judicial districts of the Commonwealth, after due inquiry, to release on parole any convict confined in the county jail, house of correction, or work-house of their respective districts, as provided in section one of an act, approved the nineteenth day of June, one thousand nine hundred and eleven (Pamphlet Laws, one thousand fifty-nine), entitled 'An act extending the powers of judges of courts of quarter sessions and of oyer and terminer, in relation to releasing prisoners in jails and workhouses on parole,' its amendments and supplements: And provided further,* That no person sentenced for an indeterminate term shall be entitled to any benefits under the act, entitled 'An act providing for the commutation of sentences for good behavior of convicts in prisons, penitentiaries, workhouses, and county jails in this State, and regulations governing the same,' approved the eleventh day of May, Anno Domini one thousand nine hundred and one:

"*And provided further, That, before any parole shall be granted pursuant to the terms hereof, notice of an intention so to do shall be given, at least ten days prior thereto, by the board of prison inspectors to the judge of the county who imposed the sentence, if he be still in office, but otherwise to the judge or judges of the court of oyer and terminer or the court of the quarter sessions then in session, or if there be no current term, then to the next ensuing term thereof, and having jurisdiction of cases of the like character. Similar notice shall also be given to the district attorney then in office in said county.*"

Though the 1911 amendments to the indeterminate sentence law greatly lessened its usefulness and thwarted some of its chief principles and aims, the system of parole was at least partially saved from the wreckage. Even the parole system was handicapped by the amendment of 1911 which allowed the sentencing judge to fix the minimum sentence. This, as Doctor Ohl pointed out in the preceding passage, has made it possible for the judge rather than the paroling board to determine when the prisoner shall be paroled. The minimum sentence, which must expire in all cases before paroling is legally possible, is normally too long for those who deserve to be paroled at all and too brief for that well defined class who require life-long segregation and confinement. This arbitrary power given to the judges makes it impossible for the paroling board to release a prisoner on parole as soon as his conduct has justified such action; in other words, it abrogates the whole principle of the preparatory phases of the parole system. But within these irritating limitations the parole system has made notable progress in the two state penitentiaries. The following analysis of the parole system in the state penitentiaries will be based upon the practice of the Western Penitentiary, not with any desire to disparage the commendable administration of this department in the Eastern Penitentiary, but because the Western Penitentiary has given more specific attention to the development of this work and has special advantages not possessed by the eastern institution, in that the farm site in Centre County makes it possible to give the convicts a transitional period of partial freedom before they receive total freedom on parole.

The parole system was introduced in the Western Penitentiary almost synchronously with the induction of Mr. Francies as warden, and its development has been one significant aspect of his constructive administrative policy. He was peculiarly fortunate in securing as his chief parole officer, Mr. John M. Eagan, who has combined to an unusual degree real administrative capacity with a sympathetic insight into the aims of the newer penology. Preparatory to organizing their parole department Mr. Francies traveled widely, advising with the leading prison officials and penological experts as to the desirable elements of a successful parole system, and Mr. Eagan made a personal inspection of the more important institutions which had parole systems in operation. After about a decade of developmental experience the parole system at the Western Penitentiary operates essentially as follows.[320] A prisoner is eligible for parole at the expiration of his minimum sentence if his conduct and other elements in his past record are such as to justify the parole officer and the inspectors in believing that the convict would live in freedom without violating the conditions of his parole or the laws of the commonwealth. Since the progress of the new institution at Rockview during the last few years has enabled the warden to send a large number of convicts to this site to labor on construction work and on the extensive farms, it has been the practice to send men to the new site some time in advance of the expiration of their minimum sentence, so that they may have a preliminary training in partial freedom. Three months before the expiration of his minimum sentence each convict is allowed to apply for release on parole, irrespective of his conduct or his mental and physical condition. Every convict who so applies must also be given a hearing by the parole board, which in both state peniten-

---

[320] This description is based upon the personal investigation of the writer.

tiaries, consists of the board of inspectors of the institution. The action that the board will take on the granting of any particular application from a convict will depend on his past criminal history, on the record of the convict while incarcerated and on his mental and physical condition. This information is furnished to the board by the chief parole officer and by the warden. Unless there are evident reasons why the application for parole should not be granted the inspectors will normally recommend favorable action on the petition. The board does not, however, have power to parole directly, but can only make recommendation on this point to the above-mentioned board of pardons and the governor. If they deem that the application shall not be granted they must submit their reasons for this decision to the Board of Pardons and the governor, exactly as in the case of recommending positive action.

In spite of this complicated formal process of securing action on parole, which requires that the Parole Board shall recommend action to the Board of Pardons which, in turn, is required to advise the governor as to his decision, there has never yet been an instance where either the Board of Pardons or the governor has reversed the decision of the local Parole Board. The duration of actual supervision of a paroled convict and the thoroughness of the inspection of his conduct depends entirely upon the individual convict. If his criminal record is not serious, if his conduct in prison has been commendable and if his record while on parole has been wholly satisfactory, discharge from parole is likely to be speedy, coming after about eighteen months' time in the most favorable cases. On the other hand, if the convict has had a suspicious criminal past, has exhibited indifferent conduct while in the penitentiary and has give no conclusive demonstration of complete reformation on parole, he will be likely to be retained on parole under more or less active supervision until the expiration of his maximum sentence. In many cases the relatives of the prisoners request that the period of parole and supervision be extended as long as legally possible because it furnishes an additional incentive to good conduct on the part of the convict. While on parole the convict is required to submit reports monthly to the chief parole officer on blanks furnished each month by the institution. These reports are examined by the chief parole officer and by the head clerk of the prison, and if any personal inspection is deemed necessary they inform the field parole officer who will visit the convict in question. Final discharge comes automatically at the expiration of the maximum sentence, but may come sooner if the paroled convict applies for discharge and the officials deem his request reasonable and sustained by the facts in his case. Normally, however, the initiative in securing the discharge of a deserving paroled convict is taken by the parole officer, who makes such a recommendation to the Parole Board and the same steps are taken and the same administrative machinery is used as in obtaining the original grant of parole. Final discharge restores the convict to the enjoyment of his civil rights as an inhabitant of the state of Pennsylvania, except in cases where the conviction has been for treason or perjury.

The violation of the conditions of parole requires the return of the convict to the institution where he must serve the remainder of his maximum sentence unless sooner reparoled, discharged or pardoned. In case of the conviction of crime while on parole, the convict must serve out the remainder of the maximum sentence and then the sentence imposed for the crime committed while on parole. The period of partial freedom at the Rockview site is safeguarded by the rather over-severe Pennsylvania penalty for escapes or attempted escapes, which condemns a prisoner who has been apprehended after escape to serve double his previous sentence after his apprehension. The office and recording phase of the parole department of the Western Penitentiary approaches perfection in the thoroughness, system and efficiency of its organization, but the parole work is rendered a farce by the lack of a sufficient field force. Only one field officer for visiting paroled prisoners has been provided by the state, though four such officers would find it difficult to care for this work as it should be attended to, there being nearly seven hundred men under formal supervision on parole from that institution. This condemns the field supervision to hopeless superficiality and calls for an immediate remedying by the legislature. The need for added field supervisors is also great in the Eastern Penitentiary where over six hundred paroled convicts are left to the supervision of one man, aided by two office clerical assistants.[321] Out of 4,795 inmates of the Western Peintentiary released on parole eleven per cent. have been returned for violation of parole or the commission of crime, while twelve per cent. have

---

[321] Mr. Albert H. Votaw calls attention to the scientific advantage of relieving the Boards of Inspectors of the burden of supervising the paroling of prisoners and giving this to a Parole Board made up of paid specialists. He says on this point: "We are placing an immense burden upon the Inspectors of our Penitentiaries who in this State constitute the Boards of Parole. They are men with a high sense of civic responsibility who do a large amount of faithful service without financial remuneration. They will not ask for release from duties which the State may impose on them, but in justice to them we submit that the time has come for at least consideration of a proposition to appoint a special Board of Parole who shall receive compensation for their services. This work, if properly performed, demands a large amount of care and study." *Penal Legislation of 1917 in the Commonwealth of Pennsylvania*, p. 20.

disappeared and failed to report. Most of the latter were foreigners who dropped out of sight during the war. On May 14, 1925, an act was passed creating a Parole Commission, to which was delegated the authority to investigate the systems and methods of parole and commutation of sentences in Pennsylvania and other states and to recommend new legislation on this subject for the state of Pennsylvania.

In a hearing before the Parole Commission, thus described in the *Prison Journal* for January, 1927, we discover the opinion of Doctor Potter and Warden Ashe as to the imperfections of the present parole system in Pennsylvania and the suggestion that the travesty can be eliminated only through the creation of a central parole board composed of real experts:

"Dr. Ellen C. Potter, Secretary of the State Department of Welfare, the only woman member of Governor Pinchot's Cabinet, really startled the commission composed of Representative Philip Sterling of Philadelphia, chairman, District Attorney Charles Edwin Fox, of Philadelphia and State Senator William Mansfield of McKeesport, in her advocacy of an indeterminate sentence and elimination of the present law giving juries in capital cases the privilege of recommending death or life imprisonment. This was generally assumed to mean the proposed change would abolish the death chair and death sentences in the state.

"She favored a state parole board, which would eliminate the present state pardon board, and the release of prison wards only when competent experts decided they were fit both mentally and physically to go back to society. The assumption relative to the abolishment of the death sentence came in her proposal to include persons convicted of murder among those given indeterminate sentences.

"The centralized, or state parole board, was recommended as perhaps the only solution to the prison parole problem, which has become a paramount issue in the nation to-day. Such a board and its subsequent subsidiary boards necessarily would cost heavily, for in the plans suggested to the parole commission only those with a psychological understanding of the criminal, such as social workers and psychiatrists, would be in charge of the supervision of the paroled prisoner.

"There is not enough supervision in the present parole system and consequently, as it was admitted, it has been a partial failure. Yet, there is none to blame for the failure to supervise and direct the man or woman just released from incarceration. The local prison parole boards in most cases have issued paroles, but had no way of supervising the needful direction over the prisoner following his release.

"Warden Stanley Ashe, of the Western Penitentiary, told the commission that the present parole system was a bluff—a parole was merely a scrap of paper. For after the prisoner once left the institution, the prison authorities seldom heard from him unless he got into trouble. And this was because there was only one man available to give part time looking after the supervision of 700 released convicts."

The friends of a rational and efficient parole system in Pennsylvania met a severe set-back when the state legislature, in 1927, killed a measure which would have provided state-wide supervision of those on parole by a central parole commission. The bill was defeated chiefly because of the opposition brought to bear by the trustees of the various institutions. They held that the present system of supervising parolees, which is solely by correspondence, is adequate and satisfactory. In this way what is, perhaps, the weakest link in the reformatory and correctional system of the state was left unremedied for an additional two years at least.

To be sure, a truly scientific parole procedure must be based upon a systematic and scientific classification of prisoners according to their past biological, psychological and sociological history, their mental traits and their behavior while in prison. Attention may now be turned to an investigation of the progress which Pennsylvania has made in this all-important phase of the newer penology.

D.   The Differentiation, Separation and Progressive Classification of Convicts

Before there can be any effective and scientific progressive classification of prisoners on the basis of their conduct while incarcerated, it is absolutely essential that there shall be provided some machinery for differentiating those convicted of crime into classes each of which will have enough uniformity so that a system of grading and promotion will be a fairly accurate reflection of the behavior of the individual convict and will afford some comparable indication of his desire for, and progress toward, reformation. For example, any scheme for grading and advancing convicts on the basis of their conduct, however admirably worked out and standardized, would fail utterly if applied indiscriminately to a group of convicts of every age, both sexes, all grades of criminality and varying degrees of mental abnormality. Class and type differentiation of some general nature, at least, must precede the application of behavior tests which will possess any validity for deciding as to the relative fitness of an individual convict for freedom. While the advances in this respect in Pennsylvania have been slow and painful and have not as yet attained to anything like relative perfection, the progress has been gratifying when the conditions of the present day are compared with those which existed at the close of the colonial period. At that time persons convicted of crime, debtors, vagrants and witnesses of all ages, of both sexes and of all mental and social states and conditions were generally herded promiscuously in one institution. Only in some of the larger and more progressive jails did there exist that elementary differentiation and separation of the accused and witnesses from the others.

With the reorganization of the administrative system of the Walnut Street Jail following 1789 there were some very important results achieved in this field of differentiation.[322] Separate rooms and portions of the building were assigned to the accused, the vagrants, the debtors and the convicted criminals. Further, the women were separated from the male prisoners and assigned to a particular section of the jail, the debtors were given a separate building, and the worst types of criminals were separated from the lesser offenders and put in the solitary cells in the distinct building erected to contain them. The opening of the Arch Street Jail in the second decade of the nineteenth century provided a separate institution for accused, debtors and vagrants. With the erection of the state penitentiaries, following 1818, this process was carried still further; not only were these new institutions limited to convicted criminals, but they were also reserved solely for those guilty of the more serious types of delinquency.[323]

Up to this time, however, there had been no classification on the basis of age groups, but with the opening of the Philadelphia House of Refuge in 1828 there was provided in a semi-public institution a type of differentiation based upon both age and criminality, the institution being intended for juvenile delinquents not convicted of the major crimes. This separation according to both age and degree of formal criminality was developed further by the establishment of the Western House of Refuge in Allegheny in the middle of the century and by the creation of the two reformatories at Huntingdon and Muncy, following 1889 and 1913, respectively.

The first and almost the only formal attempt to introduce a system of differentiation and separation on the basis of color came in 1849, when the House of Refuge for Colored Children was opened in Philadelphia. Other institutions have often introduced some separation of white from negro prisoners as an element of administrative procedure, but this has been wholly a voluntary and local practice lacking any official legal sanction and recognition.

The next departure in point of time was with respect to the

---

[322] See above, pp. 119ff., 134ff.
[323] See above, pp. 134ff.

differentiation of criminals on the basis of mental states, though in its origins this process was most crude and incomplete. As a result of the work of Dorothea L. Dix, the Pennsylvania Society for Alleviating the Miseries of Public Prisons and other philanthropic societies and individuals, a state hospital for the insane was established at Harrisburg in the decade following 1840. Though this made no provision for the reception of insane prisoners, except as the result of a difficult process of transfer from the state penitentiaries, it was the initial step in a process which was carried on in the creation of more state hospitals for the insane and in the simplification of the machinery of transfer from penal institutions. It finally culminated in the opening of the state hospital for the criminal insane at Fairview in 1912. The first movement toward providing distinct institutions for the feeble-minded and idiotic came with the establishment in 1853 of the semi-state institution, now known as the Pennsylvania Training School for Idiotic and Feeble-Minded Children at Elwyn, in Delaware County. Not until 1897 was there provided a distinct state institution for the feeble-minded and idiotic, that at Polk created by the act of June 3, 1893, and opened four years later. The only attempt to provide a differentiation of convicts on the basis of the degree of criminality has been that mentioned above in the case of the juvenile institutions and the reformatories, where, however, the matter of separation according to age plays as great a part as the consideration of the type of criminal character of the inmates.

There has not been provided anything like a system of different institutions through which convicts may pass in progressive stages on their way to earning absolute freedom, as in the famous Irish system of prison organization. A slight step in this direction may be detected in the practice initiated by former Warden Francies of sending men to the new Rockview site preparatory to release on parole, but if the Riverside prison is abandoned this will no longer be possible. The separation according to the sexes has been fairly well provided for. In the state penitentiaries the women are confined in a separate building or wing. In 1925 the Legislature appropriated $100,000 for an additional building at the State Reformatory for Women at Muncy. This building is to receive older delinquent women; in other words, to be an institution for female criminals which would allow doing away with the women's wards in the state penitentiaries. The reformatories for men and women are wholly distinct institutions. In dealing with the juvenile delinquents the Glen Mills Schools have separate institutions for the boys and girls, while at Morganza the buildings for both sexes are on the same general grounds, but are grouped at

THE PHILADELPHIA HOUSE OF REFUGE, 1860

a considerable distance from each other. While the process of differentiating the delinquent class into its well-defined types and divisions has, thus, in Pennsylvania, only passed through the more rudimentary stages as yet, great progress has been made over the conditions which existed a century ago. This process of separation has at least gone far enough so that a system of progressive classification within each type of institution can have some validity as a mode of testing the fitness of the convicts for freedom.

The term "progressive classification of prisoners" was invented by Sir Walter Crofton, who, in his capacity as organizer of the Irish prisons after 1853, first perfected a comprehensive plan for conducting a prison system in a manner which would provide for the advancement of prisoners from the stage of solitary confinement to freedom on parole by means of successive promotion in definite classes, the progress being determined by the conduct of the convict. Crofton combined Maconochie's method [324] of determining the conduct of convicts by the "marks" which they earned, with the English procedure of advancing the convicts through three definite stages of confinement. The result was the famous "Irish" system of prison discipline. According to this ingenious and remarkably successful mode of prison administration and discipline the prisoner was gradually advanced from a condition of solitary confinement to parole through stages which permitted a progressively greater degree of freedom, the rapidity of the advancement depending upon the efforts of the convict to demonstrate his progress toward reformation and his willingness to conform to the rules of the system. Frederick H. Wines gives the following excellent summary of the system of progressive classification worked out by Crofton:

"The period of cellular incarceration was served at Mountjoy, where there was a prison in two departments, one for men and one for women. The second stage was that of 'progressive classification,' a phrase of which he was the author. His male prisoners were transferred from Mountjoy to Spike Island, where they were divided into five classes; the probation class, third, second, and first classes, and the advanced class. The probation class could be skipped by prisoners who had a good record at Mountjoy. The majority of those transferred were placed in the third class, where they had to earn nine marks per month for six months, or fifty-four marks in all, as the condition of promotion. The number of marks to be earned in the second class was the same; and in the first class, twice as many, so that they could not pass from the first to the advanced class in less than one year. Under the English

[324] See below, p. 399.

system, they would then have been entitled to a ticket-of-leave (i. e. parole), but Sir Walter would not grant it until after a test had been applied, in a condition of comparative freedom, at a third prison, called an intermediate prison, at Lusk, where they slept in movable iron huts and were occupied almost precisely as freemen would have been, in farming and manufacturing. The prison at Lusk had neither bars, bolts, nor walls. Its aim was to make practical proof of the prisoner's reformation, his power of self-control, his ability to resist temptation, and to train him for a considerable period—never less than six months—under natural conditions, and so to prepare him for full freedom by the enjoyment of partial freedom as a preliminary step." [325]

This advanced and enlightened procedure naturally attracted the favorable attention of the leading exponents of prison reform in this country. The publications of the New York Prison Association from 1866 to 1870 were in part devoted to expositions of this system and recommendations of its adoption. Gaylord B. Hubbell, the warden of Sing Sing, made a personal investigation of the system and published a favorable report in 1866. In their notable report on the prison systems of the United States and Canada E. C. Wines and Theodore W. Dwight stated in 1867 that they believed the Irish system the best type of prison administration yet devised. In the next year Z. R. Brockway, then of Detroit, and later Superintendent of the Elmira Reformatory, strongly urged the introduction of a system of sentencing and treatment similar to that worked out by Crofton. In 1869 New York State passed the bill which led to the establishment of the justly renowned Elmira Reformatory, which first applied in this country in a permanent and effective way the essentials of the Irish system of classification. At the same time when the New York Prison Association was working for the acceptance of the classification system in that state, Mr. Frank B. Sanborn, perhaps the most ardent American advocate of the Crofton system, prepared a detailed report on the Irish system for the Board of Charities of his own state of Massachusetts and for the New Jersey Commission on Prison Discipline of 1869, while at the epoch-making Cincinnati Prison Congress of 1870 he delivered the chief address in favor of bringing the Irish system into the United States. The Congress placed itself upon record as holding it both desirable and

---

[325] Wines, *Punishment and Reformation*, p. 190. The women prisoners passed through the same disciplinary system, though at different institutions. For the best brief treatment in English of the "Irish" system see Mary Carpenter, *Reformatory Prison Discipline as Developed by the Rt. Honorable Sir Walter Crofton in the Irish Convict Prisons.*

possible to apply this system to the prison administration of the United States. Its point of entry, however, came not in its general adoption by the state prisons, but in the reformatories for younger adult offenders guilty of the less heinous crimes, of which the Elmira institution, opened in 1876, was the first and most famous. From its successful operation in these institutions it has made some headway toward a timid and partial reception in a number of state prisons.

As was the case with nearly all of the progressive movements in prison reform in Pennsylvania the attitude with which the Irish system of classification was viewed differed widely on the part of the controlling authorities of the Eastern and Western Penitentiaries. The authorities of the Eastern Penitentiary opposed the Irish system from the first, primarily, no doubt, because its introduction would unquestionably have meant the abrogation of the Pennsylvania system of separate confinement and individual treatment. In their report for 1868 the inspectors said on this point:

"We feel justified in here suggesting the doubt, that, when the 'Irish system' is thoroughly investigated it will maintain the character now sought to be given to it. Like all novelties or expedients it is highly estimated. Experience will divest it of all its attractions. Just now, it is the newest phase of convict treatment, and most applauded where least understood. It is odd that so much invention is necessary to devise means to sustain the opposition to the Pennsylvania system. At last the philosophy of our penitentiary discipline and the laws essential to its integrity, as a system, must conquer opposition." [326]

Nor were the Cherry Hill officials any more enthusiastic in regard to the American application of the classification principle at Elmira. In 1883, Warden Cassidy, who had been so vigorous an opponent of the indeterminate sentence and parole,[327] attended a convention of prison officials at New York City in which the Elmira system received much attention. Mr. Cassidy maintained that he could arouse little enthusiasm in his own mind for this new type of prison administration. He summed up his reaction to the meeting in the following words:

"After hearing so much of herding and grading, congregation and classification, I am the more fully convinced that the individual treatment for people that have to be cared for in prisons for punishment for crime, is the simplest and most philosophical, and is productive of better results." [328]

---

[326] Annual Report of the Eastern Penitentiary, 1868, p. 80.
[327] See above, p. 317, note 305.
[328] Annual Report of the Eastern Penitentiary, 1883, p. 80.

The nineteenth century passed without any semblance of the system of classification in the Eastern Penitentiary. Had Joseph P. Byers remained long as warden following 1904, there is little doubt but that he would have established a true system of classifying and promoting prisoners, but his term of office was too short to be able to accomplish this feat. Only during the term of Mr. Robert J. McKenty, who became warden in 1909, was even a rudimentary form of classification adopted. Mr. McKenty established a general system of classification whereby convicts were entered in class "B" and might earn their advancement to class "A" by six months of good conduct. They were not eligible to parole at the expiration of their minimum sentence unless they were at that time in class A. Persistently bad conduct or gross violation of prison rules carried the penalty of reduction to class "C," from which the convicts had to earn their way back into class A. Because of the enforced idleness of the great majority of the convicts, for which the administrative officials were not responsible, this system of classification could have little positive value. No systematic arrangement for grading and promotion can be devised without an adequate industrial organization and the uniform employment of the convicts. Hence, about all that this system of classification and promotion could be said to accomplish was the retention for a longer period than the expiration of the minimum sentence of those who had been guilty of serious misconduct. The vast majority passed automatically into the advanced class and their promotion to this class meant little or nothing as regards their relative fitness for complete freedom. Nor did this method of promotion afford any real incentive to the prisoner for strenuous efforts for reformation and better conduct. After passing, almost without any positive effort, into the most advanced class he remained there until the expiration of his minimum sentence. Nothing that he could do would hasten his release and only marked and persistent misconduct could lose for him his position. At best, then, this was but a most elementary and essentially negative system, offering little positive inducements for the progressive improvement of the convict. For this condition, however, the officials of the institution were in no sense to be blamed, as they had done about as well as possible within the limitations imposed by the abominable laws regulating prison industry and the almost equally-to-be-condemned indeterminate sentence law of 1911.

In the Western Penitentiary the official setting was much better adapted for an open-minded and favorable reception of the system of classification associated with Crofton's methods. As has been pointed out above,[329] a new and more progressive board of inspect-

---

[329] See above, pp. 333-34.

ors had been appointed in 1864, and in 1866 had made the first significant attack on the Pennsylvania system of separate confinement. Mr. Theodore H. Nevin became president of this board in 1867 and for the next seventeen years held the inspectors in line with the developments in progressive penology. In 1869 there was appointed to the office of chaplain the Reverend John Lynn Milligan, who held that office for exactly forty years, and was during that time the mightiest force in the western part of the state in working for the cause of prison reform.[330] He attended most of the national and international prison congresses during his term of office, was thoroughly in sympathy with the newer penology, and his work stands out as the analogue in the western part of Pennsylvania of the achievements of the Pennsylvania Prison Society in the East. In the same year Mr. Edward S. Wright was appointed warden and he gave hearty support to all reform proposals which were not likely to arouse sufficient opposition to threaten his tenure. In such an environment the advanced procedure of classifying prisoners received an enthusiastic reception. The laws of the state would not, of course, permit the complete adoption of the Irish system, but some significant steps were taken to introduce many of its essential principles. In 1870 the officials of the institution visited the Cincinnati Prison Congress and listened to the exposition of the virtues of the method of classifying prisoners.[331] In their report for 1871 the inspectors stated that a plan had been devised for at least a rudimentary system of classification and promotion according to the conduct of the convicts. It was held to be a combination of the Pennsylvania, Auburn and Irish systems and was described in the following manner:

"We are not allied to either of the extremes of separate or congregate government: avoiding the rock of Scylla on the one hand, as well as the whirlpool of Charybdis on the other. We have endeavored to select from each that which was good, and by engrafting the one on the other, have, we think, hit upon the correct idea of an American prison.

"We have introduced three grades of cells:

"First. The punishment (not dark) cell, for the incorrigibles, where the prisoner is completely isolated—*severely let alone*—and has nothing to do.

"Second. The separate, or Pennsylvania cells; (a portion of one wing being appropriated for this purpose) where the occasional insubordinates are placed; they have work and books, but none of the other privileges of the institution.

---

[330] See also below, pp. 354ff.
[331] *Annual Report of the Western Penitentiary*, 1871, pp. 13, 77-8.

"Third. The ordinary cells, where all the well-behaved prisoners are kept, when not at work in the shops or yards.

"The idea of *disgrace* incurred and *promotion* secured, is encouraged in this way, and thus far with satisfactory results." [332]

A further development of this principle of a grading of prisoners on the basis of merit was urged by both the inspectors and Chaplain Milligan in 1872, both stating their warm advocacy of the Irish system.[333] Some progress in this direction is indicated by the following excerpt from the annual report of the institution for 1873:

"The combined system of congregate and separate imprisonment, as recently inaugurated in the management of this penitentiary, has thus far worked to our immediate satisfaction. The convict's prison life is a graded one, his promotion depends entirely upon himself; when he enters the prison he is placed in the first or lowest grade of privileges, in the solitary cell; and then step by step, as he shows himself worthy, he is advanced, until he reaches the highest point of honor and trust in the institution, among which are attendance upon the Church and Sabbath School services, the day school exercises, the congregate workshop and the coveted benefits of the commutation law. For misbehavior he goes back, on the downward scale, to the place of beginning." [334]

After the classification system had been generally adopted in the Elmira Reformatory its success attracted the attention of the liberal authorities of the Western Penitentiary and, as far as legal limitations would permit, they worked over their earlier system of grading into a method of classification consciously modeled after that employed by Mr. Brockway in Elmira. The details of this system were described by Warden Wright in his report for 1889-90. All convicts entered the prison in the so-called "second grade." Six months of good conduct entitled them to advancement to the first grade, in which they enjoyed special privileges. They were housed in the larger cells of the new south wing; they were allowed one hour more of light in their cells at night; they were freed from the necessity of marching in lock-step and of wearing the stigmatic prison stripe; and they obtained the benefits of the commutation law. Serious misconduct or gross violation of the prison rules operated to cause the reduction of the prisoner to the third grade, from which he was compelled to work himself back to the first by good conduct. In this third grade even the ordinary privileges enjoyed by those in the entering or second grade were

---

[332] *Annual Report of the Western Penitentiary,* 1871, p. 8.
[333] Ibid., 1872, pp. 11-2, 99-101.
[334] Ibid., 1873, p. 6.

denied to the convict.[335] This arrangement has been retained with but few changes to the present day. Since the beginning of the work on the Rockview site, marked good conduct by the convicts has been rewarded by a transfer to the much more desirable environment of the open country of Centre County. This has constituted a most important source of stimulation to better conduct, but it has been offset to some degree by the fact that since the law of 1897 has paralyzed the prison industries, the more or less general idleness at the Riverside site has tended to nullify much of the importance of the system of classification as applied to the convicts retained there.

At least a passing reference should be made here to the progress of the principle of classification in the reformatory and correctional institutions of Pennsylvania. As far as there is any evidence available nothing indicates that there was any system of progressive classification adopted in the Philadelphia House of Refuge opened in 1828. By 1870 it appears that in the second House of Refuge, erected in Philadelphia between 1850 and 1854, a very crude method of classification had been adopted. Class "A" consisted of the boys under fifteen years of age and class "B" of those older. A rather naïve attempt was also made to make these into something after the nature of behavior classes through putting incorrigible boys under fifteen in class B and boys over fifteen with a record of very good conduct in class A.[336] Two years later it was reported that this system had been displaced by a more extensive and scientific one devised to indicate and stimulate moral improvement.[337] When the boys were removed to the country site at Glen Mills in 1891 this system of classification was modified by the introduction of the cottage plan of housing and organization and to-day almost no form of definite behavior classification exists at Glen Mills. The girls' department, however, which was moved to its country location at Sleighton Farms in 1910, has judiciously combined the cottage system with that of classification on the basis of behavior. Neither the Western House of Refuge at Allegheny nor its successor, the Pennsylvania Training School at Morganza, has ever developed an adequate behavior classification, though the latter has adopted the cottage form of organization and a very liberal form of administrative discipline. The first Pennsylvania institution dealing with delinquents which made a thorough-going, systematic and effective application of the system of pro-

---

[335] *Annual Report of the Western Penitentiary,* 1889-90, p. 17.
[336] *First Annual Report of the Board of Commissioners of Public Charities of the State of Pennsylvania,* 1871, p. 43.
[337] Ibid., 1872, p. xxxii.

gressive classification of inmates was the Pennsylvania Industrial Reformatory, which, since its opening in 1889, has operated its disciplinary system according to the Elmira system of progressive classification and promotion. A similar method of differentiating inmates has been adopted in the new women's reformatory at Muncy.

E. The Separation of Mentally Abnormal Convicts and Their Psychological Analysis and Study under Clinical Observation

In no phase of penology has the progress been greater in the last century than in the growing recognition of the intimate correlation between mental abnormalities and criminal conduct.[338] This advance has, of course, been primarily a result of the unparalleled progress of psychiatry or medical psychology during this period. As long as insanity was regarded as produced by demoniacal possession, and idiocy was believed to be a divine curse on the individual due to ancestral indiscretions, it was no more possible to entertain a rational conception of abnormal mental states than it was to hold a valid notion of criminality when all types of criminals were indiscriminately viewed as "perverse free moral agents"—the victims of their own self-willed folly. Two influences, which had a somewhat parallel development, tended to destroy this barbarous theological heritage and make possible the present-day attitude on these questions. Both sprang from the contributions of the English *Deists* and the French *Philosophes* of the seventeenth and eighteenth centuries, who shattered the theological epic that had benumbed the human mentality for more than a thousand years, asserted the amenability of man to scientific study and investigation, and declared a healthy confidence in man's inherent decency and worth, which was the indispensable preliminary for humanitarian efforts to improve the earthly lot of mankind.[339] The beginning of a really scientific insight into the nature and problems of insanity is usually associated with the work of the Frenchman, Pinel (1745-1826), and there is no more honorable chapter in the history of medical and social science than the progress of psychiatry from Pinel to Charcot, Janet and Freud. The humanitarian current was continued in the work of reformers, such

---

[338] See the very authoritative and interesting treatment of this subject in William A. White's *Principles of Mental Hygiene,* Chapter V; and M. H. Smith, *The Psychology of the Criminal.*

[339] A brilliant and sympathetic treatment of the origin of this type of thought is contained in Robinson and Beard's *Development of Modern Europe,* Volume I, Chapter IX; and A. C. McGiffert, *Protestant Thought before Kant,* Chapter X.

Cottage at Sleighton Farms

as John Howard and Elizabeth Fry, and in the multifarious activities of the Quakers in social and penal reform. In the introduction of the humanitarian impulse into the treatment of the insane the name of an American woman, Dorothea Lynde Dix (1802-87) stands out beyond all others in this country or Europe. To her prodigious labors and untiring devotion to the cause of a more rational and humane treatment of this class of unfortunates is mainly due the establishment of hospitals for the insane in the United States during the second third of the last century.

As early as 1835 the inspectors of the Eastern Penitentiary complained of the administrative difficulties caused by the presence of insane convicts. The warden stated that "a minute inspection of the character of the unhappy inmates of prisons, has developed another interesting fact, that many more of them than was supposed are really irresponsible beings." He recommended the provision of a state institution for such individuals.[340] Nothing was done to remedy the situation and a decade later another vigorous complaint was made regarding the same problem.[341] That the same condition existed in the Western Penitentiary is apparent from a protest of its officers in 1845 against the necessity of having to house insane convicts in the institution.[342] In the year 1844 Miss Dix made a detailed investigation of the number of insane in the state penitentiaries, the county penal institutions and the alms houses, and set forth the amazing but deplorable conditions thereby revealed in a powerful "Memorial" to the state legislature requesting legislative sanction for the erection of a state hospital for the insane in Pennsylvania.[343] The Philadelphia Society for Alleviating the Miseries of Public Prisons ably seconded Miss Dix's plea in a supplementary "Memorial" to the legislature urging immediate action in establishing a state hospital for the insane.[344] Primarily as a result of these memorials the legislature passed the act of April 14, 1845, providing for the establishment of the Pennsylvania State Lunatic Hospital at Harrisburg.[345] The original act, however,

---

[340] *Annual Report of the Eastern Penitentiary,* 1835, *Senate Journal,* 1835, II, p. 326.

[341] Ibid., 1844, p. 23.

[342] *Annual Report of the Western Penitentiary,* 1845, *Senate Journal,* 1845, II, pp. 186-87.

[343] *Journal of Prison Discipline and Philanthropy,* Vol. I, Number 3, 1845, pp. 211-53. In January of the same year Miss Dix had submitted a similar "Memorial" to the legislature of New Jersey.

[344] Ibid., Vol. I, Number 2, 1845, pp. 190-99.

[345] *Laws of the General Assembly,* 1845, pp. 440ff; J. H. Fertig and Frank M. Hunter, *A Compilation of the Laws Relating to the Board of Public Charities with Important Provisions of the Laws Relating to the Several State Institutions and the Rules and Regulations of the Committee on Lunacy,* Harrisburg, 1916, pp. 115ff. (This was compiled for the Legislative Reference Bureau.)

made no adequate arrangements for the transfer of insane prisoners from the state penitentiaries to the hospital for the insane. In 1850 and 1851 the inspectors of the Eastern Penitentiary complained once more of the necessity of retaining insane prisoners in the institution.[346] By the provisions of an act of May 4, 1852, it was made possible for the authorities of the Eastern Penitentiary to transfer insane prisoners to the Harrisburg hospital, which had been opened in the previous October.[347] This privilege was, however not extended to the Western Penitentiary at this time.[348] The acts of March 24, 1858, and March 31, 1860, made a partial attempt to remedy this defect, but not until the passage of an act of May 14, 1874, was systematic provision made for the transfer of insane prisoners from both state penitentiaries to the appropriate state hospitals. The significant section of this act reads as follows:

"Whenever any person is imprisoned within the Commonwealth convicted of any crime whatever, or charged with any crime and acquitted on the ground of insanity, application in writing may be made by the warden, superintendent, physician or any inspector of the penitentiary or prison in which such person is imprisoned, or by the General Agent of the Board of Public Charities, to the court hereinafter named, or any law judge thereof, which application shall certify under oath or affirmation that such prisoner is believed to be insane, and shall request that such prisoner shall be removed to a hospital for the insane; whereupon it shall be lawful for any judge learned in the law of any court within this commonwealth having immediate cognizance of the crime with which such prisoner is charged, or of the court by which such prisoner has been convicted, to appoint a commission of three citizens of this Commonwealth, one of whom shall be of the profession of medicine, and one of the profession of the law, whose duty it shall be to inquire into and report the mental condition of such prisoner; and if in a report signed by a majority or all the members of such

---

[346] *Annual Report of the Eastern Penitentiary,* 1850, p. 28; Ibid., 1851, p. 14. The warden complained in 1851 that the Harrisburg hospital was designed to accept only the curable insane criminals and asserted that he would have to retain the incurables.

[347] *Laws of the General Assembly,* 1852, pp. 542f.; Fertig and Hunter, p. 117.

[348] The early provisions for the transfer of criminal insane from the Western Penitentiary were both crude and complicated. The Western Pennsylvania Hospital, a private institution, was incorporated by an act of March 18, 1848, and was allowed to establish an insane department, which was opened on January 18, 1853. By an act of March 19, 1856, the institutions took on a semi-state character through a provision allowing the state to appoint three members of the board of managers. The new buildings were opened at Dixmont in Allegheny on November 13, 1862. An act of March 24, 1858, allowed the Western Penitentiary to send insane prisoners to this institution, but another act of April 22, 1863, permitted the hospital to return all incurable insane convicts to the penitentiaries.

commission it shall appear that the prisoner inquired of is of unsound mind and unfit for penal discipline, it shall be lawful for the judge issuing such commission, or for any other judge of the same court learned in the law, to make an order under the seal of such court, directing the removal of such prisoner from the place of his or her imprisonment, and that he or she shall be received, maintained and cared for by the hospital for the insane, nearest to such place of imprisonment, and which shall or may receive aid or support from the treasury of the State, and that such patient shall be detained in such hospital, until an order, as hereinafter provided, shall be granted by the said court, or any judge thereof learned in the law, for the return of such prisoner to the penitentiary or prison from which he or she was removed, or for his or her discharge from such hospital: Provided always, That whenever any hospital shall be established especially for the care of insane patients who shall have been convicted of crime, or whenever separate accommodations shall be made for such patients, in any hospital aided from the treasury of the State, the order, as aforesaid, for the removal of any such person from his or her place of imprisonment, shall direct that he or she shall be received, maintained or cared for in such special hospital, or in the separate accommodations of any hospital prepared for such purpose." [349]

Elaborated to some extent by the act of May 8, 1883, this act of 1874 remains to the present day the law governing the transfer of insane convicts from the state penitentiaries to the state hospitals for the insane.[350]

Since the establishment of the original hospital for "lunatics" at Harrisburg, Pennsylvania has made provision for a number of similar institutions which can make at least a moderately decent pretention to housing the insane of the state. These additional state hospitals for the insane are: the State Hospital for the Insane at Danville in Montour County, established by an act of April 13, 1868, and opened on November 6, 1872;[351] the State Hospital for the Insane at Warren in Warren County, established by an act of August 14, 1873, and opened on October 6, 1880;[352] the State Hospital for the Insane at Norristown in Montgomery County, established by an act of May 5, 1876, and opened on July 12, 1880;[353] the State Asylum for the Chronic Insane at Wernersville

---

[349] *Laws of the General Assembly,* 1874, pp. 160ff; Fertig and Hunter, op. cit., pp. 41-2.

[350] *Laws of the General Assembly,* 1883, pp. 21ff; Fertig and Hunter, pp. 61-2.

[351] *Laws of the General Assembly,* 1868, pp. 90ff.; Fertig and Hunter, pp. 123f.

[352] *Laws of the General Assembly,* 1873, pp. 333ff.; Fertig and Hunter. pp. 124ff.

[353] *Laws of the General Assembly,* 1876, pp. 121ff.; Fertig and Hunter, pp. 126-27.

in Berks County, established by an act of June 22, 1891, and opened on June 28, 1893;[354] the Homeopathic State Hospital at Allentown in Lehigh County established by an act of July 18, 1901, and opened on October 3, 1912;[355] and the Western State Hospital for the Insane established by an act of July 18, 1915, and recently built and opened at Blairsville Intersection in Westmoreland County.[356] After a half-century of delay there has at last been provided a distinct state hospital for the criminal insane; this was established by an act of May 11, 1905, and was opened in a partially completed condition at Fairview in Wayne County on December 17, 1912.[357] To this institution may be sent the criminal insane from all parts of the state and from all state penal institutions. In addition to the above institutions of a public nature caring for the insane, there is the semi-state institution at Dixmont in Allegheny County. This existed down to July, 1907, as the insane department of the Western Pennsylvania Hospital of Pittsburgh, the partial state control dating from an act of March 19, 1856. By a judicial decree of July, 1907, it was made a distinct institution known as the Dixmont Hospital for the Insane.[358]

Nothing like as complete provision has been made for the care of the allied class of idiotic and feeble-minded, which is a much more numerous and, on the whole, a more difficult class than the insane.[359] The first step in this direction was taken by an act of April 7, 1853, which incorporated what is now known as the Pennsylvania Training School for Idiotic and Feeble-minded Children at Elwyn in Delaware County.[360] Like the Philadelphia House of Refuge this originated and has remained a semi-private institution. The first state institution of this type created in Pennsylvania was the State Institution for the Feeble-minded of Western Pennsylvania at Polk in Venango County, established by an act of June 3, 1893, and opened April 21, 1897.[361] Two others have since been provided, namely the Pennhurst State School for the Feeble-minded and Epileptic at Pennhurst in Chester County,

---

[354] *Laws of the General Assembly*, 1891, pp. 379ff.; Fertig and Hunter, pp. 127-29.

[355] *Laws of the General Assembly*, 1901, pp. 737ff.; Fertig and Hunter, pp. 129-30.

[356] *Laws of the General Assembly*, 1915, pp. 1055ff.; Fertig and Hunter, pp. 132-33.

[357] *Laws of the General Assembly*, 1905, pp. 400ff.; Fertig and Hunter, pp. 131-32.

[358] *Laws of the General Assembly*, 1856, pp. 135ff.; Fertig and Hunter, pp. 163ff.

[359] See on this subject, H. H. Goddard, *The Criminal Imbecile*.

[360] *Laws of the General Assembly*, 1853, pp. 341ff.

[361] Ibid., 1893, pp. 289ff.; Fertig and Hunter, op. cit., pp. 133ff.

established by an act of May 15, 1903, and still uncompleted, though it has been opened for the reception of patients; [362] and the Pennsylvania Village for Feeble-minded Women at Laurelton in Union County, established by an act of July 25, 1913, and still in process of construction.[363]

Pennsylvania is making provision for two institutions for defective delinquents. The Laurelton State Village, opened about a decade ago, has been transformed into an institution which receives feeble-minded delinquent females of the child-bearing age. In other words, it is for women and girls above the juvenile court age. Another institution is now in process of erection at New Cumberland. This is to be for defective male delinquents. "This institution, when built, will receive all mentally defective men who have run afoul of the law, except those who have been convicted of murder in the first degree. They may be committed when charged with a criminal offence, or after arraignment and conviction, or may be transferred there if already serving in a penal institution."

In recent years the progress in abnormal psychology has definitely demonstrated that chronic inebriety is but a form of psychic instability and aberration rather than a special and obstinate form of voluntary perverseness. In accordance with the recognition of the significance of this undoubted fact the legislature passed an act on July 25, 1913, authorizing the establishment of a state institution for inebriates, but unfortunately little has been done to carry out this laudable intention.[364]

While no one would deny enthusiastic support to the movement for a better and more thorough care of the more grossly mentally abnormal types, such as the insane and the idiotic and epileptic, it is coming to be generally recognized that this is but the feeble beginning of the desirable application of medical psychology to the solution of the problems of penal administration. To remove from the prison the violently insane is but to prepare the way for the examination of the psychic characteristics of those who remain and may be suffering from less obvious mental and nervous disorders. Though it is impossible to deny a considerable weight to the economic and social factors in the causation of crime [365] it has now come to be generally recognized that to a hitherto wholly

---

[362] *Laws of the General Assembly,* 1903, pp. 446ff.; Fertig and Hunter, pp. 136ff.

[363] *Laws of the General Assembly,* 1913, pp. 1319ff.; Fertig and Hunter, pp. 140ff.

[364] *Laws of the General Assembly,* 1913, pp. 1306ff.; Fertig and Hunter, pp. 143-44.

[365] Cf. W. A. Bonger, *Criminality and Economic Conditions.*

unsuspected degree, crime is the product of mental abnormality and instability. Even those convicts whose criminality seems traceable to adverse economic status or unfavorable social environment often fall into these strata or circumstances which invite crime because of mental conditions which prevent them from making a normal adjustment to the problems of existence. Doctor William A. White, one of the most eminent of living psychiatrists, has thus summarized the very significant prevalence of mental and nervous disease in the convict population:

"A considerable proportion of the prison population are not normal in their developmental possibilities. Upwards of fifty per cent as they are admitted have demonstrable disease at the central nervous system level. That is, they are mentally defective, psychotic, or have gross central nervous system disease such as arteriosclerosis or syphilis. This does not include bodily diseases other than those of the central nervous system." [366]

This estimate given by Doctor White is not only conservative, but is based on fairly concrete and scientific evidence which is continually being confirmed by every investigation in this field. Doctor William Healy by his close personal study of delinquency in Chicago and Boston, particularly among juveniles, has found a close correlation between psychic aberration and criminal behavior.[367] Among the most thorough and convincing studies which have been made in this field is one which has been carried on in the psychopathic clinic opened at Sing Sing Prison in New York State, in August, 1916, under the direction of Doctor Bernard Glueck. A careful investigation of the psychic state of six hundred and eight convicts consecutively admitted revealed the significant fact that three hundred and fifty-nine, or fifty-nine per cent., were so abnormal or subnormal in mentality as to be readily detected, while there was reason to believe that a more extended analysis of the remaining forty-one per cent. would have demonstrated many of them to be mentally unstable.[368]

Another simultaneous investigation was carried on by Doctor A. L. Jacoby at the United States Naval Prison at Portsmouth, New Hampshire, following November 1, 1917. After a careful and exceedingly comprehensive examination of the court-martialed sailors sent to the prison Doctor Jacoby arrived at the conclusion that fifty-four per cent. were suffering from serious mental or

---

[366] W. A. White, *The Principles of Mental Hygiene*, p. 143. Cf. P. A. Parsons, *Crime and the Criminal*, Chaps. vii-viii.
[367] William Healy, *Mental Conflicts and Misconduct; Pathological Lying and Swindling; Delinquents and Criminals.*
[368] Bernard Glueck, in *Mental Hygiene*, January, 1918, pp. 85-151; April, 1918, pp. 177-216; October, 1918, pp. 546-56.

nervous disorders which should have been detected at the time of enlistment, and that an additional twelve per cent. had developed mental or nervous disease subsequent to their entry into the naval service. In other words, at least two-thirds of those naval prisoners were distinctly abnormal, mentally or nervously, and one-third of this abnormal group was of distinctly subnormal mentality. These statistics are of particular significance as being based upon the examination of a special class of prisoners drawn from what would be theoretically at least a select group from which the unhealthy or inferior individuals had been eliminated by severe tests at the time of enlistment.[369]

Another very reliable investigation which has been made in America of the psychological state of criminals was that conducted by Doctors Healy and Bronner embodying some 4,000 selected cases. They found the distribution to be as follows:

Normal (including border-line cases)..............63%
Psychopathic 23%
Feeble-minded (low-grade morons, imbeciles and
    idiots) 14%

Ten years ago it was believed that feeble-mindedness would account for most criminality, because it was found that in prisons around half of the population was below the line separating the dull normal from the average normal person. The army mental tests, however, revealed a similar condition for the population at large, and the tests made at Leavenworth and by Doctor Carl Murchison have definitely proved that feeble-mindedness is not markedly more prevalent among even the apprehended criminals than among the general population. Nevertheless, this does not tell the whole story, because, with only fourteen per cent. of the criminal feeble-minded, Healy and Bronner found that among the more serious types of delinquents feeble-mindedness appears to from five to ten times as frequently as among the normal population. Professor William T. Root recently made an interesting study of 1,916 prisoners in the Western Penitentiary which revealed the following distribution:

Superior types 67
Normal 296
Border-line and dull normal 822
Morons 661
Imbeciles 70

---

[369] *Mental Hygiene,* January, 1919, pp. 137-41.

In the matter of providing for this more advanced and scientific entry of psychiatry into the solution of the problems of successfully dealing with the criminal class, Pennsylvania has not made any progress comparable to that achieved in the erection of hospitals for the insane and in making it possible to transfer the insane convicts to these institutions. In this respect, however, Pennsylvania is not different from most of the other commonwealths of the United States. There has been little or nothing done to make a psychiatric clinic a part of the administrative mechanism of the penal institutions of the country. Even that at Sing Sing was merely tolerated by the state of New York while being supported by a private foundation for scientific research.[370] Attempts to introduce this indispensable element into penological practice have normally done little more than to furnish the occasion for coarse and ignorant banter and buffoonery by legislators wholly unacquainted with the essentials of the question at issue.[371] Though it will doubtless require many years to educate the public as to the vital significance of the careful psychological examination, differentiation and treatment of the inmates of all penal institutions, the evidence at hand to-day justifies the assertion that until this innovation is accepted American penology can scarcely be held to have penetrated beyond the most superficial externals of a scientific curative or reformatory treatment of the delinquent class.

Of the six state penal, reformatory and correctional institutions in Pennsylvania only one—the Girls' Department of the Glen Mills Schools—had up to 1918 made the slightest attempt to make use of the progress of modern psychology in the study and treatment of the inmates of these institutions. Here a psychologist had been added to the staff in order to study the mental conditions of the children committed and to suggest the best method of dealing with

---

[370] To the writer's knowledge only the state of Illinois has created an office of state criminologist in order to make possible the development of a systematic study of the mental traits of convicts. A Massachusetts law passed in 1921 and subsequently strengthened provides for the compulsory psychiatric examination of: (1) those indicted for capital offenses; (2) those indicted for any other offense more than once; (3) those previously convicted of a felony.

[371] A fair sample of the difficulty of obtaining adequate legislative support for this essential department of penological research and procedure was brought out in a bill introduced in the Massachusetts legislature in 1919 to provide for the psychiatric examination of the inmates of the state penal institution. The discussion of the bill consisted in almost unrelieved buffoonery which culminated in the remark of Senator Cavanaugh that "a psychiatrist is a nut employed to chase another nut." It is needless to remark that the bill was rejected. In 1921, however, a law was actually passed in Massachusetts providing for the psychological examination of the inmates of the penal institutions and jails of the state.

the various types while at the institution and of fitting them in the best manner for ultimate freedom.[372] It should be noted, however, that some of the more progressive officials of the other institutions had expressed their sympathy with the employment of psychiatry in penal administration and their willingness to make use of this valuable aid to their disciplinary and reformatory system when legislative sanction makes it possible for them to do so.[373] The gulf which separated the state penal institutions from an adequate appreciation and utilization of medical psychology a decade ago is apparent from the statement in the report of the Eastern Penitentiary for 1917 that only twenty out of five hundred and seventy-two convicts admitted during the year were mentally abnormal in any degree.[374] In other words, only a little over three per cent. were designated as mentally unsound. Under the system introduced by the Department of Public Welfare the scheme of providing for mental examinations of inmates has been extended from the institutions for children to the state reformatories for men and women at Huntingdon and Muncy respectively, and has now been introduced into the Western Penitentiary through the cooperation of Warden Ashe and Professor William T. Root of the University of Pittsburgh.

F.   The Sterilization and Segregation of the Feeble-minded Classes and the Habitual Criminal

Owing to the alarming increase of this class and its special menace to the community, much of the best social investigation in recent years has been devoted to a study of the defective and degenerate element in the general population. A number of classic investigations of congenitally defective and degenerate families by Dugdale, Goddard, McCulloch and Blackmar have revealed with a wealth of incontrovertible evidence the disastrous results which attend the promiscuous and unrestricted breeding of defectives and degenerates.[375] The general dissolution of the theological view of the causation of defective and degenerate personalities and the development of the scientific knowledge regarding the transmission of congenital defects has at last indicated the only possible method

---

[372] *Annual Report of the Glen Mills Schools,* 1916, pp. 50-3.
[373] This attitude was expressed to the writer by Warden Francies of the Western Penitentiary and Superintendent Penn of the Training School at Morganza.
[374] *Annual Report of the Eastern Penitentiary,* 1917, p. 61.
[375] Cf. R. L. Dugdale, *The Jukes;* H. H. Goddard, *The Kallikak Family;* F. W. Blackmar, *The Smoky Pilgrims;* O. C. McCulloch, *The Tribe of Ishmael;* P. A. Parsons, *Responsibility for Crime,* Chapter V.

of ridding society of this small but ever increasing degenerate element, from which a considerable proportion of the paupers, criminals and other social derelicts are recruited. The sole manner of procedure whereby this class can be speedily eliminated, before it becomes so large as to drag down the normal population in a common destruction, is to segregate or sterilize all of its members. The former expedient, while arousing less traditional resistance and opposition, is attended with great expense, and the much simpler and more humane method of sterilizing those members of the defective class that can be safely trusted outside of an institution has of late met with favor among biologists and physicians.

It should, of course, be pointed out that we no longer believe that the sterilization and segregation of defectives is the complete panacea for crime which they were believed to be ten years ago. In the first place, the best investigations have shown that feeble-mindedness is no more important than psychopathic mental states, for the most part non-hereditary, in accounting for crime. In the second place, it has now been pretty clearly demonstrated that not all feeble-mindedness is hereditary and capable of obstruction through sterilization.[375a] At the same time, this is no argument against the wholesale sterilization of the feeble-minded types. From the standpoint of both eugenics and population limitation this practice is most desirable, and its aid to the repression of criminality can not be denied.

If this policy were systematically pursued it would be a conservative prediction to state that in fifty years the defective and degenerate classes would be greatly reduced and the criminal class proportionately diminished. Most states have begun to make some pretense at custodial segregation of the worst types of the idiotic and the feeble-minded, and seventeen [376] have legalized the sterilization of the hopelessly defective and the habitually criminal, but the law has been applied even partially only in California and Wisconsin. In the case of Carrie Buck vs. the State of Virginia in the spring of 1927, the United States Supreme Court upheld the constitutionality of sterilization laws as applied to the feeble-minded.

The progress made by Pennsylvania in regard to the segregation of the feeble-minded and idiotic has been summarized in a preceding section, but it will be apparent from this sketch that only the most elementary beginning has been made even in this

---

[375a] Cf. Abraham Myerson, *The Inheritance of Mental Diseases.*

[376] California, Connecticut, Indiana, Iowa, Kansas, Michigan, Nevada, New Jersey, New York, Washington, Wisconsin, North Dakota, South Dakota, Colorado, Nebraska, Oregon and Virginia.

field of endeavor, as provision is made for the segregation of only a part of the juvenile defectives and very little provision has been made for the proper detection and segregation of the adults belonging to this class. The sterilization of the defectives, degenerates and habitual criminals has never yet received even serious consideration by the legislature. It is, however, worthy of note that perhaps the best study yet made of convict mentality has just been executed in the Western Penitentiary by William T. Root and G. Giardini, *A Psychological and Educational Survey of 1916 Prisoners in the Western Penitentiary of Pennsylvania* (1926).

G. The Progress of Educational Policy in the State Penitentiaries

(1) MORAL AND RELIGIOUS INSTRUCTION

The provision of moral and religious instruction in the Eastern Penitentiary takes its most remote origin in the beginning of preaching in the Walnut Street Jail, as a part of the general reform movement in that institution following 1787.[377] Down to 1838, however, all religious and moral instruction which was given was the work of volunteer clergymen from Philadelphia and neighboring towns and of the visitors from the Philadelphia Society for Alleviating the Miseries of Public Prisons. In 1838 the legislature authorized the appointment of a moral instructor.

"It shall be lawful for the Inspectors of the Penitentiary of the Eastern District of Pennsylvania to elect or appoint, as soon after the passage of this resolution as they may deem proper, an officer in the said Penitentiary, who shall be called a Moral Instructor, whose duty it shall be to advise and instruct the prisoners therein confined in their moral and religious obligations, and perform such other services as shall, in the opinion of the said Inspectors, appertain to his station, and the said officer shall receive, as a remuneration for his services, a sum not exceeding eight hundred dollars per annum; the said officer to hold his situation during the pleasure of the said Inspectors." [378]

The religious services in the Eastern Penitentiary, except for some special exercises in the small improvised chapel recently provided, have always been held in the corridors of the institution. Not until 1913 was it legal for the prisoners to be congregated for any purpose whatever, and this made impossible any general chapel services, even if such a structure had been available in which to have the convicts assembled. The unfavorable circumstances

---

[377] See above, pp. 85ff.
[378] *Laws of the General Assembly,* 1837-38, p. 690.

under which these sermons were delivered, allowing the convicts to sleep or read during the preaching and preventing them from seeing the preacher or hearing him distinctly, have served to destroy most of whatever value may be held to reside in these religious exercises. In addition to the preaching, other methods of disseminating religious ideas were utilized, especially the distribution of literature. In 1846 it was stated that over thirty thousand religious tracts had been distributed to the prisoners.[379] Bibles were also distributed among the prisoners, as is indicated by the following excerpt from the report of the inspectors for 1885:

"A copy of the 'Holy Scriptures, which is able to make wise unto salvation,' is placed in each cell, and very generally read. Some of the prisoners commit large portions to memory. These Sacred writings with other devotional books liberally supplied contain the 'good seed sown,' even the 'bread cast upon the waters which shall be found after many days.' "[380]

The prison library, established in 1844, was also heavily stocked with religious books, though it seems that great difficulty was met in persuading the prisoners to make an extensive use of this type of literature. In 1853 the moral instructor complained that books were often given to the prison library which were not "of a strictly religious kind," and stated that this resulted in an alarming decline in the call for religious books; "the religious department of our Library, crowded with unused books, is a standing proof to the reality of this result."[381]

There seems little doubt, however, that in spite of all the religious work accomplished by the prison authorities much the most important factor in the religious life of the institution was the visits carried on by the representatives of the Philadelphia Society for Alleviating the Miseries of Public Prisons.[382] From the erection of the Eastern Penitentiary to the present day this society has not only been the chief force in Pennsylvania prison reform, but also the main influence in the moral guidance of the prisoners. To this fact the prison authorities have been the first to testify.[383] It was stated that in 1862 the visitors from the society had about nine thousand interviews with prisoners, these averaging fifteen minutes in duration.[384] While there are many honorable names

[379] *Annual Report of the Eastern Penitentiary,* 1846, p. 71.
[380] Ibid., 1885, p. 108.
[381] Ibid., 1853, p. 36.
[382] Ibid., 1855, pp. 16, 31-2, 44; Ibid., 1873-74, p. 192; Ibid., 1890, p. 121; Ibid., 1896, p. 143; Ibid., 1904, p. 12.
[383] Ibid.
[384] *The Journal of Prison Discipline and Philanthropy,* 1862, pp. 53ff.

among the members who gave liberally of their time to visiting the convicts, the most indefatigable of all was Mr. John J. Lytle, general secretary of the society from 1887 to 1909.[385] In recent years these religious conferences with the convicts have also been carried on by representatives of the American Society for Visiting Catholic Prisoners, the Protestant Episcopal City Mission, the Salvation Army and several other religious and benevolent organizations.[386] The moral instructor has also been aided in conducting religious services by visiting Catholic and Jewish clergymen, who have charge of the religious services for their co-religionists.

The Western Penitentiary was not provided with a moral instructor until a year later than the Eastern institution. In their reports for 1837 and 1838 the inspectors requested the provision of a moral instructor and in 1839 exhorted the legislature to "give us, we beseech you, a moral instructor with adequate compensation." [387] An act of March 25, 1839, accordingly declared:

"It shall be lawful for the inspectors of the Western Penitentiary to elect or appoint, as soon after the passage of this act as they deem proper, an officer of the said penitentiary, whose duty it shall be to communicate intellectual and moral instruction to the convicts, in such manner as may be directed by the inspectors, and said officer shall have such sum as may be agreed upon by the inspectors, not to exceed seven hundred dollars, and said officer is to hold his position during the pleasure of the said inspectors." [388]

In their report for 1840 the inspectors stated that they had selected as moral instructor, "Rev. Joseph Banks, whose capacity for the gracious work and unremitting zeal in behalf of the highest interests of the unhappy subjects of his charge, the Inspectors take pleasure in offering their testimony." [389] The moral instructor himself further stated that there was preaching in each cell block on Sunday and that he made personal visits to the convicts in their cells.[390] In their next report the inspectors stated that the moral instructor was unable to submit his report on account of illness, but they assured the legislature that "his benign labors have blessed us with

---

[385] *The Journal of Prison Discipline and Philanthropy,* 1887, p. 27; Ibid., 1911, pp. 69-71; *Annual Report of the Eastern Penitentiary,* 1904, p. 12.

[386] *Annual Report of the Eastern Penitentiary,* 1904, p. 12.

[387] *Annual Report of the Western Penitentiary,* 1837, in *House Journal,* 1836-37, Vol. II, p. 411; Ibid., 1838, *Senate Journal,* 1837-38, Vol. II, pp. 247ff; Ibid., 1839, *Senate Journal,* 1838-39, Vol. II. p. 225.

[388] *Laws of the General Assembly,* 1838-39, Chap. 66.

[389] *Annual Report of the Western Penitentiary,* 1840, *Senate Journal,* 1840, Vol. II, p. 256.

[390] Ibid., pp. 263-64.

some hopeful results." [391] In his report for 1846 the moral instructor described his labors in the following manner:

"According to the directions given me, I have regularly visited all the prisoners shut up within these walls, passing from cell to cell, in daily connection with them, teaching the ignorant and uneducated the first rudiments of learning, and directing the attention of all to the Lamb of God which taketh away the sins of the world. If any fruits unto everlasting life have followed these labors it is because the spirit of God worketh by such instrumentality." [392]

Another phase of the duties of the moral instructor was touched upon in his report for 1850:

"Seven prisoners died within the year. They were all visited during the time of their severe illness. Their attention was often and earnestly directed to Jesus Christ, the only Savior. Some of them gave evidence of repentance towards God, and faith in the Lord Jesus Christ, and others seemed to die as the fool dieth." [393]

That the moral instructors capitalized the convicts' condition to aid in their campaign for the saving of souls is evident from the statement of the moral instructor in 1854 that he aimed especially to "impress upon the prisoners the need of a savior in order to obtain everlasting life, which is a *life of freedom*." [394] Unlike the Eastern Penitentiary, the Allegheny institution was early provided with a chapel. As soon as it was made legal to congregate prisoners by the law of 1869 a chapel seating six hundred and fifty was immediately erected.[395] When the new structure was built at Riverside a chapel was provided. Though it was soon outgrown, it has been adequate in the last few years on account of sending many prisoners to the new site at Rockview.

In 1869 Doctor John Lynn Milligan began his forty years of service as moral instructor at the Western Penitentiary. A student at college under E. C. Wines, Doctor Milligan was one of those early philanthropists who, like Louis Dwight, E. C. Wines and F. H. Wines, came to the field of prison reform with a theological or ministerial background. He was a leading figure in American prison reform, serving for twenty years as secretary of the American Prison Association, and also took part in most of the international prison congresses of his day. He combined to a rare

---

[391] *Annual Report of the Western Penitentiary*, 1841, *Senate Journal*, 1841, Vol. II, pp. 411-12.
[392] Ibid., 1846, *House Journal*, 1846, Vol. II, p. 164.
[393] Ibid., 1850, *Senate Journal*, 1850, Vol. II, p. 629.
[394] Ibid., 1854, *Legislative Documents*, 1854, p. 287.
[395] See above, pp. 208, 308-9.

degree a strong spiritual impulse, free from sanctimonious hypocrisy, with a practical sense of the necessity of better administrative and disciplinary machinery in order effectively to carry out any program of convict reformation. He recognized that prayer, exhortation and personal conferences must be supplemented by a classification of prisoners, commutation for good behavior, education and the indeterminate sentence and parole. In his later years he tended toward reminiscence in his reports, and in that for 1906 he included a most valuable survey of the changes he had noted in the Western Penitentiary during nearly a half-century of personal contact with it:

"When I assumed my duties it was in the old castle-like prison in West Park—there then, and for long years previously, the fundamental control was based on the 'solitary confinement plan.' Each cell was a costly little prison in itself.

"The unnatural isolation was not looked upon favorably by the progressive Board of Inspectors and the kind hearted warden. The character of the industries was cellular and antiquated. The financial returns were meager, but the methods were honored by age, and hence firmly fixed. 'They long bore the ills they had rather than fly to others they knew not of' with increasing resentment.

"They well knew that the proposed and desired changes which lay in their minds would be a severe jolt to the old methods.

"The architectural construction had aimed only to secure the safekeeping of the prisoners, regardless of sufficient natural light and fresh air necessary to the cure of the morbid mental condition invoked by the surrounding of the inmates of the cells.

"Two strong doors, one of oak plank lined with iron, and the other door solid boiler plate iron, opened from the corridors to the cell—the prisoner's home for the period of his sentence. A small opening near the top of the inner door, closed by an adjustable slide, was where the daily food was passed to the inmate. The ceilings and floors of the cells were solid stone, so also the outside wall in which a narrow vertically inclined gash was cut for the purpose of admitting all the air and natural light that the prisoner enjoyed.

"Here in this tomb-like limitation he lived and ate and did the work appointed to him. On Sabbath day here was also his church.

"The old crazy loom for weaving cloth was his constant and only companion.

"All these conditions served to more deeply depress his mind and certainly unfit him for manful conflict in free life competition at the end of his sentence.

"At the Sunday services which were conducted in each corridor, with the prisoners standing in cell with their ears at the opening of the slide in the inner iron door and the outside door ajar a few inches and held on a short chain, he might catch some of the music and the words of the speaker through the limited avenues of stone and iron.

"It was not to be expected that the Hon. Charles Dickens in his American notes would fail to tell England what he saw in our prisons.

"This was my environment for public religious services for a few Sabbaths after I began my life work in prison. Its short duration was a great relief.

"The application which the brave inspectors made, strengthened by the conjointed appeals of some true philantropists to the legislature, brought the enactment of a law, brief in words but mighty in its transforming power of the old regime.

"This law gave to the inspectors the privilege to congregate the prisoners for 'labor, learning and worship.'

"Then both cell doors were thrown wide open: The prisoners bringing their stools came out and seated themselves in the corridor at their cells where they could see each other and hear all the services.

"To them, these new and free methods of public religious services much more emphasized the meaning of liberty and love.

"Under this strange condition to them, the order and attention were perfect.

"Soon a commodious chapel was erected and the prisoners were assembled for hearing the Gospel on Sabbath morning; under more natural and normal conditions, classes for the study of the Bible were formed for the Sabbath afternoon.

"A schoolroom was improvised and a day school started for elementary instruction.

"Workshops followed and soon the inspectors realized that they had met loyal approval for the good that had come even amid the unfavorable buildings.

"Then with the same courage, they proposed a new prison in which the old past conditions should have no place. That great wish has been accomplished. 'Riverside,' as they called the enlarged prison, now stands as monument to their memory." [395a]

As the Western Penitentiary has increased in population and its inmates have been divided between the Riverside and Rockview sites the number of moral instructors has been increased to four, a Catholic and Protestant clergyman at each site. In addition, Jewish rabbis make regular visits to the institution to conduct services for the Hebrew inmates. No aid in this field comparable to that of the Philadelphia Society for Alleviating the Miseries of Public Prisons in the Eastern Penitentiary has been rendered

---

[395a] *Biennial Report of the Western Penitentiary*, 1905-06, pp. 92-4.

to the Western Penitentiary. For some time the Allegheny Prison Society gave effective assistance in visiting prisoners and aiding discharged prisoners,[396] but their work has long since ceased.

(2) ACADEMIC EDUCATION

While the moral instructor at the Eastern Penitentiary rendered important assistance in teaching ignorant convicts, and the visiting members of the Philadelphia Society for Alleviating the Miseries of Public Prisons also gave aid in this way, the educational facilities of the Cherry Hill institution have from a very early date been in the hands of a special teacher for illiterates and those with a meager education. His efforts have, however, always been handicapped by the system of solitary confinement which, until 1913, forbade the congregation of prisoners for educational, as well as for religious and industrial purposes. This has made impossible the more effective and expeditious method of teaching the illiterate convicts in classes where the same explanation and exposition of the lesson would suffice for a score or more of students. Information has necessarily been imparted through private lessons in separate cells down to very recent times. The office of teacher began as one to which the incumbent gave only a part of his time, the rest being occupied in the capacity of an inspector of prison industries. As the number of prisoners gradually increased he transferred more and more of his attention to teaching. Until the last few years the instruction was limited almost wholly to teaching reading, writing and arithmetic—the "3 R's"—to illiterates; only in the last ten or fifteen years has there been any consistent attempt to give advanced academic or vocational instruction. The beginnings of a distinct educational department in the Eastern Penitentiary go back to 1844, when a teacher was appointed to give a part of his time to imparting elementary instruction to the unschooled convicts, the remainder of his time being devoted to supervising a part of the industrial operations of the institution. The inspectors commented on this innovation in their report for the year, "a schoolmaster has, thus, been successfully introduced into the prison, whose chief duty it is to teach the ignorant to read and write, and practical arithmetic." [397] That these modest beginnings were at least successful on a small scale is evident from the numerous references in the annual reports of the institution to the successful work of the teacher.[398] By 1859 about

---

[396] Cf. *Annual Report of the Western Penitentiary*, 1878, p. 22.

[397] *Annual Report of the Eastern Penitentiary*, 1844, p. 15.

[398] Ibid., 1845, p. 13; 1846, p. 29; 1852, p. 15; 1854, pp. 9-10, 33-4; 1858, pp. 10-1.

eighteen hundred lessons were given annually to the convicts, and in the following year it was reported that twenty-three hundred lessons had been given.[399] The activities of the teacher increased until, by 1874, about sixty-seven hundred lessons were given by the teacher in the years 1873-74.[400] By 1881 it had become necessary to have a separate teacher who gave all of his time to instructing illiterate prisoners in reading, writing and arithmetic and to caring for the greatly augmented library.[401] In 1881 the teacher had two hundred and forty-seven pupils on his list, and by 1895 this number had increased to three hundred and thirty-five, though there is no doubt but that this increase was in part due to the growth of the prison population during this interval.[402] Under Warden McKenty the educational facilities in the Eastern Penitentiary were notably strengthened and the school ranked well with those of the average person of the country. The instruction extended from the beginning class for illiterates through the grammar school grades. The sessions were held daily from eight-thirty to eleven-fifteen in the forenoon and from twelve-thirty to four in the afternoon. All uneducated prisoners were required to attend the sessions of the school. At the close of the year 1917 there were six hundred and thirteen on the prison school list. The prison school at the Eastern Penitentiary has been continued, with inmate instruction, under Warden Groome. In addition to the work of the regular teacher, the visitors of the Philadelphia Society for Alleviating the Miseries of Public Prisons have rendered valuable assistance in giving instruction to the illiterate convicts.

Next to the work of the prison school the most effective educational agency has been the library. This was also established in 1844 through a gift of a number of books by one of the inspectors, Mr. J. Bacon. The inspectors remarked that through this innovation "punishment is made a positive blessing to the ignorant." [403] The number of volumes in the library has had a steady growth from this time. In 1854, 2,000 volumes were reported.[404] This number had grown to 8,500 in 1881; [405] to 9,000 in 1895; and to 10,499 in 1926. The increase in the size of the library has required the services of a special librarian, no less than 54,000 books being issued in 1917.[406]

---

[399] *Annual Report of the Eastern Penitentiary,* 1860, pp. 50-1.
[400] Ibid., 1873-74, p. 223.
[401] Ibid., 1881, p. 97; 1883, pp. 108-11.
[402] Ibid., 1881, p. 97; 1895, pp. 142-43.
[403] Ibid., 1844, pp. 15-6.
[404] Ibid., 1854, p. 29.
[405] Ibid., 1881, p. 95.
[406] Ibid., 1917, p. 77.

While no special teacher of prisoners was appointed in the Western Penitentiary until 1873, the instruction of convicts goes back to a much earlier date. In the first report of the moral instructor, that for 1840, it was stated that each convict able to read was supplied with a spelling-book, an arithmetic and a slate.[407] In their report for 1844 the inspectors asserted that "the moral instructor has devoted as much time to teaching reading, writing and the simple rules of arithmetic, as appeared to him compatible with his moral and ministerial obligations to the institution." [408] The next year they reported that the moral instructor "teaches the unlettered to read and write, and comprehend the beauty and usefulness of their mother-tongue." [409] In 1856 the inspectors said that "aside from the regular ministration of his sacred office on Sunday, during the residue of the week the moral instructor visits the prisoners from cell to cell, teaching the illiterates to read and write; exhorting the vicious, infusing into their hardened natures wholesome truths, and preparing them not only for their final responsibility, but upon their discharge hence to encounter the world's criticism and the world's charity." [410] The law of 1869, allowing the congregation of convicts in the Western Penitentiary, made it possible for the first time to organize classes for instruction in any Pennsylvania penal institution. As might have been expected from so ardent an apostle of prison reform, Chaplain Milligan at once organized a class for instruction in "the rudiments of knowledge," but complained of the lack of an adequate schoolroom. In addition to those pursuing the more elementary studies, it was asserted that six were studying algebra, one geometry and four Latin and Greek.[411] In 1873, as a part of the general reform movement following 1869, a prison day school was established with a regular teacher for this purpose. The teacher was Mr. Joseph S. Travelli, who filled the position with eminent success until the school was temporarily abandoned in 1881.[412] By 1875 there were about three hundred in the prison school and in the year 1880 about seven hundred received instruction.[413] In 1881 the flourishing day school was for some reason abandoned, probably because of the demand for the labor of the prisoners by the contractors. By 1886, however, contract convict labor had come to an end in Penn-

---

[407] *Annual Report of the Western Penitentiary*, 1840, *Senate Journal*, 1840, Vol. II, p. 263.
[408] Ibid., 1844, *Senate Journal*, 1844, Vol. II, p. 56.
[409] Ibid., 1845, *Senate Journal*, 1845, Vol. II, p. 186.
[410] Ibid., 1856, *Legislative Documents*, 1856, p. 375.
[411] Ibid., 1869, pp. 83-5.
[412] Ibid., 1873, pp. 35-6.
[413] Ibid., 1875, pp. 62-3; 1880, p. 71.

sylvania and the day school for prisoners was revived with eighty-nine enrolled and some of the adequately trained prison officers as teachers.[414] Since this time the prison school has been in session, but, down to the appointment of Warden Ashe, it was never as successful as it was in the late seventies. During this recent period a teacher was provided, though the teaching was sometimes done by scholastically inclined officers and by the moral instructor.[415] At the close of the war [416] the educational facilities at the Western Penitentiary were less extensive and efficient than in the Eastern Penitentiary, this being the weakest element in the generally excellent management of the institution. During the year 1918 no regular teacher was provided, the teaching being done by educated convicts under the general oversight of the moral instructor.

The academic instruction in the Western Penitentiary has been revolutionized under the wardenship of Mr. Stanley P. Ashe, who was appointed in 1924. Mr. Ashe was formerly a superintendent of schools and considers his function as warden to be primarily a matter of education rather than of repression and punishment. He has introduced a rule according to which no inmate of the Western Penitentiary is regarded as eligible for pardon unless he can pass certain minimum educational requirements. There were four hundred twenty-seven convicts enrolled in the school in 1926. Remarkable work has also been done at Rockview by the enlightened criminologist who is in charge of that institution, Mr. Jesse O. Stutsman. In fact, he has made provision so that competent convicts at Rockview may pursue extension courses given by the staff of Pennsylvania State College which is located near by. Annual commencement exercises are conducted at which graduates of courses are formally awarded diplomas.

The first mention of a library in the Western Penitentiary is found in the report of the moral instructor for 1840, in which he stated that the institution possessed a library of about one hundred volumes, making possible a monthly exchange of books. He called attention to the obvious need of a larger library.[417] The library facilities increased gradually through gifts and some slight purchases until, by 1877, it was reported that there were about four thousand five hundred volumes in the library and that it had become so famous in the prison world that it had received the favorable comment of

---

[414] *Annual Report of the Western Penitentiary*, 1885-86, pp. 74-5.
[415] Ibid., 1887-88, pp. 71-2; 1889-90, pp. 73-4; 1895-96, p. 107; 1899-1900, p. 101; 1902, p. 103.
[416] September, 1918.
[417] *Annual Report of the Western Penitentiary*, 1840, *Senate Journal*, 1840, Vol. II, p. 263.

the *New York Tribune*.[418] By 1896 the library had nearly doubled in size, and in 1902 it was stated that the number of volumes had increased to eleven thousand five hundred.[419] By 1918 there were about fourteen thousand volumes in the library of the Western Penitentiary with very liberal rules governing their use.

(3) VOCATIONAL EDUCATION

While provisions for some systematic vocational instruction in the Eastern Penitentiary have only been made in recent years, the value of such instruction has long been recognized. For more than a half-century after the establishment of the Pennsylvania system one of the chief arguments for that system had been the fact that the separation and individual instruction of the prisoners had allowed the teaching of a trade to each. This defense of the system lingered long after it possessed any validity, for after 1860 the handicraft trades taught in the penitentiary had become antiquated through the competition of mechanical industry.[420] Further than contending that the separate system was based on vocational instruction, the inspectors of the Eastern Penitentiary vigorously maintained that a properly organized trade school for juvenile delinquents would do more than any other single factor to effect their reformation and prevent them from becoming habitual criminals and prospective inmates of the state penitentiaries.[421] In spite of this verbal recognition of the reformative value of vocational education little or nothing was ever achieved in this direction in the Eastern Penitentiary until recently, when Warden McKenty made provision for correspondence courses in technical and vocational subjects. Particularly significant have been extension courses in engineering and agriculture which have been arranged in cooperation with Pennsylvania State College. However praiseworthy this innovation may have been, it has done but little to introduce any comprehensive system of vocational education, such as is in operation at the Huntingdon Reformatory. At the close of the year 1917 only sixty-eight out of over fourteen hundred convicts were receiving instruction of this sort, and little practical training was given in these lines except such as was possible in connection with the engineering operations involved in the maintenance and administration of the penitentiary plant.[422] No one could fail, however,

[418] *Annual Report of the Western Penitentiary,* 1877, pp. 63-4.
[419] Ibid., 1895-96, p. 107; 1902, p. 99.
[420] See above, pp. 222ff.
[421] *Annual Report of the Eastern Penitentiary,* 1870, p. 37; 1880, p. 31; 1881, pp. 75ff; 1886, pp. 10ff.; 1891, pp. 35ff.
[422] Ibid., 1917, p. 76.

to commend the administration of the penitentiary for their recognition of the fact that vocational instruction is a vital part of an adequate system of prison discipline. Under the administration of Warden John C. Groome much progress has been made in vocational instruction, incidental to the reconstruction of the industrial system of the Eastern Penitentiary. There now exist at the institution a printing shop, a shoe shop and an automobile repair shop. Men are given an opportunity to work at these trades, and, if they do not know them, are taught to master these types of work. Unfortunately, only about 160 out of 1,500 inmates can be employed at these three industries at any one time.

Only recently has anything of consequence in the way of vocational instruction been accomplished in the Western Penitentiary. Down to 1869 the conventional arguments in favor of the virtues of the Pennsylvania system in the way of industrial training were solemnly repeated by the officers in their annual reports. The extensive development of mechanical industry under the contract or lease system following 1870 made any successful vocational education quite out of the question. The anti-prison-labor legislation following 1883 made it impossible to embody any industrial education in the manufacturing system of the penitentiary, and the state and local authorities have never been impressed with the value of the establishment of a non-productive and purely educational system of vocational education. Since the appointment of Warden Stanley P. Ashe in 1924, and the gradual rehabilitation of the prison industries, provision for vocational instruction at the Western Penitentiary has been slowly instituted. Warden Ashe has been handicapped by the few industries which could be maintained up to very recently, but his penchant for education as a solvent of the crime problem has led him, in cooperation with Professor Root, to make the most of the opportunities. Warden Stutsman has been equally enlightened and desirous of providing vocational education, but he has been likewise hampered by the fact that the chief industries at Rockview are those connected with agricultural operations, namely, farming, dairying, gardening, horticulture and canning of vegetables and fruits. The handing over of prison industries to the Bureau of Restoration of the Department of Public Welfare has been a notable step forward in promoting attention to vocational training in connection with prison industry. Provision has thus been made for centralized stimulation and supervision of vocational instruction in the state penitentiaries.

The greatest progress in vocational guidance has not been made at the state penitentiaries, but at the State Industrial Reformatory at Huntingdon. When the anti-convict labor legislation was enacted, the superintendent established a manual training school which has been subsequently maintained and is one of the best in the country. It has, however, lacked a realistic touch, to some extent, because of its separation from actual productive industry.[422a]

(4) Social Education

Crime in its most fundamental sense being an anti-social act, the true reformation of the criminal consists in his effective socialization—in preparing him to live in accordance with the social, moral and legal rules prescribed for individual conduct by the group of which he is a part. The older penology of the last century maintained that this essential goal of a reformatory system of penal discipline could best be attained simply through a more or less savage system of punishment, which made the individual feel very keenly the painful results of an infraction of the legal regulations of the community. This notion, however, could only endure while the old metaphysical notion of crime was accepted which represented the criminal as a perfectly normal individual—a "free moral agent" who perversely chose to commit crime rather than to lead a law-abiding existence. Now that this view of criminality and the criminal has totally passed away among scientific students of the crime problem, and the criminal—at least the habitual offender or recidivist—has been shown to be an abnormal being whose normal conduct is criminal activity, it has become apparent that no system of prison discipline can be regarded as likely to be genuinely reformative unless it provides for the adequate training of the prisoner in the duties of citizenship and social responsibility. In other words, the fundamental success or failure of any modern system of prison discipline must be judged upon the basis of its effectiveness in preparing the inmate for the assumption of the normal responsibilities of social life upon his release.

It has long been recognized by psychologists and sociologists that no effective system of social education can be based wholly on eloquent sermons or rhetorical addresses dealing with personal salvation or the duties of citizenship. The discipline of man in social groups has been achieved in quite a different manner through concrete and personal experiences which have been often repeated and bring out forcibly and clearly the rewards which may be expected to attend conformity to group rules for conduct and the

---

[422a] For an excellent statement of the principles and practices involved in this problem see Douglas Fryer, "Psychology and Vocational Guidance for the Criminal," in the *American Review*, May-June, 1926.

penalties for deviation from these.[423] It has become evident that any significant plan for the social rehabilitation of convicts must be based upon a similar system, to impress upon the mind of the prisoner the advantages of acquiescence in the rules of conduct imposed for the government of the prison community and the dire results which attend their violation. Only in this manner can the convict be prepared for a subsequent life of freedom with any promise of success. Most of the advances in prison administration in the nineteenth and twentieth centuries have had as their fundamental aim the achievement of this result. The penological doctrine of the deterrent value of punishment was at once the most popular and the most crude of all these attempts to socialize the prisoner. Much more rational and effective were the system of commutation for good behavior, which had its origin chiefly in Maconochie's "mark" system, and the method of grading, promoting and paroling prisoners, which was first extensively practiced by Sir Walter Crofton in his Irish system of prison administration and came into American penology chiefly through the medium of the American adaptation and improvement of the methods of Crofton in the Elmira system. A further development of social education came in the gradual introduction of the honor system in some phases of penal discipline, particularly with respect to prisoners who had earned the respect and confidence of the authorities through good conduct. The reliance upon honor was a prominent part of the Irish system, particularly in the final stage of incarceration at Lusk, and was gradually introduced into American penal practices, especially by Gideon Haynes, the able and progressive warden of the Massachusetts State Penitentiary at Charlestown.

The latest and most advanced phase of social education in penal discipline has been associated with systems of convict self-government designed to train the prisoners for a normal social life by practical experience in self-government in an environment as nearly like that into which they will go upon release as it is possible to maintain within a penal institution. Quite contrary to general supposition, the notion and practice of inmate self-government in penal and reformatory institutions is not a wholly recent innovation. As early as 1831 De Beaumont and De Tocqueville reported a very advanced system of self-government in the "House of Reformation" for juvenile delinquents in South Boston.[424] But in spite

---

[423] See on this point especially W. Trotter, *The Instinct of the Herd in Peace and War;* W. G. Sumner, *Folkways;* E. A. Ross, *Social Control.*

[424] De Beaumont and De Tocqueville, *On the Penitentiary System in the United States,* translated by Francis Lieber, Philadelphia, 1833, pp. 216-23. This is discussed at length by Winthrop D. Lane in his revised edition of F. H. Wines' *Punishment and Reformation,* 1918.

of early and sporadic instances of the introduction of systems of inmate self-government in penal institutions, the first systematic and fearless attempt to institute a system of convict self-government was made by Mr. Thomas Mott Osborne in Sing Sing Prison following 1915. The essence of Mr. Osborne's "Mutual Welfare League" consisted in the practical application of the doctrine that a convict could not be trained for normal social life in the paralyzing environment of the conventional repressive system of prison discipline, but required for this social education a set of surroundings calculated as much as possible to bring to bear the influences of normal life in a social group, and thereby to fit the inmate for such an existence upon the expiration of his sentence. Accordingly, the rules of discipline of the institution were chiefly left to a body of delegates composed of fifty convicts elected by the inmates on the basis of the representation of the several work gangs. Infractions of discipline were dealt with by a board of five judges chosen by the delegates, though an appeal might be taken from their decision to the warden. The decision of the judges was carried out by the regular officers of the prison. No keepers or guards were allowed in the shops, discipline here being wholly in the hands of convicts. A system of token money was introduced in the shops. A convict commissary was organized from which inmates could purchase articles of comfort. An employment bureau was maintained by the members of the League. Outdoor recreation, lectures and entertainments were provided. The position and privileges of the inmates depended upon the excellence of their obedience to the regulations of the self-governing system. It was further provided that released members of the League should attempt to find employment for their fellow members upon the expiration of their sentence and should attempt to sustain the efforts at reformation which had been initiated while at Sing Sing. In this way it was hoped that an adequate system of social education might be provided which would restore to a normal life the great majority of convicts who had hitherto been released only to be returned for another offense after a brief period of freedom.[425] A number of influences combined to bring Mr. Osborne's régime to a premature end at Sing Sing. Among these may be mentioned Mr. Osborne's failure to comprehend that his system was applicable only to non-defective convicts, and that it must be preceded by an adequate system of clinical observation, classification and promotion of convicts; his own unyielding and uncompromising attitude, so

---

[425] The whole subject is best discussed in Mr. Osborne's published lectures, *Society and Its Prisons,* and in his *Prisons and Common Sense.* He obtained his notions from the George Junior Republic.

characteristic of the ardent reformer on the defensive; the opposition of the keepers and guards who had been trained wholly in the savage methods of the conventional repressive penology; the bitter enmity of grafting contractors who found Mr. Osborne as little susceptible to dishonesty as to conventionality; the opposition of political rivals among the notorious "rounders" of the machine politicians; and the jealousy of leading penologists of a more conventional and conservative cast. These facts, however, should not blind one to the certainty that Mr. Osborne's innovation was the most significant advance in American penology since the introduction of the Elmira system and is likely in its essence to be universally adopted within the next century for application to such convicts as it can in any way be hoped to reform.[426]

The degree to which commutation, classification and promotion have been introduced into Pennsylvania penology has been already discussed.[427] The honor system was widely and generously developed by Warden McKenty at the Eastern Penitentiary and by Warden Francies at the new penitentiary site in Centre County. Indeed, it is doubtful if there is another place in America where the honor system is more extensively and successfully applied to adult delinquents than at Rockview.

Almost no progress has been made in the way of introducing the self-government plan into the Pennsylvania penitentiaries. At the Eastern Penitentiary there exists an admirably efficient and impartial administration of the old type of repressive discipline of a semi-military character. By these methods, Colonel John C. Groome, a former army officer and for fourteen years head of the state police of Pennsylvania, has brought order out of the somewhat chaotic state of affairs which existed at the close of the administration of the affable and easy-going McKenty. The warden at the Western Penitentiary, Stanley P. Ashe, an enlightened educator, has little faith in the repressive system, and relies widely upon the reformative influence of education, but he has not deemed it feasible to introduce the self-government plan. Jesse O. Stutsman, who has just retired as warden of the Rockview Penitentiary is one of the most enlightened and best informed penologists in the country. While Superintendent of the Detroit House of Correction he conducted a self-government plan successfully for five years, and in his book, *Curing the Criminal,* he comes out as a discriminating exponent of the Osborne self-government scheme, but he has not been able to put the plan into operation at his institution. Only at the

---

[426] Mr. Osborne later applied his methods with success at the United States Naval Prison at Portsmouth, New Hampshire. He died in the autumn of 1926.
[427] See above, pp. 311ff., 330ff.

Sleighton Farm School for Girls has self-government had much of a trial in Pennsylvania.

H. Probation and the Non-Institutional Care of Delinquents

The beginnings of the non-institutional care of delinquents may be traced to the ticket-of-leave or parole system, which originated in the middle of the nineteenth century and has come to be a cardinal feature of modern penological theory and practice. This, however, merely made possible the removal of the convict from imprisonment during the latter portion of his term and in no way attempted to do away with imprisonment altogether. With the gradual growth among careful students of penology of the conviction that in many, if not in most cases, the convict issued from prison a worse character than he was upon entry, especially in the case of young first offenders, there has arisen a determined movement to secure the introduction of a system of suspended sentence and probation, to be applied to those first offenders and others, who, it seems reasonable to believe, can be most effectively treated outside of a penal institution. As has been the case with nearly all of the radical innovations in penology, this progressive practice was first applied to juvenile delinquents, especially in connection with the creation of a juvenile court system in the more advanced municipalities of the country, a movement which originated in Illinois in 1899 and in which Judge Benjamin B. Lindsey of Denver was a pioneer and the most picturesque figure.

While there were earlier approximations to a juvenile court system in Pennsylvania, the basis of the present system was laid by acts of 1903. That of March 26, 1903, directed that "no child under the age of sixteen years shall be committed by any Magistrate or Justice of the Peace to any institution for the purpose of correction or reformation, but all applications for such commitment shall be made to the Court of Quarter Sessions of the county." [428] The powers of the court of quarter sessions in dealing with these cases of juvenile delinquents under sixteen years of age were defined in an act of April 23, 1903. The premises and purposes of this act were set forth as follows:

"The welfare of the State demands that children should be guarded from association and contact with crime and criminals, and the ordinary process of the criminal law does not provide

---

[428] *A Comprehensive Review of the Work of the Juvenile Court of Philadelphia,* 1903-08, Philadelphia, 1908, p. 58. An earlier act, that of June 12, 1893, had provided for the separate and distinct trial of juvenile delinquents.

such treatment and care and moral encouragement as are essential to all children in the formative period of life, but endangers the whole future of the child.

"Experience has shown that children, lacking proper parental care or guardianship, are led into courses of life which may render them liable to the pains and penalties of the criminal law of the State, although, in fact, the real interests of such child or children require that they be not incarcerated in penitentiaries and jails, as members of the criminal class, but be subjected to a wise care, treatment and control, that their evil tendencies may be checked and their better instincts may be strengthened.

"To that end, it is important that the powers of the courts, in respect to the care, treatment and control over dependent, neglected, delinquent and incorrigible children should be clearly distinguished from the powers exercised in the administration of the criminal law." [429]

It was also decreed that a judge of the court of quarter sessions should hold a juvenile court for the purpose of carrying out the provisions of the act.[430] He was to exercise his powers when, in the opinion of a magistrate, justice of the peace, district attorney or judge involved in the case, the interests of both the child and the state could no longer be served by allowing the child his ordinary liberties or by committing him to a conventional institution for juvenile delinquents.[431] In such cases the judge of the juvenile court was authorized to "commit such child to the care of its parents, subject to the supervision of a Probation Officer, or to some suitable institution, or to the care of some reputable citizen of good moral character, or to the care of some training school, or to an industrial school, or to the care of some association willing to receive it." [432] The parents, institution, association or individual to which the child was committed became by that fact its guardian.[433] The commitment could not, however, extend beyond the age of twenty-one years. [434] It was further specifically ordered that no child under twelve years of age should be sent to a reformatory or correctional institution unless the suspended sentence and probation failed to operate successfully in such a case.[435] The court was authorized to appoint suitable probation officers to investigate the circumstances connected with the cases of all children

---

[429] *A Comprehensive Review of the Work of the Juvenile Court of Philadelphia,* pp. 53-4.
[430] Ibid., p. 54.
[431] Ibid., pp. 54-5.
[432] Ibid., p. 56.
[433] Ibid.
[434] Ibid., p. 57.
[435] Ibid.

brought before the court in accordance with the provision of the act. The possibility of readily obtaining competent probation officers was, however, made exceedingly remote by the stipulation that they should receive no salary.[436]

Since the passage of the act of 1903 several important additions have been made to the legal basis of the probation of juveniles in Pennsylvania. An act of July 12, 1913, established a Municipal Court for the city of Philadelphia and gave it the jurisdiction over cases involving juvenile delinquents and their probation.[437] The jurisdiction was confirmed and further defined in an act of June 17, 1915.[438] An act of March 15, 1915, gave the county court of Allegheny County jurisdiction over cases involving juveniles in that county.[439] It also provided for the securing of competent probation officers by making it possible to pay the chief probation officer three thousand dollars per year and his subordinates one-half of that sum.[440] The absurd provision in the act of 1903 that probation officers should receive no public salary in Pennsylvania was wiped out by an act of April 1, 1909, which allowed the court of quarter sessions to pay probation officers a salary of not to exceed one hundred dollars per month.[441] As the municipal court of Philadelphia contemplated a rather extensive application of the principle of probation to both juvenile and adult delinquents in accordance with the laws of April 23, 1903, May 10, 1909, and June 19, 1911, an act of June 15, 1915, made provision for a salary for probation officers in Philadelphia which would make it possible to secure officers of high capacity who might be expected to devote all of their time to their duties. The president judge of the municipal court was authorized to appoint a chief probation officer for the city who would receive a salary of not to exceed five thousand dollars and subordinate to receive not over half that amount.[442]

The actual mode of operation of the act of 1903 and its subsequent revisions is thus set forth by Judge William H. Staake, who has long been the leader among Philadelphia jurists in the cause

[436] *A Comprehensive Review of the Work of the Juvenile Court of Philadelphia*, pp. 55-6. The laws relating to juvenile courts, probation, and juvenile institutions are conveniently brought together by John H. Fertig and S. Edward Hannestad in *A Compilation of the Laws Relating to Juvenile Courts and Dependent, Neglected, Incorrigible and Delinquent Children*, Harrisburg, 1916.
[437] *Laws of the General Assembly*, 1913, pp. 711ff.
[438] Ibid., 1915, pp. 1017ff.
[439] Ibid., pp. 5ff.
[440] Ibid.
[441] Ibid., 1909, pp. 89ff.
[442] Ibid., 1915, pp. 988ff.

of the reform of criminal procedure in cases dealing with juvenile delinquents:

"There are no classes specifically entitled to probation instead of 'incarceration.' What is meant by this is: The whole Juvenile Court idea is, that the offender is only a delinquent, and not an intentional violator of the law, or in fact a criminal. He is not incarcerated in the sense of imprisonment. He may be, and is, liable to detention in the care of an individual, or, in some cases, in the care of an institution.

"The person or official who is to decide what shall be the disposition made of the delinquent juvenile was formerly the Judge of the Court of Quarter Sessions but is now the Judge of the Municipal Court, so far as Philadelphia is concerned; that Court having as a statutory, and not as a constitutional court, taken over all matters incidental to the Juvenile Court, as well as matters affecting domestic relations, such as making orders for the maintenance of the wife by the husband or of the wife and children by the husband, or of the children alone by the husband.

"It should be stated that the Municipal Court, in Philadelphia and another analagous court in the County of Allegheny, are the only special courts which have charge of this work. In the counties, other than Philadelphia and Allegheny, the Court of Quarter Sessions for such individual county or Judicial District would have the jurisdiction and the authority in connection with juvenile delinquents.

"The Judge, who under the calendar of the particular Court, exercises the discretion, whether to detain the delinquent juvenile offender, or whether to place him on probation in his own family under the oversight or superintendency of a probation officer, or whether to place him in the case of some private person, who would be willing to undertake the responsibility for such supervision, or to place him in a suitable institution such as the institutions at Glen Mills, or under the supervision of an officer of certain well known charities, such as the Children's Aid Society and the Society for the Prevention of Cruelty to Children, or other recognized societies having the same object in view.

"In Philadelphia and Allegheny, and in other counties, the probation officers appointed by the respective courts would investigate the conduct of juvenile delinquents, and then report regularly to the tribunal appointing him.

"The results of violation of probationary conditions would be either a continuance of the probation by the Court, instead of a discharge of the probationer, on the recommendation of the probation officers, or in some cases, where it was found the delinquent was a hopeless case, and was not to be controlled by the court's probation officers, there might be a commitment to an institution for juvenile delinquents, or even to the Huntingdon Reformatory, so far as male juvenile delinquents are concerned, when the seriousness of the offense of the delinquent was of a character to submit the case to a formal trial in the courts." [443]

As has been the case with almost every progressive prison reform practice in the past, so with probation, its application to juvenile delinquents was soon followed by its introduction into the methods of treating adult delinquents not convicted of major crimes. At the present time some twenty-six states now have probation systems which are applied to adult delinquents with a greater or less degree of thoroughness. Probation on suspended sentence for most convicted persons except the more defective and degenerate types seems to be dictated by both science and common sense. Probation, linked up with proper guidance and psychiatric aid, presents a double advantage over the house of correction, jail and prison. It gives the individual a strong incentive to reform and provides intelligent guidance and encouragement. It also saves the person from the stigma, humiliation, degradation and demoralizing association which is everywhere to be found in our penal and correctional institutions. For the time being the extension of probation is one of the most promising immediate steps which can be taken in criminal science and jurisprudence.

Adult probation was first permitted in Pennsylvania according to the provisions of an act of May 10, 1909, and was continued practically unchanged by an act of June 19, 1911. As a part of the acts also establishing the parole and indeterminate sentence systems in Pennsylvania, it was the product of the agitation of the same group of reformers that has been described above in connection with the establishment of the indeterminate sentence in that state.[444] That portion of the act of 1911 which deals with the subject of probation still governs that practice in Pennsylvania and is given in the following paragraphs:

"Be it enacted, etc., That whenever any person shall be convicted in any court of this commonwealth of any crime, except murder, administering poison, kidnapping, incest, sodomy, buggery, rape, assault and battery with intent to ravish, arson, robbery or burglary, and it does not appear to the said court that the defendant has ever before been imprisoned for crime, either in this state or elsewhere (but detention in an institution for juvenile delinquents shall not be considered imprisonment), and where the said court believes that the character of the defendant and the circumstances

---

[443] From a memorandum kindly furnished to the writer by Judge Staake at the request of Doctor J. F. Ohl.
[444] See above, pp. 317ff.

of the case are such that he or she is not likely again to engage in an offensive course of conduct, and that the public good does not demand or require that the defendant should suffer the penalty imposed by law; said court shall have power to suspend the imposing of the sentence, and place the defendant on probation for a definite period, on such terms and conditions as it may deem right and proper, said terms and conditions to be duly entered on record as a part of the judgment of the court in such case.

"In any case where a fine only is imposed, and the defendant might be imprisoned until such fine be paid, the court may direct, as one of the terms of the probation, that such fines shall be paid in certain instalments at certain times: Provided, however, that upon payment of the fine, judgment shall be satisfied and probation cease.

"Whenever or wherever the court may deem it necessary and desirable, it may appoint a discreet person to serve as probation officer, for the performance of such duties as the court shall direct. The salary of such officer shall be determined by the court, and this, together with the necessary expenses incurred while in the actual performance of duty, shall be paid by the county, upon vouchers approved by the court and county commissioners. In no case, however, shall a defendant be committed in the custody of a probation officer of the opposite sex.

"Whenever a person placed on probation, as aforesaid, shall violate the terms of his or her probation, he or she shall be subject to arrest in the same manner as in the case of an escaped convict; and shall be brought before the court which released him or her on probation, which court may thereupon pronounce upon such defendant such sentence as may be prescribed by law, to begin at such time as the court may direct.

"Whenever it is the judgment of the court that a person on probation has satisfactorily met the conditions of his or her probation, the court shall discharge such defendant and cause record thereof to be made: Provided, That the length of such period of probation shall not be more than the maximum term for which the defendant might have been imprisoned." [445]

Though the provisions of this act make possible a very liberal use of the principle of adult probation and the suspended sentence in Pennsylvania, the fact that their application has been made optional rather than obligatory has made the operation of the law in this respect as variable and inconsistent as the application of the parole and indeterminate sentence law in that state. Just as educated and sensible judges make a wise and liberal use of their power to fix the minimum sentence, so they frequently apply their power to suspend sentence and admit the convicted person to probation,

---

[445] *Laws of the General Assembly,* 1911, pp. 1055-56.

and in the same manner that reactionary and short-sighted judges make a vicious use of the minimum sentence provision, so they rarely or never admit a convict to probation. Without either the compulsory probation of certain classes of lesser offenders or a more universally intelligent judiciary the suspended sentence and probation can meet with only limited success in Pennsylvania, as elsewhere. Only in the probation department of the Philadelphia municipal court under the direction of Chief Probation Officer, Louis N. Robinson (recently resigned) has any notable progress been made in Pennsylvania, but here the prospects for a successful application of the principle of the suspended sentence and parole to delinquents are unexcelled in this country. Whatever the short-comings in its use in Pennsylvania at the present time there can be no doubt but that it will come to be one of the vital features of the penology of the future. Its value and its desirability have been admirably summarized in the report of the Committee to Investigate Penal Systems in 1919:

"Conceived as a mere incident of the sentencing power, to be exercised only in exceptional cases, the suspended sentence and probation are beginning to disclose themselves as a momentous, not to say revolutionary step in the progress of penology, not less important in its ultimate consequences than the substitution a century ago of imprisonment for the death penalty and other forms of physical punishment. Like the older forms of punishment which it superseded, imprisonment too has proved a failure, so far at least, as the newer aim of punishment, the reformation of the wrong-doer is concerned. As we are coming to see the protection which society enjoys through the imprisonment for a few months or years of a small portion of the criminal class is dearly purchased by a system which returns the offender to society less fitted than before to cope with the conditions of a life of freedom. More and more, as we develop a probation service worthy of the name, will the courts be reluctant to commit men, women and children to the demoralizing associations and discipline of institutional life and will give them their chance to redeem themselves under competent guidance and supervision among the associations and activities of everyday life." [446]

On May 7, 1925, an act was passed providing for some extension of the use of probation in Pennsylvania. It is to be hoped that this will make possible the adoption on a wide scale of the successful methods employed in this respect in the city of Philadelphia by Doctor Robinson:

---

[446] *Report of the Commission to Investigate Penal Systems,* Philadelphia, 1919, p. 25.

"Section 1. Be it enacted, &c., That whenever any person shall be convicted in any court of this Commonwealth of any crime, except murder, administering poison, kidnapping, incest, sodomy, buggery, rape, assault and battery with intent to ravish, arson, robbery, or burglary, and it does not appear to the said court that the defendant has ever before been imprisoned for crime, either in this State or elsewhere (but detention in an institution for juvenile delinquents shall not be considered imprisonment), and where the said court believes that the character of the defendant and the circumstances of the case such that he or she is not likely again to engage in an offensive course of conduct, and that the public good does not demand or require that the defendant should suffer the penalty imposed by law, the said court shall have the power to suspend the imposing of the sentence, and place the defendant on probation for a definite period, on such terms and conditions, *including the payment of money for the use of the county, not exceeding, however, the fine fixed by law for conviction of such offense,* as it may deem right and proper; said terms and conditions to be duly entered of record as a part of the judgment of the court in such case. *No such condition for the payment of money shall be considered as the imposition of a fine or a sentence nor prevent the court from thereafter sentencing any defendant under the act under which he or she was convicted upon violation of his or her parole.*"

A bill was introduced in the State Legislature in 1927 to provide for the establishment of a State Probation Bureau. The bill was based on a state-wide study of court procedure and probation made by Mr. Leon Stern for the National Probation Association and the Pennsylvania Committee on Penal Affairs. The proposed system of state supervision of the probation activities was to be very much like that existing at the present time in the states of New York and Massachusetts. The bill provided, further, for a method of examining probation officers whenever the judges desired to have the probation commission give examinations. The bill was, very unfortunately, defeated. The opposition came chiefly from the probation officers, who did not desire state supervision of their work. Another point to which they objected strenuously was the examination system proposed, even though it was not mandatory.

VI. PRISON INVESTIGATIONS AND PRISON REFORM MOVEMENTS

1. The Criticism of the Pennsylvania System by Louis Dwight

From the time of the establishment of the Pennsylvania system until the middle of the century the most vigorous and persistent enemy of the separate system of prison discipline was Louis Dwight, the active secretary of the Prison Discipline Society of Boston. His critical comments on the Pennsylvania system, while violently partisan, are worthy of note as constituting a basis for comparison with the equally partisan contentions of its apologists. As early as 1827 he presented a lengthy and vigorous protest against the desirability of establishing solitary confinement in the Eastern Penitentiary.[447] In 1828 he stated that he and a companion had just visited a completed cell block in the new penitentiary building at Cherry Hill and had experienced no difficulty in conversing from cell to cell and from yard to yard.[448] In 1835 he condemned the cruel methods of punishments practiced in the Eastern Penitentiary, such as the gag and douche. He also declared that there was an unjustifiable mortality and an abnormal degree of insanity in the institution.[449] The next year he made the sweeping assertion that the Pennsylvania system was a proved failure with respect to the elements of health, reformation, earnings from industry, and moral and religious instruction.[450] In 1839 he accused the authorities of the Eastern Penitentiary of attempting to suppress the information regarding the abuses in discipline in that institution which had been revealed by Mr. McElwee and others in 1835. He complained that it had taken him four years to obtain a copy of McElwee's volume describing the cruelties practiced.[451] In 1842 he stated that the authorities of the institution had persuaded the legislature to pass a law in 1833 taking away the right of the grand jury to visit the Eastern Penitentiary and to submit a report upon the conditions revealed by their investigation.[452] The most thorough-going of Dwight's attacks upon the Pennsylvania system is to be found in the report of his society for the year 1843. Following a

---

[447] *Report of the Boston Prison Discipline Society*, 1827, pp. 121-28.
[448] Ibid., 1828, pp. 39-47.
[449] Ibid., 1835, pp. 20-2.
[450] Ibid., 1836, pp. 38-40.
[451] Ibid., 1839, pp. 48-53.
[452] Ibid., 1842, p. 62.

voluminous condemnation of the Pennsylvania system, accompanied by a large number of citations from reports and other documents, and a recital of the instances of its failure before and after 1829, Dwight made a most categorical arraignment of the solitary system:

"1. The Pennsylvania system fails to answer the expectations and designs of its friends in dispensing with labor.

"2. The Pennsylvania system fails to answer the expectations and promises of its early friends in preventing evil communication.

"3. The Pennsylvania system fails to answer the promises and expectations of its early friends in deterring from crime and preventing recommitments.

"4. The Pennsylvania system fails to answer the promises and expectations of its early friends in regard to its effects on health and life.

"5. The Pennsylvania system fails to answer the promises and expectations of its early friends in regard to its effects on the mind.

"6. The Pennsylvania system fails to answer the promises and expectations of its early friends in regard to self-support.

"7. The Pennsylvania system fails to answer the promises and expectations of its early friends by dispensing with severe punishments for misdemeanor in Prison.

"8. The Pennsylvania system fails to answer the promises and expectations of its early friends in regard to its extension in America." [453]

In his reports for 1849 and 1850 Dwight made a special attack upon the Pennsylvania system for what he alleged to be its production of an abnormal degree of insanity among convicts. He maintained that ten convicts had developed insanity in 1848, while the Canadian penal commission which had visited the Eastern Penitentiary in 1849 had asserted that out of the total of three hundred convicts no less than fifty were insane.[454] In 1854 Louis Dwight died and with his death the Pennsylvania system lost its most implacable enemy. There is little evidence for believing that his criticisms did more than to stir the exponents of the Pennsylvania system to a more determined defense of their methods.

2. SPECIAL INVESTIGATIONS OF PRISON CONDITIONS

The most conspicuous fact concerning special investigations of prison conditions in Pennsylvania has been their almost total absence. With the exception of a very few investigations of special

---

[453] *Report of the Boston Prison Discipline Society,* 1843, pp. 44-103, particularly pp. 49ff.

[454] Ibid., 1849, p. 70; 1850, p. 37.

charges of cruelty or corruption in a particular institution, there have been no penetrating examinations of the situation in the state penitentiaries of Pennsylvania. In fact, from the establishment of the system in 1829 to the appointment of the Commission to Investigate Penal Systems in 1917 there was no systematic and comprehensive examination of the administration of the penal and correctional institutions of the state designed to secure a thoroughgoing revision, improvement and coordination of the institutions and the practice of penology in the state. This remarkable circumstance is to be explained by several conditions and factors. In the first place, for nearly a half-century after its establishment the system of separate confinement was a matter of local pride to the citizens of Pennsylvania, and to those of Philadelphia in particular. Any public investigations which would have revealed gross abuses in the state penitentiaries would have been a reflection upon the Pennsylvania system and would have been eagerly pounced upon by Louis Dwight and other protagonists of the Auburn system. Again, the state penitentiaries have frequently been administered or controlled by men prominent in political circles whose personal influence would make a public investigation difficult. Further, and probably most important of all, the function of investigating commissions has been exercised to a very considerable extent by the Philadelphia Society for Alleviating the Miseries of Public Prisons and (since 1870) the State Board of Public Charities. Both of these groups have carried on with a varying degree of vigor the program of criticizing existing conditions and suggesting improvements, which is normally associated with investigating commissions. One thing, however, is certain, and that is that the general absence of investigations is no proof of a uniform and general excellence of administration and discipline in the penal institutions of the state.

The first significant investigation of abuses in the state penitentiaries came in the years 1834 and 1835, when serious charges were brought against the administration of the Eastern Penitentiary. These charges are especially interesting and significant as being made at a time when the formal public reports of the institution were proclaiming the extreme perfection in penal discipline which had been attained in the institution. The charges specifically advanced were as follows:

"Against the Warden, Officers and Agents of the Eastern Penitentiary, for investigation by the joint committee of the Senate and House of Representatives of the Commonwealth of Pennsylvania, on so much of the Governor's message as relates to abuses in the economy and management of that institution; drawn up and preferred by the Attorney General, conformably to the resolution of the committee, dated the 8th of December, 1834.

"First. Practices and manners among the officers, agents and females, licentious and immoral; attested by indecent conversations, gross personal familiarities, sexual intercourse, and the existence of a filthy disease; generally known to and participated in by the Warden, one John Holloway, one Richard Blundin and his wife, and others unknown.

"Second. Embezzlement and misapplication of the public provisions and public property, and of the public labor, to the private and unauthorized use and advantage of various persons connected with the institution, and of others unconnected with it; on the part particularly of the said wife of Richard Blundin, and to the knowledge and with the connivance of the Warden; as also to the use and advantage of the Warden, for the improving and working of a farm and factory belonging in whole or in part to the said Warden.

"Third. Cruel and unusual punishment inflicted by order of the Warden, upon refractory convicts; exemplified in the two following cases: the case of one Seneca Plumly, who, in the depth of winter, was tied up against the wall attached to his cell by the wrists, while buckets of extremely cold water were thrown upon him from a height, which partly froze on his head and person, and he was shortly after discharged as incurably insane; and the case of Matthias Maccumsey, in whose mouth an iron bar or gag was so forcibly fastened, that his blood collected and suffused up in his brain and he suddenly died under the treatment.

"Fourth. Known practices and habits inconsistent with the object and principles of a penitentiary and its system, subversive of its order, regularity and security; such as the giving of large entertainments within the prison, by the warden, carousing and dancing late at night at the apartments of the said wife of Richard Blundin, within the walls, frequent intoxication, habitual intercourse with lewd and depraved persons, and irregular hours also on the part of the said wife of Richard Blundin, and with the knowledge and connivance of the Warden.

"Fifth. A frequent and illegal practice in the treatment of convicts by the Warden, of departing from, and in effect disregarding the sentences of the courts of justice; relaxing their severity, commuting their inflictions, or evading their real meaning: thus substituting his individual caprice or discretion for the decisions of the law, and defeating the regularity and precision which ought to characterize the penitentiary system." [455]

A joint committee was appointed to investigate the charges; and it examined witnesses in Philadelphia from December 16, 1834, to

---

[455] *A Concise History of the Eastern Penitentiary of Pennsylvania, together with a detailed Statement of the Proceedings of the Committee Appointed by the Legislature, December 6, 1834,* By a Member of the Legislature, Philadelphia, Neall and Massey, Printers, 1835, pp. 34-5.

January 22, 1835.[456] The committee disagreed concerning the findings and a majority [457] and a minority [458] report were submitted. Much of the questioning turned on the matter of the immoral actions of Mrs. Blundin and exhibits more of a morbid curiosity than of a real desire to discover fundamental abuses in the administration of prison discipline in the Eastern Penitentiary. The majority of the committee endeavored with little success to "whitewash" the administration but even they could not disprove the charges of cruel punishments, especially in the cases of Plumly and Maccumsey. They could only plead that such methods of punishment were common in the general prison world at that time.[459] A careful and unbiased examination of the published testimony tends to support the report of the minority rather than the majority of the investigating committee.[460] The minority summarized their views on the results of the investigation as follows:

"The conviction left on the mind of the undersigned, by facts adduced in evidence, is that in the Eastern Penitentiary there existed

"First—Frequent misapplication of the public property and public labor to the private advantage of various persons connected with the institution.

"Second—Cruel and unusual punishment inflicted on refractory convicts, resulting in one instance in the death of the sufferer.

"Third—The indulgence in great irregularities and immoralites on the part of those concerned in the management of the institution.

"Fourth—Violation of the laws of the commonwealth, which require the convicts to be kept singly and separately at labor in the cells or work yards." [461]

Especially significant is the undoubtedly accurate assertion of the minority that the charge of "cruel and unusual punishments was established to a frightful extent." [462]

The importance of the whole investigation, while most significant as revealing very serious abuses in almost every department of the administration and discipline of the Eastern Penitentiary, lies not so much in this alone as it does in the fact that these conditions were discovered during the first flush of enthusiasm over the

---

[456] *A Concise History of the Eastern Penitentiary,* etc., p. 35.
[457] Ibid., pp. 29ff.
[458] Ibid., pp. 103ff.
[459] Ibid., pp. 42-3.
[460] Ibid., pp. 144ff. See especially pp. 176-80.
[461] Ibid., p. 108.
[462] Ibid. See pp. 16ff. for a description of the punishments, which included "ducking," the "mad chair," the strait-jacket and the iron gag, in addition to some other less brutal methods and practices.

Pennsylvania system and at a time when the public reports and descriptions were declaring that perfection itself reigned supreme in the disciplinary system of the prison at Cherry Hill. It shows that little dependence can be placed in the public reports in so far as they deal with the details of the discipline of the institution and brings out the truth of an observation recently made by a distinguished penologist that the "inside" and detailed history of the disciplinary aspects of the Eastern Penitentiary can never be written unless unknown records can be discovered in the private papers of citizens of the time who were acquainted with the real facts involved. It further goes to show that the criticisms of Louis Dwight can not be wholly assigned to his personal bias against the Pennsylvania system.

An exposure which should have led to an investigation of the Pennsylvania system was contained in the message of Governor W. F. Johnston in 1850, in which the governor stated that he and his predecessors had been so frequently approached in the effort to secure pardons for prisoners afflicted with "ill-health or insanity" that a change should be made in the laws, so as to modify the severity of the system of solitary confinement.[463] Nothing was done about this assertion, however; primarily, no doubt, because of the violent denial of the charge by the officials of both penitentiaries.

No important prison investigation took place after 1834-35 until 1897, when Judge Gordon charged the officials of the Eastern Penitentiary with excessive cruelty and serious irregularities in the administration of the institution.[464] A legislative investigating committee was appointed which examined the two penitentiaries and made the following recommendations:

"After a careful examination of both penitentiaries, the committee offers the following as the principal objects to be sought in any general prison legislation, to-wit:

"1. That the State assumes charge of all the county prisons and the expense of maintaining all the convicted prisoners therein.

"2. That all the prisons be organized in one system, under the supervision of a board of unpaid prison commissioners, with power to consolidate and reduce the number of prisons, to make general regulations concerning them, and to transfer both officers and prisoners from one prison to another.

"3. To establish at some centrally located prison, a ward or hospital for insane prisoners, and to secure the detention of those under proper safeguards, regardless of their terms of sentence.

"4. To abolish all power driven machinery from every prison

---

[463] *Senate Journal,* 1850, Vol. II, p. 608. See also *Governor's Message,* 1850.
[464] Ibid., 1897, Vol. II, pp. 2298-2305.

in the State, but would recommend that all goods used in the different State institutions of the Commonwealth, be made by the convicts of the two penitentiaries.

"Should these objects be accomplished by suitable legislation, the committee believes it would be entirely unnecessary to erect a separate and independent asylum for insane convicts." [465]

The next investigation of prison conditions came about a decade later when, in 1908-09, the State Board of Public Charities conducted an investigation of the charges made against Warden Johnson of the Western Penitentiary.[466] The investigation was conducted from October 13, 1908, to February 10, 1909. The board reported great difficulty in carrying out the investigation because Warden Johnson attempted with no little success to intimidate the witnesses, who were in part prison officers, and prevent them from giving evidence damaging to the warden's case.[467] The investigators stated that the accepted evidence proved the warden to have been guilty of the following acts not in harmony with a sound system of prison administration. The warden, while not an habitual drunkard, was often intoxicated when on duty. He invariably let the contract for the prison meat to the same contractors, even though the meat was often in a decayed state and always under weight. Other contracts for prison supplies were found to be irregular, and the warden obtained all the food for his own family without cost from the prison supplies. Further, the warden let the contracts for the officers' uniforms without consulting the officers. Some of the clothing for the warden and his family was made by prison labor without cost; all of the repairing and cleaning of the clothing of the warden and his family was done by the prisoners without pay, and the same was true of the laundry work, even that of visitors at the warden's apartments. The warden's family was given free range of the entire prison at all times, to the detriment of the general discipline of the institution. Mr. Henry Phipps had given five thousand dollars to the prison for a conservatory to furnish flowers for the prisoners, but the male prisoners never received any and even the female prisoners and the patients in the hospital were neglected, while the warden annually took for his own use about one thousand dollars' worth of flowers and

---

[465] *Senate Journal*, 1897, p. 2305.

[466] While one must be continually on his guard against an obvious bias, much can be learned from Alexander Berkmann's *Prison Memoirs of an Anarchist* concerning the administration and discipline of the Western Penitentiary during the latter part of Warden Wright's period as warden of the prison.

[467] *Report of the State Board of Public Charities*, 1909, pp. 78-9.

utilized them as gifts to secure personal favors from prominent citizens. The fire insurance of the prison plant was let to the warden's father without any bids being asked for. The warden kept a cow and hens on the prison property and sold a large number of eggs on his own account. Prisoners were allowed to talk over the telephone to advance the political fortunes of officers. A very expensive carriage, harness and team were purchased for the warden, and the latter was very frequently absent from the institution on "business tours which appear to be largely pleasure excursions." The warden exhibited little interest in investigating the circumstances connected with a threatened escape of convicts. The board of inspectors often met and transacted business with only two, or less than a quorum, present. The officers were not allowed to make complaints to the inspectors without first submitting them to the warden.[468] On the basis of the above findings the investigators arrived at the following conclusions:

"This completes the list of specific charges. While some of them, considered alone, would seem trivial, yet, taken as a whole, they show incompetence, a remarkable looseness of discipline and accounting, general mismanagement, and, in many respects, other failures on the part of the Warden and the higher officials to perform the duties imposed upon them by law. The investigation of these charges brought to light other serious irregularities and violations of law, some of them of more importance than the specific charges under investigation. . . .

"In short, the Warden seems not only to have failed in filling his proper position efficiently, but he has undertaken to perform the duties of other officers to the neglect of his own. The testimony shows him to be lacking in many, if not all of the essential qualities that make for competence of an officer charged with administrative functions. Justice to the prisoners and the good of public service point clearly to the necessity for the removal of Warden Johnson for reasons above stated." [469]

The inspectors were proved to be equally, if not more, culpable in the matter by the fact that they reelected Johnson as warden of the Western Penitentiary after the investigation had closed and after the inspectors had themselves admitted that the testimony during the investigation had revealed "an astounding state of affairs." [470] They later made some amend for their delinquency by appointing John Francies warden of the institution.

With the exception of a thorough investigation of the industrial

---

[468] *Report of the State Board of Public Charities,* 1909, pp. 80-7.
[469] Ibid., pp. 86, 89.
[470] Ibid., 1909, pp. 86-90.

aspect of the penal system of the state during 1913-15 by Professor Louis N. Robinson, there was no movement for an investigation of the penitentiary system of Pennsylvania until the passage of an act on July 25, 1917, authorizing the governor to appoint a commission to investigate prison systems and their organization, with the end in view of recommending improvements in the penal, reformatory and correctional institutions of Pennsylvania. This act specifically declared that:

"The Governor is hereby duly authorized to appoint a commission of five persons, two of whom shall be learned in the law; and at least one of whom shall be an active official of a correctional institution within this Commonwealth, to investigate the prison systems and the organization and management of correctional institutions within this Commonwealth and elsewhere; to recommend such revision of the existing prison system within this Commonwealth and the laws pertaining to the establishment, maintenance, and regulation of state and county correctional institutions within this Commonwealth, as it shall deem wise, and to report the same to the general Assembly at the session of one thousand nine hundred and nineteen." [471]

The act was unique in the history of Pennsylvania penology. There were no distressing special circumstances to be investigated other than the labor situation, and this had been fully covered in Professor Robinson's report submitted two years earlier. Rarely, if ever, had the various state institutions been under the control of more competent management or more efficiently administered. For the first time public recognition was given to the fact that the whole penological theory and practice in the state was in need of a systematic overhauling and reorganization that would give to it uniformity, would eliminate from it vestiges of barbarism which had lingered on through no special fault of any one, and would bring into the practice of Pennsylvania the advances in penological theory and application made in the more progressive states of the Union in the last generation. Not since the reorganization at the close of the colonial period was a more promising opportunity opened to prison reformers than that which faced this "Commission to Investigate Penal Systems."

The commission as appointed by the governor was composed of Fletcher W. Stites, Chairman, Alfred E. Jones, Martha P. Falconer,

---

[471] The commission, as appointed, consisted of Fletcher W. Stites, Alfred E. Jones, Louis N. Robinson, Albert H. Votaw and Martha P. Falconer. Doctor George W. Kirchwey, of New York City, who had just completed the direction of a similar investigation in New Jersey, was engaged as the counsel to the commission.

Louis N. Robinson and Albert H. Votaw. The commission engaged as its counsel and director of investigation, Doctor George W. Kirchwey, formerly Dean of the Columbia University School of Law, and at that time Professor of Criminology and Penology at the New York School of Social Work. Doctor Kirchwey had just served with success as counsel and director to the New Jersey Prison Inquiry Committee, whose report in 1918 had led to a revolutionary reconstruction of the system of charities and corrections in New Jersey. The brunt of the work in directing the investigations undertaken by the commission was borne by Mr. Votaw and Doctor Kirchwey. The scope of the work of the commission, together with its final recommendations, is indicated by the following excerpts from the Report of January 1, 1919:

"COMMONWEALTH OF PENNSYLVANIA

"REPORT OF COMMISSION TO INVESTIGATE PENAL SYSTEMS

"To the General Assembly:

"Your Commission duly appointed pursuant to Act of the Legislature, No. 409, 1917, 'to investigate the prison systems and the organization and management of correctional institutions within this Commonwealth and elsewhere; to recommend such revision of the existing prison system within this Commonwealth, and the laws pertaining to the establishment, maintenance and regulation of State and County correctional institutions within this Commonwealth as it shall deem wise, and to report the same to the General Assembly at the session of 1919,' respectfully submits the following report of its proceedings, together with its conclusions and recommendations and proposed bills for carrying the same into effect.

"The Commission was constituted as follows:
"Fletcher W. Stites, Narberth, Chairman,
"Alfred E. Jones, Uniontown,
"Mrs. Martha P. Falconer, Darling P. O.,
"Louis N. Robinson, Swarthmore,
"Albert H. Votaw, Philadelphia.

"On November 1, 1917, the members of the Commission met in the City of Philadelphia, for the purpose of organization and assigned the work of investigation which had been committed to it to the several members thereof. On July 1, 1918, the Commission retained Dr. George W. Kirchwey, of New York City, as its counsel to direct the subsequent course of the investigation and to aid the Commission with his counsel and advice.

"SCOPE OF INVESTIGATION

"The Commission was fortunate in having in its personnel as thus constituted four members, including its counsel, who had through long experience and previous investigations acquired considerable information as to penal institutions and their management in this and other States. The investigation covered:

"(1) A careful study and analysis of the laws governing penal conditions and institutions in this Commonwealth;

"(2) An examination of the six correctional institutions directly controlled by the State, namely:

"The Eastern Penitentiary, at Philadelphia;
"The Western Penitentiary, at Pittsburgh;
"The New Central Penitentiary, at Bellefonte;
"The State Industrial Reformatory, at Huntingdon;
"The Pennsylvania Training School, at Morganza;
"The State Industrial Home for Women, at Muncy;

"(3) A similar examination of the Glen Mills Schools—the Girls' Department, Sleighton Farms, at Darlington, and the Boys' Department at Glen Mills;

"(4) A similar examination of the Philadelphia House of Correction and of the County Convict Prison at Holmesburg, Moyamensing Prison in Philadelphia, the Allegheny County Workhouse at Hoboken and many other county institutions;

"(5) A study of the constitution, organization and functions of the State Board of Public Charities, and specifically of those of its Committee on Lunacy;

"(6) A study of the powers and activities of the Prison Labor Commission instituted under the Act of June 1, 1918;

"(7) A careful survey of the entire history of the penal system of the Commonwealth of Pennsylvania from the colonial period down to the present time, based on the historical research of Professor Harry E. Barnes of Clark University, Massachusetts;

"(8) An investigation of significant correctional institutions in several other States, notably in New York, New Jersey and Ohio.

"To supplement and enlarge the range of these inquiries and studies, the Commission was permitted to avail itself of the results of previous investigations conducted by two of its members; on the 'Employment and Compensation of Prisoners in Pennsylvania,' by Professor Louis N. Robinson, as Secretary of the Penal Commission of 1913-15, and on the county jails and workhouses, made periodically from 1914 to 1918 by Albert H. Votaw, as Secretary of the Pennsylvania Prison Society. . . .

"RECOMMENDATIONS

"Upon the foregoing facts and conclusions the Commission submits the following recommendations, which are herewith submitted for such action as the General Assembly may deem proper:—

"*First.*—The Commission recommends that the General Assembly provide for the enlargement of the Board of Public Charities by the addition of two members thereto, at least one of whom shall be a woman, and by the institution of a standing committee of five members of such Board, at least one of whom shall be a woman, such committee, which shall be chosen annually by a majority vote of the Board, to be known as the 'Committee on Delinquency' and to be vested with the following powers:—

"(*a*) To inspect and investigate the condition and management of all penal, correctional and reformatory institutions within the Commonwealth and inquire into all complaints against the same and report thereon, with recommendations of appropriate action, to the Board of Public Charities, the Governor, the General Assembly, or the Courts, as the circumstances may require;

"(*b*) To institute, maintain and supervise a medical service adapted to the examination of the inmates of such institutions and the proper professional treatment of all such as are mentally or physically afflicted or deficient;

"(*c*) To make recommendations to the governing authorities of all such institutions for the improvement of the sanitary and hygienic conditions, the medical and hospital equipment, and the medical service thereof;

"(*d*) To transfer inmates of institutions within its jurisdiction to other institutions owned, managed or controlled by the Commonwealth or any political subdivision thereof, or, if suitable arrangements can be made, to other institutions, where such inmates may receive treatment more suitable to their mental and physical condition;

"(*e*) To institute, maintain and supervise in institutions within its jurisdiction a system of correctional and reformatory education;

"(*f*) To institute, maintain and supervise a system for the employment of the inmates of institutions within its jurisdiction;

"(*g*) To prepare and submit to the Board of Public Charities not later than the first day of December of each even-numbered year, a biennial budget for the Committee and such of the institutions within its jurisdiction as are wholly or partly supported by the Commonwealth, and for that purpose to require of such institutions such reports from time to time as the Committee shall deem necessary; and

"(*h*) To make rules and regulations establishing a uniform system of accounting and bookkeeping in all institutions within its jurisdiction.

"It is also recommended that the Committee on Delinquency be authorized and directed to choose a Secretary, not a member of the Board of Public Charities, at a salary of $7,500 per annum, who shall be the executive officer of the Committee and an expert in the care and treatment of delinquents, and who shall be known as the 'Commissioner of Delinquency.'

"*Second.*—The Commission further recommends that the General Assembly provide by appropriate legislation for the employment of all the able-bodied convicts of the Commonwealth in useful and, so far as possible, in productive labor, and especially, that it vest in the Committee on Delinquency the powers of the Prison Labor Commission and the functions of the Business Agent of such Commission and enlarge such powers and functions as suggested on page 15 of this report.

"*Third.*—The Commission further recommends the enactment of a law establishing four State Industrial Farms, to receive, care for and provide for the useful employment of the inmates of county prisons and jails and of persons hereafter convicted of any offense punishable by imprisonment in any county jail or prison who have been or shall hereafter be sentenced for a term of thirty days or more.

"*Fourth.*—The Commission further recommends that the Act of Assembly approved July 17, 1917 (No. 337), providing for the employment, during the continuance of the war, of inmates of county jails at agricultural labor on any county or almshouse farm, be amended so as to continue its operation indefinitely after the conclusion of peace.

"*Fifth.*—The Commission further recommends that the General Assembly provide for the purchase of a tract of land, of not less than 600 nor more than 1200 acres, to be used for the benefit of the Eastern Penitentiary as a prison farm.

"*Sixth.*—The Commission further recommends that a law be enacted prohibiting fees or allowances and contracts for furnishing meals to the inmates of county jails or other penal institutions of the Commonwealth.

"*Seventh.*—The Commission further recommends that the Act approved June 19, 1911, authorizing the courts in the case of a person sentenced to a penitentiary to fix as the minimum term of imprisonment any period less than the maximum prescribed by law for the offense of which such person was convicted, be amended by a provision that the minimum limit of the sentence imposed shall never exceed one-third of the maximum prescribed by the Court.

"In the foregoing recommendations the Commission has confined itself to matters requiring legislative action and to such only as seem to it to be essential to a consistent, integrated policy of penal administration. All other matters with respect to which the Commission has given expression to its views are either subsidiary to those on which immediate legislative action is recommended or are such as may be properly referred to the wisdom of the proposed Committee on Delinquency for consideration and action. The greatest abuse of the prevailing prison system—the lack of imagination and of understanding which keeps alive in most of our penal establishments the methods of a severe and repressive discipline—cannot be abolished by legislative decree. The greatest reform of which the system is capable—the awakening in the inmates of the new life which comes from active, responsible participation in the life of the prison community—is equally beyond the reach of legislative action. These will be the fruits of a keener intelligence and of a deeper understanding than have yet, except in a few rare instances, been brought to bear on the problem. But your Commission believes that the plan of penal administration which it has recommended, and which provides for the most thoroughgoing study and the most intelligent treatment of the individual delinquent which has yet been attempted, will gradually prepare the way for these and other reforms in the penal system of the Commonwealth.

"Respectfully submitted,

"January 1, 1919.

> "FLETCHER W. STITES, *Chairman,*
> "ALFRED E. JONES,
> "MARTHA P. FALCONER,
> "LOUIS N. ROBINSON,
> "ALBERT H. VOTAW,
> > *"Commissioners.*

"GEORGE W. KIRCHWEY,
"Counsel to the Commission."

The majority of the recommendations of the commission have since been realized through the reform legislation which has been described above in connection with the establishment of the Board of Public Welfare, the abolition of the restrictive labor legislation, the securing of a partial indeterminate sentence law, the extension of the probation system, the provision for employment of the inmates of jails and workhouses, and the act of 1925 appropriating money for the purchase of a large tract of land as the site of a new Eastern Penitentiary. Much of the credit for the execution of the advanced penal legislation of Pennsylvania in recent years has been due to the support of the reform program by Governor Gifford Pinchot, who has retained Doctor Kirchwey as his adviser. An admirable Secretary of Public Welfare has been appointed in the person of Dr. Ellen C. Potter. No phase of the work of Governor Pinchot and the Board of Public Welfare has been more creditable than the choice of new wardens for the three state penitentiaries. Colonel John C. Broome was made warden of the Eastern Penitentiary; Mr. J. O. Stutsman, warden of the Central Penitentiary at Rockview; and Mr. Stanley P. Ashe, warden of the Western Penitentiary. All three of these men have proved enlightened criminologists and penologists.[471a]

[471a] The writer is aware of the recent dismissal of Mr. Stutsman, but he does not concur in the wisdom of the action. It is somewhat akin to the attitude toward Mr. Osborne at Sing Sing.

The remarkable progress which has been made since 1923 with respect to the improvement of prison administration, the organization and centralization of the state penal and correctional institutions, the solution of the problem of convict unemployment, the establishment of industrial training, the scientific overhauling of institutional finances, the study of social conditions related to criminality, and the beginning of the utilization of scientific knowledge in Pennsylvaina penal institutions is well described by Doctor Ellen C. Potter in an address delivered in February, 1927:

"Four years ago you asked me as the newly appointed Secretary of Welfare to appear before you at the State Convention to tell you what I hoped to do. The time which had elapsed from the date of my appointment to the date of the meeting was, as you know, very short, but having helped to bring up the infant Department of Welfare through its first summer, I had the advantage of familiarity with its problems. There were a few principles which appeared to me to stand out as fundamental to the success of public social work in Pennsylvania which it seemed possible to lay down as a 'platform' from which we might proceed and this I ventured to do with the approval of Governor Pinchot. . . .

"*First*—to develop and strengthen local responsibility for local social welfare, 'Home rule in Welfare Work.'

"*Second*—to improve standards of social work by an educational process and not by police methods of compulsion. Incidentally to promote mutual understanding and confidence between all those engaged in social work.

"*Third*—to keep the Department of Welfare out of politics and to put the state charities on a sound social basis.

"*Fourth*—to give a business-like administration of the Department in order that the people might be well served.

"*Fifth*—To take official action only on the basis of assembled facts; and to do our best to add to the sum of human knowledge by social research.

"*Sixth*—to ascertain our legal powers; to administer with discretion; and to ascertain the points at which the laws relating to social welfare needed to be strengthened.

"Whether we have 'kept the faith' on the basis of these principles you shall say; at all events this is what we attempted to set as a platform and guide for the development of social work in Pennsylvania. . . .

"We were glad that we had committed ourselves to a policy of education, diplomacy and conciliation rather than to 'big stick' methods of securing corrective results. Such methods are slow but if they are continued over a series of years, and they now have been for four years, some substantial results are bound to be realized. I am glad to be able to report to you that the physical equipment and administration of the county alms houses and county prisons of the state, has, with very few exceptions, improved enormously during this period.

"To be sure the Secretary has sometimes been called 'impractical' and a 'visionary' when she suggested that a bath tub be provided for the cleanliness and safety of the inmates of the alms houses, and has been told that the inmates can go to the brook for a bath; or when the Secretary suggested that vagrants accepted at the county jail should be given cots instead of being allowed to sleep on burlap in the coal bin, and that they should be given work (a stone pile being suggested) instead of being fed free at cost to the taxpayers, she sees, according to the Sheriff, that she is asking for the 'best hotel accommodations' for these wanderers; or when she suggests that one article of diet be added to the prison breakfast and supper menu, which at the time consists of coffee and bread, she is charged with wishing to waste the tax-payers' money on riotous living for convicts.

"However, patience and persistence in *reasonable* recommenda-tions with the suggestion that the story must go to the newspapers in obdurate cases, has secured corrective results, and we have a sense of satisfaction that the more than 8,500 persons who are supported daily in our county homes and the 6,000 daily supported in our county prisons (14,500 total) are more decently housed, more suitably fed and more humanly treated than they would have been had not the Department been continuously attending to the people's business in the field of social welfare. . . .

"With the enactment of the Administrative Code the responsi-bility for budgetary control of state-owned institutions became one of the duties of the Department. Here again our power was by indirection, the trustees of institutions being appointed directly by the Governor and superintendents being appointed by the trustees without any obligation to the Secretary of Welfare. If an institu-tion wilfully failed to live within its budget the compulsion to reform was vested in the Governor who might advise the state fiscal officers not to pay out any funds under the appropriation acts until the trustees did conform.

"In making the provisions of any new law effective, especially relating to financial affairs, there is a mass of detail in procedure and records which must be set up and made effective if satisfactory results are to be obtained.

"When, in 1923, the Administration came into office there was no standard system of cost accounting in force in any state owned institution; there was no standard system of specification and pur-chase of supplies; no standard system of drawing up building plans, specifications and handling contracts.

"Today a standard system of cost accounting is in force in all state owned institutions; standard specifications covering the major items purchased by institutions are set up with a modified form of central purchasing established; standard procedure in regard to plans, specifications and building contracts are in force resulting in the saving of hundreds of thousands of dollars (not to say millions) to the State.

"Moreover the state institutions are rendering a higher type of professional service at no greater per capita cost than when the Department was given the responsibility of controlling expenditures.

"As concrete evidence of improved business administration I may cite the fact that for the 1921-23 biennium, deficiencies of $582,056 had to be met for the Welfare institutions while for 1925-27 there is but one deficiency incurred during our administration, amounting to less than $35,000 and incurred in the operation of a newly created institution, Locust Mountain Hospital, for which no previous operating costs were available as a basis for estimate. . . .

"But if business methods were at loose ends in our state institutions in 1923 there were two acutely bad professional problems involving our state owned general hospitals and our penitentiaries, which were crying for solution even more insistently.

"These two problems, representing as they did the end results of maladministrtaion, highly colored with political corruption, demanded most of the time and thought of the Secretary of Welfare during the early months of 1923.

"When institutional conditions become unutterably bad it is interesting to note how few persons there are within a state who are ready to study the situation and to lend a hand in providing a remedy. I am therefore always impelled to take off my hat to Colonel John C. Groome who was willing and able to undertake to bring order out of chaos in the Eastern State Penitentiary, where conditions during the winter and early spring were indescribable.

"With 'hootch' freely for sale, even manufactured within the institution; with dope easily available; with the woman's section of the prison a brothel, with the building itself infested with filth and vermin, there were no lower depths to which it could sink; while the control of the institution itself was actually in the hands of 'The Four Horsemen,' four convicts running the institution in their own interest and that of some of the prison officers.

"While license and gross depravity were rampant at the Eastern end of the state, at the Central and Western Penitentiaries there was to be found the hard boiled type of utter restraint with shackles, dungeons, 'solitary' and mental torture; with depravity and deterioration of men quite as marked as in the east.

"In addition no industrial, recreational, educational, or spiritual program was under way in these institutions.

"Needless to say many months of careful study of the situation had to be made, experts such as Hastings Hart and Whitman and later Arthur Dean were brought in to advise on the situation as a whole and as a result we have today a group of prisons and reformatories whose administration is second to none in the United States.

"The buildings are clean, though antiquated and overcrowded; educational, recreational, religious, industrial and trade training programs are in force and a solid foundation has been laid for future progress.

"More than 92 per cent. of the inmates are employed either in Welfare industries, handicrafts or in the domestic work of the institution and are receiving compensation while those employed in the Welfare shops are receiving trade training carefully organized and supervised as contrasted with absolute unemployment of more than a third of the prison population in 1923.

"As a matter of policy, four years ago, we committed ourselves to the principle of conducting prison industries on a self-supporting basis, for purposes of trade training and in such a manner as to minimize competition with the free manufacturer and organized labor.

"I am able to report today that the operation of our industries has not cost the taxpayer one penny during the past four years; as a matter of fact out of net earnings approximately $200,000 has gone back into the industries for capital outlay.

"We have trained a goodly number of graduates who now hold responsible jobs and we have been gratified to find our policies approved both by representatives of organized labor and the U. S. Chamber of Commerce. We have associated with our shops committees composed of men representative of labor and of the Philadelphia Chamber of Commerce whose advice is invaluable independent of these industries. . . .

"During the past four years under the Bureau of Mental Health the mental health clinics have been increased from 20 to 51 and lack of funds alone has prevented further expansion; thorough mental examinations are now made of all admissions to the Huntingdon Reformatory and at Muncy, the State reformatory for women, this contributing materially to the simplification of the administrative problems in those institutions; the waiting lists which were tremendous at our schools for the feeble-minded have been carefully studied and constructive planning for those unable to secure admission has been undertaken; provision has been made for the care and training of juvenile insane at the Allentown State Hospital; and an approved school for the training of attendants has been established at the Harrisburg State Hospital and is meeting a crying need in that field."

Three new commissions relating to penology and criminal jurisprudence were created by the State Legislature in their session of 1927. The nature and import of these new commissions are well set forth in the June, 1927, *Bulletin of the Pennsylvania Committee on Penal Affairs*:

"Three Commissions having to do with penal matters issued from the recent Legislative session. A *Commission on Penal Institutions* of five persons—qualifications not specified—is allowed $20,000 for the purpose of inquiring into the advisability of making Rockview a separate penitentiary, and of investigating 'the several State and local penal institutions, their method of administration, and the commitment, employment, care and maintenance of inmates therein, and to suggest methods for the improvement of the same, to study and make recommendations relative to the transfer and retransfer of inmates to and from such institutions, and to inquire into the advisability of providing for the construction of district or central prisons or workhouses for the confinement of prisoners now confined in county and city prisons and workhouses.'

"Here is a Commission capable of much weal or woe to the penal system of our State! Its recommendations may determine the nature of Pennsylvania's prison system for generations to come. It is therefore of most vital concern to the citizens of the State that its personnel shall consist of men and women qualified by training and experience to deal with this technical and complex problem. The ordinary legislative commission would work havoc indeed—and it is highly essential to urge upon the Governor the great concern of the public in his wise choice of this Commission.

"Two other commissions are given less immediately practical, but nevertheless important duties. One is virtually a continuation of the *Penal Code Commission* which has been working for four years on a revision of the penal laws of the Commonwealth. The other is a *Crime Commission* charged with the duty of studying 'the laws, conditions and practice of this Commonwealth relating to crimes, criminal procedure and criminals, to examine the crime situation in the Commonwealth of Pennsylvania, the procedure, methods and agencies concerned with the detection of crime, the apprehension, bailing, prosecution and trial of persons accused of crime, and the punishment, treatment and pardon of convicted persons, and all other matters which have relation directly or indirectly to the crime situation in this Commonwealth, and such additional laws as may be made to embody the best thought and experience on these subjects, and to suggest revisions and amendments to the statutes of Pennsylvania which relate to any of the foregoing matters.'

"Here again, the value of the Commission depends wholly on its personnel; whether it is to be a superficial survey responding to public emotions by a series of recommendations for drastic punishment, or a careful inquiry into the causes and possible methods of preventing and dealing with crime, and protecting the public from its depredations—utilizing all the instruments which progress has made possible in psychiatric and social science."

3. The Work of the Philadelphia Society for Alleviating the Miseries of Public Prisons.
(The Pennsylvania Prison Society)

The part played by the Philadelphia Society for Alleviating the Miseries of Public Prisons in the reconstruction of penal conditions in Pennsylvania at the close of the colonial period and in the creation of the Pennsylvania prison system has been described in an earlier part of this work. At the close of nearly a century after these reforms had been achieved the society still exists [472] as the most powerful agency for prison reform in the state, and its labors in this field since 1835 have been more productive of permanent good than the combined efforts of other critics and investigators. Very little has been achieved in improving the conditions in penal and reformatory institutions in Pennsylvania which has not been due in a very large degree to the activities of this organization.[473]

The following summary review of the work of this organization can not be regarded as anything more than an account of a few of its more conspicuous achievements and activities. A full account of their multifarious labors would constitute a treatise in itself.[474] The first notable service rendered by the society following 1835 was the aid it gave to Dorothea L. Dix in agitating for the establishment of a hospital for the insane which would allow the removal of insane convicts from the state penitentiaries. A vigorous memorial was sent to the legislature in 1845 urging such action.[475] In 1850-51 the society devoted its main efforts to an attempt to compel the practice of solitary confinement in the county jails of the state.[476] The first law in Pennsylvania ordering the granting of commutation of sentence for good behavior—that of 1861—was passed as a result of the agitation of the society, especially of Townsend Sharpless.[477] From 1853 to 1870 the society labored to have a workhouse provided for the city of Philadelphia.[478]

---

[472] Its name was changed to that of *The Pennsylvania Prison Society* in 1886.

[473] Good surveys of the work of the society in the last century are provided in *The Journal of Prison Discipline and Philanthropy,* Volumes for 1862, 1887, 1900 and 1910.

[474] The full account of the labors of the society can be obtained from the files of the *Journal of Prison Discipline and Philanthropy,* the organ of the society. It can be obtained in the society offices, and a full set has also been collected for the library of the Russell Sage Foundation in New York.

[475] *Journal of Prison Discipline and Philanthropy,* Vol. I, No. 2, 1845, pp. 190-99.

[476] Ibid., Vol. VI, No. 3, 1851, pp. 129-32.

[477] Ibid., Vol. XVI, No. 4, 1861; Ibid., 1887, p. 17.

[478] Ibid., 1862, pp. 39-40.

One of the most important achievements of this organization was the leadership that it took in securing the legislation creating the State Board of Public Charities in 1869.[479] In 1872 it secured the creation of the State Board of Pardons, thus taking the important pardoning powers out of the hands of the governor alone.[480] It lent its aid after 1885 to the struggle for a special state hospital for the criminal insane.[481] In the period of discussion accompanying the establishment of the Huntingdon Reformatory the majority of the members of the society ranged themselves in favor of the adoption of the advanced Elmira system of prison administration.[482] In the period from 1909 to the present, which has been characterized by the greatest penological progress of the last century, the society has led in the program of education and agitation which secured such notable innovations as the practices of probation, parole and the indeterminate sentence, made a vigorous attempt to remedy the intolerable industrial situation in the state penitentiaries, and obtained legislation creating a general prison investigating commission. Particularly worthy of mention in this more recent period have been the labors of Albert H. Votaw, the general secretary of the society, and Doctor J. F. Ohl, the chairman of the standing committee on legislation.

Beyond these activities more or less directly related to reform in the state penitentiary system, the society has done valuable work in allied fields. Particularly significant has been its investigation of the jails. While its study of jail conditions has been less steady than the investigations by the State Board of Public Charities, it has been much more penetrating, especially in the decade before 1921 when the work of the state board has been perfunctory and mechanical, while that of the prison society has been especially thoroughgoing and conscientious.[483] The most notable humanitarian efforts of the society have been expended in aiding discharged prisoners and in visiting the prisoners in the Eastern Penitentiary. Not since 1895 has the state given any aid to discharged prisoners, both money and clothing being furnished by the prison society.[484] This type of work was given a more systematic and permanent basis when the "Department of Released Prisoners" was created by the Society in 1925. The nature and results of its work are well described in the *Prison Journal* for January, 1927.

[479] *Journal of Prison Discipline and Philanthropy,* 1872, pp. 50-3; 1873, p. 65.
[480] Ibid., 1887, p. 19.
[481] Ibid., 1885, pp. 18-20.
[482] Ibid., 1891, pp. 36-46.
[483] Ibid., 1865, pp. 3-14; 1883, pp. 43-5; 1912, p. 12; 1914, Supplement 53; 1916, Supplement 55.
[484] Ibid., 1912, pp. 9-10.

Many thousand visits have been made to inmates of the Eastern Penitentiary; in this phase of the work the most active member of the society was Mr. John J. Lytle, secretary of the society from 1860 to 1909.[485] The work of the society is now supplemented by that of the even more alert Pennsylvania Committee on Penal Affairs directed by Doctor Louis N. Robinson and Mr. Leon Stern.

4. Some Important Reform Movements in Pennsylvania Penology Not Immediately Connected with the State Penitentiaries

There are several important developments in the reform of penology in Pennsylvania, which represented the labors of various progressive movements and organizations and constituted advances of great significance, but were not directly connected with the state penitentiaries.

One of the most conspicuous and significant phases of the progress of prison administration in the last century has been the development of a scientific differentiation in the institutions designed to treat the criminal classes. In the early modern prisons which prevailed before the Pennsylvania and Auburn Prisons came into existence, all alleged and real delinquents were herded together in an enclosure, generally in one room or group of rooms, containing accused and convicted, debtors and criminals, male and female, young and old, insane, idiotic and those of normal mentality, first offenders and hardened recidivists. The reformation of the offender was rendered hopeless at the outset under such conditions.

The rise of the Pennsylvania and Auburn systems marked a great step in the way of progress. The accused were separated from the convicted, and separate portions of the prison were assigned to the male and female prisoners. The next step came in the erection of Houses of Refuge for young offenders, their condition in the prisons of the time naturally giving rise to much sympathy on the part of reformers. The historical background of their development is a long one. The origins of institutions for juvenile delinquents must be sought in the juvenile departments of the English workhouses of the sixteenth and seventeenth centuries. The movement reached its highest early development in

---

[485] *Journal of Prison Discipline and Philanthropy*, 1911, pp. 69-71. Along with the work of the Pennsylvania Prison Society should be mentioned the valuable efforts in recent years of the Protestant Episcopal City Mission and the Philadelphia branch of the American Society for Visiting Catholic Prisoners.

Holland, where, by the seventeenth century, a famous system of such institutions for the neglected and delinquent youth had developed. From an observation of their operation William Penn is said to have derived in part his notion of imprisonment as a method of treating the criminal.

The beginning of the modern movement is normally taken to date from the building of the House of Refuge at Danzig, in 1813, under the direction of one John Falk. In London, also, similar institutions were developing, in part out of earlier progress there and in part from imitation of continental methods. The introduction of such institutions into the United States was due to the work of Professor John Griscom, a Quaker who traveled extensively in Europe in the early twenties and was struck with the importance of these "child-saving institutions." He brought back his impressions to New York City and Philadelphia, where they were appropriated by the reforming groups. The first House of Refuge for juvenile delinquents in this country was opened at Madison Square in New York City on January 25, 1825. It was built far north of the center of the city, in the hope that a century of municipal expansion would not disturb it. The second institution of the kind was opened in Boston in 1826, and the third in Philadelphia in 1828. But these were private institutions, though in part open to the use of the commonwealth. The first state institution for juvenile delinquents was opened at Westboro, Massachusetts, in 1847.

These early houses of refuge, however, were nothing more than prisons for young offenders. In neither architecture nor administration did they differ from the conventional prison, though an exception must be made in the case of the Boston House of Refuge, where, as early as 1831, De Beaumont and De Tocqueville discovered the existence of a crude but real system of classification, promotion and inmate self-government. The origination of the more modern and humane method of handling juvenile delinquents in the cottage or family arrangement was due to the work of the French publicist and reformer, Frédéric Auguste Demetz. Looking upon the problem as a French judge, Demetz was shocked by the conventional method of handling juvenile delinquents. Aided by the Vicomte de Courteilles, a wealthy Touraine landholder, who gave Demetz the necessary farming land, the latter opened at Mettray in 1840, his first agricultural colony for juvenile delinquents administered according to the "Family system." His system spread rapidly, being first introduced into this country at the state reform school in Lancaster, Ohio, in 1855. But the family system of housing and administration, initiated by Demetz, was only a beginning in the right direction. Long hours and heavy work were prescribed for the inmates with the avowed aim of making them too tired to desire to play or engage in mischief. The progress has been a long and gradual one from these early "cottage institutions" to such a system as that of the George Junior Republic or that now practiced in such a reform school as the girls' institution at Sleighton Farms in Pennsylvania, where inmate self-government and an extremely close approximation to normal family life prevail.

The circumstances connected with the origins of the Philadelphia House of Refuge in 1828—the first Pennsylvania institution to be differentiated from the state penitentiaries—have already been briefly described. While an annex for colored inmates and new buildings for white inmates were erected in the middle of the last century, no important administrative or disciplinary progress occurred until 1892, when the boys' department was moved to Glen Mills and the example of Ohio, New Jersey and other states was followed in adopting, in place of the barbarous and prison-like "house of refuge" architecture and organization, the more humane and advanced "cottage-farm" system, which had been originated by Demetz and De Courteilles at Mettray, France, in 1840. The girls' department was moved to Darlington in 1910, and, under the direction of Superintendents Martha P. Falconer and Emily F. Morrison, has become one of the most progressive institutions in this county. The system of inmate self-government has attracted special attention and approval. Notable progress has been made in the way of institutions for juvenile delinquents in the western part of the state. The House of Refuge of Western Pennsylvania was opened at Allegheny in 1854. Its name was changed to the Pennsylvania Reform School in 1872. In 1876 it was removed to Morganza and the cottage system adopted. In 1912 its name was changed once more, this time to the Pennsylvania Training School. Under the management of Superintendent W. F. Penn it has become in recent years a rival of the Darlington (Sleighton Farms) institution in the enlightened nature of its correctional methods.

The first step of importance in differentiating the criminal classes, technically so-called, was the above described provision of institutions for juvenile delinquents. The next advance came in the form of institutions for the group of youthful offenders between the juveniles and adults.

In his two works, *The Penitentiary Systems of Europe and America* (1828) and *The Theory of Imprisonment* (1836), that wise and progressive French penologist, Monsieur Charles Lucas, had clearly taken the advanced position that a curative reformatory

The School at Sleighton Farms

type of prison discipline ought to be substituted for the contemporary repressive prison system. It was a long time, however, before this aspiration was adequately realized. It was only achieved and then imperfectly, in the Elmira Reformatory system introduced into New York State following 1870.

A number of significant currents of reform in penology converged in producing this system. An important element was contributed by the new methods of prison discipline introduced in the British penal colony in Australia. Captain Alexander Maconochie came to Norfolk Island in Australia in 1840, and was able to bring about a tremendous improvement in penal methods by eliminating the old flat-time sentence and introducing the beginnings of commutation of sentence for good behavior. Every convict, according to the seriousness of his offense, instead of being sentenced to a given term of years, had a certain number of marks set against him which he had to redeem before he was liberated. These marks were to be earned by deportment, labor and study, and the more rapidly they were acquired the more speedy the release.

At about the same time the notion of an indeterminate time sentence was originated and given popularity through the writings of Archbishop Whately of Dublin, the Scotchman, George Combe, and especially the English reformers, Frederick and Matthew Davenport Hill. Its supplement, the famous parole system, while anticipated by a number of other reformers, was most systematically and effectively advocated by the French publicist, Bonneville de Marsangy. Maconochie's system of determining the period of incarceration upon the basis of the behavior of the convict was combined with the notion of the indeterminate sentence and parole in the famous Irish system of prison administration, which was introduced by Sir Walter Crofton in the decade following 1853. To these earlier progressive innovations he added the practice of classifying convicts in graded groups, through which each convict had to pass before obtaining his freedom on parole, his advancement being determined by his conduct.

The notion of productive and instructive prison labor, which goes back to the Pennsylvania Quakers, was also developed by a number of progressive penologists during the second quarter of the nineteenth century, especially by Montesinos in Spain and Obermaier in Bavaria.

All of these liberal and progressive innovations, which have been only too briefly and casually mentioned above, attracted the attention of the leading American reformers, most notably Theodore W. Dwight and E. C. Wines of the New York Prison Association, F. B. Sanborn of Concord, Massachusetts, Z. R. Brockway, Superintendent of the Detroit House of Correction, and Gaylord Hubbell, Warden of Sing Sing Prison. All of these men prepared able, vigorous and widely read public reports or private monographs, urging the adoption of these advanced methods in the American prison system, but they were able to secure the introduction of these innovations only for the treatment of younger first offenders. A law authorizing the creation of such an institution at Elmira, New York, was passed in 1869, and the institution was opened in 1877, with Mr. Brockway as its first superintendent. A decent preliminary approximation to the principle of the indeterminate sentence was secured, and the inmates were divided into classes or grades through which they might advance to ultimate parole by virtue of good conduct, if they did not desire to remain in the institution for the maximum sentence.

The great advance which the Irish and Elmira systems mark over Pennsylvania and Auburn systems, was the fact that in these later types of penal discipline the term of incarceration was at least roughly made to depend upon the observable progress made by the prisoner on the road to ultimate reformation. It was, thus, a system which chiefly stressed reformation rather than either retaliation or deterrence. As far as its application in the United States is concerned, however, even this method of discipline possessed serious and grave defects. In the first place, it was scarcely at all introduced into the prisons which confined the adult offenders, thus not being applied to the great bulk of the prison population. In the second place, while it was based primarily upon the idea of effecting the reformation of the convicts, it failed signally to provide the right sort of psychological surroundings to expedite this process. The whole system of discipline was repressive, and varied from benevolent despotism, in the best instances, to tyrannical cruelty in the worst. There was little, if anything, done to introduce into the mind of the individual convict, or into the groups of the convicts generally, any sense of individual or collective responsibility for the conduct of the prison community, nor was any significant attempt made to provide any education in the elements of group conduct and the responsibilities of the citizen. There was little, if any, grasp of that fundamental fact which is basic in the newer penology, namely, that a prisoner can be fitted for a life of freedom only by some training in a social environment which bears some fair resemblance in point of liberty and responsibility to that which he must enter upon obtaining his release. Finally, there was no wide acceptance of the present position that the general body of delinquents can not be treated as a single unified group. There was no general recognition that criminals must be dealt with as individuals or as a number of classes of individuals of different psychological and biological types that must be scientifically differentiated through a careful psychiatric study, as well as a detailed sociological study of their environment, preliminary to the major part of their treatment while incarcerated. These last conditions have only been very recently and very incompletely realized in systems of convict self-government, such as those which Mr. Thomas Mott Osborne has introduced, and in such careful psychiatric studies of the criminal class as were attempted in the psychiatric clinic introduced in the Sing Sing prison by Doctors Thomas W. Salmon and Bernard Glueck. It is a significant fact that when the present writer visited the parent institution at Elmira in the spring of 1926 the officials boasted that convicts eligible to either institutions preferred to be sent by the judge to the Auburn Prison rather than to the Elmira Reformatory, the discipline being less severe in the state prison at Auburn. The officials believed this to be a tribute to Elmira.

Pennsylvania was some ten years or more behind New York State in adopting the reformatory principle and embodying it in a concrete institution for delinquents. In 1889 the Huntingdon Industrial Reformatory was opened, and provided an improved correctional institution for the younger male offenders guilty of the less serious offenses. It had been recommended by Governor Henry M. Hoyt that a special commission be appointed to investigate the Elmira Reformatory, the Pennsylvania Prison Society and the State Board of Public Charities. Modeled directly after the Elmira system, it adopted in its administrative organization nearly all of the great reforms in nineteenth century penology, including the reformatory idea of Charles Lucas, the commutation system of Maconochie, the classification and promotion methods of Crofton, the indeterminate sentence, as recommended by Whatley, Combe and the brothers Hill, the parole system of Marsangy, and the notion of the value of instructive labor, which had been developed by the Pennsylvania Quakers, by Montesinos in Spain, and by Obermaier in Bavaria.

The Huntingdon Reformatory has remained true to the Brockway ideal of benevolent despotism and has never capitulated to the self-government scheme in any degree. It has, for the most part, been an economically and efficiently conducted institution of the repressive type, with emphasis placed upon a rigorously severe disciplinary system. The problem of discipline has been intensified by the absurd anti-convict labor laws of Pennsylvania, which for a long time practically disrupted inmate industry at Huntingdon. In part this was compensated for by the presence of an unusually well equipped and efficient system of manual training. Of late the state-use system has helped the authorities to solve the industrial situation to a certain degree through the manufacture of automobile registration plates, and institutional furniture. Architecturally and administratively speaking, the Huntingdon Reformatory, like its Elmira prototype, still remains a vestige from the past with respect to the facts and ideals of scientific penology. Some steps toward modernization have been taken, however, by the new superintendent, Mr. James W. Herron.

A somewhat more modern institution for women of a comparable type was authorized by an act of 1913 creating the State Industrial Home for Women, subsequently located at Muncy. Among those most active in the campaign for the establishment of this institution should be mentioned Mrs. Edward Biddle, Mrs. S. Gordon McCouch, Mrs. Franklin P. James, Mrs. Martha P. Falconer, the Pennsylvania Prison Society and the State Board of Public Charities. Here the self-government plan has made much greater headway than at Huntingdon. Under the original act only girls and women between the ages of sixteen and twenty-five were admitted to Muncy on a general sentence of not more than three years, unless the maximum term prescribed by law exceeded three years. In 1925 the Legislature appropriated $100,000 to build a new department for older women. This act also provided that these women over twenty-five years of age might be sent to Muncy for any term to which they were sentenced by the judge in accordance with the penal code. Muncy has, thus, become both an institution of the reformatory type for young women and a penal institution for older women who formerly have been sent to the state penitentiaries.

Finally, attention should be called to the admirable industrial farm organized by Mr. A. H. Leslie in recent years at the Allegheny County Workhouse. It is a model institution of its kind and serves as an example of what may be expected from that which seems destined to be one of the pivotal institutions of the penology of the future, when the archaic county jail shall at last have passed to its deserved oblivion.

Real progress was made in regard to relieving the vicious situation in the archaic county jail system through two acts passed by the Legislature in 1927. One allowed the transfer of women serving a sentence of one year or less from the jails to appropriate institutions. The other permitted the counties to acquire land up to five hundred acres for the purpose of establishing a jail farm and to transfer the inmates of the county jails from the county-seats to these farm sites.

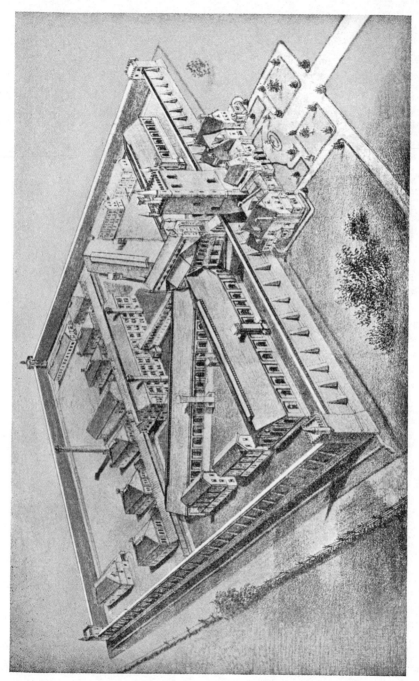

The State Industrial Reformatory at Huntingdon

VII. POLITICS AND PRISON ADMINISTRATION

Any discussion of the part played by considerations of party politics in the administration of the state penitentiaries of Pennsylvania must be based upon an understanding of the nature of the party system and history in Pennsylvania. Few states in this country north of Mason and Dixon's line have been more completely and permanently controlled by one political party than has Pennsylvania by the Republican party. This party has never lost its predominance even temporarily, except when it has been divided by factional strife. Therefore, while political factors have played as great a part in administrative appointments in Pennsylvania as in most states of the Union, the excessive evils of the spoils system, which appear with a frequent change of party control, have been very generally absent from Pennsylvania. While offices have been uniformly bestowed as a reward for political services, the incumbents have tended to hold these offices for a relatively long period, displaced as a usual thing only as the result of gross incompetence, publicly revealed, or as a result of insurgency. Even the latter cause has been discouraged because of the improbability of a successful revolt against the dominant party and party leaders. While this "mono-partisan" system has resulted in the desirable lengthening of the tenure of public officials, it should not be forgotten that it has possessed one drawback; namely, that it has made it possible to keep in office for a longer period many incompetent men who, with a party change, would have been ousted with a possibility, if not a probability, of being replaced by better officials.

The nature of the political control over the officials of the state penitentiaries has not differed radically from the situation with respect to the mode of filling the other appointive offices, except that it has been somewhat less of a strictly partisan type. The fact that the inspectors have been in control of the appointment of the chief officers of the prisons has had a beneficial result in many cases. As the inspectors have received no salary their position has not been eagerly sought by politicians, and the men appointed have generally been those who had a relatively high devotion to public service and some real interest in penological problems. To some extent this situation has led to the lessening of the entry of the political system into the administrative control of the state penitentiaries. It would, further, seem safe to assert that the degree of political control has been less in the East than in the West. In Philadelphia the local interest in prison problems has been greater and this has induced leading citizens to assume the burdens of the office of prison inspector and to keep competent men in charge of the Eastern Penitentiary. The close contact of the Philadelphia Society for Alleviating the Miseries of Public Prisons with affairs in the Eastern Penitentiary has also made it less easy to put incompetent political lieutenants in important offices in that institution. Writing in 1880, Richard Vaux, for more than a generation president of the Board of Inspectors of the Eastern Penitentiary, contended that political considerations had no part in appointments to the offices in the institution at Cherry Hill.[486] Not only the eminence of the man, but also the fact that he was a Democrat or minority party man, would serve to make one trust the veracity of that statement, though there is little doubt that matters have changed to some degree since 1880. The long period of service of Warden Cassidy in the Eastern Penitentiary would also indicate the absence of any extreme prevalence of political favoritism.

While there has been less evidence of deviation from party lines in the appointment of inspectors and officers in the Western Penitentiary, the record for long tenure within the party fold has been excellent. With the exception of about a decade between their terms, two men, Armstead Beckman and Edward S. Wright, served as wardens of the Western Penitentiary from 1837 to 1902. It is to be doubted if this record of continuous service can be surpassed in the country. As far as the possibility of continuity and permanence of administrative policy is concerned, it would be doubtful if the strictest observance of the civil service system could have produced a better opportunity. Further, it can not be said that obviously political appointments to chief offices in the state penitentiaries have always had unfortunate results. Warden John Francies, an efficient if repressive warden, was one of the most important politicians in Western Pennsylvania. McKenty, another politician from the East, proved less efficient. The establishment of the Board of Public Welfare was certainly a step forward of great importance in the way of supplanting politicial favoritism by considerations of specialized training and administrative competence. Under Governor Pinchot the system was kept clear of political corruption. What this means may be seen in the presence of such persons as Secretary Potter and Warden Stutsman, Broome and Ashe in the place of the conventionally affable but untrained political henchman. No informed students of penology doubts that when, in the more or less distant future, the facts of penal science shall have gained general acceptance among the mass of the

[486] *Annual Report of the Eastern Penitentiary,* 1880, p. 43.

citizens, the chief administrative officer of a state penitentiary will have to qualify for his position through the possession
of as great technical knowledge and as long a professional experience
as are now demanded of the superintendent of the most important
hospitals. Until this time arrives political considerations will doubtless determine such appointments, and the history of this aspect of
Pennsylvania penology is, on the whole, relatively complimentary
to that state when studied in comparison with the general situation
in the United States during the nineteenth century.

There is another aspect of the general field of political control
over prison administration, however, namely the passage of legislation concerning penitentiary administration in the interest of
obtaining votes rather than with the end in view of improving
the situation in the state penitentiaries. This type of political
prostitution of the penitentiary system is even more insidious
and detrimental than a partisan distribution of penitentiary offices,
and here it can accurately be maintained that the record of Pennsylvania is among the worst in the history of American penology.
In Pennsylvania this disastrous and unpardonable practice has taken
the shape of legislative catering to, and cringing before, the monstrous demands of unprincipled labor agitators concerning the
elimination of convict labor. This moral capitulation to the vote-
getting phobia was exemplified chiefly in the anti-convict labor
legislation of the eighties, which culminated in the notorious Muehlbronner Law of 1897. This has paralyzed the prison industries in
the state for more than a score of years, has greatly increased the
expense of maintaining the state penitentiaries, has brought untold
agony to thousands of convicts, has lessened, if not wholly eliminated, the reformatory effects of incarceration, and has not to the
slightest degree improved the condition of honest labor within
the state.

Finally, there should be mentioned the entry of politics into
prison administration through the awarding of contracts for construction, repairs and supplies to those who have rendered political
support to penitentiary officers or whose favor is desired by such
officers for various reasons. While there is little evidence that
Pennsylvania has suffered from this common practice more than
other states, the testimony in the investigation of the conduct of
Warden Johnson of the Western Penitentiary indicates that it has
not been absent from this commonwealth. The centralized budget
system introduced by the Board of Public Welfare will certainly
curb this type of abuse in the future.

VIII. GENERAL SUMMARY OF THE DEVELOPMENT OF THE STATE PRISON SYSTEM OF PENNSYLVANIA

The two preceding sections have described the process through which Pennsylvania has passed in developing a penal system out of the primitive chaos which existed at the close of the colonial period. It has been shown that Pennsylvania has exemplified most of the significant advances in nineteenth-century penology, though some of the more recent and most significant steps in progress have not found much footing here. It should further be clear that Pennsylvania has long since ceased to be a pioneer, an innovator, and a leader in penological progress and has become content to follow more or less tardily, progressive departures initiated elsewhere. It must, nevertheless, be admitted that, with the exception of the industrial situation in the state penitentiaries, the penological theories and practices of Pennsylvania are not widely different from those which prevail in most of the states throughout the country, but are fairly well on a level with the general situation which exists in this field. Hence, the cause of the backwardness of Pennsylvania, when compared with the expert penological knowledge of the leaders in prison reform, is to be sought not in any special conditions existing in that state, but in the faulty opinions and information possessed by the general public throughout the United States regarding the causation of crime and the treatment of the criminal. While more progress has been made in the real scientific basis of criminology and penology in the last forty years than was previously achieved since the dawn of history, these advances are scarcely known to the general public and, consequently, can not have modified their views. Hence, it is not surprising that the level of public intelligence with regard to the theory and practice of penology is beneath the status of the reforms proposed by Plato more than two thousand years ago.

It should, therefore, be evident that the ultimate solution of the problems of penology in both Pennsylvania and the United States can not be scientifically solved except through a thoroughgoing and persistent campaign of public education along this line. Such a program is easier of fulfillment now than ever before. The old theological and metaphysical obstacles to a rational view of the "crime problem" are gradually dissolving, social reform in a general way, at least, has finally become respectable and somewhat popular, and not only has the scientific knowledge which must form the foundations of the penology of the future become assured, but also practical experiments in enlightened penal administration have been carried out with eminent success. It is not enough, however, that a knowledge of such facts should be prevalent among .experts and reformers. It must be diffused among the general body of citizens upon whom the reformers must depend for the constructive legislation and the sentimental support which is indispensable to permanent progress. Again, this campaign of education can not be adequately conducted merely through the work of penological experts, technical journals of criminology and penology, or even in general periodicals dealing with social reform. It must be carried on in good faith and with energy by the general press, the lecture platform, and the pulpit until the whole public is as thoroughly educated along this line as it has become, for example, in matters of public health and hygiene. Until such a situation has been brought about, progress in penology is doomed to be sporadic, local and generally ineffective. The solution of prison problems, then, seems to be fundamentally a problem of conscientious and scientific publicity.

THE END

INDEX

INDEX